# MONEY

# MONEY

FRANCIS A. WALKER

GYAN

*Published by*

Gyan Publishing House
5, Ansari Road
Daryaganj, New Delhi-110002
Phone: 011-47034999, 9811692060
E-mail: books@gyanbooks.com

*Distribution Network*
gyanbooks.com
India, USA, Canada, UK, Australia, France



ISBN : 978-81-212-9506-2 (PB)
First Published, 1877

2nd Impression 2023

*Printed at:* Gyan Press, Delhi.



**MONEY**
Author: FRANCIS A. WALKER

# MONEY

BY

FRANCIS A. WALKER

*Professor of Political Economy and History in the Sheffield Scientific School of Yale College, and Lecturer in Political Economy in the Johns Hopkins University; author of "The Statistical Atlas of the United States," "The Wages Question," etc.*

1891.

# PREFACE.

This volume contains the substance of a course of lectures delivered last spring in the Johns Hopkins University, Baltimore. The most considerable change which has been made in preparing the lectures for the press is the definitive abandonment of the term *Currency*. After carrying that word around for twenty years I have in the present work rid myself of the incubus, and have experienced somewhat the same feeling of relief as did the Ancient Mariner when the dead body of the Albatross dropped from his neck and disappeared in the sea. There is in my humble opinion not one thing to be said for this ill-omened word, except that it forms its plural rather more agreeably than does *Money*. Some awkwardness of expression has doubtless resulted from my first attempt to substitute that good old-fashioned word for the mischievous "Yankeeism," as Mr. McLeod calls it, which in the early part of this century obtained so strong a hold upon the public ear. Perhaps it does not savor too much of abusiveness to say that the new-fangled term made its way to general acceptance in no small degree because its own vagueness answered well to the cloudiness of the popular mind on the subject of Money; and that its vagueness has, in turn, done much to obscure the truth during the seventy-five weary years of economical discussion since it became current.

Something more, however, than a correct terminology is needed to resolve the deep, dark questions which constitute what Gen. Craufurd, in his "Reflections on the Circulating Medium," calls "the most intricate, abstruse, complex and subtile parts of political economy." It is, indeed, as Prof. Price declares, "a fatal theme." "I have found no branch of my subject," wrote Sir James Steuart, "so difficult to reduce to principles as the doctrine of Money."

It is strange that an institution wholly of man's devising should so baffle man's research,[1] but it seems, as Prof. Jevons has remarked, that a kind of intellectual vertigo attacks all writers on this theme. Nor is it a fault of the head alone which is apt to appear in such discussions. Sir Walter Scott, in his "Letters on the Currency of Scotland," puts into the mouth of a surly critic a complaint which Sir Walter manifestly intended for the whole race of writers on Money. "In your ill-advised tract you have shown yourself as irritable as Baalam, and as obstinate as his ass." If this volume makes no great contribution to the philosophy of the subject, the author trusts he will be judged to have shown no excess of controversial zeal, no lack of courtesy towards those writers of reputation from whom he is compelled to differ.

A great degree of originality is not claimed for the present work. If it shall be found to assist the reader in his study of this difficult subject, it will probably be in the following way:

1. By rejecting the word *Currency* and extending the term *Money* to include bank-notes [pp. 395–400]; by a new analysis of the function of Money in recording and

---

[1] Perry's Elements of Pol. Econ., p. 205.

registering for mutual comparison the values of all commodities in the markets, and the substitution thereupon of the term "common denominator in exchange" for the inappropriate and misleading term "measure of value" [pp. 280–90]; and by supplying the omitted proviso to Ricardo's propositions respecting the circulation of debased coins and inconvertible paper [pp. 198–9; 279], the doctrine of Money is relieved of certain factitious features which have obscured or partially concealed the nature and office of that great economical agent.

2. At the risk, perhaps the actual cost, of not a little repetition, topics which are usually blended in treatment are here separately taken up and subjected to an individual discussion. "Nothing," says Edmund Burke, "is so great an enemy to accuracy of judgment as a coarse discrimination, a want of such classification and distribution as the subject admits of." The author has sought not only to trace out the bearings of all distinguishable parts of the general subject, but, by arts of arrangement and even by artifices of typography, to emphasize distinctions and call attention sharply to discriminations which he has learned by experience are likely to be overlooked by the casual reader and even by the faithful student.

3. If any subject has presented to the author's mind peculiar difficulties, he has taken special pains to set forth the questions involved therein stripped to the kernel, with the arguments and authorities on either side fully and fairly arrayed. At but a single point have I been conscious of any bias of judgment arising from prepossession. The doctrine that paper money, nominally or really convertible into coin, is liable to be issued in excess under speculative impulses from trade, was maintained with religious earnestness for more than thirty

years by my honored father, and I cannot claim to be free from a strong desire, not of a purely philosophical origin, to establish the truth of that doctrine. I trust it will not be found that I have, on that account, failed fairly to present and argue the questions involved.

The philosophy of money owes little to the cultivation of systematic political economy in modern times. "If," says M. Wolowski, "political economy has within a century become a distinct science, the fundamental doctrines which it teaches were in great part familiar to the eminent minds of antiquity." In no department of economical inquiry does this hold true to so large an extent as in that which is now before us. Aristotle's theory of the Money-function is, even to-day, accepted by a large school of economists as containing the full essence of truth on this subject. The same theme was among the first to command the attention of the thoughtful upon the intellectual revival of Europe. In 1360 Nicole Oresme, Bishop of Lisieux, moved by the abuses of the French coin, wrote his treatise on Money, a work which, after being long lost to the world, was about 1862 discovered[1] by the eminent German economist, Roscher, of Leipzig, and has since been put out by M. Wolowski in the original Latin text, with an introduction and a French translation. No work extant expresses more justly and strongly the pernicious effects of that *morbus numericus* which wrought such misery among the peoples and caused such weakness in the governments of Europe, and had afflicted France with especial virulence,

[1] See his communication to the French Academy, in M. Wolowski' edition of Oresme's work.

preparing the way for the arms of Edward III and Henry V. Oresme sets forth the principles of coinage and seigniorage with a precision nowhere surpassed.

At the beginning of the sixteenth century the astronomer Copernicus addressed to the king of Poland his treatise, "Monete Cudende Ratio," which opens with this broad declaration: "Numberless as are the evils by which kingdoms, principalities and republics are wont to decline, these four are, in my judgment, most baleful: civil strife, pestilence, sterility of the soil, and corruption of the coin. The first three are so manifest that no one can fail to apprehend them; but the fourth, which concerns money, is considered by few, and those the most reflective, since it is not by a blow, but little by little and through a secret approach, that it destroys the state."

But it was Italy that made the largest of the early contributions to the philosophy of the subject. That country, it has been remarked, was long noted for the worst money and the best writers on money.[1] The coin of Italy was sunk into a rayless abyss of discredit while Beccaria and Verri were expounding the true laws of monetary circulation; and the works of Scaruffi and Néri were manuals for the mints of the Continent. Nor was the association accidental. It was the sight of flagrant abuses which set Nicole Oresme in France to pondering the laws of money. It was the almost inconceivable degradation of the coin of Italy that drove its publicists to investigate the cause of the evil and to reflect upon the means of cure. Let us hope that the losses and sufferings to which the people of the United States have been subjected during the past sixteen years will at

---

[1] Colwell, Ways and Means of Payment, p. 106 n.

least bring about some good result by enlightening the public mind as to the nature and the laws of money, and by firmly establishing certain principles at once of public faith and public policy from which no temptation of present advantage nor even the stress of warlike exigency shall ever again be able to move the nation.

While this work aims at being a systematic treatise on Money, and has been written without special reference to the existing financial situation, I cannot forbear, in view of the propositions now pending in Congress for altering our coinage laws, to quote the words which a great English statesman addressed to his countrymen during the period of the Bank Restriction:[1] "A very little reflection will satisfy every reader that, in the present state of things, and so long as we have no fixed standard of value for our currency, it would be absurd to send into circulation any new coinage."

[1] Huskisson, The Depreciation of the Currency.

# CONTENTS

## *PART I.*

## METALLIC MONEY.

### *CHAPTER V.*



### *CHAPTER VI.*



### *CHAPTER VII.*



### *CHAPTER VIII.*



### *CHAPTER IX.*



### *CHAPTER X.*



### *CHAPTER XI.*

## *PART III.*

## CONVERTIBLE PAPER MONEY.

# PART I.

# METALLIC MONEY.

# MONEY.

## CHAPTER I.

### THE PRIMITIVE FUNCTION OF MONEY.

TRADE arises out of the Division of Labor.
The need of Money comes from the fact of Trade. [1]

Trade, in its beginnings, assumes the form of direct exchange, commodity for commodity; what we call Truck or Barter. But trade cannot proceed far without serious obstacles to direct exchange being encountered through the failure of what Prof. Jevons in his admirable work, "Money and the Mechanism of Exchange" (1875), terms Coincidence in Barter. The difficulty is "to find two persons whose disposable possessions mutually suit each other's wants. There may be many persons wanting, and many possessing those things wanted; but to allow of an act of barter, there must be a double coincidence, which will rarely happen."—[P. 3.]

Illustrations of the difficulty noted are so familiar that I need not dwell upon it in order to show the importance of the Money-function. The griefs of the boot-maker

---

[1] "Currency has its origin in the Division of Labor."—Prof. Price, Principles of Currency, p. 38.

wanting a hat, who found many who had hats but did not, at the time, want boots, and many more who wanted boots badly enough but were quite as ill off, temporarily or permanently, respecting hats, have been related by every writer upon money. Prof. Jevons notes what he regards as a distinct, though minor, inconvenience of barter, namely, the impossibility of dividing many kinds of goods, without impairing or destroying their utility. "A store of corn, a bag of gold dust, a carcass of meat may be portioned out, and more or less may be given in exchange for what is wanted. But the tailor, as we are reminded in several treatises on political economy, may have a coat ready to exchange, but it much exceeds in value the bread which he wishes to get from the baker, or the meat from the butcher."—[P. 6.] It is evident that the inconveniences of barter, arising out of the difficulty noted by Prof. Jevons, of securing the required coincidence of wants and of possessions, call loudly, even in the most primitive condition of industrial society, for some

MEDIUM OF EXCHANGE,

some commodity which every one shall freely receive in exchange for what he has but does not desire personally to consume, in the confident assurance that, with it, he can, at any time, and of kinds and in quantities to suit his immediate wants, obtain from others what they have but do not desire to use.

Such an "interposed commodity," to employ Prof. Price's phrase,[1] would be money, whatever its material or form. This is the first Money-function: to facilitate exchanges by obviating the necessity of the double coin-

---

Principles of Currency, p. 44.

cidence which is required in Barter.[1] An exchange where money is thus introduced becomes, it will be observed, a twofold[2] transaction. "Every sale for money," says Prof. Price, following J. B. Say, "is only half a transaction." Goods are sold for money, in order that money itself may, at the time and in the place most suitable and convenient, be, in turn, sold for goods.

"It is not," says Mr. Mill, "with money that things are really purchased. Nobody's income (except that of the gold or silver miner) is derived from the precious metals. The pounds or shillings which a person receives weekly or yearly, are not what constitute his income; they are a sort of tickets or orders which he can present for payment at any shop he pleases, and which entitle him to receive a certain value of any commodity that he makes choice of. The farmer pays his laborers and his landlord in these tickets, as the most convenient plan for himself and them; but their real income is their share of his corn, cattle and hay, and it makes no essential difference whether he distributes it to them direct, or sells it for them and gives them the price; but as they would have to sell

---

[1] "Une fois que l'usage du numéraire est devenu général, chaque individu ne doit plus s'inquiéter, pour satisfaire tous ses besoins, que de fournir une chose ou un service répondant à un besoin quelconque, certain qu'il est d'obtenir, en échange de cette chose ou de ce service, une quantité déterminée de numéraire, avec laquelle il pourra se procurer les autres choses et les autres services dont il aura besoin."—[A. E. Cherbuliez, Science Écon., i, 241].

[2] "Ce sont deux échanges au lieu d'un. Mais, grâce à ce dédoublement, on peut effectuer des échanges innombrables sans attendre le hasard d'une coincidence, presque impossible, de besoins inverses et réciproques; grâce à ce dédoublement, on peut céder et acquérir toute sorte de bien par quantités très-exactes et sans qu'il faille jamais établir l'équivalence du marché par l'introduction d'objets qui lui sont étrangers."—[H. Cernuschi, Mécanique de l'Échange, p. 24].

it for money if he did not, and as he is a seller at any rate, it best suits the purposes of all, that he should sell their share along with his own, and leave the laborers more leisure for work and the landlord for being idle. The capitalists, except those who are producers of the precious metals, derive no part of their income from those metals, since they only get them by buying them with their own produce; while all other persons have their incomes paid to them by the capitalists, or by those who have received payment from the capitalists, and as the capitalists have nothing, from the first, except their produce, it is that and nothing else which supplies all incomes furnished by them. There cannot, in short, be intrinsically a more insignificant thing, in the economy of society, than money; except in the character of a contrivance for sparing time and labor. It is a machinery for doing quickly and commodiously what would be done, though less quickly and commodiously, without it; and, like many other kinds of machinery," adds Mr. Mill, "it only exerts a distinct and independent influence of its own when it gets out of order."—[Principles of Political Economy, iii, 7, 3.]

## II. MONEY AS A MEASURE OF VALUE (?)

"But a second difficulty," says Prof. Jevons, "arises in barter. *At what rate* is any exchange to be made? If a certain quantity of beef be given for a certain quantity of corn, and in like manner corn be exchanged for cheese, and cheese for eggs, and eggs for flax, and so on, still the question will arise—how much beef for how much flax, or how much of any one commodity for a given quantity of another? In a state of barter, the price-current list would be a most complicated document,[1] for each commodity would have to be quoted in terms of every other commodity, or else complicated rule-of-three sums would become necessary. Between 100 articles there must exist no less than 4950 possible ratios of exchange. . . . All such trouble is avoided if any one commodity be chosen and its ratio of exchange with each other commodity be quoted. Knowing how much corn is to be bought for a pound of silver, and also how much flax for the same quantity of silver, we learn without further trouble how much corn exchanges for so much flax. The chosen commodity becomes *a common denominator or common measure of value*, in terms of which we estimate the value of all other goods, so that their values become capable of the most easy comparison."—[Pp. 5–6.]

By some writers this function of money is treated as even more important than that of a medium of exchange. Thus, Prof. Bowen writes:[2] "We can do without money as a medium of exchange, and can even barter commodities for other commodities without the use of any medium. But we cannot do without money as a common standard, or measure, of value. A measure must be homogeneous with the thing measured. As that which measures length or capacity must itself possess length or capacity, so *that which measures value must have value in itself, or intrinsic value.*"

---

[1] "L'évaluation directe de chaque bien par chaque bien est une opération presque impossible. . . . La monnaie simplifie tout: au lieu d'évaluer chaque bien par chaque bien, on évalue tous les biens par un seul. La monnaie est le bien évaluant; tous les autres biens sont des biens évalués."—[H. Cernuschi, Mécanique de l'Échange, p. 19.]

[2] American Political Economy, p. 293.

And Prof. Rogers says:[1] "A little reflection will show that some common measure of value must needs be adopted in all societies whose condition is superior to mere barbarism. . . . Even if money were not a physical object it would still be necessary as a symbol or calculus. We need some common measure of value *as we need measures of length and capacity*, even though we never transfer that which is designated by the name, money. . . . So necessary is this process to trade, that we are told of nations who have no money, properly so called, but who have been constrained to invent *a fictitious measure* in order to express values. In short, the functions of money in the act of exchange present a close analogy to the functions of language in relation to thought. As there may be a rude barter, so there may be a rude language of signs. But there is no true communication of thought except by articulate speech, and similarly there can be no real and effectual trade except by the use of *a common measure*."

And Mr. Mill:[2] "In order to understand the manifold functions of a circulating medium, there is no better way than to consider what are the principal inconveniences which we should experience if we had not such a medium. The first and most obvious would be the want of a *common measure for values* of different sorts. If a tailor had only coats and wanted to buy bread or a horse, it would be very troublesome to ascertain how much bread he ought to obtain for a coat, or how many coats he should give for a horse. The calculations must be recommenced on different data, every time he bartered his coats for a different kind of article; and there could be

---

[1] Political Economy, p. 22.

[2] Principles of Political Economy, iii, 7, 1.

no current price or regular quotations of value. Whereas now, each thing has a current price in money, and he gets over all difficulties by reckoning his coat at £4 or £5, and a four-pound loaf at 6*d.* or 7*d.* As it is much easier to compare different lengths by expressing them in a common language called feet and inches, so it is much easier to compare values by means of a common language called pounds, shillings, and pence. In no other way can values be arranged one above another in a scale; in no other can a person conveniently calculate the sum of his possessions; and it is easier to ascertain and remember the relations of many things to one thing, than their innumerable cross-relations with one another. This advantage of having *a common language in which values may be expressed*, is, even by itself, so important, that some such mode of expressing and computing them would probably be used even if a pound or a shilling did not express any real thing, but a mere unit of calculation."

There is to be observed, extending through the statements here quoted from these four justly celebrated writers, an unfortunate confusion of the functions of a common denominator and of a common measure of value. And I make bold to say that the failure of nearly all writers on this subject, to discriminate between the two offices, has caused no small part of the contradiction and confusion of the popular, and even of the scientific discussion of the subject.

"A common denominator *or* common measure of value," says Prof Jevons; but surely a common denom-

So Prof. Rogers follows up the just remark, "Even if money were not a physical object, it would still be necessary as a symbol or calculus," by the wholly inconsistent assertion, "We need some common measure of value as we need measures of length and capacity."

inator and a common measure of value are not equivalent; indeed, they have no necessary relation to each other. That which is to measure must, as Prof. Bowen says, be of a kind with the thing measured; of a kind, that is, in the respect of which the comparison is made. Not that we need cloth to measure cloth; but to measure the weight of cloth, we must have that which itself possesses weight; and to measure the length of cloth, that which itself possesses length. So to measure value, an article must possess value. But values being measured may be expressed, relatively to each other, by a simple scale of numbers; just as the ratios between lengths that have been measured may be expressed without reference to feet or inches. If I say that three objects are, in length, respectively, as 1, 7 and 4, I use no fictitious measure of length. And so, if I say that the values of three commodities are as 1, 7 and 4, I am using no "fictitious measure of value" (Rogers). I take a unit, and say that there are in the one case 4 of these, in another 7, in the last only 1. This is the function of the common denominator, not of the common measure.

The distinction is vital. In it lies the germ of the whole controversy between the advocates of Ideal Money and the advocates of Real Money. The former admit all that is claimed for the importance of having a common denominator through which to register the relative values of the 100 commodities, for instance, of which Prof. Jevons makes account, and thus save the necessity of 4950 quotations in the price-current; but for this, they

---

But a mere symbol or calculus cannot be a measure of length or of capacity. In like manner Mr. Mill shows the importance of having "a common *language* in which values may be *expressed*" under the title "the want of a common *measure* for values."

say, and they say justly, no distinct article, as a measure of value, is necessary. The articles are measured against each other, in respect of their several values, and it is only necessary that there should be some common denominator in which the values, thus determined, may be expressed.

If, for example, it takes five times as much labor to produce a wheelbarrow as to produce a bushel of wheat, the value of the wheelbarrow will be to that of the wheat as 5 to 1. And if a cart costs five times as much labor as a wheelbarrow, the respective values of the three com modities may be expressed as 25 : 5 : 1.

To measure values we must, of course, use values; but, in the instances given, we have the amounts of labor embodied, so to speak, in the several articles, compared directly with each other, and the resulting ratios, expressed in pure numbers, are quite sufficient for a basis of exchange. It is not necessary to the comparison that there should be an article distinct from the wheelbarrow, the cart, and the bushel of wheat, itself costing one day's labor, against which each of these three articles might by turns be measured, in order that "exchanging proportions" should be established between them.

We shall return to this subject at a later period in our discussion,[1] when we shall undertake to show that it is not even necessary that the amounts of labor respectively embodied in the several commodities to be exchanged should be compared against each other; but that articles possessing no "intrinsic value" (Bowen) whatever, mere bits of colored paper, perhaps, may afford the common denominator needed for the expression of a list of values as long as the diversification of modern industry shall

[1] Pp. 190; 281-8.

require. For the present, it is sufficient to point out the distinction between the common denominator and the common measure of values; and to note that the writers quoted only establish the need of

A COMMON DENOMINATOR

for the various commodities to be exchanged in any market. This, then, we accept as the second Money-function.

III. But something more still is required in the development of industrial society.

"A third function of money," says Prof Jevons, "soon develops itself. Commerce cannot advance far before people begin to borrow and lend, and debts of various origin are contracted. It is in some cases usual, indeed, to restore the very same article which was borrowed, and in almost every case it would be possible to pay back in the same kind of commodity. If corn be borrowed, corn might be paid back with interest in corn; but the lender will often not wish to have things returned to him at an uncertain time, when he does not much need them, or when their value is unusually low; a borrower, too, may need several different kinds of articles, which he is not likely to obtain from one person; hence arises the convenience of borrowing and lending in one generally recognized commodity, of which the value varies little. Every person making a contract by which he will receive something at a future day, will prefer to secure the receipt of a commodity likely to be as valuable then as now. This commodity will usually be the current money, and it will thus come to perform the function of a *Standard of Value*."—[P. 14.]

The office which Prof. Jevons thus indicates is actually performed in industrial society by that which we call Money; but the title applied by Prof. Jevons to this office, or function, is unfortunate, both as being little descriptive and as arousing the antagonism of those who advocate the concurrent circulation of gold and silver as money. These economists find themselves galled by the use of this term, since, if money serves as a standard of value, then the use of two metals indifferently as money constitutes a *double-standard of value*, a phrase which savors of absurdity, and which the bi-metallists resent as applied to their scheme. They assert that there can be no such thing as a standard of value, single or double,[1] value being nothing but a relation between commodities, a ratio of exchange varying in the nature of the case with the incessant fluctuations of supply and demand.

There is no reason why the prejudices, if they are nothing more, of so large and respectable a body of writers should not be regarded in this instance, since the phrase in dispute is but little descriptive, if not actually misleading. Bearing in mind, then, Prof. Jevons's statement of this function, but changing its title to suit the case more precisely, we say that money performs the part in industrial society of a

STANDARD FOR DEFERRED PAYMENTS.

IV. But Prof. Jevons attributes to money still another function in industrial society:

---

[1] The German economist Rau thus writes to M. Wolowski: "La confusion d'idées qui a été occasionnée en France par le terme *étalon* n'existe pas chez nous, parce que nous ne désignons pas par le même mot l'unité de mesure pour les choses matérielles, soit le volume et le poids des corps, et celle des prix."—[L'or et L'argent, p. 42.]

M. Wolowski proposes *Évaluateur*, instead of *Étalon*.

"It is worthy of inquiry whether money does not also serve a fourth distinct purpose—that of embodying value in a convenient form for conveyance to distant places. Money, when acting as a medium of exchange, circulates backwards and forwards near the same spot, and may sometimes return to the same hands again and again. . . . But at times a person needs to condense his property into the smallest compass, so that he may hoard it away for a time, or carry it with him on a long journey, or transmit it to a friend in a distant country.

"Something which is very valuable, although of little bulk and weight, and which will be recognized as very valuable in every part of the world, is necessary for this purpose. The current money of a country is perhaps more likely to fulfill these conditions than anything else, although diamonds and other precious stones and articles of exceptional beauty and rarity might occasionally be employed."—[P. 15.]

It appears to me that this suggestion of Prof. Jevons[1] cannot be received favorably. Money does not serve as a store of value. When a commodity comes to serve as a store of value, it ceases to be money. Gold and silver in hoards, or as treasure, are no more money than gold and silver in plate, or on the roof of a temple, or in a statue of Jupiter. The fact that gold and silver may be used as a store of value constitutes, indeed, one of the important facts which go to qualify them for service as money, just as their usefulness in the arts and in industry goes, as we shall see, to the same object; but in

---

[1] Mr. Horton, in his excellent work, "Silver and Gold" (1877), adopts this view of Money: "It is largely used for the peculiar purpose of preservation of value, and this both in space and time."—[P 66, cf. p. 103].

neither case are they performing the functions of money, which have reference exclusively to exchanges, arising out of the division of labor.

Such is the analysis of the operation of Money made by Prof. Jevons. Reserving our exception to the fourth function, and to the titles given to the second and third, we may fully accept the remark with which he closes his analysis: "It is in the highest degree important that the reader should discriminate carefully and constantly between the four functions which money fulfills, at least in modern societies. We are so accustomed to use the one same substance in all the four different ways, that they tend to become confused together in thought. We come to regard as almost necessary that union of functions which is, at the most, a matter of convenience, and may not always be desirable. We might certainly employ one substance as a medium of exchange, a second as a measure of value, a third as a standard of value, and a fourth as a store of value. In buying and selling we might transfer portions of gold; in expressing and calculating prices we might speak in terms of silver; when we wanted to make long leases we might define the rent in terms of wheat, and when we wished to carry our riches away we might condense it into the form of precious stones.

"This use of different commodities for each of the functions of money has, in fact, been partially carried out. In Queen Elizabeth's reign, silver was the common measure of value, gold was employed in large payments, in quantities depending upon its current value in silver; while corn was required by the Act 18th Elizabeth, c. VI (1576), to be the standard of value in drawing the leases of certain college lands."—[Pp. 16–7.]

"There is, however," adds Prof. Jevons, "evident

convenience in selecting, if possible, one single substance which can serve all the functions of money."

But while we recognize the truth of Prof. Jevons's remark that two and even more articles may at the same time, in the same community, be performing the offices of money, we hardly accept Turgot's proposition that all commodities are, in some sense, money.[1] Any article may become money: all cannot. Money must always be, in the phrase of the logicians, particular. That one article should at any time and in any place be money, it is essential that all others, or even many others, should not.

Such, as it has been described, is the primitive function of money.

Its importance can scarcely be exaggerated. "It has been wisely said," remarks Chevalier, "that there is no machine which economizes labor like money, and its adoption has been likened to the discovery of letters."[2] —[On Gold, p. 28].

The illustrations taken to show the inconveniences of barter have been drawn from a primitive condition of in-

---

[1] "Ces deux propriétés de servir de commune mesure des toutes les valeurs, ct d'être un gage représentatif de toute marchandise de pareille valeur, renferment tout ce qui constitue l'essence et l'utilité de ce qu'on appelle monnaie, et il suit des détails dans lesquels je viens d'entrer que toutes les marchandises sont à quelques égards monnaie, et participent à ces deux propriétés essentielles plus ou moins à raison de leur nature particulière."—[Sur la formation et la distribution des richesses, xli.]

[2] "The value of money has been settled by general consent to express our wants and our property, as letters were invented to express our ideas; aud both these institutions, by giving a more active energy to the powers and passions of human nature, have contributed to multiply the objects they were designed to express."—[Gibbon, chap. ix.]

dustry; the artisans were men known to each other, each working by himself and producing by his own labor the whole of the article he desired to exchange for others; the articles assumed for the purposes of illustration were simple necessaries, in universal request.

If, however, we step at once forward to the most highly organized forms of modern industry, and consider the inconveniences of universal barter, even after the introduction of the credit system, to be hereafter described,[1] we shall find them such as to constitute a most onerous and oppressive tax upon the production of the community, amounting, in many cases, to absolute prohibition. Hence when Mr. Huskisson said of the crisis of 1825–6, that England approached "within twenty-four hours of barter,"[2] he represented a state of things dangerous in an appalling degree to the welfare of the kingdom. So that, even in combating doctrines deemed perilous heresies, like those of the Inflationists of the Western States, I must deem it always unwise to make statements like that contained in Mr. Wells's able paper entitled "The Cremation Plan of Resumption."

"Were all the currency in the country absolutely swept out of existence to-morrow morning, there would doubtless be much inconvenience experienced, the same as though all the yard-sticks, foot-rules, and bushel measures were to disappear; but in either case, *there would not probably be one less acre of land cultivated, yard of cloth made, ton of coal dug, or pound of iron smelted, in consequence.*"—[P. 7.]

How differently Mr. Wells viewed the Money-function

---

[1] Pp. 65–9.

[2] Lord Normanby wrote from Paris, in 1848, that the city was "reduced to a condition of barter."

when dealing directly with the practical inconveniences of barter, we see in the following sentence from his tract entitled "Robinson Crusoe's Money," in which he describes the embarrassment of his islanders in carrying on production without a medium of exchange :

"The people on the island—both laborers and employers—were, however, fully agreed that life was too short[1] to *waste a good part of it* in a game of blind-man's-buff, on a large scale, for such this attempt to conduct exchanges on a basis of direct barter substantially was; but they nevertheless also clearly perceived that the game would continue to be played *to the interruption of all material progress*, unless some other method of exchanging could be devised and adopted."—[P. 20.]

In his "Nutrition of a Commonwealth," Hobbes has briefly but strikingly exhibited the importance of the Money-function in the State :

"By means of which measures, all commodities, movable and immovable, are made to accompany a man to all places of his resort, within and without the place of his ordinary residence, and the same passeth from man to man, within the Commonwealth, and goes round about, nourishing as it passeth, every part thereof; in so much as this concoction is, as it were, the sanguinifaction[2] of the Commonwealth; for natural blood is in like manner made of the fruits of the earth, and, circulating, nourisheth by the way every member of the body of man.

. . . . . . .

"By concoction I understand the reducing of all com-

---

[1] "Les heures et les jours ne suffiraient pas à cherchér, soliciter, offrir, combiner des trocs."—[H. Cernuschi, Méc. de l'Éch., p. 25.]

[2] "La monnaie est appelée à remplir dans l'économie publique, le rôle du sang dans l'économie animale: elle commence par dissoudre

modities which are not presently consumed, but reserved for nourishment in time to come, to something of equal value, and withal, so portable as not to hinder the motion of men from place to place, to the end a man may have in what place soever, such nourishment as the place affordeth. And this is nothing else but gold and silver and money."

In a very judicious work on "Money and Banks," published in 1839, Prof. Tucker, of Virginia, well expressed the advantages to be derived from the use of money:

"By reason of the readiness with which money enables every producer to dispose of his redundant products—that is, to convert them into what has a more varying and universal value—it is a great incentive to industry. Were the practice of barter to prevail, the fear felt by a tradesman that he might not find persons who would both want his commodities, and have such as he himself would take in return, would check his industry, and he would generally wait, as is often the case with country workmen, for articles to be ordered before they were made.

"There is also, from the use of money, a great saving of time, which the industrious class can appropriate to the business of production.

"Money is moreover favorable to that separation of trades[1] which is of itself so propitious to increased production, and to an improvement in the quality of the articles produced. If there was no general medium of ex-

---

tous les moyens de subsistance pour en extraire la partie nutritive et répandre ensuite dans les diverses parties du corps les éléments de conservation et de vie."—[Roscher, Wolowski's Translation, §117.]

[1] "Money is essential to the subdivision of labor and services, and the organization of society."—[Prof. Rogers, Political Economy, p. 23.]

change, men would often fabricate articles for themselves, from the trouble and delay of obtaining them by barter.

"As every article has its known market price in the general measure of value, where there is one, every producer can thereby better adapt his supply to the varying demands and diversified tastes of the community. Money furnishes a very sensitive barometer of these variations, by consulting which the industrious classes will be less likely to misdirect their labor, and create redundancy on the one hand, or subject the community to scarcity on the other.

"The introduction of money has also a manifest tendency to beget frugality and encourage accumulation.[1] Without such a convenient and unchanging representative of value, or mode of investment, many things would be wastefully consumed, supposing them to be produced, which would be saved if convertible into money. The practice of saving is so much encouraged by the facilities which the precious metals afford, that it occasionally grows to be one of the strongest human passions; and misers, who are instances of the abuse of frugality, and who are, in part, the creatures of a metallic currency, furnish striking proofs of its power over human action, a power which, excessive in their case, exerts a healthy influence on the rest of the community."

---

[1] "L'avantage principal de l'or et de l'argent pour la formation des capitaux a été de favoriser les plus petites économies, et de les capitaliser de façon qu'elles devinssent au bout d'un certain temps applicables à des acquisitions de meubles et de vêtements d'un usage durable, ou même à solder des travaux utiles. Avant l'introduction de ces métaux dans le commerce, un homme ne pouvait se former de capital que par la multiplication de ses bestiaux ou l'emploi de son travail qui n'etait pas absolument nécessaire à sa subsistance, à se fabriquer des choses durables qui fussent à son usage, ou qui pussent être vendues.' —[Note of Dupont de Nemours to Turgot, Des Richesses, lii].

Prof. Perry expands one of the ideas suggested by Prof. Tucker, as follows:[1]

"The fact that such a medium is in universal circulation, and that the holders of it are ready to exchange it against any sort of services adapted to gratify their desires, exercises a kind of creative power, and brings a thousand products to the market which would otherwise never have come into existence.

"Since money will buy anything, men are on the alert to bring forward something which will buy money, and since money is divisible into small pieces, an incredible number and variety of small services are brought forward to be exchanged against these pieces, which services we have no reason to suppose would ever be brought forward at all were it not for the strong attraction of the money. . . .

"Money is a form of capital which stimulates and facilitates all the processes of production, without exception."

This is treading on perilous ground. To speak of money as exercising a kind of creative power and as stimulating the processes of production, is to use language which might, without a great deal of violence, be wrested to serve the argument of those who, at the present juncture, are clamoring for increased issues by the government, as a means of reviving industry. Strictly taken, however, Prof. Perry's statement is true. We shall have occasion, at a later stage[2] of our discussion, to consider the effects of an increase in the amount of money circulating in any community.

Still another consideration, bearing not so much upon

---

[1] Political Economy, 213–4.

[2] See chap. iv.

the production as upon the distribution of wealth, may be presented in the language of the eminent German economist, Roscher.[1] It is that, under the system of barter, "the party which is, in an economical view, the stronger, would, in every bargain, possess an advantage much greater than he enjoys at present." The truth of this proposition will be seen if we imagine two persons, one strong and active, the other feeble and lame, to be required to travel in company, first along a smooth road, and afterwards over a rough and broken country. Both will suffer from the irregularity of the ground in the second case; but the weak and lame person will experience relatively the greater disadvantage. He will fall further behind, as well as accomplish his task with much more of weariness and pain.

If then, as there is reason to assert, every industrial community is divided among the economically weak and the economically strong; if, in the exchange of products or services, some classes are, in their best estate, at a disadvantage by reason of their inability to resort, with promptitude and assurance, to the best market, whether from poverty, from ignorance, from social ties and domestic burdens, or from apprehensions, reasonable or superstitious, of the effects of change, clearly it is true that any cause, like the introduction of money, which facilitates the exchange of products or services, does not merely advantage the community as a whole, but relieves the weaker classes from a portion of their disabilities and raises them more nearly to an equality with those whom they have to encounter in the competitions of industry. All classes derive a benefit from the use of money; but that which the poorest and the economically feeblest receive is relatively greater.

---

[1] Lib. ii, cap. 3.

But while we thus magnify the services rendered by money to industrial civilization, it must not be overlooked that barter is still retained in many transactions, even in the most advanced communities, especially in the payment of wages, "in kind." This fact is exceedingly important to be noted, as will hereafter appear.[1] The question of a direct exchange or of the use of "an interposed commodity," is not always one of necessity, but sometimes one of convenience merely; of convenience, too, in such a degree only, that a positive reason, perhaps of no great force, may lead to a considerable extension of barter.

Can the analysis which we have obtained of the facts of exchange in a primitive industrial state be applied with assurance to the conditions of modern society without adding to or subtracting from the conclusions we have reached?

Prof. Price, in his "Principles of Currency," remarks that he writes first of metallic currency, or coin, "not only because it is the most ancient, the most general, and the most easily understood form of currency, but also because it furnishes peculiar facilities from its simplicity for ascertaining the fundamental principles of all currency."—[P. 37.] Again he says: "We arrived at first principles in the investigation of coin. Our duty is to adhere to them closely and to apply them firmly, under the conviction that money, currency, whether made of paper or metal, in its leading features is always the same, and that its various forms all work out the same general result."—[P. 98.]

It is yet too early to criticise this assumption of Prof.

---

[1] See pp. 199–204.

Price, that the analysis of the Money-function in a primitive condition of industrial society yields all the elements which are found in a state of highly organized production and trade;[1] but let us leave our minds open on this side.

The savage builds his canoe of materials every part of which would float of itself. The civilized man builds his broadside ship-of-war of material which, of itself, would drop like a plummet to the bottom.

We may find, in our further investigation, that there is something more in the philosophy of money than comes out in the primitive trade between the tailor, the butcher and the baker.

To obtain such large advantages as we have seen result from the use of money, no small sacrifice may willingly be submitted to.

"There is no doubt," says Mr. James Wilson, "that the time and labor which are saved by the interposition of coin, as compared with a system of barter, form an ample remuneration for the portion of capital withdrawn from productive sources, to act as a simple circulator of commodities, by rendering the remainder of the capital of the country so much the more productive."—[Capital, Currency and Banking, p. 15].

"The portion of capital," says Mr. Wilson. Is money capital? We have, unfortunately, on this point, great looseness of statement among economists, due more, I am disposed to believe, to carelessness of expression than to faults in thinking.

Mr. Wilson says: "Whatever coin is actually used in

---

[1] "The vast operations of commerce, when dissected, only reproduce the action of the tailor and his two fellow-tradesmen."—[P. 43.]

circulation, although it may aid the productiveness of the general capital of the country, is itself so much withdrawn from productive uses"[1] [*ibid.*]; and he elsewhere speaks of money withdrawn from circulation, as *restored to productive uses.*—[Cf. pp. 16, 39, 41, 228.]

If gold and silver are capital before their use as money it is difficult to see how they lose this character by being applied to a use in which they facilitate production in a high degree. It would be quite as correct to speak of a railway locomotive as withdrawn from productive uses because employed only in the transfer of commodities, and as restored to capital when laid up for repairs.

---

[1] In the same way, Prof. Newcomb, of Washington, who has written admirably in Political Economy, in the special departments of Money and Taxation, says: "Gold and silver coin is, in the strictest sense, unproductive capital, whether lyiug in the vaults of banks, or locked up in a miser's chest, or circulating as money."—[Financial Policy of the United States, p. 48.] "Stérile mais nécessaire," says M. Cernuschi [Méc. de l'Ech.] On the other hand, M. Wolowski says [La Question des Banques, p. 27n]: "La partie du capital consacrée à la monnaie produit autant et plus que celles qui se trouvent engagées dans l'autres mécanismes. Il n'est pas de machine qui côute relativement moins et qui donne des résultats plus considérables."

## CHAPTER II.

### THE ELEMENTS OF MONEY: THE METALS AS MONEY.

HAVING seen the occasion which exists, even in a primitive state, and increasingly in communities as they advance industrially, for "an interposed commodity" to facilitate exchanges, it will be profitable to inquire what qualities a commodity should possess to fit it for such a use.

And first, it may be said, the one condition which is absolutely essential, is general acceptability.[1] Specific material qualities may be noted, partly as contributing to this fact of acceptability, partly as offering independent advantages for the use, as money, of the commodities in which these are found; but, however important the uses of an article, however admirably suited in its properties to perform such an office, unless the fact of general acceptability is secured, whether with or without reference to such qualities, an article cannot serve in this capacity. It is the disposition, or the indisposition, of the great majority of the community to receive it in payment which

[1] "Il danaro è la merce universale: cioè a dire è quella merce la quale per la universale sua accettazione, per il poco volume che ne rende facile il trasporto, per la commoda divisibilità e per la incorruttibilità sua è universalmente ricevuta in iscambio di ogni merce particolare."—[Count Verri, Della Pol. Econ., § 2.]

settles the question whether a particular commodity shall become money or not. The reasons, if indeed they reason at all in the matter, which actuate individuals or the community in their preferences, may be mistaken, or the appetencies to which they yield may be such as the moral philosopher cannot approve. The economist has only to do with the fact that, however it comes about, the willingness of the mass of the people to receive one article rather than others in payment for whatever they have to sell, furnishes the prime, the one essential, condition of a true money.

The carved pebbles formerly used by the Ethiopians, the wampum which circulated between the New England colonists and the natives, the glass beads used in small payments even down to this day along the Arabian gulf, the shells and the red feathers employed throughout the islands of the Indian ocean, were good money, though serving no purpose but ornament and decoration.[1] They were desired by the community in general;[2] men would give for them the fruits of their labor, knowing that with them they could obtain most conveniently in time, in form and in amount, the fruits of the labor of others.

---

[1] "Vanity, which among some peoples, makes its appearance before the need of clothing is felt."—[Wolowski, notes to Roscher, § 119.]

[2] It is not enough that a few individuals may greatly desire an article. Sir Hans Sloane might be willing to give five guineas for an overgrown toad; but were a hundred gentlemen of the county to share his degraded taste, that would not constitute toads money. It is hazardous to say however, what may not become money at some time and place. Milburn, in his "Oriental Commerce," tells us that at St. Jago "old clothes, particularly black," form the best medium for obtaining supplies of food from the natives.

It is in view of its general, or universal, acceptability that certain writers speak of money as a pledge or security for whatever the holder may wish, now or at a future time, to obtain.

Thus Aristotle, in the "Nicomachian Ethics," says: "With regard to a future exchange [if we want nothing at present], money is, as it were, our security."

Mr. McLeod, in the same connection, quotes from Baudeau, Adam Smith, and Henry Thornton, as follows:

Baudeau: "It is a kind of bill of exchange, or order payable at the will of the bearer."

Adam Smith: "A guinea may be considered as a bill for a certain quantity of necessaries or conveniences, upon all the tradesmen of the neighborhood."

Thornton: "Money, of every kind, is an order for goods."

Bastiat develops the same idea in the following illustration:

"You have a crown-piece, what does it mean in your hands? It is, as it were, the witness and the proof that you have at some time done some work, which, instead of profiting by, you have allowed society, in the person of your client, to enjoy. This crown-piece witnesses that you have rendered a service to society, and moreover, it states the value of it. It witnesses, besides, that you have not received back from society a real equivalent service, as was your right. To put it in your power to exercise this right when and how you please, society, by the hands of your client, has given you an Acknowledgment, a Title, an Order of the State, a Token, a Crown-piece, in short, which does not differ from titles of credit, except that it carries its value in itself, and if you can read with the eye of the mind the inscription it bears, you can distinctly see these words: 'Pay to the bearer a service equivalent to that which he has rendered to society, value received and stated, proved and measured by that which is on me.'

"After that you cede your crown-piece to me; either it is a present, or it is in exchange for something else. If you give it to me as the price of a service, see what follows: your account as regards the real satisfaction with society is satisfied, balanced, closed. You rendered it a service in exchange for a crown-piece, you now restore it the crown-piece in exchange for a service: so far as regards you the account is settled. But I am now just in the position you were before. It is I now who have done a service to society in your person. It is I who have become its creditor for the value of the work which I have done for you, and which I could devote to myself. It is into my hands therefore that this title of credit should pass, the witness and the proof of this social debt."

Now, these are striking and picturesque expressions of the universal acceptability of money. But Mr. McLeod has proceeded to deal with them as if literally true, and issues from his discussion of the subject with the strange statement that "Money is the representative of debt" [Econ. Phil., i, 198], adding that "where there is no debt, there can be no currency" [p. 196], and at last formulates his definition of money as "Any economic quantity which a debtor can by law compel his creditor to take in discharge of a debt."[1]—[*Ibid.*, 276.]

---

[1] Again, "Among all civilized nations, gold or silver bullion is the acknowledged representative of debt," [ii, 370]—"the symbol of debt."—[*Ibid.*]

He denies that money is an interposed (or as he terms it, an intermediate) commodity. "It is the essential quality of currency that it is a *general* charge of debt upon the person of the debtor, or obligant.

Of which it may be enough at the present time to say, that the perfect form of money would be one which the creditor would be as desirous of receiving as the debtor could wish him to be, and thus the element of legal compulsion would become entirely inconsequential, and hence no proper part of a definition; and, secondly, that such money has in fact circulated, at one time or another, over pretty much the whole inhabited world, not even the nominal compulsion[1] of the creditor existing in no small proportion of instances.

There could scarcely be a grosser case of the perversion of the plain meaning of a writer than in the use which Mr. McLeod here makes of the expressions he quotes. Dr. Smith intended to convey this thought: that the acceptability of the guinea was so complete that the tradesman, though free to sell his goods or to withhold them, would gladly take it in exchange for any equivalent part of his stock; and that the holder of the guinea would therefore be just as sure of obtaining, through its agency, what he might desire, as if he had an obligation which could be enforced at law. Dr. Smith uses, thus, the entire freedom of the tradesman to show more strikingly the universal purchasing power of money. Mr. McLeod twists this around, with what violence it is needless to say, to make it fit into his proposition that it is of the essence of money that the creditor should be obliged by law to receive it.

---

and is not a title to any specific or particular articles."—[i, 206.] "In all cases whatever, it involves the idea of personal liability." "This distinction is of the utmost importance and it seems to show that the transferability from hand to hand is not the fundamental conception of a currency."

[1] "Our paper is of value in commerce, because in law it is of none; it is powerful on 'Change, because in Westminster Hall it is impotent."—[Burke, French Revolution.]

Even Prof. Price, whose conception of the primitive function of money is very strong and clear, makes use of an unfortunate mode of expression regarding it.

He says, speaking of money, as compared with bank-notes, bills of exchange, promissory notes, etc.: "The distinction I would suggest would place coin in a class by itself, and would group in a second and collateral class all the other instruments of exchange. The two classes of the instruments of exchange would then be guarantees by a commodity and guarantees by account. The basis of this division is the fact that coin constitutes an actual payment."—[Principles of Currency, p. 177.] But, if coin constitutes an actual payment, why call it a guarantee at all?

I must suppose Prof. Price's reason in so doing to be that this form of statement best consists with the proposition upon which his theory of the exchanges of modern industrial society is built up, that money is an instrument for the transfer of debts—of which we shall inquire more hereafter; but, surely, in the view we have obtained of the Money-function in primitive industrial society, and in view of Prof. Price's admission that coin constitutes an actual payment, the use of the word *guarantees* is of very doubtful propriety.

If I have parted voluntarily with the fruit of my labor and received therefor the fruit of another man's labor—gold—being "an actual payment," it is not easy to see what further is guaranteed me, or who should guarantee me anything. It is true that with the gold I expect to be able to obtain, at any time, an equivalent portion of the product of any other man in the community; and this expectation constitutes my reason for being willing to receive it; and everybody's willingness, on similar grounds, to receive it, constitutes it money; but if we go far enough back, we note that when I produced the article with which I obtained this money, I probably did so not because I wanted that specific article (my parting with it would seem to be a proof of that), but in the expectation that with it I could obtain the money, with which, in turn, I could obtain the particular articles I should wish to consume. If, then, the money which the tailor receives for his coat is a guarantee (that he will receive from other members of the industrial community that which his personal wants demand), the coat itself was a guarantee. With his labor he gets the coat; with the coat he gets the money; with the money he gets bread and meat for his family. If the money was a guarantee for bread and meat in this case, so was the coat a guarantee for the money.

At the same time, it is well to enforce strongly the thought that men take money with the expectation of parting with it; that this is the use to which they mean to put it, and it is for this reason they receive it; that the real object is something other and further on; and that money is always truly *a medium*, a means to an end.

In this view, and anticipating the adoption of gold as money and its coinage for higher convenience, we can fully assent to these words of Prof. Price:

"Gold, in the form of money or coin, is simply a commodity, employed for bartering, as a ship for carrying, or a plow for farming. . . . It is not sought for its own sake, as an article of consumption, but purely as a machine. It is wealth only in the identical sense that a cart is; for its action is very similar to a cart's; it fetches for its owner the things he is in want of. . . .

"It is nothing but machinery and must never be regarded as valuable, except for the work it performs, so long as it remains in the state of coin. It can be converted at pleasure into an end, into an article of consumption, by being sold as metal; till then it is a mere tool, and wealth only in the sense that tools are wealth. Its specific worth, the work for which money is made, is to supersede single by double barter; for the exchanges which are indispensable to civilized life could not be carried on by direct barter. Selling is the first half of double barter; the second half is obtained when the coin got by the sale is itself sold for something else. Whenever gold buys, it is also itself sold. The goods and the gold fare exactly alike in every sale and every purchase. Men take money in selling solely in order to sell that money again in buying."—[Principles of Currency, p. 65.]

Looking at the history of money, we notice that two conditions, now united and now separated, have served to give to a considerable number of commodities a local and temporary acceptance, in the degree necessary to bring them into use as money.

The first is the general consumption of the article throughout the community. Thus, in many countries the staple cereal crop has come into use as money. However inconvenient in other respects, the fact that every family had occasion, during the year, to use considerable portions of it, has often given to such a commodity a good degree of currency. Wheat, corn and rye, have extensively fulfilled this office. Cattle, also, were used as money from the earliest days. With the Greeks of the Homeric period, oxen served as the medium of exchange; and after the abandonment of Britain by the Romans we find the inhabitants, in the scarcity of coin, returning to the use of "living money," especially in Scotland and Wales. "It is very possible," says Sir

Henry Maine,[1] "that kine were first exclusively valued for their flesh and milk; but it is clear that, in very early times, a distinct and special importance belonged to them as the instrument or medium of exchange." The fact of general use made copper skewers[2] once good money in Greece; and the many adaptations of iron have given it currency in countries and in ages when it was not so plentiful that its weight, for a limited value, became embarrassing.

But even more than the fact of general consumption at home, the fact that an article forms the staple export of a region gives it acceptability for the purposes of an "interposed-commodity." Thus in the early colonial days, we find tobacco in Virginia and Maryland, and rice[3] in Carolina, constituting the ordinary money of the people; and they served this purpose reasonably well. At every country-store, tobacco or rice was always freely taken every week or month the storekeeper sent his stock down to the seaboard, where his wagons were loaded with West India goods, hardware, etc., for the planters' use. The fact that these articles of produce were always and freely received at the country-store, gave them a high degree of acceptability in all the ordinary transactions of exchange. Even professional fees and salaries were paid in rice and tobacco. For a similar reason, dried cod were, during the same period, used in Newfoundland as

---

[1] Early History of Institutions, p. 149.

[2] Adam Smith speaks of a village in Scotland in his day, where nails were used as money. The general use of bullets, in the chase and in warfare against the Indians, made them good "change" in the early days of New England.

[3] At Porto Novo, on the Coromandel shore, accounts are kept in "collums" of paddy, *i. e.*, rice in the husk.—[Milburn, Oriental Commerce, 213.]

money, and sugar in the West Indies. Tea is still used in the settlement of transactions at the great Russian fairs, and small compressed blocks of that article still circulate in China, as, according to Mr. McLeod, dates, in definite measures, do in the oases of Africa. Furs have always been a good money, in regions from which they are exported. Thus the Massachusetts Court of Assistants, in 1631, ordered that corn at the usual rates should pass for payment of all debts, unless money *or beaver*[1] were expressly named in the contract. Furs play an important part in the history of Russian money.

Among the material properties fitting articles for use as money, we note the following:

Portability.—Doubtless one reason for the preference given to cattle among the ancients was the fact that they would carry themselves, instead of requiring to be carried, like most other forms of property, whenever the chieftain had occasion to move his abode, for purposes of gain, or to avoid a threatened attack. And of articles which cannot be classed as "living money," preference will naturally be given, in any state of society, to such as contain much value in small bulk, and which can thus be easily transported, and for the same reason, easily stored and concealed.

A second desirable quality is uniformity. In this, the living money referred to was particularly deficient. If Glaucus stipulated, in advance, to give 100 oxen for his

[1] "Of all the articles, the products of the country, which our fathers used as currency, that which was most available and convenient was the skin of the beaver. Furs were in demand in Europe, and could always, without much loss, be converted into coin or its equivalent."—[Bronson, Connecticut Currency, p. 7.]

golden armor, there is too much reason to fear that it was a sorry lot of "lean kine" that were turned in for payment. The public records of the Colony of Massachusetts bear amusing testimony to the depravity of human nature, in culling out the worst of the flock in settlement of taxes; and no one who is familiar with the frontier life of our day but has had occasion to be astonished at the capabilities of some of the animal species, in the way of furnishing gaunt and puny specimens for consumption by the "wards of the nation." Not a few articles, otherwise reasonably well suited to use as money, fail in this important respect of uniformity of size and quality.

Again, it is desirable that the article which is to be used as money should be such as will cost little or nothing for keeping, and will not readily deteriorate. The mention of the first condition reveals how poorly fitted cattle are for use as money[1] in any but a pastoral state of society (where they, in fact, keep themselves), owing to their remarkable physiological property of being able to "eat their heads off," every little while. Especially did the good people of Massachusetts find cattle unsuited for receipt into the public treasury. It is astonishing how much a cow can eat without either giving milk or gaining flesh, if she belongs to a government or a corporation.

Liability to deterioration is so far common to most forms of wealth as to leave but few without serious disadvantages in their use as money. Rust, insects, excessive moisture, undue heating, even mere exposure to the air, work mischief more or less rapidly to most of the

---

[1] "Usage qui suppose la possession facile de riches pâturages."—[Roscher, Wolowski's translation. § 118.]

treasures of earth. In the degree, therefore, in which any article is subject to waste or deterioration, is it unfitted to serve as money. This, however, was not the view of Peter Martyr, who, contemplating the bags of cacao used by the early Mexicans in their exchanges, was led to exclaim, "Blessed money! which exempts its possessors from avarice, since it cannot be long hoarded or hidden under ground!" In his cheerful optimism this writer deserves to take rank, at least approximately, with those philosophers of to-day who, after discovering all sorts of good things about our greenbacks, have declared it to be their crowning excellence that no other nation can, or will, take them from us.

Still another thing which is to be desired in that commodity which is to serve as money, is that it shall be susceptible of division, according to the ever varying necessities of exchange, without any important loss of its own utility thereby. Grain, and not a few others of the articles which we have referred to as used for money, in one country or another, at one period or another, have possessed this property. The lack of it would prove a fatal objection in the case of many commodities in other ways well adapted to such uses. It was reported by some early travelers that the Tartars, when in want of meat, would take a steak from the living animal, and by some means close the wound till the exigencies of the larder demanded another cut off the flank. If the Tartars ever had this knack of serving up beef as occasion required, other peoples have not derived it from them, but have found it necessary to deal with the living animal as a whole. This difficulty or impossibility of a division without loss, clearly would throw out many commodities from possible use as money. The tailor, while he could put on a patch of any required dimensions, corresponding to a loaf of any size of the baker's bread, could not well split a coat down the back to make change, or sell one pantaloon without its fellow.

So much for money as a medium of exchange; but further, it is evident that, to enable an article to perform the function of a standard for deferred payments, a certain steadiness in value is essential. That men may safely promise to pay down, at a future date, definite quantities of a specific commodity, it is highly important that a given quantity of that commodity shall then represent approximately the same cost of production as at the time the bargain is made. Otherwise, grave uncertainty will be introduced into every contract, with the strong probability that one or the other party will suffer serious loss, to the discouragement of industry and trade.

Thus, through the capriciousness of the seasons, a bushel of wheat may represent, in one year, an amount of labor greater or less by fifty per cent. than in the preceding or the succeeding year. For the payment of rents, through terms of years, the lessor may perhaps take the chance of good years with bad (though a long succession of bad or of good harvests is a not unfamiliar occurrence); but ordinary commercial transactions could not be carried on amid the uncertainty as to the value of payments to be made or received, which would be involved in the use of an article varying so greatly in cost of production within a brief term.

Such being the material properties most important in any article which is to be used as money, we note that the metals have been found to possess them in a higher degree than any other considerable class of commodities.

Iron, lead, tin or copper, early became the money of nearly all the nations whose history we know. Of these the first[1] possesses perhaps the fewest advantages; yet when we compare it with cattle or wheat, we find ample reason for the preference given to it, over them, in use as money, in very early times. It is, indeed, subject to deterioration by exposure to the atmosphere; but it has a life of many years, even in the worst conditions. This fact gives it comparative stability of value. In early times, moreover, iron possessed considerable value for its bulk. The art of mining being in its infancy, a comparatively small amount of the metal represented the labor of days;[2] while its numerous uses in the economy of life, whether civilized or savage, contributed to its general acceptability among all classes and between different communities.

Lead was used as money both by the Romans and the early English, and is still received in Burmah, by weight, in small payments.[3]

Tin served the Mexicans[4] as money, even after gold and silver were known among them, and was in extensive use for personal ornament and in the arts of decoration. It was long and extensively used as money in Sweden, and is still so employed among the Chinese, along the shores of the Malay Peninsula, and in Prince of Wales Island.

But of the metals named, copper has the greatest im-

---

[1] The money of Lacedæmon was of iron; Sweden was reduced to iron money during the wars of Charles XII; money of this metal is still used by the inhabitants of Senegambia.

[2] Lead was cheaper than iron, in England, down to the Grea' Plague.—[Rogers, Hist. Agriculture and Prices, i, 599.]

[3] E. Seyd, Bullion and the Foreign Exchanges, p. 368.

[4] Prescott, Conquest of Mexico, ii, 140.

portance in the history of money. From its higher cost of production, it very generally superseded iron, as the latter came, in the progress of the mining art, to possess a value for its bulk unsuited to the office of exchange; while silver was yet too rare and precious for the use of the humbler classes. During the silver famine of the Middle Ages copper again returned to be the principal and most valuable money in common circulation, silver and gold being found only in the cabinets of nobles and the caskets of bankers. The employment of copper as an actual money has continued down even to our day, though we have seen it reduced to the less honorable office of small change, and even, within the last few years, degraded to a mere ingredient of coin-metal, as in France, or dispensed with entirely in favor of the cleaner nickel, as in the United States.

## SILVER AND GOLD.

Two metals, however, gold and silver, have enjoyed a pre-eminence in the history of Money, which has earned for them the proud title, the Precious Metals.

Not that they are the most costly of all; several[1] metals surpass both of them in this respect; but this is true only of metals found in extremely limited quantities.

Of the two, silver first came to be used as money. We hear of it in the early history of the Hebrew race. We find it coined among the Greeks and Romans while, for long ages, gold remained merely treasure, devoted almost exclusively to regal or sacerdotal uses.

"Silver," says Mr. Seyd,[2] "ranks next after gold, in the

---

[1] Eight, I believe. Vanadium I have seen quoted at more than eight times its weight in gold.

[2] Bullion and the Foreign Exchanges, pp. 111-5. Mr. Seyd gives an interesting description of the properties of silver.

class of noble metals, though platinum and its kindred metals are less liable to alteration, and less subject to the influence of chemical agents. But silver, on the other hand, possesses many most valuable properties which the metals of the platinum group lack altogether."

The extreme beauty of silver, and its numerous uses in the economy of life make it an object of admiration and desire among people in all degrees of social advancement. The brightest of all metals, its surpassing brilliancy almost justifies the preference expressed by the barefoot boy of Sir Walter Scott, "Give me the white money, please." Practically imperishable (since the sulphide which forms over silver in impure air, veiling its beauty, protects it from further action of the atmosphere), a high degree of steadiness in value is secured by the large volume of existing metal in comparison with the results of current production. Easily fusible, highly ductile, silver would have filled our utmost conception of a money-material had not the earth yielded one transcendent metallic product, in comparison with which even silver fades from desire.

In Oriental worship, the temple of the Moon is inlaid with Silver; the temple of the Sun is resplendent with Gold.

The advantages which this royal metal possesses for use as money have been so often illustrated, and have been so far intimated in what has been shown of the defects of other commodities and even of the other metals, that it will not be necessary to dwell upon them here at length.

The practical indestructibility of gold—for it can only be attacked by agents which have to be specially prepared for the purpose—at once gives assurance to him who receives it that he can suffer no loss from natural causes through taking it, and imparts to it, when used as money, the highest attainable steadiness in value.

"The price of all metals," says Adam Smith, "though liable to slow and gradual variations, varies less from year to year than that of almost any other part of the rude produce of land; and the price of the precious metals is even less liable to sudden variations than that of the coarse ones.

"The durableness of metals is the foundation of this extraordinary steadiness of price.[1] The corn which was brought to market last year will be all or almost all consumed long before the end of this year. But some part of the iron which was brought from the mine two or three hundred years ago may be still in use, and perhaps some part of the gold which was brought from it two or three thousand years ago. The different masses of corn which in different years must supply the consumption of the world will always be nearly in proportion to the respective produce of those different years.

"But the proportion between the different masses of iron which may be in use in two different years will be very little affected by any accidental difference in the produce of the iron mines of those two years; and the proportion between the masses of gold will be still less affected by any such difference in the produce of the gold mines. Though the product of a greater part of metallic mines therefore varies perhaps still more from year to year than that of the greater part of corn-fields, those variations have not the same effect upon the price

[1] "Tandis que des moissons plus ou moins abondantes font rapidement osciller le prix du blé, parce que la portion conservée n'atteint pas le chiffre d'une seule récolte, les alluvions d'or et d'argent n'expriment qu' une fraction minime des existences de métaux précieux." —[Wolowski, L'Or et l'Argent, 11.]

of the one species of commodities as upon that of the other."—[Wealth of Nations, i, 221.]

The fusibility, ductility and malleability of gold form a group of properties of the highest importance, as we shall have occasion farther to note when we come to speak of coinage, while they add vastly to its uses in the arts industrial and decorative. One cubic inch of gold, Mr. Seyd tells us, may be drawn out to cover fourteen millions of square inches. Gold may be refined and alloyed, united and divided, with absolutely no loss of the pure metal[1] in the repeated process. Practically a slight loss is experienced in a corresponding treatment of silver.[2] Silver, on the other hand, has a certain advantage over gold in respect to tenacity.

"The compendious value of gold," to use Mr. Jacob's phrase, allows a vast amount of purchasing power to be concentrated, for conveyance or for concealment, in small bulk. In his memoir upon the Production of Gold and Silver, Humboldt states that at then existing prices, one kilogram of gold would purchase 1611 kilograms of copper, 9700 of iron, 20,794 of wheat, 27,655 of rye or 31,717 of barley.

But while gold is thus precious, it is found in sufficient quantity to allow of its convenient use as an every-day medium of exchange in all highly advanced industrial communities. Were gold as costly as vanadium, the piece in which a workman received his day's wages might,

[1] "Si, par rapport à la société, la monnaie peut à bon droit être assimilée aux machines, cette machine-là se distingue de toutes les autres, en ce que les matières dont elle est faite sont très précieuses et possèdent, à très-peu près, la même valeur que la machine toute confectionnée. Le bois, la fonte, le fer, le cuivre, qui entrent dans la composition d'un mécanisme quelconque, si vous brisez celuici, perdent beaucoup de ce qu'ils valaient ajustés ensemble."—[Chevalier La Monnaie, p. 591.]

[2] Jacob, Inquiry into the Precious Metals, p. 166.

as Mr. McAdam says, be carried off and lost through an inadvertent sneeze, and would habitually require to be handled with delicate pincers. While it is true that the value of any commodity varies with the quantity in which it is supplied; and that, were there less gold, each portion would bear a higher purchasing power, and thus, theoretically, all the commodities of the world's commerce might be exchanged through the agency of the gold which is found in a half-eagle; yet, practically, it is of consequence that the metal or metals employed, while possessing great value for a given bulk and weight, should be found in quantity to afford pieces of such purity as to remain clean and bright, and of such size as to be conveniently handled and carried about, in number sufficient to achieve the highest convenience of exchange, according to the spending-habits of the community, habits which will vary much with the social condition of the people, the ratios obtaining in the distribution of wealth among the several classes, the facilities of intercourse, the characteristics of the local industry (as when a community produces mainly that which itself wishes to consume, or the reverse), etc., etc. It is evident that in every varying condition of society and industry there must be, between the body of potential purchasers—those, that is, who have occasion and the means to buy goods offered in the markets—and the body of coins or money-pieces of a given size, a numerical proportion which best answers the requirements of the community; and that, as this proportion is departed from, either in the way of excess or of deficiency in the number of coins or money-pieces, through using a material too cheap or too costly, the convenience of exchange will be impaired, very slightly indeed at first, and perhaps for a long time not appreciably, but to the certain annoyance and obstruction of trade and industry should this course of things proceed to extremity in either direction. The iron of the Lacedæmonians would be an impossible money to-day. Copper, an ounce of which, speaking roughly, is worth a pound of iron, has become too bulky to serve as the sole, or the most valuable, money of highly civilized countries, and is hence remitted to those less advanced, or is confined to use as the smallest of change. And within the present decade several nations have resorted for the first time, upon an extensive scale, to the coinage of gold, on the plea that silver has become too cheap a material for the common coin of commerce.

We have seen that the precious metals derive a remarkable degree of steadiness in value through their high degree of durability, from which it results that great changes in the amount of current production have only a slight effect upon the total volume in the possession of mankind. We have now to note in closing, that money of gold and silver receives an additional support in maintaining its value uniform, through the rapid extension of demand for the use of these metals in the arts,[1] which is the sure concomitant of an increase of supply threatening to reduce their power in exchange.

---

[1] Looking to this demand for gold and silver from the arts, industrial or decorative, Prof. N. W. Senior, in his lectures on "The Cost of Obtaining Money," declares that "the value of the precious metals, as money, must depend ultimately on their value as materials of jewelry and plate, since, if they were not used as commodities they could not circulate as money." [In the Edinburgh Review of July, 1843, Prof. Senior wrote: "The primary cause of the utility of gold is, of course, its use as the material of plate; the secondary cause is its use as money."] Prof. Senior appears here to be in error. The value of money (with a given supply) is governed by the aggregate demand for it from all sources, both for use in the arts and for service as money.

## CHAPTER III.

### THE TERRITORIAL DISTRIBUTION OF MONEY.

WE have noted the material properties which have given to gold and silver their special fitness for use as money. In part, these properties may be said to contribute to that universal acceptability which is the prime condition of a medium of exchange. In part, they may be regarded as affording advantages, especially in the way of coinage, which are independent of and additional to that acceptability, since we know that the passion for gold and silver appeared, to curse or to bless mankind, before the art of coinage was known. But while the universal acceptability of these metals has fitted them to perform their great service to trade, and through trade to production, a false apprehension of the advantages of their possession has led peoples, philosophers and statesmen into errors of the gravest practical consequences.

The so-called Mercantile Theory, which, nearly down to the present century, exercised undisputed sway over the councils of every commercial state, the influence of which survives in some measure to our day, defying the power of reason, is a growth out of this root.

"Midas," says Mr. McLeod, "was the parent of the Mercantile System: and for centuries every government in Europe was imbued with his ideas. . . . .

"Midas saw that, with treasure in his hand, he was wealthy,—he could obtain whatever he wanted, and could command the services of others. He quite forgot that gold was only of use while it could *command something else*, and that if that something else were changed to gold, his gold would be of no use whatever. Gold, therefore, was only of use because of the multitude of things which were not gold. The very same ideas gradually grew up in Europe. Sovereigns saw that their chief power consisted in the treasures they could accumulate. It then became a cardinal point of their policy to encourage the importation of money as much as possible and to prohibit its export.[1] From about the beginning of the 14th Century the laws of nearly every country in Europe endeavored to prevent the export of money. Statesmen and merchants were all infected with this delusion, which was greatly fostered by the discovery of the New World. The Spaniards, dazzled with the brilliant prospect of securing the greatest part of the wealth in the world, without labor, imagined that the well-being of the country consisted in amassing enormous heaps of gold and silver. But they wholly mistook the means for the end, not discerning that the precious metals are only precious so

---

[1] The usual method taken by kings and parliaments to increase the stock of money within their respective countries was to prohibit the export of gold and silver, the penalty not infrequently being death; but, in addition to this, acts of the legislature, in both England and Scotland, decreed that merchants, foreigners as well as natives, should import a certain quantity of coin or bullion in every ship, in proportion to the value of the other goods, and should expend that coin and bullion, with all the money received for their imports, in purchasing the commodities of the country. These laws were, however, soon repealed. By a treaty with Sweden cited by Hume, the Swedes were permitted to export English commodities free of duty, provided the price was paid in bullion.

long as they are used for setting industry in motion, while they encourage the tilling of the land—the mother of increase—or the building of ships to promote the commerce of nations, or plying the loom to produce clothing for mankind."—[Economical Philosophy, i, 50.]

Upon the consequences of this delusion, to Spain first and most heavily, and to the other countries of Europe, in restraints laid upon trade and in wars waged for a commercial supremacy which should enable the victor to control the movement of the precious metals, which had come to be regarded as the true and sole wealth, it is not necessary to dwell.

To Adam Smith the world owed its deliverance out of the power of this monstrous delusion, which had for centuries been more potent for evil, perhaps, than any other which has afflicted mankind. Dr. Smith's refutation of the Mercantile Theory will ever remain the great monument of his fame, for what a century ago was the standing policy of all the statesmen of Europe, has now scarcely an apologist or defender.[1]

Nothing has been added to Adam Smith's great argument. It has required no expansion, no corroboration, no further illustration, no adaptation, even, to popular comprehension. At once and forever, the Mercantile Theory fell out of the intellectual sympathy of mankind.

Yet, unfortunately, it has not wholly lost its hold upon the imagination and the sensibilities of the masses, and

---

[1] "Even countries retaining a highly protective or restrictive system," says Chevalier, "now allow the exportation of money." Of Russia, however, Mr. Seyd says: "The exportation of silver has for a long time been prohibited; that of gold is periodically allowed, but just now [1868] it is prohibited."—[Bullion and the Foreign Exchanges, 332.]

even of the refined and educated. "There are few," says Prof. Cairnes,[1] "even among professed economists, who are free from the influence of the Mercantile Theory of Wealth."

So deeply rooted is this instinct respecting gold and silver, that Prof. Price is drawn to use this vigorous language respecting it: "The greatest of commercial delusions is the wonderful apostasy about gold. I call it apostasy because the light was made to shine, and men willfully shut their eyes against it. Adam Smith exposed in undying words the emptiness and the absurdity of that inveterate fallacy of the trading world which has been called the Mercantile Theory. Many writers of great ability followed him in the same path, and this famous theory became almost a by-word for ridicule. Men for a time were shamed out of such a preposterous illusion: but for a time only. Truth in this region proved itself to be no match for error; the tendency to backslide into the old thoughts, into the old habit of looking only at what was visible and on the surface, was irresistible. Money buys goods; with money debts are paid; money opens shops and warehouses; loans and advances are counted in money: therefore, money is the true riches; money is the one thing of which there never can be too much; money is the soul and essence of all trade; money is the wealth of nations." "I confess," continues Prof. Price, "that I never address myself to the examination of such language without some feeling of humiliation: to have to repeat Adam Smith's refutation of the Mercantile Theory to the whole trading world, in an age remarkable for intellectual activity, is a spectacle far from gratifying to the believers in the power of truth and genius. How

---

[1] Essays in Pol. Econ., p. 98ⁿ.

can one hope for the victory of truth, when an exploded delusion can re-appear in such force, and assert its mastery over a whole community? What confidence can be placed in the success of new arguments when reasoning of the most powerful order has served only to flash a brief outbreak of light, to be followed after by darkness more universal, more deeply settled down, than ever?"

The image with which this quotation closes is manifestly too strong justly to represent the phase of the public mind which Prof. Price deprecates. Far from the darkness having become more universal, more deeply settled down after the lightning flash, the influence of the Mercantile Theory was never so slight as now. That any of its effects survive such universal admission of its falsity, only affords another instance of the tenacity of popular prejudice and superstition.

The complaints which Profs. Cairnes and Price make respecting the persistence in popular feeling of the refuted notion that money is a means and not an end; that it is something more or other than a tool for a specific and highly technical purpose, brings us squarely up against the question:

## HOW MUCH MONEY DOES AN INDUSTRIAL COMMUNITY REQUIRE?

I say industrial, instead of commercial, because I desire strongly to insist on the distinction with which I started out, that the function of trade is to allow the division of labor to be carried out to its economical maximum; and that money confers a benefit, not because it facilitates trade, as if that were an end in itself, but because, by facilitating exchanges, it allows the division of labor in production to be carried as far as industrial reasons exist for its extension.

How much money, then, does an industrial community require?

To be in a position to answer this question, we must ascertain the law of the distribution of the precious metals.

Perhaps no doctrine is more truly entitled to be called Ricardian than that which is generally accepted on this subject, with or without qualification, by the whole body of economists. Not that Mr. Ricardo first conceived the doctrine, or first taught it; but it may well be called his, on account of the breadth of statement and power of expression with which he advanced it, in the memorable pamphlet "On the High Price of Bullion," (1809), which preceded, and in a certain sense brought on, the great Bullion Controversy.

"The precious metals employed for circulating the commodities of the world, previously to the establishment of banks, have been supposed by the most approved writers on political economy to have been divided into certain proportions among the different civilized nations of the earth, according to the state of their commerce and wealth, and, therefore, according to the number and frequency of the payments which they had to perform. When so divided, they preserved everywhere the same value, and as each country had an equal necessity for the quantity actually in use, there could be no temptation offered to either for their importation or exportation.

"If the quantity of gold and silver in the world employed as money were exceedingly small, or abundantly great, it would not in the least affect the proportions in which they would be divided among the different nations —the variation in their quantity would have produced nc other effect than to make the commodities for which they were exchanged comparatively dear or cheap. The smaller quantity of money would perform the functions of a circulating medium as well as the larger."

. . . . . . .

If, in the progress towards wealth, one nation advanced more rapidly than the others, that nation would require and obtain a greater proportion of the money of the world. Its commerce, its commodities, and its payments would increase, and the general currency of the world would be divided according to the new proportions. All countries, therefore, would contribute their share to this effectual demand.

"In the same manner, if any nation wasted part of its wealth, or lost part of its trade, it could not retain the same quantity of circulating medium which it before possessed. A part would be exported, and divided among the other nations till the usual proportions were re-established."

"If a mine of gold were discovered in either of these countries, the currency of that country would be lowered in value in consequence of the increased quantity of the precious metals brought into circulation, and would therefore no longer be of the same value as that of other countries. Gold and silver, whether in coin or in bullion, obeying the law which regulates all other commodities, would immediately become articles of exportation; they would leave the country where they were cheap, for those countries where they were dear, and would continue to do so as long as the mine should prove productive, and till the proportion existing between capital and money in each country before the discovery of the mine were again established, and gold and silver restored everywhere to one value."

"Thus, then, it appears that the currency of one country can never, for any length of time, be much more valuable, as far as equal quantities of the precious metals are concerned, than that of another; that excess of currency is but a relative term."

From no logical consequence of his doctrine did Mr. Ricardo shrink.

"The exportation of the specie," he says, in the same pamphlet, "may at all times be safely left to the discretion of individuals. It will not be exported more than any other commodity, unless its exportation should be advantageous to the country. If it be advantageous to export it, no laws can effectually prevent its exportation."

"The exportation of coin," he says again, "is caused by its cheapness." "We should not import more goods than we export, unless we had a redundancy of currency." Again: "Specie will be sent abroad to discharge a debt only when it is superabundant; only when it is the cheapest exportable commodity." "*Money can never be exported to excess;*"—never to such an extent "*as to occasion a void in the circulation.*"

Not only did Mr. Ricardo insist that the exportation of specie might safely be left to the natural course of trade, in the assurance that it could never be carried to excess, never to such an extent as to produce a void in the circulation; and that all outflow of specie certainly indicated an excess of money, the reduction of which was wholesome to trade, and through trade, to production; but he daunted many of his followers by advancing boldly to the extreme case of a large subsidy to be paid suddenly abroad, in time of war, when foreign ports were closed and commerce in a large degree suspended, and declared, without hesitation or qualification, that such a subsidy to a foreign country would not be paid in specie unless the circulating medium at home were redundant.

This doctrine was attacked by Mr. Malthus in the "Edinburgh Review" (Feb., 1811), with arguments of which the following extracts contain the gist. Mr. Malthus supposes the necessity arising for importing corn largely, or for paying a subsidy abroad, and proceeds as follows.

"A part of the debt will be paid in these metals [gold and silver], and a part by the increased exports of commodities. But, as far as it is paid by the transmission of bullion, this transmission does not merely originate in redundancy of currency. It is not occasioned by its cheapness. It is not, as Mr. Ricardo endeavors to persuade us, the cause of an unfavorable balance, instead of the effect. It is not merely a salutary remedy for a redundant currency; but it is owing precisely to the cause mentioned by Mr. Thornton,—the unwillingness of the creditor nation to receive a great additional quantity of goods not wanted for immediate consumption, without being bribed to it by excessive cheapness; and its willingness to receive bullion—the currency of the commercial world—without any such bribe.

"It is unquestionably true as stated by Mr. Ricardo, that no nation will pay a debt in the precious metals if it can do it cheaper by commodities; but the prices of commodities are liable to great depressions from a glut in the market; whereas, the precious metals, on account of their having been constituted by the universal consent of society the general medium of exchange and instrument of commerce, will pay a debt of the largest amount at its nominal estimation, according to the quantity of bullion contained in the respective currencies of the countries in question."

I have said that in carrying his doctrine out without

qualification to the case of a foreign subsidy in case of war, Mr. Ricardo daunted some who held with him up to that point. Mr. Henry Thornton, subsequently one of the authors of the Bullion Report[1], in his important work on "Paper Credit," published in 1802, had admitted that in case of a disastrous failure of successive harvests, an exportation of money might take place, without reference to the state of the domestic circulation, and to the detriment of trade. The following are his words:

"Though the value of the commercial exports and imports of a country will have this general tendency to proportion themselves to each other, there will not fail occasionally to arise a very great inequality between them. A good or a bad harvest in particular will have a considerable influence in producing this temporary difference. The extra quantity of corn and other articles imported into Great Britain in this and the last year, with a view to supply the deficiency of our own crops, must have amounted in value to so many millions, that it may justly excite surprise that we should have been able, during an expensive war, to provide the means of canceling our foreign debt so far even as we have done; especially when the peculiar interruptions to our commerce are also considered."

Mr. Thornton dwells for several pages on the causes thus tending to produce an unfavorable balance, and resumes: "The fair statement of the case seems to be this: At the time of a very unfavorable balance (produced, for example, through a failure of the harvest), a country has occasion for large supplies of corn from abroad; but either it has not the means of supplying at the instant a sufficient quantity of goods as a return, or,

---

[1] See pp. 353–4.

which is much the more probable case, and which, I suppose, is more applicable to England, the goods which the country having the unfavorable balance is able to furnish as means of canceling its debt are not in such demand abroad as to afford the prospect of a tempting or even of a tolerable price; and this want of a demand may happen possibly through some political circumstance which has produced, in a particular quarter, the temporary interruption of an established branch of commerce. The country, therefore, which has the favorable balance being, to a certain degree, eager for payment, but not in immediate want of all that supply of goods which would be necessary to pay the balance, prefers gold as part, at least, of the payment, for gold can always be turned to a more beneficial use than a very great overplus of any other commodity."

Mr. Thomas Tooke, again, in his pamphlet on the "State of the Currency," published after the Panic of 1825, discusses the practicability of meeting large and unexpected balances of payments by the shipment of goods, in which he adduces considerations to show that an increased export of ordinary commodities cannot always be made with the promptness which a sudden exigency may demand, the disturbing causes being, in his view, of considerable extent and duration.[1]

It is to be noted that since the date of these several publications, the importance of the exceptional causes contemplated by Messrs. Thornton, Ricardo, and Tooke

[1] Thus Mr. Tooke states that "taking the time occupied in the shipment, the transmission, the interval between arrival and sale, and again between the sale and the expiration of the credit, a period of a year and a half, or two years, may elapse before the funds arising from such shipments can be made available to foreign payments."—[P. 106.]

has been greatly diminished. The railway car and the ocean steamship to convey freight, with the telegraph by land and sea, to convey information of commercial demand and to carry back orders for goods, have much reduced the scope of the retarding forces, while the almost universal reduction in the term of commercial credit has rendered the proceeds of exportation available at a much earlier date.

A second cause which has operated within the same interval to take away much of the importance which the participants in this high debate, in the early part of the century, attached to any sudden and extensive disturbance of trade or demand for foreign expenditure, is the remarkable extension, coincidently with the reduction in the term of commercial credit, of the national borrowing-system, under which any organized government, however poor its credit, can borrow, at a price; while governments of resource and reputation are enabled to contract loans to an almost unlimited extent upon favorable terms.

Such is the law of distribution of the precious metals as expounded and enforced by Mr. Ricardo. In his view, gold and silver keep their due proportions, the world over, as the waters of a lake preserve their level. If any force operates to disturb that level, every particle in the whole mass moves instantly to restore the equilibrium. So long as the movement of the precious metals is not restrained by force of law (and Mr. Ricardo holds the force of law in this respect to be very slight[1]), no country can retain

[1] "It is by all writers indiscriminately allowed that no penalties can prevent the coin from being melted when its value as bullion becomes superior to its value as coin."—[High Price of Bullion.]

Mr. Mill, however, is drawn to remark: "The effect of the prohi-

an excess, or suffer a deficiency, above or below its own just share.

That a country has no mineral wealth of its own puts it at no disadvantage for the securing of its proper part of the world's supply of money. "For gold," said John Locke, in his glorious paper on "The Value of Money," addressed to the Lord-Keeper Somers, "For gold grows not that I know in our country, and silver so little that one-hundred-thousandth part of the silver we have now in England was not drawn out of any mines in this island." "The power of manufacturing at a cheap rate," wrote Henry Thornton, "is far more valuable than any stock of bullion." And Prof. Senior, in his lectures (1830) on "The Cost of Obtaining Money," writes: "The mine worked by England is the general market of the world. The miners are those who produce those commodities by the export of which the precious metals are obtained."

It will be observed that Mr. Ricardo makes Price the agent in effecting this movement of gold and silver. It is because the purchasing power of money falls when it is supplied in excess, that the excess tends to run away.

---

bition cannot, however, have been so entirely insignificant as it has been supposed to be by writers on the subject. The facts adduced by Mr. Fullarton show that it required a greater percentage of difference in value between coin and bullion than has commonly been imagined, to bring the coin to the melting-pot."—[Political Economy, III, ix, 1.]

"The conscience of the exporter, and the value of a false oath,' says Mr. Bosanquet, "are correctly stated by the committee at four and one half per cent."—[Practical Observations, etc., p. 30.] The market price of consciences would seem to have fallen in the course of a century, for "A. V.," in his letter to Lord Godolphin, in 1696, speaks of twenty per cent. as "a good alloy for any scruple of conscience" in the melting of the coin.

It is because the purchasing power of money rises where its quantity is deficient, that gold and silver set in like a tide[1] towards whatever country lacks its due distributive share of the volume in existence. And in the case of a new supply, as from an opened mine, the added amount, wherever produced, is swiftly and surely apportioned among all the nations having commercial relations, just as a bucket of water poured upon the centre of a lake will not long disturb the general level.

Whether Mr. Ricardo does not attribute an undue degree of mobility to the precious metals, under the agency of price; whether the retarding influences have not more power than this great thinker attributes to them; whether, during the delays attending the redistribution of the precious metals following any important disturbing cause, effects may not be produced which we cannot afford to overlook in our philosophy of money, are questions we shall yet have to discuss.[2] The general truth of the doctrine is not to be disputed, nor can its importance be disparaged. It sets justly forth the tendency of great forces which never cease to operate, whatever obstruction they may encounter, throughout the world of commerce.

"The amount of money in a country" is, therefore, in Mr. Ricardo's words, "regulated by its value."—[Reply to Bosanquet.] And, conversely, the value of money in any country is determined by the amount existing.

We are now in a position to undertake the inquiry how much money a country requires? It is that amount

---

[1] Mr. Tooke's favorite illustration, frequently repeated in his works

[2] See p. 150.

which will keep its prices (after allowance is made for the cost of transporting goods[1]) at a level with those of the countries with which it has commercial relations.[2] Thus, if it costs $2 (including charges for freight, insurance, interest, commissions, etc.,) to carry a barrel of flour from New York to London, and flour of a given quality sells in London at $12, there should be money enough in New York to allow and to enable $10 to buy a barrel of flour of that quality.

But what determines whether $10, or more or less, shall buy a barrel of flour in New York? Why will not $8 buy it? Why will less than $12 do it?

This brings us to the question, what is the relation between the amount of money in a country and the general scale of prices existing therein? a question which, if not the most difficult in Political Economy, is perhaps the one upon which the most contradictory opinions have been expressed by economists of reputation.

The following is Mr. John Stuart Mill's statement of

---

[1] Il peut arriver que le prix de l'argent diffère d'une manière durable de pays à pays, lorsque des obstacles permanents s'opposent au mouvement de va-et-vient, qui rétablirait le niveau. Ainsi les métaux précieux se maintiendront à un prix élevé dans les contrées qui ne peuvent se les procurer qu'en livrant en échange des biens d'un transport très-difficile."—[Roscher (Wolowski's Tranl.), § 125.]

[2] "Every country (temporary fluctuations excepted) will possess, and have in circulation, just that quantity of money which will perform all the exchanges required of it, consistently with maintaining a value conformable to its cost of production. The prices of things will, in the average, be such that money will exchange for its own cost in all other goods; and precisely because the quantity cannot be prevented from affecting the value, the quantity itself will be kept at the amount consistent with that standard of prices—at the amount necessary for performing, at those prices, all the business required of it." —[J. S. Mill, Political Economy, III, ix, 3.]

the relation between money and commodities:[1] "The supply of money is the quantity of it which people are wanting to lay out: that is, all the money they have in their possession, except what they are hoarding, or at least keeping by them as a reserve for future contingencies. The supply of money, in short, is all the money in circulation at the time.

"The demand for money, again, consists of all the goods offered for sale. Every seller of goods is a buyer of money, and the goods he brings with him constitute his demand. The demand for money differs from the demand for other things in this, that it is limited only by the means of the purchaser. The demand for other things is for so much and no more; but there is always a demand for as much money as can be got. . . . As the whole of the goods in the market compose the demand for money, so the whole of the money constitutes the demand for goods." . . .

[Mr. Mill then supposes an increase of money to take place and prices thereupon to rise.]

"It is to be remarked that this ratio would be precisely that in which the quantity of money had been increased. If the whole money in circulation was doubled, prices would be doubled. If it was only increased one-fourth, prices would rise one-fourth.[2] . . .

---

[1] The following is the statement made by Montesquieu: "Si l'on compare la masse de l'or et de l'argent qui est dans le monde avec la somme des marchandises qui y sont, il est certain que chaque denrée ou marchandise en particulier pourra être comparée à une certaine portion de la masse entière de l'or et de l'argent. Comme le total de l'une est au total de l'autre, la partie de l'une sera à la partie de l'autre."—[De l'Esprit des Lois, xxii, 7.]

[2] "That commodities would rise or fall in price, in proportion to the increase or diminution of money, I assume as a fact which is incontrovertible."—[Ricardo, Reply to Bosanquet.]

"The very same effect would be produced on prices, if we suppose the goods diminished instead of the money increased; and the contrary effect, if the goods were increased or the money diminished. . . .

"So that the value of money, other things being the same, varies inversely as its quantity; every increase of quantity lowering the value, and every diminution raising it in a ratio exactly equivalent.

. . . . . . .

"From what precedes, it might for a moment be supposed that all the goods on sale in a country at any one time are exchanged for all the money existing and in circulation at that same time; or, in other words, that there is always in circulation in a country a quantity of money equal in value to the whole of the goods then and there on sale. But this would be a complete misapprehension. . . .

"If we assume the quantity of goods on sale, and the number of times these goods are resold, to be fixed quantities, the value of money will depend upon its quantity, together with the average number of times that each piece changes hands in the process.

. . . . . . .

"The propositions we have laid down . . . must for the present be understood as applying only to a state of things in which money, that is, gold or silver, is the exclusive instrument of exchange and actually passes

---

"If the quantity of gold in a country whose currency consists of gold should be increased in any given proportion, the quantity of other articles and the demand for them remaining the same, the value of any given commodity measured in the coin of that country would be increased in the same proportion."—[Huskisson, The Depreciation of the Currency.]

from hand to hand at every purchase, credit in any of its shapes being unknown.[1] . . . .

"In no commodity is it the quantity in existence, but the quantity offered for sale, that determines the value. Whatever may be the quantity of money in the country, only that part of it will affect prices which goes into the markets for commodities, and is there actively exchanged against goods. . . . Money hoarded does not act on prices. Money kept in reserve by individuals to meet contingencies which do not occur, does not act on prices. The money in the coffers of the bank, or retained as a reserve by private bankers, does not act on prices until drawn out, nor even then, unless drawn out to be expended in commodities.

"It frequently happens that money, to a considerable amount, is brought into the country, is there actively employed as capital, and again flows out, without having ever once acted upon the markets of *commodities*,[2] but only upon the market of *securities*, or, as it is commonly though improperly called, the money market."

---

[1] By overlooking this proviso, Prof. Price, in his "Principles of Currency," was led to do grave injustice towards Mr. Mill, characterizing his proposition that all the goods on sale constitute the demand for money as "absolutely and glaringly untrue" [p. 162], and goes forward to show how cotton is sold for iron and iron for cotton without the intervention of money. No one, however, has more justly described (in the appropriate place) the office of barter and of credit in saving the use of money, than Mr. Mill; and in the above series of propositions he carefully guards himself against misconstruction by the proviso which Prof. Price so strangely overlooked.

[2] Mr. Ricardo appears to doubt whether this can occur, at least in an important degree. "There can," he says in his reply to Bosanquet, "be no great addition to the bullion of a country, the currency of which is of standard value, without causing an increase in the quantity of money." We shall meet the question further on.

"This is a case," continues Mr. Mill, "highly deserving of attention, and it is a fact now beginning to be recognized that the passage of the precious metals from country to country is determined much more than was formerly supposed[1] by the state of the loan market in different countries and much less by the state of prices."

In the above paragraphs Mr. Mill shows very clearly the fallacy of the popular notions which have crept into many a treatise not without merit, that the volume of money is in some way to be compared with the volume of accumulated wealth, or with the volume of annual production, or with the numbers of the population. The use of money, we have seen, arises out of trade. Hence it is the amount of trade, and not of production, that must determine price, the volume of money being fixed. But production and trade have no necessary or constant relation to each other. A community may have large production and little trade; or it may have great trade with relatively small production. If, as is conceivable, the entire product were to be consumed by the identical producers, no exchange at all would take place and no use of money whatever would be required.

But Mr. Mill's propositions require to be still further qualified. Let us suppose we are making arrangements for the transportation from Chicago to Baltimore of a large part of the wheat of the Northwest. It is evident that the number of cars of a given capacity will bear some necessary ratio to the bulk of grain to be carried; but it is also evident that we cannot ascertain how many cars will be needed to carry so much wheat till we know how often the cars can, on the average, make the trip.

---

[1] See Ricardo's statement of the law of the distribution of the precious metals.

So we must say of the supply of money: it is a quantity of two dimensions. We need to know not only its volume, the number of coins of a given weight and fineness of metal, but also its rate of movement, or, as is usually said, its rapidity of circulation.[1]

What have we thus far obtained? We have seen that the quantity of money required in any community bears no constant ratio to population, and that it is not determined by the amount of accumulated wealth, nor by the extent of the annual production;[2] but that, as the need of money arises wholly out of the fact of trade, we must look to the demands of trade to ascertain the quantity of money which a community shall employ, the question as to the demand for money being merely the question what goods are offered for money.

We have further seen that the supply of money is a quantity of two dimensions, the volume of the precious metals circulating—the number of pieces of a given weight and fineness—and the rate of their movement. "Engineers," says Mr. McLeod, "usually call the quantity of the motion of an engine its duty; so we may call the circulation of the currency its duty."[3]

---

[1] Mr. Mill severely criticises this phrase, and makes the following suggestion: "Rapidity of circulation being a phrase so ill adapted to express the only thing which it is of any importance to express by it, and having a tendency to confuse the subject by suggesting a meaning extremely different from the one intended, it would be a good thing if the phrase could be got rid of, and another substituted more directly significant of the idea meant to be conveyed. Some such expression as 'the efficiency of money,' though not unexceptionable, would do better."

[2] For similar reasons, not by the amount of taxation: a favorite view of some writers.

[3] Economical Philosophy, i. 211.

And this requires us to observe that, in the view of those who hold that money acts as a Measure of Value,[1] it performs this function in respect to a vast bulk of commodities where it is not called on to become a medium of exchange. It is its use as a medium of exchange which determines its value; yet its value, so determined, becomes the means of estimating values, without reference to actual exchanges.[2] It costs nothing to measure values, in this sense. It costs something to exchange them. It requires the actual use of money, for a longer or shorter space of time, to effect those double exchanges which we call buying and selling; but the prices resulting from such exchanges may be applied to far greater bodies of wealth, without the use of money. For example, a farmer sells a cow to be sent to the city for beef. It is only in the actual sale that money is used: but he takes the price—the money-value—thus determined, as the means of estimating the value of his herd; and so does the government in taxing him; so also do his neighbors in deciding how much of a man he is. Our farmer sells another cow, this time to a mechanical neighbor, and takes his pay in work. No money passes, and hence money serves here as a measure of value either for the cow or the work, only, if at all, in the way indicated, namely, the farmer compares his cow with the one he has just sold for money, and, knowing it to be as good a cow, or better, or poorer, fixes her price, in denominations of money, for the purposes of the contemplated ex-

---

[1] See pp 4-9.

[2] "The cotton must be calculated and expressed in money, and so must the iron, before they can be exchanged for one another; in other words, they must be measured, and that is done by money: but the actual money is not wanted at all."—[Prof. Price, Principles of Currency, p. 163.]

change, the same, or higher, or lower, to correspond with the facts of the case, while the mechanic, having worked the month before at money wages, and knowing his ability to render an equal service in the new relation, fixes the price of his labor, in denominations of money, for the purposes of the contemplated exchange, at the same amount per day or per week.

It will be observed that every time a barter transaction is substituted for buying and selling, the demand for money is thereby diminished and its value thereby lowered (the supply remaining the same), while the higher prices of commodities which result from the sales actually effected by the use of money, are carried over, in estimation, to the commodities remaining unsold, or to those whose transfer is accomplished by a direct exchange of goods for goods.

And conversely, just so far as sales for money are substituted for barter transactions, the demand for money being thereby increased, the value of money rises, and the lower prices which result are carried over, in estimation, to the commodities directly exchanged, or remaining in store.

But it is not alone the continuance, in part, of the barter system which reduces the demand for money. The introduction of the Credit System has an effect in the same direction. We saw that one great reason for the use of money was found in the want of coincidence in exchange, both as to times and quantities. The farmer harvests his crop within the space of a few weeks. But that which he purchases he requires now and then, week by week, throughout the year. In the discussion of the need for money which was quoted[1] from Prof.

---

[1] See p. 2.

Jevons's work, it was assumed that the farmer would not part with his produce until he had the material equivalent therefor actually in hand; and that the shop-keeper would be equally lacking in confidence towards the farmer. But if the farmer and the shop-keeper can agree to trust each other, this failure of coincidence in the times at which their respective needs are felt, will involve merely a little book-keeping, and no use of money. The farmer will take groceries, clothing, etc., as he requires them; and at the end of the season will haul down fifty bushels of wheat to the grocer, twenty to the tailor, etc., and the accounts are squared.

The tailor and the boot-maker no longer are plunged into that embarrassment in which we have contemplated them, arising out of a want of coincidence between the value of integral portions of their respective products. The tailor is no longer obliged to say: One coat is worth two pairs of boots; you have brought me a pair of boots: good; take half of this coat and wear it while I wear your boots; when I have worn them out I will take another pair, and then I will let you have the other half of the coat. The tailor credits the boot-maker with one pair of boots, bought, charges him with one entire coat, sold, and when the second pair of boots is brought in, gives credit for that also, squaring the transaction.

The above illustration may represent all that large body of exchange-transactions where the parties become mutually indebted; obligations very irregularly incurred as to time and amount, canceling each other, leaving a small balance, or perhaps none at all, to be paid in money. It does not for our present purpose matter whether such indebtedness is witnessed only in the memory of the parties, or takes the form of current book accounts, or is more formally evidenced and secured by notes of hand. Mr. McLeod states a case as follows:

"Let us suppose that A and B are reciprocally indebted to each other for the sale of goods. Let us suppose that A has bought goods from B to the amount of £10, and B has bought goods from A to the amount of £13. Then it is quite clear there are three ways of settling their dealings: First, each may send a clerk to the other to demand payment in full of his debt. This would require £23. Second, A may send £10 to B to discharge his debt and B may send it back to A with £3 more to discharge his debt. This method would require £13. Third, they may meet and set off their mutual debts against each other and pay only the difference in coin, requiring £3."—[Economical Philosophy, i, 208.]

But the credit system has a still wider application in economizing the use of money. The more minute the subdivision of labor, the more complicated become the relations of exchange, and the larger the proportion of obligations which are not mutual. The cotton manufacturer, perhaps, does not sell to a single person from whom he buys. Must he, therefore, receive a material equivalent every time he sells, and yield up a material equivalent every time he buys? Here again we find room for an expedient which vastly economizes the use of money. In the advance of civilization, the promissory note is made transferable.[1]

Of the efficiency of this agency for dispensing with the use of money, it is scarcely necessary to speak. I give to my creditor my note for the value of what I have received. In the fullness of time it is offered to me, not

---

[1] Some of our readers may not know that this is a very modern expedient. In England it was not introduced till the reign of Anne

by my creditor with a demand for payment, but by my debtor, who says, in effect, to me, here is your note again; now give me back that I gave you. He has bought my note from my original creditor, has put himself in the place of the creditor, and being thus at the same time both debtor and creditor to me, as I am both creditor and debtor to him, the transaction is complete. As Mr. Colwell remarks, "no currency can be more suited to pay a man with than that which he has issued himself."—[Ways and Means of Payment, p. 8.]

In this cancellation of indebtedness the banks perform a most important service,[1] saving a vast amount of time and labor, of annoyance and disappointment.

---

[1] In the first edition of this work, exception was taken to Prof. Price's definition of a bank, given in his "Principles of Currency" (1869), viz.: as "an Institution for the Transfer of Debts."

I was not aware, when that note was written, that in his work on Currency and Banking (1876), Prof. Price had proposed another and a wider definition of banking, which is not only beyond technical criticism, but which sets forth the function which the banker performs in modern industrial society with all the freedom and force which distingnish the writings of that eminent economist.

"He it is," says Prof. Price, "who selects the men into whose hands the wealth moved by his agency is to be committed. He neither created the wealth which his depositors sold, nor does he touch the other wealth which his borrowers purchase; but it signifies immensely to what sort of borrowers he gives the means of buying, by empowering them to draw cheques upon his bank. On him mainly depends whether the men who acquire the wealth of the nation will employ it wisely and preserve it by making use of it as capital in processes which will reproduce its consumption, or to men who will waste and destroy it in prodigal expenditure, or in unskilful trade, or in reckless speculations in mines, or in making railways in the wilds which cannot for a long period of years reproduce to the country the food, clothing, and materials which their construction consumed. This is the sole range of the banker's action—his selection of the men to whom the country's wealth shall be entrusted—and it is a mighty one."

In this view, the bank is a third party who, by putting itself now in the debtor's and now in the creditor's place, that is, becoming debtor and creditor alternately, at the request and on the warrant of the trading individuals concerned, effects that mutuality of obligations which is the condition of cancellation. It is in the bank that the claim of the creditor and the obligation of the debtor meet and are simultaneously discharged.

The Clearing-House, with its gigantic operations is, in respect to the cancellation of indebtedness, only the Banker's Bank, doing that for its constituent banks which the banks do for the individuals of the trading community. When it is said that the annual Clearing-House transactions of London now stand at or above £6,000,000,000, while those of New York are even greater, the importance of this contribution to the economy of money will be apparent.

While thus, through the operation of the Credit System, the occasion for the use of money is largely reduced in modern industrial society, and thus the demand for money is diminished, the efficiency of a given body of money is continually being heightened by improvements in the art of banking, and thus the supply of money is practically increased. For the present we leave out of account the substitution of paper for coin as a circulating medium, and keep in view a purely metallic currency. Even in 1809, Mr. Ricardo noted "the daily improvements which we are making in the art of economizing the use of the circulating medium," and Mr. Norman, in his "Remarks on Currency and Banking" (1838), states that notwithstanding the vast increase of production, England probably possessed less coin than she had fifty years before, while France had less than before the Revolution. Since that time, the telegraph and the steam-car, with the extension of the banking system, have still further increased the rate of movement which money is able to attain in the purchase of commodities and the payment of debts.

It has been shown that the Bank and the Clearing-House, through their agency in securing the Cancellation of Indebtedness, greatly diminish the amount of money which requires to be used in effecting the exchanges of a people. The Bank, through the Check System, also gives a higher efficiency to any given amount of money, by diminishing the necessary Reserves of the trading community. It will appear that if each man is to carry around in his pocket, or keep in his house or shop, all the money which he apprehends he may need to use before it will be possible or convenient to get a new supply, the aggregate amount of such reserves will necessarily be very large. But, through the Deposit and Check System, the aggregate reserves of the commercial community may be greatly reduced. Instead of each man keeping money by him, in anticipation of a call, for weeks it may be, the banker is able, with a fifth or a tenth part the ready money which his customers would in the aggregate have required, to serve each in his turn. Only one man could have a given piece of money in his pocket at a time; but a dozen men may be checking upon the same gold in the banker's vaults, with perfect safety. The adoption of this system, therefore, diminishes the amount of money which, in a given state of trade, will be needed to make purchases and effect payments. "If," says Lord Overstone, "a state of things be supposed in which no deposit business existed, and there is a certain state of prices under that condition of things; if you then suppose the sudden introduction into the country of the deposit system, to the extent to which it now exists in this country, the effect of that great change will be a greater economized use of the precious metals, and consequently a new distribution of the precious metals throughout the world."—[Tracts, p. 473.]

But this economy in the use of money extends even further down in industrial society. "Not only," wrote Mr. Tooke, "are improvements daily taking place among the bankers in their payments on the largest scale; not only is the practice of lodging money with a banker becoming more general, as including a large proportion of the smallest classes of tradesmen; but there is less detention in the very minutest channels of circulation, inasmuch as, by the institution of savings banks, the most inconsiderable sums, which must, but for this mode of investment, have been dormant as petty hoards in the hands of mechanics and menial servants, have become and are becoming daily more available to swell the amount of currency applicable to general purposes."—[History of Prices, i, 145.]

The causes which Mr. Tooke here indicates are continually operating to economize the use of money, though, in spite of all these improvements, there is still inevitably more or less, everywhere, of waste or loss. "Some of it," says Locke, "leaving the channels of trade, will unavoidably be drained into standing pools."

But while, as Chevalier has remarked,[1] "it is well to give prominence to the fact of the nearly stationary character of the metallic currency in countries where the commercial machinery is well organized," it is easy to overstate the case. Thus Prof. Price, in his book on the

[1] On Gold, Cobden's translation, p. 96.

"Principles of Currency," gives an analysis of the sum of £19,000,000 paid into Sir John Lubbock's bank, from which it appears that only £605,000, or about three per cent., was paid in coin or notes; and Prof. Price thereafter argues[1] on the assumption that this fairly represents the proportion of payments made in England with ready money. There is, however, reason to doubt whether Sir John Lubbock's bank affords accurate indications of the character of the whole body of commercial transactions throughout England, taking city and country together; while it is notorious that no other people approach the English in the economy of the precious metals, the check, for example, being thus far almost exclusively an English and American institution. Were Prof. Price to make an analysis of the payments into many a German or French, or even Scotch, bank, he would find the payments in coin and notes to be, not three parts in a hundred only, but thirty or even sixty. So that this able writer must not be taken too seriously when he says that gold and silver and even bank-notes are "only the small change of commerce" [p. 164]; and again, when he says that "it is only for small payments, for the small retail business of the country, and what may be called 'change,' that gold is wanted and used in England," there is danger that the mind of the reader shall receive an erroneous impression of the importance of this function. In a philosophical sense retail business can hardly be called small. "The value," says Adam Smith, "of the goods circulated between the different dealers never can exceed the value of those circulated between the dealers and consumers, whatever is

[1] Cf. pp. 68, 75, 78, 83, 86, 87, 88, 116, 117, 173.

bought by the dealers being ultimately destined to be sold to consumers."[1]

From this long review we see that the amount of money which any country should possess, or to put it otherwise, will possess under the free operation of the laws of distribution, depends not alone upon the amount of its trade, the number and frequency of payments to be made, but also upon the habits of the people, commercial and even domestic;[2] upon the degree in which credit exists between man and man, and between city and city; upon the efficiency of the laws for the collection of debts; upon the amount of traveling which takes place (for the traveler, notwithstanding the letter-of-credit, uses more money for a given expenditure than the stay-at-home); upon the state of the roads, upon the celerity and certainty of the postal and telegraph[3] services, and the degree in which express companies are permitted to impose upon the public; and upon the commercial and banking organization which exists.

Hence, in respect to no community can we say, in ad-

[1] Wealth of Nations, i, 323.

[2] I am surprised to find Prof. Tucker holding of the former slave-holding States that, though on so many accounts they required little money in proportion to their capital or their income, they yet had in the institution of slavery an occasion for money which made a large addition to their circulation.—[Money and Banks, p. 28.] I should suppose that, notwithstanding the demands of the domestic slave-trade, the fact that the masters made all the purchases and held all the money-reserves for their artificial families of 100, 200 or 500 souls, would have made the occasion for money less rather than greater, by reason of the institution of slavery.

[3] On the influence of the telegraph in a panic, see the "Economist,' 1875, p. 609.

vance, what amount of money it should possess in order satisfactorily to perform its exchanges, at prices corresponding to those which rule in the communities with which it has commercial relations.

Nor is it necessary that it should be known. Such inquiries, for example, as those of Locke, who reaches the conclusion that not less than "one-fiftieth part of the laborers' wages, one-fourth part of the land-holders' yearly revenue, and one-twentieth part of the traders' yearly returns, in ready money," can be enough to drive the trade of a country, and of Sir Wm. Petty, who thought the money needed in his time was one-half the rent of land, one-fourth the rent of buildings, and one-fifty-second part of the annual wages,[1] such inquiries as these are of merely curious interest.

If no interference with the natural distribution of the precious metals is allowed, each country, each county, and each town, throughout the trading world, will receive its due distributive share: that amount of money which will best perform its exchanges, an amount which could not be exceeded without raising prices unduly and disturbing the relations of trade.

This clearly means that, in general, poor countries must have little money, and, of course, they will not relish such a dispensation. It would be too much to expect of human nature that the inhabitants of such countries should not complain bitterly of the lack of money, and resort to many devices to attract and retain it in defiance

[1] "In the calculation of Mr. Jevons on the one hand, and various statisticians on the other, who have estimated the annual produce of capital and labor in the United Kingdom, the proportion between the circulation and the annual income of the country is 1 to 6, 7, or 8."—[Prof. Rogers's Notes to Adam Smith's Wealth of Nations, i, 295.]

of the law of distribution which has been pointed out, not seeing that the real evil from which they suffer is poverty of capital and paucity of production, due to soil, to climate, to vices of industrial character, or to the newness of settlement; and that the true cure for the evil is to be found in the extension and diversification of production which will bring trade, and, with it, money, correspondingly.

Not only does the law which has been stated govern the distribution of the precious metals, as between separate countries, but it applies with equal force, and even, perhaps, against less of resistance, to the several sections of the same country. Each will receive, each will retain, that portion of the money of the whole country which the necessities of its trade demand. It is in view of this tendency of gold and silver to seek their best market, that Sir Walter Scott, in his "Letters of Malachi Malagrowther, on the Currency of Scotland," compared Great Britain to the Image in Belshazzar's Dream:

"London, its head, might be of fine gold; the fertile provinces of England, like its breast and arms, might be of silver; the southern half of Scotland might acquire some brass or copper, but the northern provinces would be without worth or value, like the legs, which were formed of iron and clay.

"What force is to compel gold to circulate to these barren extremities of the island I cannot understand; and, when once forced there, I fear its natural tendency to return to the source from which it issued will render all efforts to detain it as difficult as the task of the men who attempted to hedge in the cuckoo.'

## CHAPTER IV.

### THE IMPORTANCE OF THE MONEY SUPPLY.

SUCH being the operation of the law of the distribution of the precious metals through the agency of Price, and such the relation of the volume of money to prevailing prices, we have now to meet the much vexed question, how far it is of consequence that the volume of money in the world should be maintained at its present dimensions, or increased above them.

It is argued that the law of distribution as stated by Mr. Ricardo, applies with the same force, whatever—within reasonable limits[1]—the volume of the precious metals. A reduction of quantity would result in a corresponding enhancement of the purchase-power of each integral portion of the remainder; while an increase would

---

[1] In his "Cremation Plan of Resumption," Mr. Wells says: "A three-cent piece, if it could be divided into a sufficient number of pieces, with each piece capable of being handled, would undoubtedly suffice for doing all the business of the country, if no other instrumentality was available."

On the grounds of those who hold the theory of an Ideal Money, [see pp. 290–91] the statement may be accepted; but if Mr. Wells, as I understand, holds with M. Chevalier, that money must be "a material equivalent" for the things with which it is to be exchanged, such an amount of silver as he indicates would be an impossible currency for a country. Such a quantum of value, like the drop of

as surely result, other things remaining the same, in a diminution of the purchase power of each ounce of silver, each grain of gold.

Bastiat, in his airy way, thus treats the question:

"Ten persons were at play. For greater ease they had adopted the plan of each person taking ten counters, and placing against these a hundred francs under a candlestick so that each counter corresponded to ten francs. After the game, the winnings were adjusted and the players drew from the candlestick as many ten francs as would represent the number of counters. Seeing this, one of them—a great arithmetician, perhaps, but an indifferent reasoner, said, 'Gentlemen, experience invariably teaches me that, at the end of the game, I find myself a gainer in proportion to the number of my counters. Have you not observed the same with regard to yourselves? Thus, what is true of me must be true of each of you, or what is *true of each must be true of all.* We should, therefore, all of us gain more at the end of the game if we all had more counters. Now, nothing can be easier; we have only to distribute twice the number.' This was done; but when the game was finished and they came to adjust the winnings, it was found that the thousand francs under the candlestick had not been miraculously multiplied according to the general expectation. They had to be divided accordingly, and the only result obtained (chimerical enough) was this: every one had, it is true, his double number of counters, but every counter, instead of corresponding to ten francs, only represented five.

---

water in a small tube, would fall within the law of capillary attraction, where the tendency to adhere to the wall of the tube becomes stronger, through the smallness of the matter on which it cperates, than the tendency, through the force of gravitation, to seek the general level below.

"Thus it was clearly shown, that what is true of each is not always true of all."—[Essays in Political Economy.]

What matters it, then, whether the amount of money be increased or decreased?

This question has been the subject of controversy down to our day. The result with which we shall issue from the inquiry will be found of immediate application to the Silver Problem, now agitating the political and economical world.

Let Prof. Cairnes represent the views of those economists who deprecate the increase, or, at any rate, the considerable increase, of the precious metals.

"I am aware, indeed, that there are writers[1] who regard gold not simply as a convenient medium for the exchange of commodities independently produced, but as, in itself, a source of productive energy, as the 'motive power of all industry and commerce,' and who accordingly consider 'an addition to the quantity of money to be the same thing as an addition to the fixed capital of a country,' as equivalent in its effects upon industry to

---

[1] Prof. Cairnes has especially in view Mr. William Newmarch, the distinguished coadjutor of Thomas Tooke in his "History of Prices," and himself the actual author of the later volumes of that invaluable series.

That ingenious author, Sir Wm. Petty, in his tract entitled "Verbum Sap," thus writes: "For money is but the fat of the body politic, whereof too much doth as often hinder its activity, as too little makes it sick. 'Tis true that, as fat lubricates the motion of the muscles, feeds in want of victuals, fills up uneven cavities and beautifies the body, so doth money, in the state, quicken its action, feed from abroad in the time of dearth at home, even accounts by reason of its divisibility and beautify the whole, especially the particular persons that have it in plenty." Hume's oft-quoted image has a sort of family resemblance to that of Petty: "It is the oil which renders the motion of the wheels more smooth and easy."

'improved harbors, roads, and manufactories.' According to such views, the influence of the gold discoveries must be universally beneficial—beneficial not merely in relation to the countries which produce the cheap money, but in a still more eminent degree in relation to those which permanently retain it. But, in spite of the plausibilities of the Mercantile Theory, common sense no less than economic science will continue to ask how the world is enriched by parting with its real wealth? how the well-being of Europe and Asia is promoted by parting with the materials of well-being, receiving in return, not materials of well-being, not augmented supplies of wool and tallow, corn and provisions, not those commodities which new countries are specially fitted to produce, and of which old countries are pressingly in need, but what? increased supplies of the precious metals: a more cumbrous medium of exchange!" And again he asks: "Are the other nations of the world destined to continue forever laboring in the service of the gold countries, for no other than the barren reward of an addition to their circulation?"—[Essays on Political Economy, p. 45.]

Such is the objection of one of the ablest of recent economists, one, moreover, who made a special study of the effects of the Californian and Australian gold discoveries. What can be opposed to this view of the case? The following is the serious and weighty statement of Mr. Hume, a favorite quotation among the advocates of increased quantities of money:

"It is certain that, since the discovery of the mines in America, industry has increased in all the nations of Europe, except in the possessors of those mines; and this may be justly ascribed, amongst other reasons, to the increase in gold and silver.

"Accordingly we find that, in every kingdom intc which money begins to flow in greater abundance than formerly, everything takes a new face; labor and industry gain life; the merchant becomes more enterprising, the manufacturer more diligent and skillful, and even the farmer follows his plow with greater alacrity and attention. This is not easily to be accounted for, if we consider only the influence which a greater abundance of coin has in the kingdom itself by heightening the price of commodities and obliging every one to pay a greater number of these little yellow or white pieces for everything he purchases. And as to foreign trade, it appears that great plenty of money is rather disadvantageous, by raising the price of every kind of labor.

"To account, then, for this phenomena, we must consider that, though the high price of commodities be a necessary consequence of the increase of gold and silver, yet it follows not immediately upon that increase; but some time is required before the money circulates through the whole state and makes its effect to be felt on all ranks of people. At first no alteration is perceived; by degrees the price rises, first of one commodity and then another, till the whole at last reaches a just proportion with the new quantity of specie which is in the kingdom.

"In my opinion it is only in this interval, or intermediate situation, between the acquisition of money and rise of prices, that the increasing quantity of gold and silver is favorable to industry. When any quantity of money is imported into a nation it is not at first dispersed into many hands, but is confined to the coffers of a few persons, who immediately seek to employ it to advantage.

. . . . . . .

"It is easy to trace the money in its progress through

the whole commonwealth, where we shall find that it must first quicken the diligence of every individual before it increases the price of labor."

But the largest claim for the advantages of an increased production of the precious metals is that put forward by Sir Archibald Alison:

"The two greatest events which have occurred in the history of mankind have been directly brought about by a successive contraction and expansion of the circulating medium of society. The fall of the Roman Empire,[1] so long ascribed, in ignorance, to slavery, heathenism, and moral corruption, was in reality brought about by a decline in the silver and gold mines of Spain and Greece. . . . . . . And as if Providence had intended to reveal in the clearest manner the influence of this mighty agent on human affairs, the resurrection of mankind from the ruin which these causes had produced was owing to the directly opposite set of agencies being put in operation. Columbus led the way in the career of renovation; when he spread his sails across the Atlantic, he bore mankind and its fortunes in his bark. . . . . The annual supply of the precious metal for the use of the globe was tripled; before a century had expired, the prices of every species of produce were quadrupled. The weight of debt and taxes insensibly wore off under the influence of that prodigious increase; in the renovation of industry, the relations of society were changed; the weight of feudalism cast off; the rights of man established. Among the many concurring causes which conspired to bring about this mighty consummation, the

[1] Contrast with this the striking fact that the copious index to Merivale's work does not contain either of the titles, Coin, Currency, or Money.

most important, though hitherto the least observed, was the discovery of Mexico and Peru.

. . . . . . . .

"That Great Britain, and every state largely concerned in industrial enterprises, has suffered grievous and long continued distress since the peace [1815], is unhappily too well known to all who have lived through that period.

. . . . . . . .

"The thoughtful in all countries had their attention forcibly arrested by this long succession of disasters, so different from what had been anticipated during the smiling days of universal peace, and many and various were the theories put forward to account for such distressing phenomena. The real explanation of them is to be found in a cause of paramount importance and universal operation, though at the time unobserved—and that was the simultaneous contraction of the monetary circulation of the globe, from the effects of the South American revolution, and of the paper circulation of Great Britain. . . .

"If the circulating medium of the globe had remained stationary, or declining, as it was from 1815 to 1849 from the effects of South American revolution and English legislation, the necessary result must have been that it would have become altogether inadequate to the wants of men; and not only would industry have been everywhere cramped, but the price of produce would have universally and constantly fallen. Money would every day have become more valuable—all other articles measured in money, less so; debts and taxes would have been constantly increasing in weight and oppression: the fate which crushed Rome in ancient, and has all but crushed Great Britain in modern, times, would have been that of the whole family of mankind.

"All these evils have been entirely obviated, and the opposite set of blessings introduced, by the opening of the great reserve treasures of nature in California and Australia. . . . Three years only have elapsed since Californian gold was discovered by Anglo-Saxon enterprise, and the annual supply has already come to exceed £25,000,000. Coupled with the mines of Australia and the Ural mountains, it will soon exceed thirty, perhaps reach forty millions! Before half a century has elapsed, prices of every article of commerce will be tripled, enterprise proportionally encouraged, industry vivified, debts and taxes lessened."—[History of Europe, 1851–52, ch. i, §§ 33–40.]

I have given the text of Sir A. Alison's remarks, though with some abridgment, because any paraphrase of a claim so extensive would necessarily have been deemed a caricature. In the view of this writer, the decline of the Roman Empire was caused by the failing production of the mines of Spain and Thrace; the long life in death of the Middle Ages was due to the scarcity of the circulating medium; the revival of political and industrial activity in the 16th Century had its origin and motive force, not in the invention of the printing press and the mariner's compass, but in the discovery of Potosi; the rapid increase of pauperism and the decline in the condition of the working classes after the Napoleonic wars, was the result, primarily, not of the exhaustion of Europe by that long and desperate struggle of the Old against the New, not of vicious systems of taxation, but of the suspension of gold and silver mining industry in Mexico and the Spanish South American states.

And from the condition of abject misery into which the world was plunged by this cause, relief could, in the constitution of things, have come in but one way, not through increase of public or private virtue, not by advances in the industrial arts, not through industry or through international peace, but, as it in fact came, through the accidental discovery of gold at Sutter's Mill in California, in 1847.

Nor must Sir A. Alison's views on this subject be regarded as singular and exceptional. A large party in England, all through the controversy on the resumption of specie payments and the successive renewals of the Bank Charter, down to 1841, maintained the vital necessity of securing the increase of the circulating medium, to keep pace with, and even to run ahead of, the demands of trade for money, regarding the consequences of a failure to effect this object as involving the worst industrial and social disasters.

Nor is the view of the importance of maintaining the volume of the circulating medium which is taken by a large party in the United States, for which Mr. Henry C. Carey[1] furnishes the arguments, less pronounced than that of the so-called "Birmingham School," of which the eloquent Mathias Attwood was the leader in the English Currency battles of 1819, 1822, and 1832. But as the attention of this party is directed to the increase of Paper Money, we may defer the consideration of their position.

How much of economical truth is there in the claim that the volume of Money should be kept good from age to age?

---

[1] See his tract: "The Finance Minister and the Currency," a review of Mr. H. McCulloch's administration of the Treasury Department.

In the first place it must be admitted—what is too apt to be overlooked—that the advocates of Hard Money, so called, are in fairness estopped from treating with contempt as they are prone to do, claims like those of Sir Archibald Alison. Writers who regard an inflation of the currency through excessive issues of paper money as the sufficient cause of overwhelming national disaster, paralyzing the nerves and sinews of industry, corrupting public and private morals, and perverting every instinct, social or economical, to mischievous effects, have no right to treat as absurd the largest assertion respecting the evils of a reduction of the volume of money, through a stoppage of the sources of supply, such as took place in consequence of the invasion of the Roman Empire by the barbarians, and of the Mexican and South American revolutions.

Perhaps we shall get a better view of the subject by confining ourselves to the claim made in favor of a progressive increase of money, keeping in advance of the demands of trade, and hence effecting a gradual reduction of its value.

To this, it will be observed, three distinct advantages are attributed by the writers we have quoted.

The first is that indicated by Mr. Hume. Whereas Mr. Ricardo assumed, for the purposes of his argument in the bullion controversy, that the distribution of the precious metals would take place throughout the whole commercial world, and among the industrial classes of each nation by turns, with no appreciable interval, Mr. Hume asserts that some time is actually required before the new money circulates through the commercial body and makes its influence felt on all ranks of people and all sorts of commodities. In this Mr. Hume anticipated the best results of recent thinking and investigation.

Such an effect, says M. Chevalier, must proceed, as it were, by jerks; and he elsewhere uses the figure, as translated by Mr. Cobden, "a series of rebounds"—perhaps we might say, successive action and reaction—to describe the progress, between 1849 and 1859, of the diffusion of the money from the Californian and Australian mines. Prof. Cairnes, in his able essays on the "Gold Question," published in 1859 and 1860, has also shown that the effects of gold discoveries proceed, not only from one class of commodities to another, but from one country to another, with appreciable intervals, allowing important economical effects to be produced meanwhile.[1]

Now, in the course of this retarded distribution, Mr. Hume discovers the possibility of an influence highly beneficial, while it lasts, upon the industry of a country. In the interval, or intermediate situation, between the acquisition of money and the rise of prices, a stimulus is given to enterprise which causes everything to take on a new face; labor and industry to gain life; the merchant to become more enterprising; the manufacturer more diligent and skillful, and even the farmer to follow his plow with greater alacrity and attention.

It seems to me that this view of the subject commends itself as both rational and thoroughly practical.

The Ricardian economist, looking at money as a tool for a specific and highly technical purpose—and, in general, we cannot too strongly insist upon this view—declares that he sees no advantage in an increase of money above its former level. If money gains in amount, it loses in value; more of it only purchases the same quantity of commodities. On the other hand, Mr. Hume, as a moral philosopher, having his attention strongly fixed

---

[1] See pp. 150–7.

on the power which hope and courage have to call forth the utmost energies of men, finds in an increase of money the possibility of a gain which may more than compensate mankind for the labor expended in raising the additional gold and silver from the mine. It does not need to be said that Mr. Hume had in view an increase of money not so great as to bewilder the producer and the trader through a fiercely rapid advance of prices, or to render sober business calculations impossible. When courage and enterprise are exalted to rashness, through a stimulation proceeding to intoxication, the effects are only prejudicial. Within certain limits, however, and these not necessarily narrow, there are illusions which inspire exertion because they dignify and beautify the objects of exertion; evoking efforts which would not otherwise be put forth, yet from which there are no injurious reactions, inasmuch as they are thoroughly compatible with the moral and physical nature of man.

It is to be observed that Mr. Hume confines the advantage of a given increase in the volume of the precious metals to the interval required to secure its uniform diffusion among all classes, and its equal effect upon all prices. This view is taken by Mr. Jacob, the author of the "Inquiry into the Precious Metals," who declares that "an impulse would be given to the productive powers which would continue so long as the increase of the precious metals should continue to lessen their relative value to other commodities."—[P. 251.]

We may conceive such an increase of the precious metals as Mr. Hume has in contemplation, through discoveries of new mines, or through the invention of new mechanical or chemical agencies for working mines, as occurring once in a human generation, quickening enterprise, inciting to mental activity and breaking up the scale of habit which tends to form over social and industrial organizations; or, we may conceive such a relation between the current production of the precious metals and the volume in existence, that the process which Mr. Hume describes may be continually, though quietly, going forward from age to age.

It may be said: were such a cause to operate continuously, it would come to be anticipated, would be taken into account in business calculations, and hence, the incentive which Mr. Hume discovers in the occasional increase of the precious metals would cease to be exerted by a continuous enlargement of the volume of money.

To a certain extent this would prove true in the situation supposed; but the objection, which is in the spirit of a great deal of accepted reasoning upon economical subjects, fails to recognize the limitations of the human mind. The operations involved in mental discount, or enlargement to a scale, are among the most difficult which ordinary men are called to perform; and in either of these most persons fail entirely. It is in this way, as we shall have occasion to note hereafter,[1] that the principal mischiefs of fluctuating paper money are inflicted.

A second advantage would seem to be claimed by Sir Archibald Alison for an increase of the precious metals in use as money, namely, a diminution in the rate of taxation, as, according to this writer, it was the reduction of the volume of money, from the time of Augustus forward, which increased the taxes of the Empire; while a like cause enhanced the burden of taxation in England after the Napoleonic wars.

Except so far as taxation results from the necessity of paying the interest or principal of public debts, it is diffi-

---

[1] See pp. 385–7.

cult to see how the cause adduced can have any considerable effect in this direction. Taxes are the means of furnishing the revenue of government. The revenue of government is to meet current expenditures for a vast range of commodities and services. If the volume of money is increased and its purchasing power diminished, the prices of the commodities purchased by government will, it is to be presumed, advance correspondingly. During the interval spoken of by Mr. Hume, the prices of services—wages—may indeed not advance with equal rapidity, and thus, in the language of Mr. Huskisson, "a saving accrue to the state from paying the wages of valor, talent, industry, and labor, in a depreciated currency," but this gain could not be long or greatly reckoned upon.

It is in the third claim made by the advocates of an increase of money, viz., the reduction in the pressure of indebtedness and of fixed charges of all kinds—rents, pensions, annuities, etc.—that the main strength of their position lies. In Mr. Hume's day, the body of indebtedness, public and private, was comparatively small; in Sir A. Alison's time it had assumed vast dimensions, and has been steadily increasing ever since, not only absolutely, but relatively to other financial interests.

The public indebtedness of the civilized world, to-day, probably stands between twenty-five and thirty thousand millions of dollars of American money. The volume of private debts, including the capitalized value of fixed charges—loans, annuities, etc.—is vastly greater. Nearly the whole of this body of obligations is payable, interest and principal (where the principal sum is to be paid[1]) in Money. The question whether the supply of money shall increase or decrease is, then, the question

[1] The English *Consols* are merely perpetual annuities.

whether the burden of these more or less permanent charges shall be diminished or enhanced.

You loan to the city of Baltimore $10,000, receiving therefor a bond payable in thirty years, with interest at six per cent. annually, meanwhile. The city expends the $10,000 borrowed in purchasing supplies for municipal purposes, brick for building, stone for paving and curbing, pipe for drainage, posts and lamps for lighting. Going back further we see that what the city really borrows is days' labor. If ordinary labor is worth $1.25 a day, you, in effect, lend to the city eight thousand days' labor, either of men in the quarries or kilns, where the stone and the brick are gotten out, or in the streets and on the partly erected walls of the public buildings, laying the stone and brick for municipal uses. You pay these men their wages now and bid them work for the city.

In return, what does the city, in effect, promise to do for you? To pay you eight thousand days' labor at the end of thirty years, and, meanwhile, to let you enjoy every year four hundred and eighty days' labor, which you take out to suit yourself, whether of men dredging for oysters in the bay, or working on your house, or raising wheat for you in Illinois.

Such, in the economical view, was your contract with the city; but, through the use of a "Standard for Deferred Payments," these quantities are expressed in terms of money, and the legal obligation of the city to you is to be satisfied with money only. If, then, while that bond is running to maturity, the supply of the precious metals is to be either decreased or increased (by supply I mean here the volume relatively to the demand), you receive more or fewer days' labor to enjoy, from year to year, and the city will pay you more or fewer days' labor at the end of the term, in final discharge of the obligation.

It is the fact of a vast body of outstanding indebtedness which gives its chief importance to the current production of the precious metals. That gold and silver should be yielded in exactly that amount, from year to year, from generation to generation, which will serve to keep the value of money uniform, is not to be expected. We have seen the causes which tend, with varying force, to reduce the use for money in trade, while other causes operate to increase "the duty" (to use Mr. McLeod's phrase) of the existing volume. At the same time, the diversification of production and the extension of trade make their urgent demand for an increased medium of exchange. While these causes operate to subject to continual change the demand for money, the production which is to furnish the required supply is, in a high degree, spasmodic, and has at times almost altogether ceased.

We are not to expect, therefore, that the value of money will remain constant through any long period. One of the two parties to long contracts[1] will, in all probability, lose while the other gains, by the change in values. The losses thus sustained may be slight; they may be serious, even ruinous.

The question arising out of the consideration of this possibility, this probability, that the burden of the body of indebtedness, public and private, existing at any given date, will be enhanced or diminished appreciably, perhaps enormously, before it comes to maturity, by changes in the value of money, whether the economist should look upon the two possible results with equal regret, or should, upon economical grounds purely, regard the one

[1] For Prof. Jevons's proposition for obviating the effects of such fluctuations, see p. 159.

or the other as preferable, or even, it may be, as positively desirable, is a question which has been made the subject of animated controversy.

Mr. J. R. McCulloch, the English economist, has perhaps taken the strongest ground in favor of the desirableness[1] of a gradual reduction in the burden of debts, through the natural increase of the volume of the precious metals. He maintains that a depreciation of the circulating medium, through this cause, promotes industry, diminishing the weight of the obligations which press upon the producing classes, whether employers or employed, giving them the use, at a lower rate in produce, (because at a fixed rate in money), of all the agents—land, buildings, stock—which they hold by hire or lease for terms of years, from those who are not themselves personally engaged in production. At the same time, all that part of the taxation of government which goes to the payment of the principal and interest of public indebtedness, is reduced in its weight upon the whole community, whether engaged in active production or not.

Now, "why," asks Mr. Maclaren,[2] "should the power to make a fortune be cherished, at the expense of a fortune when made?"

Please observe that the question here is not, whether by any act of government, or association of debtors, the burden of debts shall be reduced. That question we shall see arising in connection with the debt incurred by

---

[1] "Though, like a fall of rain after a long course of dry weather, it may be prejudicial to certain classes, it is beneficial to an incomparably greater number, including all who are actively engaged in industrial pursuits; and is, speaking generally, of great public or national advantage."—[His article on the "Precious Metals" in the Encyclopædia Brittanica.]

[2] History of the Currency, p. 312.

England in the Napoleonic wars, and that incurred by the United States in the recent civil conflict. It is quite a different matter. The scaling down of debts by a purposed depreciation of the circulation, through excessive issues of paper money, is only a form of practical repudiation, which has always the sting of injustice about it, and always draws a retribution after it.[1]

The question we are now considering is, whether such an effect, as the result of natural causes, where no ill-faith can be alleged,—purely, *ictus dei*—is a proper subject of congratulation on strictly economical considerations: whether, in short, as Mr. Maclaren puts it, the power to make a fortune should be cherished at the expense of fortunes which have been made; whether, if the mortgage which the representatives of past production, for such the holders of these obligations preponderatingly are, have upon the fruits of current industry can be paid off on reduced terms, without any violation of faith, the world may be expected to gain economically thereby.

Having conducted the inquiry to this point, we reach

---

[1] Some writers would appear to shrink from the discussion of the effects of an increase of the precious metals, lest they should give encouragement to schemes for reducing the burden of debts by acts of legislation. On this point, Mr. Horton's remark seems to me thoroughly just and manly:

"I am well aware of the demagogue spirit which is the legitimate child of the Legal Tender Acts, and which has sought to dishonor the country by appeals to the baser motives of the debtor class. I know the danger of appearing to give the support of science to that spirit. On the other hand, I have confidence in truth and in the honesty and acuteness of my countrymen; and I think the safe course for the advocates of sound currency is to grasp this nettle firmly. The truth will bear to be seen; the greatest danger is in misrepresenting it."—[Silver and Gold, p. 70.]

the strict limits of the department of money. The matter is to be decided as a question in general economics Certainly I think no one could refuse to admit that, if it were an issue between having the pressure of the whole body of indebtedness diminished by natural causes, or increased, the former result would be preferable. If it were a question between sacrificing the present to the past, or the past to the present, all would agree in saying, let the dead bury its dead. Whether it is a result positively desirable, on economical grounds, that debts should undergo a progressive depreciation, might fairly be disputed. The weight of opinion, among economical writers of reputation, seems to be in the affirmative. M. Chevalier, with great emphasis, gives his ample authority to this view:

"Such a change will benefit those who live by current labor; it will injure those who live upon the fruits of past labor, whether their fathers' or their own. In this, it will work in the same direction with most of the developments which are brought about by that great law of civilization to which we give the noble name of progress.[1]

### THE MONEY SUPPLY AND THE RATE OF INTEREST.

Still another advantage which is at times claimed for a progressive increase of the stock of money, is that it lowers the rate of interest. This opinion is so widely spread, that it deserves a careful examination:

Interest is compensation for the use of capital; not necessarily of money.[2] Money is only one of many forms

---

[1] La Monnaie, p. 760.

[2] The inveterate disposition to regard the rate of interest as depending on the supply of money is thus explained by Mr. Mill: "Money, which is so commonly understood as the synonym of

of capital; and in loans is commonly but the agent for the transfer, from lender to borrower, of other special forms of capital. In any philosophical view, it is not the money but the capital, in its special forms, which is lent and borrowed.

If I borrow a thousand dollars in money, the chances are a thousand to one that I immediately, or shortly, turn the money into articles suitable for my business, my personal necessities, etc., etc. These were what I really wanted: the money was but the means to that end. These are what I really pay interest upon, not upon the money.

In the modern commercial organization money is not always, nor even usually,[1] the agent in the transfer of capital from lender to borrower. Thus, a country mer-

---

wealth, is more especially the term in use to denote it when borrowing is spoken of. . . . Borrowing capital is universally called borrowing money; the loan market is called the money market; those who have their capital disposable for investment or loan are called the moneyed class; and the equivalent given for the use of capital, or in other words, interest, is not only called the interest of money, but, by a grosser perversion of terms, the value of money. This misapplication of language, assisted by some fallacious appearances which we shall notice and clear up hereafter, has created a general notion among persons in business, that the value of money, meaning the rate of interest, has an intimate connection with the value of money in its proper sense, the value or purchasing power of the circulating medium."—[Pol. Econ., III, viii, 2.]

[1] I am surprised to see this remark of Prof. Perry: "Value in any other form than money is not generally suitable for loaning."—[Pol. Econ., p. 236.] And again, "Thus we see the reason why governments, corporations and individuals, when they borrow, borrow money."—[P. 237.] I do not believe that two per cent. of the discounted paper in the banks of New York to-day was given for money paid. As will be said further on, money is used to a greater extent in paying debts than in contracting them.

chant comes to the city and goes about making his purchases for the month: he buys dry goods, groceries, hardware, etc., etc., and in each case he gives his note—promising, for *value received*, to pay so much *with interest*. No money has passed in the transaction. The interest is not paid upon money loaned, but upon merchandise bought.

In this distinction, that interest is paid for the use of capital, not usually of money, we see the insufficiency of Aristotle's objections to usury, viz., that, as money does not produce money, no gain or increase should be expected upon the loan of money. It is true that money does not beget money[1]; but capital does manifestly beget capital. If a man borrows a thousand ducats and ties them up in a bag, he will not find any little ducats in the bag at the end of a year; but if he purchases with the ducats a flock of sheep, he will, with proper attention, have lambs enough at the end of the year to pay a handsome interest on the loan, and make a handsome profit for himself. If he turns the ducats into corn he will find it bringing forth, some thirty, some sixty, and some an hundred fold; out of which he may abundantly compensate the owner of the ducats, the laborers who have plowed, sown, and reaped, and still retain something for himself. Very seldom does a man borrow money to use it, as money, through anything like the term of his loan. When he does so, as brokers, for example, sometimes do, he may to Antonio's question, "Is your gold and silver ewes and rams?" return Shylock's answer, "I cannot tell; I make it breed as fast."

[1] "Monstruosum est et contra naturam quod res infecunda pariat, quod res sterilis a tota specie fructificet vel multiplicetur ex se, cujusmodi est pecunia."—[Nicholas Oresme, Tractatus de Origine, Natura, Jure, et Mutationibus Monetarum.]

In the same light we see the futility of the notion that the rate of interest is to be permanently reduced by augmenting the supply of money. The rate of interest depends on the supply of capital in all forms suited to productive uses, compared with the opportunity to use capital productively. There may be a low rate of interest with little capital, in a country where industry is depressed by bad government or social disorder; there may even be a high rate of interest with great capital, where natural resources are abundant and the spirit of enterprise is continually incited by success. What "the West" wants is more capital; what it thinks it wants is more money. Capital is there relatively scarce and the rate of interest consequently high, because the country is new, the natural advantages abundant, the people enterprising. Were the people less enterprising, there might be capital enough for all their uses, and interest would then be low. Were the natural advantages less abundant, there might be capital enough to furnish all the tools and materials which labor could profitably employ, and interest would then be low; and again, when those communities shall become older, they will naturally have accumulated larger stores of tools and materials; will have their warehouses, furnaces, shops, bridges, fences, and roads constructed, and then there will be capital enough to allow a low rate of interest. Interest was high in New England two hundred years ago for the same reason that makes it high now at the West. The people had inherited little and had, therefore, much to make for themselves, and tools and materials were thus in scant supply in comparison with the demand, *i. e.*, the occasion for their use.

But while the average rate of interest is determined thus in the supply and demand of capital in its various forms, it is true that temporary effects for days, foı weeks, it may even be for months, are produced by changes in the supply of money. This is due to two considerations: first, that money is, as has been said, to a certain extent the agent in the transfer of capital from lenders to borrowers; and, secondly, because money, as the standard of deferred payments, is, to a much greater extent,[1] the means with which the maturing obligations of borrowers are met.

[1] Due to the fact that the notes given by retail dealers for goods had of the wholesale merchants are not generally paid [offset] by other notes which have come into their possession, but by the money which they have collected in small amounts through the sales of their goods.

## CHAPTER V.

### THE PRODUCTION OF THE PRECIOUS METALS.

No treatment of the subject of money can be complete which omits a survey of the existing field of gold and silver production. The monetary questions which now agitate many of the nations of the world, not sparing America, Asia, or Australia, convulsing some with the severest throes of felt or apprehended financial distress, have reference primarily to the facts, the startling facts, of the present yield of the precious metals. Nor can we fully gather the due effect of recent developments without at least a brief review of the past production of gold and silver.

### THE FIELD OF PRODUCTION.

When we consider the effects upon local prices, extending often to serious disturbances of international commerce, which attend the rapid increase of the money of the world, the wide geographical distribution of the precious metals becomes a fact, not alone of curious interest, but of positive economical importance. It would be easier to say in what countries gold or silver had not been found than to enumerate those where one or both have been produced. Even in economic quantities, there are few considerable countries which have not, at one time or another, contributed to the world's supply of these metals.

"It is probable," says Mr. Jacob, from whose "Inquiry into the Precious Metals" (1831) I shall freely quote throughout the present and the two succeeding chapters, "that the precious metals were first known to mankind in the eastern parts of Asia and in Egypt; but which of these countries is entitled to a priority in the discovery, it is almost impossible to determine."

Of all the continents, Africa, though early conspicuous for its production of both gold and silver, appears to be the one which has made, within recent times—it might almost be said within historic times—the smallest contribution to the stock of the precious metals, although the name of an obsolete British coin—the Guinea—testifies to the fame of the gold dust of a portion of the western coast.[1] "We are," says Mr. Jacob, "disposed to estimate at a very low rate the whole produce of gold from Africa, and as no silver is known to be extracted from that part of the world, in an estimate of the production and consumption of the world at large we have not thought it necessary to take any notice of either the western or the eastern shore."—[P. 372.]

Yet the mines of Africa furnished a large share of the gold and silver produced before the Christian era. It was with treasures torn from the temples of Egypt by Cambyses that the palaces of Susa and Persepolis were built. The greater portion of this metallic wealth had been obtained in commerce with the Nubians and Macrobians. There is no evidence that the valley of

[1] "The gold that has reached Europe from Africa, has consisted of small grains stated to have been collected from the streams and carried about in quills as an article of traffic."—[Jacob, p. 371.]

the Nile below the cataracts ever yielded the precious metals; while the complete abandonment of the fertile sources of metallic wealth above appears to have taken place even before the time of Alexander.

The mineral wealth of Asia Minor, which has remained to this day proverbial, made, in fact, but a slight contribution to the world's supply. The mines of Mt. Tmolus and the gold sands of the Pactolus were early exhausted. Neither gold nor silver was produced in Palestine, Phenicia, and the land reaching to the frontier of Egypt. In Arabia, no mines of the precious metals are known to exist, and Mr. Jacob remarks that, were any found, it would probably prove unprofitable to work them, on account of the scarcity of fuel. In the country now known as Persia, argentiferous lead is said to exist in great abundance; but little silver is produced. "In Afghanistan, gold," says Mr. Jacob, "is said to be found in some of the streams that flow from the mountains of Hindoo Cosh, and some silver in the country of the Caffres; but nothing is known as to the quantity of either." In the Burman empire and in Thibet, the mining of the precious metals is an important source of national wealth. In Cochin China, small quantities both of gold and silver continue to be extracted from the sands of the rivers. The extensive territory of India affords little either of gold or silver. "None is found within the government of the three great Presidencies."—[Jacob, p. 375.] The Malay Peninsula was called by the ancients Chersonesus Aurea; but if it ever yielded the precious metals in quantity to justify that appellation, little or none is now produced there. Of China, our information is indefinite, though the quantity of silver is known to be considerable. What is called Syce or Sycee silver was formerly supposed to be wholly of Chinese origin, but is now known to be indifferently either Chinese or American silver, which has undergone the process of refining in a degree making it exceptionally pure. The islands of the Indian Ocean yield some gold. It is said to have been formerly produced in Ceylon, but none is now extracted; nor, says Mr. Jacob, are there authentic accounts of that metal being found in Java. Sumatra yields gold in moderate amount, both from the washing of the river sands and from small mines in the mountains.[1] Borneo has long been celebrated for its abundance of gold, chiefly from alluvial deposits. Gold is also found in the bed of the rivers of Celebes. The Phillipine islands produce a moderate amount. Of Japan we have, from Marco Polo and early travelers, accounts which speak of large amounts of the same precious metal; but little has flowed into the channels of the world's commerce.

Mr. Jacob, writing about 1830, estimated the whole product of Asia at not above £1,400,000 annually, made up of:

| | | |
|---|---|---|
| 380,000 oz. gold | £3 5s. | £1,235,000 |
| 260,000 oz. silver | 5s. | 65,000 |
| Silver in Turkey | | 100,000 |
| | | £1,400,000 |

[1] Prof. Rogers, in his notes to Adam Smith (i, 225), quotes from Sir R. Murchison's "Siluria" the statement that gold is generally found superficially, silver in deep mines. "Modern science, instead of contradicting, only confirms the truth of the aphorism of the patriarch Job which thus shadowed forth the downward persistence of the one, and the superficial distribution of the other: 'Surely there is a vein for the silver: the earth has dust of gold.'" Considerable exceptions require to be taken to this statement. An increasing proportion of the gold produced is drawn from deep mines.

Nearly all the principal geographical divisions of Europe have, at an earlier or later age, yielded gold or silver, though in some the mining industry has never assumed importance. None of the ancient writers speak of gold or silver in Portugal, as distinct from Spain, though a little gold is now washed from the sands of the Douro, and smaller streams. Southern Italy has always been barren of the precious metals; and, while early writers record the washing of gold from the sands of the Po, none has been produced since the subjugation of that region by the Romans. The islands of Sicily, Corsica, Majorca, Minorca, and Malta are also destitute of the precious metals, but Sardinia has furnished some gold and much silver. Gold and silver were found in England and Wales centuries before the Roman conquest, and gold is still produced in economic quantities in Cornwall. In the reign of James IV and James V of Scotland,[1] gold was taken in considerable amounts from the earth washed down from the Grampian Hills. "The search," says Mr. Jacob, "is now given over; but bits are still found accidentally."—[P. 158.] In Ireland small amounts of silver have been taken out in Tipperary; and it is stated that about the close of the last century about £10,000 of gold was obtained from the alluvial soil of the county Wicklow. Both silver and gold have been mined from an immemorial period in Sweden

[1] Martin, in his "Description of the Western Islands," tries hard, in the face of discouragement, to make out a good story. "I shall not," he says, "offer to assert that there are mines of gold or silver in the Western Isles from any resemblance they may bear to other parts that afford mines; but the natives affirm that gold dust has been found at Griminis on the west coast of the isle of North Vist, and at Copreaul in Harries, in which, as well as in other parts of the isles, *the teeth of the sheep that feed there are dyed yellow.*"

and Norway, though the product yielded is not believed to have been at any time of great importance for the supply of commerce. Mr. Jacob remarks [p. 154] that the Northern nations of Europe appear to have possessed more gold and silver during the Middle Ages than was to be found in Germany, France, or the British islands, but there is reason to believe that this abundance was due to the success of the piratical expeditions which scourged the shores of so many countries, and in part, also, to a profitable trade with Russia.

The country of Europe most productive of the precious metals, but especially of silver, in early times, was Spain.[1] The "Tarshish" of Scripture is quite generally identified as a portion of this peninsula. The amount of gold obtained in Spain was probably never considerable. It is not mentioned by Ezekiel among the treasures brought from Tarshish. The productiveness of the Spanish mines continued through the period of Roman domination; but with the decline of the Empire the yield of the precious metals greatly diminished or ceased altogether. "There are no accounts," says Mr. Jacob, "of any mines being worked under the Suevic or under the Gothic monarchs who at length governed that coun-

[1] Diodorus relates an absurd story about the discovery of silver through the accidental burning of the woods on the Pyrenees, the streams of molten silver running down the sides of the mountains. Almost every place celebrated for the precious metals has some tradition, more or less improbable, respecting the first discovery of the treasure. At Potosi, it was a hunter pulling up a bush which he had seized to steady himself by in ascending the mountain. In the Hartz Mountains it was a horse pawing up the earth. In Saxony, glittering particles were observed among the dirt on the wheels of carts which had passed through the extensive forest in which the silver was concealed.

try; nor any traces of works in mines at this time to be seen, that are not evidently of Roman,[1] of Moorish, or of more modern construction."—[P. 146.] The revival of the productiveness of the Spanish mines under the Moors was probably due not more to the engineering skill of this people than to the fact that their conquests had given them vast numbers of Christian slaves who could be employed in the mines where free laborers would not consent to serve.

We know little of ancient mining operations in France. The Romans during their occupation worked mines of silver in the Pyrenees, and perhaps in Languedoc. The Frankish rulers of Lorraine opened extensive mines of silver in that territory. Silver is still found in France, in moderate amount, in connection with lead.

In what is now Prussian Silesia, mines of silver were discovered at a very early date, and were long extensively worked. The mines of Saxony[2] and the Hartz district were discovered about the tenth century of the Christian era, and are still productive. Their contributions have never ceased to be of importance to the world's supply of silver, though overshadowed after the fifteenth century by the vast resources of Mexico and Peru.

The mines of Hungary, especially at Kremnitz, began

---

[1] Mr. Bowles notes that, on both sides of the Pyrenees, the shafts dug by the Romans are easily identified, being round; while the Moorish shafts are square. This ingenious writer suggests that, in this, each people followed their habits in respect to fortifications. The Romans, accustomed to the use of the battering ram, avoided angles; the Moors, with no fear of such attacks, built their forts square.

[2] "There is no part of the world in which the operations of mining are conducted with more skill, economy and industry."—[Jacob, p. 139.]

to be worked somewhat earlier than those of Silesia and the Hartz; and have never ceased to be of importance. The mines of Austria, the richest in mineral wealth of all the countries of Europe, were among the chief sources of supply during the Middle Ages. In Transylvania, especially, the rivers, without exception, are auriferous, and numerous gold mines are still productive. In the Bohemian mountains were formerly gold washings; but the yield in recent times has been small, if, indeed, it was ever of consequence. Illyria was anciently esteemed very rich in gold, and Strabo attributes the great decline in the value of that metal in Italy to the produce of the Noric Alps. Gold in moderate quantities and small amounts of silver are still drawn from this district. Of the gold regions of Russia Herodotus has left a glowing description; but the very traces of former workings were for two thousand years lost, and gold was only rediscovered at the beginning of the eighteenth century. Greece, last to be mentioned, was probably the first of Europe in which the precious metals were systematically produced. It is believed that the Grecian mines were opened by Phenician miners and capitalists, first in the islands of the Mediterranean, next upon the mainland and especially in Attica, and lastly in Macedon and Thrace. It was with the gold of his Thracian mines that Philip bribed the orators of Athens to betray the liberties of their country.

### THE ECONOMIC CONDITIONS OF GOLD AND SILVER PRODUCTION.

Such, as we have hastily surveyed it, was the field of the production of the precious metals prior to the discovery of America. Let us, for a moment, consider the economic law which governs this branch of industry, as it is well stated by Mr. Mill:

"Of the three classes into which commodities are divided, those absolutely limited in supply; those which may be had in unlimited quantity, at a given cost of production, and those which may be had in unlimited quantity, but at an increasing cost of production: the precious metals, being the produce of mines, belong to the third class. Their natural value, therefore, is proportional to their cost of production in the most unfavorable existing circumstances: that is, at the worst mines which it is necessary to work in order to obtain the required supply. A pound weight of gold will, in the country of the mines, exchange, on the average, for as much of every other commodity as is produced at a cost equal to its own.

. . . . . . .

"If gold is above its natural or cost value, money will be of high value, and the prices of all things, labor included, will be low. These low prices will lower the expenses of all producers: but as their returns will also be lowered, no advantage will be obtained by any producer except the producer of gold, whose returns from his mine, not depending on price, will be the same as before; and his expenses being less, he will obtain extra profits and will be stimulated to increase his production.

"*E converso*, if the metal is below its natural value, since this is as much as to say that prices are high and the money expenses of all producers unusually great; for this, however, all other producers will be compensated by increased money returns; the miner alone will extract from his mine no more metal than before, while his expenses will be greater."—[Political Economy, III, ix, 2.]

The foregoing account would hold good in all production of the precious metals under the operation of the law of supply and demand. But in the early ages, especially throughout the eastern world, the production of gold and silver was, as I conceive it, chiefly non-economical. The mines, the property of the king, were worked by his subjects who were equally his property, and the products remained his peculiar possession, or were devoted to sacerdotal uses.[1] Gold and silver were regarded as an end, not as a means; as treasure, not money.[2] They were distributed not by trade, but by war. It was the hand of the conqueror that stripped them from palaces and temples. If they were taken from the store of the monarch, it was not to freight the caravans of commerce, but to fill the chariots and mule-carts, to lade the sumpter-horses or the camel-trains of a victorious army.[3]

Hence it was that the distribution of the precious metals through the agency of prices, which was described in a previous chapter, was in early ages effected so tardily, if at all; and the wealth or poverty of a kingdom, measured by its possession of gold and silver, was determined, primarily, by the fact of mines being found within its limits; secondarily, by the military prowess of the people and the ambition of their princes. Anaximenes of Lampsacus relates that Philip of Macedon, in the early part of his reign, before the mines of Thrace

---

[1] "It was deemed either a royal or a sacerdotal privilege to possess them."—[Jacob, p. 72.]

[2] Mr. Mill remarks that "in Hindostan, gold, silver and gems are most curiously hoarded, and not devoted to production."

[3] Indeed, the expectation of plunder originally formed the tie which drew the free Grecian soldier after his general. It was not until the time of Pericles that the regular payment of soldiers began at Athens, and it was not till a century later that the custom had extended itself over the whole of Greece.

were opened to him, was wont, when he retired to rest, to place under his pillow the small and only cup of gold he possessed. That Philip's son loaded with the golden spoil of Persepolis[1] ten thousand mule-carts and five thousand camels. And when Macedon, in turn, fell before the conquering rage of Rome, the treasures carried away by Paulus Æmilius sufficed for fifteen years' expenditure, without the necessity of a resort to taxation. Speaking broadly, we may say of those early times, that the law of supply and demand had little to do with the production of the precious metals; and that when produced, they were not distributed through the agency of price. To this rule there were, however, exceptions. The peasantry not infrequently extracted by patient labor small amounts of gold from sources, especially the river sands, which had not attracted the notice of their rulers. No degree of vigilance could guard against the unfaithfulness of slaves and overseers in pilfering the products of the mine. And when the vast accumulations of treasure passed from the conquered, enormous waste was certain to result; large sums were seized by the soldiery in the hour of sack and pillage, while from time to time the conqueror, perhaps the usurper, appeased his mutinous followers by donatives[2] of gold, which were speedily dissipated and passed into circulation.

Of the foregoing statement of the non-economical nature of the production and distribution of the precious metals, one other important qualification requires to be made. The Tyrians, and afterwards the Carthaginians, early directed their great commercial talents to exchang-

[1] Stated by Diodorus at £27,600,000 British sterling. The whole spoil of Persia is put by Arrian at forty millions British sterling.

[2] According to Arrian, Alexander distributed, in Susa, £4,600,000, British money, in paying the debts of his soldiery.

ing the silver of Western Europe, and especially of Spain, for gold with Arabia and the further East, perhaps with India itself. Nor could the statement be applied without large and continually increasing exceptions, after the time of Alexander. Already had the extensive coinage of Persia shown that gold was losing its character as treasure and gaining that of money; while the Romans, not so much through their commercial instincts, as through that courting of the populace and the soldiery which marked their entire history, gave a merry circulation to the spoil of Macedon and Asia.

Yet, while these exceptions require to be made, the original condition of things subsisted not only down to the period of the Roman Empire, but for centuries later, though with continually diminishing scope, as personal slavery, in its absolute form, gave way, first, before the gradual extension of Roman citizenship, and, secondly, before the free spirit of the Teutonic invaders of the Empire who came to occupy the countries, Spain and Thrace, then most productive of the precious metals.

As I conceive it, we can only explain the vast accumulations of treasure in Egypt, Persia and Judea, by reference to the political system of the age. The production of the precious metals was, in the main, especially at the East, non-economical, without reference, that is, to the cost of production. It was only because kings were as completely masters of the labor and as regardless of the lives of their subjects as the royal builders of the Pyramids, that such quantities of gold and silver could be extracted from the soil by the rude implements of that age. The treasures of Susa and Persepolis could no more have been accumulated under the operation of commercial demand, than the Pyramids have been built by free labor.

The comparison may appear extravagant: yet I cannot but think that it will serve to express very justly the non-economical character of the labor which was expended for this object during the early ages, at least down to the time of Alexander, and largely, through the East, for centuries later.

And even when gold and silver began to lose somewhat their character of royal or sacerdotal treasure, and to acquire that of money, and when, thus, their production ceased to be non-economical, when, that is, it began to have reference to the cost of production and became subject to the law of supply and demand, it still remained, in a high sense, uneconomical, by which I mean that the ordinary assumptions of economical reasoning would have to be importantly modified in dealing with this industry. The ordinary reasoning of the economist is based upon the sufficiency of the individual initiative—each man, that is, on his own instance seeking his own interest—to accomplish the largest production of wealth, and its most equable distribution among the various producing classes; and this, not for the moment merely, but through any period of time that may be taken into account, however considerable.

It is upon this assumption that the abstract doctrine of *laissez faire*, freedom of industry, freedom of trade, is built.

But while this assumption clearly has to be modified somewhat in application to almost any form of production, in respect to none do the assumed depart from the observed facts so widely as in the mining of the precious metals.

While greed, the haste to be rich, is always and everywhere the enemy of true self-interest, it nowhere obtains such a mastery over the senses of men, as where gold and silver are in sight, the immediate objects of exertion. Never do men so sacrifice the future to the present, never so disregard the larger considerations of prudence. This is not due merely to the fact that the production of the precious metals has generally been pursued at a distance from the permanent seats of population, under conditions difficult and perhaps dangerous, and hence by men more than usually reckless and subject to the force of immediate desires. Largely is it due to the mysterious attraction which these metals have exerted upon the powers and passions of men of all races and in all ages. The *sacra auri fames* of the poet is but a sober expression of the lust which has ever burned in the hearts of men in sight of gold.

But while greed, in the economical sense which I have given the word, is thus often, and almost as a rule, opposed to true self-interest; and while greed is so easily exalted to frenzy in the prospect of the precious metals, there is also no industry in which so wide a difference is made in the large, the ultimate, result, according as men work under the blind impulse of immediate acquisition, or under the direction of an intelligent sense of self-interest, extending its view beyond the present to the distant future.

Time will not serve us to go deeply into the technicalities of the production of gold and silver; but one or two simple illustrations may make this proposition seem not unreasonable.

Here is, let us suppose, a superficial deposit of gold dust in the bed of an old river. Throughout certain portions of the former channel, where the forces of the current especially directed it, the gold lies richly mingled with the sand. Over other portions of the bed of the stream it is found more and more sparsely, yielding a less and less return to labor. Is it not evident that a hundred men under intelligent direction, animated by the purpose to secure for themselves, as a body, the largest amount of the precious metal from this deposit, would proceed to work very differently from a hundred miners who should rush into the bed of the old stream, with the wild cry of "Gold!" each for himself struggling with furious haste to get the most he could before night, careless how much he wasted in his search, half washing the sands, and letting perhaps more than he obtained be carried down, to be lodged here and there in places which would escape the eye, or in quantities which would not pay the working? Does it not appear that thus a "placer" which would yield a handsome return to labor for a month, might be exhausted for economical purposes in a week, so that thereafter labor would receive a fortuitous, and at best, an inadequate return?

But let us transfer our view to the production of the precious metals, no longer from the bed of streams, but from the deep recesses of the earth, where shafts have to be driven hundreds of fathoms through solid rock, where the roof under which the miners work by the light of their torches has to be supported by beams of timber or by pillars of rock left for that purpose in the progress of the excavation; where life has to be guarded most carefully and expensively against mephitic or explosive gases; and where the mines have to be kept free of water by constant pumping or systematic drainage. Under such circumstances it is evident that, unless the present is to be strictly subordinated to the future; unless the greed for immediate acquisition is to be held strongly in hand by prudence, and all work be done in the large view of true self-interest, a great difference will be wrought, in the result, upon the production of the mine, looked upon as a resource for supplying the world of commerce from age to age with the metal which has been adopted, not only as the medium of current exchanges, but as the standard by which deferred payments are to be effected. If only indolence furnishes in insufficient quantity, or of inadequate material, the timbers which are to shore up the sides and the roof of the galleries, or if, in the haste to push the work that yields so richly its golden gains, the accumulation of fire-damp is unnoted or neglected, one awful hour may suffice to close forever that source of wealth, which, with proper care, with a due subordination of the present to the future, with a just view of self-interest, would have remained open to give employment, generation after generation, to a large population.

So much for the effects of greed upon the work; how of the worker?

The statistics of mining populations show a horrible waste of laboring power and of life arising out of recklessness in exposure and of parsimony in expenditure even where laborers are free to make their terms with their employers. If so, how rapid must have been the consumption of life and laboring force, when mines were generally worked by convicts and slaves, having no power to contract or to stipulate terms, but driven to work by gangs, in chains! Do we not see here the possibility, almost the certainty, of indefinite waste and loss in production, where the passionate greed of wealth, the consuming lust of gold, loses even the physical instincts of self-preservation to restrain the exertions of the bodily powers and the exposure of life and limb in the perilous work of mining?

But we have yet another step to take in the same di

rection. Let us suppose the mine to be worked and the body of slaves to be driven, not by the owner and master, who could never entirely forget the claims of the future, never be wholly inconsiderate of the needs of his own property, but by the farmer, cut off, by the very terms of his brief lease, from all interest in the distant future, intent only on achieving the maximum of immediate production with the minimum of outlay, utterly indifferent as to the condition in which he shall leave the mine at the expiry of his legal interest therein, and as to the labor supply of the next lessee.

Here, at last, we reach the sufficient explanation of the havoc which has been wrought upon the mining resources of the world,[1] a havoc which is eloquently witnessed, throughout Europe, Asia, and Africa, by abandoned mines never truly worked out, and by the utter sterility of regions once the sources of rich supplies of metallic wealth.

Nor can we afford to disregard the effects of war and of civil commotion upon the production of the precious metals. The fire runs over the fields and burns and blackens all around; but, another spring, nature blooms

[1] The family of the Fuggars were the best miners of Europe at the close of the sixteenth and the beginning of the seventeenth century. Their success was long witnessed by scores of noble families in Augsburg, Madrid, Antwerp, Genoa, Milan and Ghent. Yet Mr. Jacob says of their mines at Guadalcanal, in Spain: "They viewed their concessions as a temporary property from which they were to extract what wealth they could, with as much expedition as possible, and with the least expense to themselves. With this view they formed many galleries where the minerals appeared the most rich, and speedily forsook them to open others. There are now visible as many as sixteen of these openings, the roofs of which were supported by wooden posts, but so slightly that they have all rotted, and thus the passages became closed up."—[P. 150.]

with even a greener foliage and a larger fruitage, for what wasted also fertilized. The fire that sweeps over the mouth of the mine leaves blackness and the horror of a deep silence only.

Such, in a figure, is the difference between the effects of war or civil convulsion upon mining, as contrasted with agricultural industry. No cause has been more potent for closing mines not yet exhausted. Even religious persecution[1] has set its seal over the mouth of many a mine, a seal never to be broken. The mining population once scattered, the mouth of the mine fallen in, the roof here crushing the neglected timbers, the subterranean springs there filling up the vacant galleries, this once fertile source of supply is added to the almost countless number of those which have ceased to contribute to the world's stock of the precious metals.

It may be thought that the moral and material conditions of mining have been dwelt upon at undue length; but I conceive that we cannot understand the wayward course of the production of the precious metals, since the establishment of the Roman Empire, without reference to these considerations, any more than we can upon the principle of supply and demand, alone, account for the vast accumulations of treasure, prior to that period, by the unskillful labor and rude implements of the early ages.

---

[1] The Altenburg mines were abandoned by reason of Protestantism spreading among the miners. "Fallen buildings, heaps of scoriæ, open shafts and choked galleries," says Mr. Jacob, "still attest the former prosperity of the mining operations of this district."—[P. 136.] Religious differences caused the abandonment of many of the Salzburg mines.

## CHAPTER VI.

### THE PRODUCTION OF THE PRECIOUS METALS.—FROM AUGUSTUS TO COLUMBUS.

In tracing the history of the production of the precious metals, as bearing on the question of the Money-supply, we need to have in consideration three elements besides the yield of the mines.

The other elements of the problem are:

1. The consumption of gold and silver as ornaments, and in the arts, industrial and decorative.
2. The wear of the metals in use as coin.
3. The drain of silver to the East.

The consumption of the precious metals as ornaments and in the arts has long been of vast though indeterminate extent. Nor has the dedication of gold or silver to that use always prevented its return to more practical service as money. In some ages and countries these uses have been in a high degree interchangeable.[1]

---

[1] The telegraphic correspondence of the London "Times" from Calcutta, June 17, 1877, contains the following: "The Bombay papers have been drawing attention to the extraordinary increase in the amount of jewelry and personal ornaments tendered for sale at the Presidency Mint, as affording a sure test of the severity with which the famine is pressing on the people. The published figures are certainly startling. The value of silver ornaments tendered from January to October, 1876, averaged from £200 to £600, monthly. It has

As we shall see,[1] ring-money preceded coined money; and the ring and the chain have not infrequently served very well in later times as substitutes for coin. The reader recalls how the Scottish archer of Louis XI bit off some links of his gold chain, to purchase masses for the souls of his murdered kindred. On the death of Sir Thomas Gresham, the founder of the Royal Exchange of London, no small part of his wealth was found to consist of rings and chains, almost as truly ready-money, in those days, as easily appraised, as easily exchanged, as the coin of the realm.

There are other uses to which the precious metals are put which would seem to be incompatible with their further service as money; yet time and accident have served to bring about the restoration to the purposes of commerce of vast masses of gold and silver dedicated, not merely to royal uses, but to the decoration of temples and the worship of deity, whether in heathen or Christian lands.

Not only was conquest generally deemed to carry with it the right to strip the temples of their precious utensils, and even of the images and the masses of metal which gave refulgence to altar and roof and dome;[2] but the necessities of the monarch or the state might, even in Christian countries, justify a demand upon the church for its vessels of silver and of gold. When

since then increased enormously and was, in May, over £80,000. It is a well-known fact that the purchase of ornaments is the Indian peasant's usual way of investing his savings, and that he clings to these baubles as long as possible."

[1] See p. 165.

[2] The Capitol, denominated *aurea* by Virgil and *fulgens* by Horace, was gilded, or rather plated, with 12,000 talents of gold, and the same mode of decoration soon extended to temples and palaces.

Richard the Lion Heart was ransomed from captivity in 1194, "even the gold and silver cups and other vessels used in the Holy Eucharist," says Arnold, Abbot of Lubec, "were melted for the purpose."

The consumption of these metals in the arts of interior decoration, and in the form of household utensils, has varied greatly, not merely in different ages, and not merely in consequence of the scarcity or profusion with which the precious metals were supplied by the mines, but according to the prevailing tastes of each people at the time. The Romans, even when, by the victories of Paulus Æmilius and of Cæsar, they became masters of a large part of the accumulated treasures of the world, employed the precious metals but little in their homes, whether for gilding[1] or for plate.

But in public places the Romans, ever intent on impressing the populace, now by magnificence, now by generosity, were profuse in the employment of gold and silver.[2] The equipage of the senator, the *lectica*, or sedan-chair, in which he was borne, the carriage in which he rode, and even the bits and collars of his horses were, wholly or in considerable part, of gold.

Of the gold and silver applied thus to purposes of ostentation, not a little would, in times of disaster to the

[1] Gilding on metals or china, which involves great loss of the metal, was unknown to the ancients.

[2] "Though the Greeks and Romans generally were without some of our commonest implements of gold and silver, such, for instance, as watches and forks, it is probable that they indulged even more than we do in personal decoration with rings, seals and trinkets of a thousand descriptions. Their armor and even their peaceful habiliments were ornamented with the precious metals, and altogether the traffic in this particular article, which came chiefly from the Spanish mines, furnished as important an element in their commerce as in our own."—[Merivale's History of the Romans, iv, 317.]

individual or the state, find its way back to the channels of commerce. This was, however, a resource of less scope than it would be found to be now. "It has been supposed," says Mr. Jacob, "that in England, at the present day, the quantity of gold and silver in actual existence, including utensils, ornaments, jewelry, trinkets and watches, is three or four times as great as the value of those metals which exist in the form of money. In case circumstances should arise to induce the conversion of plate into money, these would be a resource which could furnish a supply; but in the Roman Empire the plate and jewels of two thousand wealthy families would have been but a feeble aid to the money circulating in that powerful Empire, which comprehended within its limits the most populous and extensive parts of the known world."—[P. 116.] During the Middle Ages, the quantity of the precious metals employed for domestic utensils, for religious uses or in personal decoration, is believed by this writer to have been very small.—[P. 165.] Gilding and plating were now the forms chiefly taken by this species of luxury.

The use of gold and silver in the arts has in some countries been caused, not so much by the abundance of the precious, as by the scarcity of the useful, metals. The Portuguese discoverers found the Brazilians using fish-hooks of gold; while in the Scandinavian tumuli opened in Denmark were swords, daggers and knives, the blades of which were of gold while an edge of iron was introduced for the purpose of cutting. Prescott, in his ' Conquest of Peru," relates that silver was mingled with copper in the manufacture of armor by the Levantine artisans employed by Almagro at Cuzco [ii, 212]; and that in the march on Xauxa, Pizarro shod the horses of his command throughout with silver.—[i, 452.]

The loss of gold and silver by abrasion of coin in use, is another element of the question of the Money-supply. The amount of this loss is a function of two variables: exposure to abrasion, as determined by the shape of the coin and the rapidity of circulation, and the power of resistance, as determined by the character of the alloy in the coin.

Thus, when the stock of the precious metals was at its height in the reign of Augustus, by far the greater portion was protected from abrasion by being held in mass, as treasure. Within the next hundred years, however, the vast bodies which had been stored in the treasure houses were thrown into active circulation among the people, and a high rate of consumption immediately resulted from the inferior character of the alloys used in the mints of the empire.

It does not appear that the ancients employed silver to alloy gold. Their alloys consisted wholly of tin, copper or iron. Now, the English mint experiments, most carefully conducted between 1798 and 1802, show that the loss on gold under the same friction but with different alloys, was as follows:

On British standard gold, if alloyed with silver alone, or with equal parts of silver and copper, on 854 grains, 4.20 grains; if alloyed with tin and copper, on 846 grains, 15.30 grains; if alloyed with iron and copper, on 825 grains, 21.60 grains.

On the other hand, when, between 800 and 1492, the quantity of the precious metals in existence had sunk to a minimum, and prices had reached the point that copper, tin and iron contained a value for their bulk adequate to effect the few and tardy exchanges of that dark age, the loss from abrasion on the surviving volume of gold and silver coins became almost indefinitely less as they were withdrawn from the uses of ordinary commerce and were found only in the caskets of princes or in the shops of goldsmiths.

It has been said that the drain of silver to the East is to be regarded as an element in the question of the Money-supply.

It will naturally be asked why, under the principle of Ricardo's law of distribution, the East should thus be separated, in our contemplation, from the West; why the silver sent to Asia should be treated by the writer on Money as lost to commerce?

It has already been intimated that the result of recent thinking and investigation has been to qualify somewhat Ricardo's statement of the diffusion of the precious metals by the operations of commerce; that it has come to be recognized that the distribution is not effected without encountering retarding causes, which allow important effects to be experienced through the occurrence of distinct intervals in the passage of a new supply from one country to another, and from one class of commodities to another. But even those economists who have most rigidly insisted on applying the principle of diffusion, without important qualification, to all the nations of Europe and America, have been wont to regard the East as, until recently, at least, almost a total exception, looking upon China and the other countries of Asia as constituting, as it were, a vast plain of sand, which drinks up the streams of the precious metals without giving them back to commerce.

The exchange of the silver of Europe, and particularly of Spain, for the gold and spices of the East, had proceeded from the earliest times. The proportionate value of silver to gold was greater in Asia than in Europe. "When gold," says Mr. Jacob, "was worth in

Asia and Africa no more than eight or nine times its weight in silver, it was worth in Europe, and especially in Western Europe, from ten to thirteen times as much."—[P. 190.] Indeed, there is reason to believe that the values of silver and of gold in Asia at earlier dates approached even nearer to equality. A fragment of Agatharchidas is preserved which assigns to silver in Arabia a value greater than that of gold, and in our own day, the opening of trade with Japan found gold valued in the coinage of that empire only as one to four of silver.

It was not, however, until the sixteenth century that the money of Europe and America began to overflow, in great streams, into what Prof. Cairnes calls "the more absorbent and impassive systems of Asia." During that and the following century, Mr. Jacob estimates that one-tenth of the treasure supplied to Europe by the mines of America was transported to India. In the eighteenth century the export rapidly increased with the European consumption of teas, silk, and other oriental productions. For the period 1700 to 1829, the conclusion of his "Inquiry," Mr. Jacob estimates the share of the product of the mines transferred to Asia to be not less than two-fifths.

Having dwelt with some fullness upon the conditions of the production of the precious metals, and having stated and briefly illustrated the other elements of the case, let us consider the main facts respecting the Money-supply of the Western world since the establishment of the Roman Empire.

By successive conquests Rome had not alone acquired possession of nearly all the mines throughout the world then yielding the precious metals. A large proportion of the whole mass of gold and silver which had been produced during preceding centuries was drawn to Italy. This result was only rendered possible by the habitual accumulation of the precious metals throughout the East in great stores of royal treasure, as has been described. Had the produce of the mines been diffused by the agency of commerce, as in subsequent ages, among the body of the people, even the force of imperial taxation at its utmost pressure must have failed to draw together so large a portion of the gold and silver of the world.

Through the non-economical character of the production of the precious metals, as discussed in a previous chapter, the volume of these metals in existence had been raised to dimensions far exceeding what would have been possible under the operation of the law of supply and demand, with the rude chemical and mechanical appliances then in use. The mass was indeed enormous. Mr. Jacob estimates the stock of money in the Empire on the accession of Augustus, at £358,000,000 sterling.[1]

But while Rome, by her military energy, seized the accumulated treasures of Carthage, Spain, Gaul, Greece, Asia, and Egypt, throwing into circulation, as money, among her people what had been hoarded as royal

---

[1] Throughout this and the following chapter I shall give the figures of production and consumption as Mr. Jacob estimates them, not because I have great confidence in estimates of this sort, prior to the present century, but because (1) Mr. Jacob's estimates are referred to very extensively by all English, French, and German writers, and the reader may therefore be interested to see them in detail; (2) Mr. Jacob's mode of tracing down the course of production and consumption affords a capital example of that sort of investigation.

treasure or devoted, in vast masses, to sacerdotal uses, thus raising the prices of all commodities throughout the Empire, but especially in Italy and the countries nearest the capital, Roman dominion, almost by the necessity of the case, proved fatal to the continued supply of the precious metals. The Romans were unskilled in mining. Italy was, perhaps, of all the countries embraced within the Empire, that which had least developed its own mineral resources. This fact undoubtedly concurred with the Roman instinct for the simplification of administration, in inducing the general adoption of the system of "farming" the mines, with the result, both upon the mines as properties and upon the laboring populations pertaining to them, which has been described as incident to that mode of working.

"The farmers," says Mr. Jacob, "took out only the best ores, and neglected those of inferior quality; leaving them in the pits, where they soon became buried in the rubbish with which they were surrounded. Their object being to enrich themselves during the term for which they held the mines, they naturally neglected the interests of future workers and suffered them to go to ruin. Whilst exhausting the mines of the richest ores, they only cut the passages and propped the roofs in so slight a manner that, if they lasted during the current leases, they would all require to be reconstructed in a short period after; which, when the best ores had been extracted, would be at an expense that could not be replaced by any product of the inferior ores which had been left behind. The various contrivances for keeping out the water from the mines, and the machines and the implements for extracting what could not be kept out, were all contrived to answer temporary purposes commensurate with the length of the period for which they were let to farm."—[P. 79.]

But the Roman dominion served in still another way to diminish the productiveness of the mines. Prior to conquest, the mines of Spain, Thrace, Asia, and other gold or silver bearing countries, had been worked, for the benefit of the local sovereigns, by convicts, by conscripts, or by serfs. The crop of convicts in those brutal days was never likely to fail; and as their labor was essentially non-economical, *i. e.*, as they had, in any case, to be confined at the public charge, for the protection of society or their own punishment, the produce of their labor bore no necessary relation to the cost of their maintenance. It was otherwise with the conscripted and the adscripted laborers in the mines, those drawn by lot and those born to the service. If the supply of these was to be kept up from generation to generation, the produce of their labor must be charged with the cost of maintaining them, together with their families. A fourth class of laborers in mines consisted of slaves, the captives of almost incessant wars. The employment of these, again, was chiefly non-economical, being without reference either to repaying the cost of bringing the present body of laborers to maturity, or to providing for the future. It was by this last means that the labor-supply of the mines of the earliest period was largely recruited; and the activity of the production of the precious metals in any country was made to depend greatly upon the good or ill fortune of the people in war. The gradual extension of the Roman dominion brought about a state of almost universal peace, merging a thousand warring tribes in the vast empire which was bounded by the ocean, the Rhine, the Danube, the Euphrates, and the Desert of Africa; a state of peace interrupted only by civil commotion, the results of which, however bloody.

could not include the reduction of the soldiers of either faction to the condition of slavery.[1] Thus war, as a source of labor-supply for the mines, practically ceased. Slaves were still, it is true, brought into the Empire as the result of piracy, or of trade with barbarous regions beyond the reach of Roman power; but these were hardly numerous enough to meet the demands for personal service, under the growing luxuriousness of the age; and purchased slaves soon became too costly to be employed in the difficult and dangerous work of mining.[2]

There remained to the Roman authorities, as a resource for working the mines of the precious metals which had been acquired by conquest, the labor of convicts and of serfs.[3] As the difficulty of securing laborers from other sources increased, labor in the mines was more and more made the penalty of crime, until this mode of punishment became almost universal; while successive decrees increased the traditional obligations of the peasantry in the neighborhood of mines.[4] The severity of these exactions coupled with

---

[1] "The legions of Pompey, when beaten by Julius Cæsar, did not become slaves, neither were those who fought under Brutus and Cassius at Philippi, nor those who contended under Marc Antony against Octavius, when dispersed as an army, sold for slaves to their fellow-citizens."—[Jacob, p. 101.]

[2] "Though numerous slaves were employed in all the offices of domestic life, in trades, in fabrics, and in agriculture, . . . there are no instances, in the time of the emperors or in the ages that followed, of their being employed in the degrading and unproductive labor of the mines."—[Jacob, p. 103.]

[3] Glebæ et metallis adscripti.

[4] "At first, one half of the inhabitants, only, were compelled to labor in the operations connected with the mines; but as the numbers decreased a law was made by which all the children of these hereditary miners were required to devote their labor to the mines."—[Jacob, p. 98.]

the cruelty of the farmers and overseers made great inroads upon these unfortunate populations. Soon a new danger presented itself. The barbarians appeared on the borders of the Empire, offering a refuge to those who had the courage, born of despair, to attempt their escape from the power of Rome. Next, the barbarians thrust themselves into the Empire, and the lands earliest invaded were those on the produce of whose mines the world was most dependent for its supply of the precious metals. The serfs became the personal slaves of the conquerors, or swelled the ranks of their armies.[1]

Such were the causes which in swift succession reduced the labor-supply of the mines of the Empire. Meanwhile, so wasteful had been the operations of the farmers of the mines, that the earlier emperors were driven to assume the charge of the mines, which were again worked by public officers on government account.

It will not be necessary to speak of the various measures resorted to by successive emperors to stimulate the failing production of the precious metals; of grants to individuals to work mines on shares; of edicts issued almost in despair, making mining as "free" as many nowadays wish banking to be; of efforts to systematize the administration of the mines and introduce scientific knowledge and technical skill into the conduct of mining operations. The production of the precious metals had received a shock from which it was not to recover for more than one thousand years.

"We may safely conclude," says Mr. Jacob, "that after the third or fourth century the labor of extracting the precious metals had gradually diminished within

[1] Dacian miners re-inforced the Goths who defeated and slew the Emperor Valens.

the limits of the Roman Empire; and that, from the fifth century, after the more afflicting irruptions of the barbarians into the weak and tottering Western Empire, it had altogether ceased."—[P. 101.] "In the period from about 480 to 670 or 680, the greatest diligence has been able to discover no trace, in any author, of the operations of mining having been carried on."—[P. 131.]

It was to the decrease thus produced in the supply of the precious metals, beginning "at the very time when the victories of the legions and the wisdom of the Antonines had given peace and security, and, with it an increase in numbers and riches, to the Roman Empire," and proceeding to such an extent as to allow the stock of money to waste away to probably less than one-tenth the amount held in the reign of Augustus, that Alison attributes the Decline and Fall of that mighty fabric of military power, legislative wisdom and administrative skill. The value of money undergoing a continual enhancement by the falling off in the yield of the mines, the producing classes were kept at a constant disadvantage in competition with the more alert and intelligent exchanging and speculative classes; while the debtor class was put at an increasing disadvantage in its relations with the creditor class through the growing aggravation of all charges fixed by custom or by contract.

From the long dearth of money which prevailed from the foundation of the Empire, the first signs of revival came with the Saracen conquests in Europe, in the eighth century. That revival, however, only proceeded so far as, by Mr. Jacob's computations, to put a stop to the waste of the stock of money, and to keep the volume in circulation good from 806 to the period of the discovery of America. "The whole period," says this writer, "was a time of hostility and turbulence. There was little security for any kind of property, and less still for that which could alone induce the working ol mines for silver and gold. None of the mines that are noticed were uninterruptedly wrought, and few of these were worked simultaneously. Some were most productive at one period, and then yielded nothing for centuries, while others were discovered, explored and speedily abandoned.

"The art of separating the precious metals from the ores and from the inferior metals with which they had been mingled had been lost[1] since the time of the Roman operations, and were recovered by the same slow and gradual steps by which the ancients had proceeded. As the mines were worked in countries very remote from each other, the improvements, either in the mechanical or scientific process, would not be speedily diffused, and though some might advance rapidly, others would do so at a slower pace."—[P. 193.]

It is in view of the general facts of production recited, and of the elements of loss and waste which have been indicated, that Mr. Jacob makes his computations, so frequently cited in economical discussions, of the quantity of the precious metals in circulation at the discovery of America.

He assumes that in the year 14 A.D., there was in existence, as money, £358,000,000. Every thirty-six years he supposes that ten per cent. was lost by abrasion in use, which would leave in the year 158 A.D., £233,-

---

[1] "L'art même des mines se perdit."—[Chevalier, La Monnaie, p 431.]

263,800; in 302, £147,374,380; in 482, £87,033,099; in 806, £33,674,256; which last figures he takes as representing the lowest point reached by the stock of money within historic times. In the seven hundred years that followed, Mr. Jacob holds that this amount was kept good, but not increased,[1] by the yield of the mines, especially those of the German Empire.

---

[1] To show the high purchase power which money had obtained in England through its scarcity, Mr. Jacob gives numerous illustrations, of which the following will suffice:

King Henry VI, being held a prisoner by Edward IV (1470), there was allowed for the subsistence of himself and his suite of ten persons, £3 10*s.* per week. Lady Anne, daughter of King Edward III, was allowed £1 11*s.* weekly "for her exhibition, sustentation, and convenient diet of meat and drink."—[Inquiry into the Precious Metals, p. 180.]

## CHAPTER VII.

### THE PRODUCTION OF THE PRECIOUS METALS.—1492–1848.

In 1492 America was discovered. The first lands reached by the Spaniards did not produce the precious metals in abundance; but enough was in the possession of the natives to excite the cupidity and inflame the imaginations of the discoverers. Their accounts of enormous quantities of gold and boundless treasure are calculated to deceive the readers of the chronicles of the early conquests. Humboldt estimates the average annual amount of the precious metals which America furnished to Europe, 1492 to 1500, at only about £52,000.

It was not until the invasion of Mexico by Cortes, in 1519, that the yield was greatly increased. The Mexican treasure consisted mainly of silver, which metal was destined to form the greater part of the New World's production during the next three centuries.

The conquest of Mexico aroused the ambition of Pizarro, and the invasion and subjugation of Peru speedily followed, bringing to the supply of the exhausted circulation of Europe at once the large annual yield of the mines of that country, and the accumulations of past production, in the temples and in the palaces of the Incas.

Estimating the annual production of the new world between 1492 and 1521 (the date of the capture of the city of Mexico) at £52,000, which is Humboldt's estimate for the period 1492 to 1500, and which it is safe to continue to 1521, we have £1,308,000

From 1521 to 1545, Humboldt estimates the annual production at £630,000, 15,750,000

1492–1545, - - - £17,058,000

In the latter part of the year 1545, the mines of the Cerro de Potosi were opened. The fame of the discovery soon attracted a large population and the mountain was pierced in every direction. The real date of the finding of the treasures of the new world is 1545, not 1492.

Of far more lasting consequence, even than the discovery of the deposits of Potosi, was the discovery by Medina[1] of the process of amalgamation by the use of mercury. The mines of Potosi, wonderful as they were, would in time be exhausted; but the process of this humble Mexican miner is practiced to-day in every quarter of the globe where silver ores are raised.

The annual supply of the American mines for the fifty-four years, 1546–1599, Mr. Jacob estimates at £2,100,000, while the miners of Europe, especially those of the Pyrenees and of Languedoc, stimulated by the fame of the trans-Atlantic treasures, redoubled their

[1] "Medina fut pour l'industrie métallurgique, ce que Triptolème avait été pour la culture du sol dans les temps primitifs" . . "Habituellement l'esprit humain n'arrive aux formules simples qu'en traversant beaucoup de complications; ce pauvre mineur fut plus heureux; du premier coup, il trouva une recette tellement simple, que pendant trois siècles on n'y a presque rien changé.'—[M. Chevalier La Monnaie.]

exertions and their production. For the entire period 1492 to 1599, Mr. Jacob makes the following computation:

| | |
|---|---|
| Stock of money current in Europe, at the discovery of America, - - - | £34,000,000 |
| Additional product, after making allowance for the loss by natural wear ($\frac{1}{300}$ per annum), - - | 138,000,000 |
| | £172,000,000 |
| Deduct from it what had been conveyed to Asia ($\frac{1}{10}$) and what had been applied to arts and industries ($\frac{1}{5}$), | 42,000,000 |
| Stock in 1599, - - | £130,000,000 |

From 1600 to 1699, the elements of the problem are increased by the contributions of Brazil; and the estimate of annual production, in which Mr. Jacob concurs substantially with Humboldt, rises to £3,375,000:

| | | |
|---|---|---|
| Stock of coin, 1600, - | £130,000,000 | |
| Deduct for abrasion and loss 1600–1699, - | 43,000,000 | |
| | | £87,000,000 |
| Produce of the mines, 100 years, - - - | 337,500,000 | |
| Transferred to India and China, - - - | 33,250,000 | |
| | £304,250,000 | |
| Deduct as converted to other uses than coin, | 60,250,000 | |
| | £244,000,000 | |
| Deduct for abrasion and loss, - - - | 34,000,000 | |
| | | 210,000,000 |
| | | £297,000,000 |

It was in the latter portion of the sixteenth, and the earlier portion of the seventeenth century, that the effects of the new supply of the metals appear to have been realized in the prices of produce in the countries of Europe. Adam Smith entertains the view that, until the year 1570, silver did not fall in value.[1] At the latter date, however, the influence of the astonishing production of silver at Potosi began to be felt. From 1570 to 1640 silver sank rapidly. Corn rose from about two oz. of silver the quarter, to six or eight oz.[2] "The discovery of the abundant mines of America seems to have been the sole cause of this diminution in the value of silver, in proportion to that of corn. It is accounted for, accordingly, in the same manner by everybody, and there never has been any dispute, either about the fact or about the cause of it."

So great a fall in the value of the precious metals could not but powerfully affect the social and industrial conditions of Europe. We have seen how far Mr. Hume and Sir A. Alison attribute to it the astonishing developments of the centuries which followed. Even so careful an economist as Prof. Cairnes declares that the produce of the mines of the New World "supplied and rendered possible the remarkable expansion of oriental trade which forms the most striking commercial fact of the age that followed."[3]

---

[1] Wealth of Nations, i, 187–202.

[2] Mr. Hume wrote: "By the most exact computations that have been formed all over Europe, after making allowance for the alterations in the numerary value, or the denomination, it is found that the prices of all things have only risen three, or at most four, times since the discovery of the West Indies." Mr. Jacob makes out the increase to have been as from 100 to 470.

[3] Essays in Political Economy, p. 110.

On the other hand, so rapid was the fall, so great the disturbance of trade and industry that followed, so wholesale the reduction in the value of fixed incomes and permanent charges, that wide-spread distress and much permanent pauperism resulted. Even in the view of those who advocate the gradual depreciation of money, the depreciation effected between 1570 and 1640 was too sudden and violent to be consistent with the best results. Mr. Jacob attributes to the overwhelming changes in the purchase power of money, at this period, that sudden increase of pauperism which gave occasion for the establishment of the English Poor Laws; and those financial embarrassments of Charles I which led to the Great Rebellion.[1] Instead of a slow and gradual diminution of the weight of indebtedness (that mortgage which the representatives of past production hold upon the produce of present labor), debts were, in many cases, almost confiscated by the rapid depreciation of the money in which they were to be paid. The creditor class was very generally impoverished, if not hopelessly ruined.

In seventy years, however, the work, so far at least as England was concerned, was accomplished. "Between 1630 and 1640, or about 1636," says Adam Smith, "the effect of the discovery of the mines of America, in reducing the value of silver, appears to have been completed; and the value of that metal seems never to have

[1] Prof. Cairnes holds the same view: "Less directly, but still intimately connected with the same event were the sudden growth and temporary splendor of the Spanish monarchy, the establishment of the Poor Laws in England, the financial embarrassments of Charles I, which resulted in the Long Parliament and the Revolution, and the rise and progress of British maritime power."—[Essays, p. 110.

sunk lower, in proportion to that of corn, than it was about this time."

Let us follow Mr. Jacob in his further inquiry into the Money-supply.

Down to the close of the seventeenth century, he had assumed the loss by wear, on the general mass of coined gold and silver, to be $\frac{1}{360}$ annually. The reason for this was, in his own language, "If the rate of loss by wear on gold money was at the rate of one part in 600, and that money was one-sixth of the circulating medium, and if the rate of loss on the silver money was at the rate of one part in 150, the mean rate of depreciation would be as near to one part in 360 as can be calculated."—[P. 300.] After 1700, however, Mr. Jacob adopts a different assumption, taking the ratio of silver to gold in use, no longer as 5:1, but as 4:1. Gold being more durable than silver, we have a lower rate of annual consumption in the total mass, which is henceforward, for the purposes of these computations, taken as $\frac{1}{420}$ annually.

The eighteenth century witnessed the comparative decline of the mines of Peru and the rapid development of those of Mexico,[1] whose production increased two-

[1] M. Chevalier, in his treatise "La Monnaie," has set in striking contrast the condition of mining in the one country and in the other. "La plupart des mines mexicaines sont dans de fertiles contrées, où la vie est facile. Les mines du Pérou occupent une terre glacée, en raison de son élévation extrême, et où les arbres même refusent de croître. On y touche de la main les neiges éternelles. . . . C'est la Sibérie sous l'équateur, la Sibérie sans ses forêts qui offrent au métallurgiste un combustible inépuisable; la Sibérie sans ses plaines aisées à parcourir; la Sibérie sans ses fleuves majestueux qui y donnent, pendant la belle saison, un système de communication plus commode encore que le traîneau sur les neiges de l'hiver."—[Pp. 379–80.]

fold, fourfold, and even fivefold, before the close of the period.

| | | |
|---|---|---|
| Stock in Europe, 1700, | £297,000,000 | |
| Deduct for friction and loss, 1700 to 1809, | 71,000,000 | |
| | | £226,000,000 |
| Add produce of mines,[1] | 880,000,000 | |
| Deduct $\frac{2}{5}$ for Asia, - | 352,000,000 | |
| | 528,000,000 | |
| Deduct $\frac{2}{3}$ as applied to other uses than coin, | 352,000,000 | |
| | 176,000,000 | |
| Deduct for wear, $\frac{1}{420}$ annually, - - | 22,000,000 | |
| | | 154,000,000 |
| Stock in 1810, - - | | £380,000,000[2] |

The year 1809 marks the beginning of a new epoch in the history of the Money-supply.

From 1492 onward, the yield of the precious metals, though varying greatly at times, had never fallen below what was necessary to keep up the supply of coin, after all the loss in wear, the consumption of the metals in

---

[1] Spanish America, about £706,000,000; Portuguese America, about £80,000,000; gold and silver from Europe and gold dust from Africa, about £94,000,000.

[2] "This computation," adds Mr. Jacob, "though by a very different process, gives a result so nearly approaching to those of Forbonnais, Gerboux, and Heron de Villefosse, that it seems more entitled to confidence than that of Necker, who rated the coin of France to be nearly equal to that of all Europe, and the collective stock not much to exceed one-half of this estimate."—[P. 315.]

the arts, and the steady and increasing drain to India; while for the entire period the excess of the supply over the requirements for these purposes had been such as to raise the amount in existence throughout the civilized world, as coin, according to Mr. Jacob's estimate, from £34,000,000 to £380,000,000.

But a change was to come. The disturbed state of Europe, and particularly the invasion of Spain by Bonaparte, incited the Spanish colonies to assert their independence. For twenty years war and civil convulsions racked the populations of Spanish America to a degree that became almost destructive of all settled industry, but produced their first and worst effects upon the mining of the precious metals. "In each district," says Mr. Ward, in his work on Mexico, "the principal mines were abandoned; the machinery was allowed to go to ruins, and the silver raised was merely the gleanings of more prosperous times, the workings, where any were attempted, being confined almost entirely to the upper levels."[1]

Yet, even in this abandonment of the mines by the capitalists and by the organized bodies of paid and trained miners, Mr. Ward notes that production did not wholly cease, even in the districts most affected. "It is a fact," he remarks, "universally admitted, that in almost all the mining districts, although the towns have been ruined by the emigration of the wealthy inhabitants, whose capitals were formerly invested in mining operations, the lower classes have throughout the revolution found means to draw their subsistence from the mines. Under the denomination of *buscones*, or searchers, they have never ceased to work; and although,

[1] ii, 21.

from the want of method in their operations, they have done the most serious injury to the mines themselves, they have in general continued to extract from the upper levels, or from the old workings, neglected in better times for others of greater promise, a very considerable quantity of silver. This desultory system is still pursued in many parts of the country and at Zirmapan, Zaculapan, El Doctor, and many of the northern districts, a large population is even now maintained by it."

Like causes, operating between 1811 to 1820, produced like effects in Chili, Peru, Colombia and Buenos Ayres. The gold product of Brazil had begun to decline, even by the middle of the preceding century, and the occasion of war between England and the United States, 1812–5, by giving an impetus to the cultivation of cotton, caused a still more rapid decrease in the yield of the mines. At the same time the product of Hungary and Austria, which had been the great resource of Europe during the money-famine of the Middle Ages, fell sharply off to one-half its former amount.

In one direction only did an increase appear. The mines of the Ural mountains in this period began to yield a large, and, after 1823, constantly increasing volume of the precious metals.

Mr. Jacob enters with much detail into the inquiry, how much of the gold and silver of Europe and America was drawn into consumption in the arts during the period 1809 to 1829, the latter date marking the close of his investigations. For the first time statistical information, more or less precise, is available to form the basis of his computations. The facts brought out in his 26th Chapter as to the use of the precious metals by the gold-beaters, the water-gilders, the jewelers and the decorators of china-ware, and in the manufacture of plate and of watches, are exceedingly interesting. Our space will not serve to present his results in detail. One item, only, deserves to be taken out of the account and separately stated:

"According to the information collected from the most considerable refiners, who are commonly the purchasers of broken pieces of gold and silver, of burned lace and picture frames, and of foreign gold and silver coins, the quantity of *old metal* used in this trade is very small.

. . . . . . .

"We cannot deem these meltings of old gold and silver goods to have contributed more than a fortieth part to the precious metals that have been applied to useful or ornamental purposes during the last twenty years."—[P. 367.]

Of the drain to the East, Mr. Jacob remarks:

"In the former part of this inquiry, in all the recent divisions of the subject, a large and rather doubtful allowance has been made for that portion of the precious metals which passed to the several parts of Asia by the channels which Humboldt has traced.

"A great change has been effected in the commerce of the East within a few late years. . . . Though large quantities have been transported there in some years, other quantities have been again returned to Europe, not, indeed, of the same species of metal, nor in equal quantities. Silver has been conveyed to Asia, and gold has been exported from thence."

After a criticism of the estimates of Humboldt, which he deems excessive, Mr. Jacob concludes: "We see no necessity for considering the whole trade of Asia, taken collectively, to have absorbed more of the stock of the precious metals which Europe had collected from the mines of America and from those within her limits, than to the amount of £2,000,000, annually, within the twenty years we have been reviewing."

Mr. Jacob issues from his investigation of the Money-supply of the period 1809–1829, with the following results:

| | | |
|---|---|---|
| Stock of coin, 1810, - - - | | £380,000,000 |
| Loss by abrasion, - - - | | 18,095,220 |
| | | 361,904,780 |
| Supply of the mines[1] - - - | | 103,736,000 |
| | | £465,640,780 |
| Converted into utensils and ornaments - | £112,252,220 | |
| Transferred to Asia - | 40,000,000 | |
| | | 152,252,220 |
| | | £313,388,560 |

So marked a diminution in the Money-supply of the world, coinciding with the vast increase of public and private indebtedness, could not but excite serious apprehension as to the future among economists and statesmen. The apprehension felt on this subject was, indeed, the motive of the investigation which Mr. Jacob undertook, with the results which have been exhibited. We have seen with what alarm the English historian of this period of European politics contemplated the threatened reduction of the Money-supply through an indefinite future.

For the period between 1830 and 1848, we have no such careful guide to follow. The general facts are

[1] Of which Spanish America furnished £76,626,768; Brazil, £4,-110,000

known. From 1823, as has been stated, the production of the Ural Mountains took on a steady rate of increase, while later still, about 1830, the auriferous sands of Siberia[1] became known, and after 1840 yielded a far larger mass of gold than that taken from the Ural region. By 1848 the annual supply of gold alone had risen to about £8,000,000, as estimated by Chevalier, a yield quite sufficient to remove all apprehension of a positive decline in the supply, and, indeed, adequate to secure a progressive increase of the stock of money.

[1] M. Leon Faucher strongly contrasts the popular character of gold mining in Australia and California, with the severe restraints and high taxes imposed on this industry by the government of Russia.

## CHAPTER VIII.

### THE PRODUCTION OF THE PRECIOUS METALS—THE CALIFORNIAN AND AUSTRALIAN EPISODE.

In 1848 the existence of rich and vast deposits of gold on the Pacific[1] coast of the United States was made known, followed quickly by the Australian discoveries of 1851. At once the annual yield of the precious metals rose to £38,000,000.

Of the disturbance of the proportions existing between the values of gold and silver, from the fact that the new supply was almost exclusively of the former metal, we shall find occasion to speak hereafter.[2] An increase so sudden, so tremendous, in the volume of the precious metals was well calculated to arouse the expectation of economists.

"The auriferous rocks and sands of California and Australia," wrote Prof. Cairnes,[3] "are as much superior, in richness and abundance, to those which rewarded the industry of the Spanish adventurers, as the latter were superior to all which had been previously known."

"The circumstances of the present time," he contin-

---

[1] Up to this time gold had been produced at several points on the Atlantic Slope, especially in North Carolina and Georgia. It was also raised in very small amounts in Virginia, South Carolina, Alabama and Tennessee.

[2] See p. 233–5.

[3] Essays in Political Economy, p. 110.

ued, "are not such as to preclude the possibility of a recurrence of events similar, or analogous, to those which the first American discoveries drew after them. Those events were of the greatest moment to mankind. They included the rapid colonization of America by European races; great and lasting changes in the channels of trade; striking vicissitudes in the fortunes of nations, and a monetary revolution, the effects of which have been felt in every quarter of the globe."

It was in a sort of panic at the effects of the new supplies to be anticipated in the immediate future that M. Chevalier wrote his well-known work on the "Probable Fall in the Value of Gold;" but as M. Chevalier directs his attention mainly to the disturbance of the relations between gold and silver, and that, too, with specific reference to the monetary legislation of his own country, dealing slightly with the changes which the new money, by altering the distribution of purchasing power in the world, should produce in the movements of trade and the fortunes of nations, I prefer to deal with the wider views of Prof. Cairnes, presented in four papers, written at various dates between 1859 and 1872, which occupy the first part of his volume, entitled "Essays in Political Economy," a work which, with the treatise by the same writer on the "Character and Logical Method of Political Economy," may be commended unreservedly to every student of the science.

What, then, were the facts with which Prof. Cairnes had to deal? In a word, the production of the precious metals had suddenly sprung into an activity, due to the discovery of mines in hitherto unsettled and but partially explored regions,[1] which seemed to show the capa-

[1] "Between the years 1849–1868 it is calculated that gold valued at £657,000,000, and silver at £345,000,000 have been added to the

bility[1] of doubling the stock of the world in twenty or twenty-five years.

What was to come of this?

Let us revert to our statement of the elements of the problem of the Money-supply. The loss of coin by abrasion in use is now reduced to a minimum, first, by improvements in coinage, especially in the matter of alloys, and, secondly, by the very general use of paper substitutes for coin in circulation.

Prof. Cairnes had next to consider the probable demand for the consumption of the metals in the arts. On this point he adds nothing to the minute and searching analysis of M. Chevalier, but adopts the conclusion reached by that economist, viz., that not much was to be expected from the extending use of gold in manufactures[2] as a means of disposing of the new supplies.

India and the East remained as the possible absorbent of the stock of silver, so far as it should be released

---

stock of precious metals in the world. Of this gold, £365,000,000 have been added from new sources."—[Rogers's Notes to Adam Smith, i, 250n.]

[1] In reading the essays of Prof. Cairnes and the work of Chevalier on "Gold," it should be remembered that they wrote at a time when California and Australia still possessed vast tracts which had not been subjected to scientific survey or even to reconnoissance; and thus the extent of the gold fields could scarcely be conjectured..

[2] Prof. Cairnes deems the use of gold for ornaments characteristic of semi-barbarous life. "The superfluous expenditure of a nation advancing in civilization is accordingly devoted less and less to objects which absorb mere masses of gold and silver, and more and more to purposes of a higher order; to the beautifying of its domains, the embellishing of its houses, the general cultivation of its tastes; and parks and mansions, pictures, sculpture and books, take the place of accumulations of plate and collections of jewelry."—[P. 133.]

from the offices of money by the superabundant supplies of gold pouring into Europe from the new mines.

The capacity of the East to absorb the precious metals in vast amounts had been amply demonstrated when Prof. Cairnes wrote. According to the computations of M. Chevalier, the exports of silver to India and China reached, in 1857, the prodigious sum of £20,145,921, "that is to say, more than double the yield of all the silver mines that supply the markets of the Western world."[1] "This exportation," continues the writer, "is independent of an exportation of probably one-tenth of the above amount in gold, which has been going on during the last few years." The closing remark introduces a new feature of the situation. The East, which from the earliest ages had never ceased to exchange its gold for the silver of the West, had itself become, in no inconsiderable degree, a consumer of gold.[2]

In spite of the apparent capacity and disposition of India and China to absorb a great portion of the new supplies of the precious metals, Prof. Cairnes was not prepared to accept this as the solution of the problem.

"In India," he wrote, "though more than a century

---

[1] On Gold, p. 65. M. Chevalier explains this increase in the shipments of silver partly by the civil war in China, causing a demand for that form of wealth which can be most easily concealed, and partly by the Indian Mutiny, involving extraordinary expenditures by the government for the supply of troops in the field. The falling off in the European grain crop had also increased the demand for the rice of the East, and the failure of the crop of silk in Italy and France had obliged manufacturers to resort to China for a much larger portion than usual of their material.

[2] The London "Economist" estimates that between 1858 and 1872 China and India received and retained £90,000,000 in gold. Little, however, of this is used as money; see the Report of Mr. Göschen's Committee, Q. 939, 1015, 1085.

under British rule, the advantages of credit, as a medium of exchange, are only beginning to be understood. The circulation of bank-notes is exceedingly limited, and is still confined to some of the Presidency towns; checks, by which so large a portion of the business of this country is carried on, are but slightly used; and the great mass of transactions is effected by a transfer of rupees bodily in every sale. The magnitude of the transactions conducted in this manner may be estimated by the fact stated by Sir Charles Napier, that the escort of treasure constituted one of the severest duties of the late Bengal army; from 20,000 to 30,000 men being constantly occupied in this manner. The quantity of the precious metals employed in thus carrying on the internal traffic of India has been variously estimated between £150,000,000 and £300,000,000. But this state of things is evidently not destined to be of long continuance. Mr. Wilson's recent minute gives grounds for believing that the Indian government are alive to this subject, and that India will soon enjoy the advantages of an effective paper system. Such an event cannot fail to be attended with important consequences on the trade and industry of that country; and among these consequences we may expect this, that, instead of requiring, as now, continuous large additions to her present enormous stock of metallic money, she will not only be enabled to dispense with these, but will find it for her interest to part with a large portion of what she now employs; the coin thus liberated will form a new tributary to swell the increasing surplus, and the influences tending to depress the value of gold will be increased."[1]

---

[1] Essays in Political Economy, p. 127.

For the above reasons Prof. Cairnes held with M. Chevalier, that "the currency offers the one sole channel by which the principal part of the enormous production of gold can find an outlet:" the population of civilized countries advancing at the rate of one and a half per cent. per annum; gold, or at least that portion which goes into general circulation, increasing by more than ten per cent. per annum.

So much for the Money-supply. How of the demand? Will the increasing requirements of trade absorb any large proportion of the new supplies without allowing a rise of prices, that is, a depreciation of money? To this Prof. Cairnes replies: "The proportion of the trade of the world which is carried on with metallic money is daily diminishing and constantly tends to diminish." In one direction only Prof. Cairnes found an occasion for an actual increase, though not an extensive one, of the Money-supply without an advance of prices; but to state this new source of demand would be to anticipate the natural development of the argument. I shall, therefore, refer to it at a later period.[1]

In general, then, we may say that Prof. Cairnes agreed with M. Chevalier in holding that "the Currency" afforded the main channel by which the new supplies must find their outlet; and, also, in holding that the wants of trade were not likely to allow such an addition to the money of the world[2] without an advance of prices, that is, without a depreciation of money: a depreciation which, if the rate of production was to be maintained, must be rapid and extensive.

---

[1] See p. 156.

[2] "It would be difficult to estimate at more than 6 milliards [£240,000,000] the sum required for the circulation, independently of silver money, of all the nations of Christendom."—[Chevalier on Gold, p 100.]

With what results to the several countries of the world and to the several classes of commodities? Prof. Cairnes's inquiry into these effects of the new Money-supply constitutes one of the most valuable of recent contributions to economical science.

It will appear that all the positive results a writer may obtain in such an investigation must be in contravention or modification of Mr. Ricardo's principle of the distribution of the precious metals. If such a distribution is to be achieved only with appreciable intervals, allowing effects of serious consequence to be wrought, as the new supplies pass, by equable process, or "by jerks," to use M. Chevalier's phrase, from one country to another, from one class of commodities to another, from one body of producers to another, we shall find the necessity, which it was intimated at the outset[1] might arise, of qualifying the principle which we provisionally accepted, as governing the relative proportions in which the money of the world is to be divided among the several nations, communities and classes of producers.

Prof. Cairnes holds strongly that it is of distinct economical consequence where the gold-supplies issue, and in what relations, geographical and commercial, other nations stand to the sources of the new production. That is, he holds that the immediate effects of that production would be importantly different were the thirty or forty million pounds yearly issuing from California and Australia to be yielded by mines scattered over the surface of Europe and Asia. "Gold and silver, like all other things which are the subjects of international exchange, possess local values;[2] and it is by a suc-

[1] See p. 57.

[2] "The lower the local value of the precious metals in any country the greater will be the advantage to that country in foreign markets.

cession of operations on the local values of gold of an unequal and fluctuating character, that its depreciation is being effected, and that (the conditions of production remaining as at present) its value will continue to decline. The twofold[1] rise of prices in the gold countries forms the first step in this progress, and it will be through a series of similar partial advances in other countries, and not by any general movement, that the depreciation of the metal throughout the world will be accomplished, if that consummation is indeed to take place."—[P. 82.]

So vast a volume of the precious metals cannot, Prof. Cairnes holds, be poured into the reservoir from which the nations draw their supplies, without producing disturbances which will be very unequally experienced by the several nations, according as they are geographically and commercially near to or remote from the place of discharge. Of the great depreciation in the 16th Century, he remarks: "This disturbance was in favor of the Spanish, the Portuguese and the Dutch, while the English, further removed from the spring-head of the new metal, received their supplies more slowly and in scantier streams. Money incomes in England therefore rose less rapidly than prices in common markets; and the population of England suffered accordingly. We have no doubt that this was a leading cause of the industrial distress which prevailed throughout a portion of the reign of Queen Elizabeth, and which led to the introduction of the Poor Laws."

---

—[P. 84.] . . . "Every country, therefore, is interested in raising as rapidly as possible the prices of its productions—in other words, in the most rapid possible depreciation of the local value of its gold."—[P. 85.]

[1] See p. 153.

"In the present gold movement, however, the tables have been turned, and the monetary disturbance is now in favor of the Anglo-Saxon. It is now England and the United States that have their hands in the till, and the money which they extract is employed in raising prices[1] against the nations which in the 16th Century were gainers at their expense."—[P. 150.]

But if such effects are to be wrought as between nations, according as they are geographically and commercially near to or remote from the sources of supply, Prof. Cairnes attributes to the gold discoveries a decided potency, also, in altering the distribution of wealth among the different producing classes of each nation by turns. Ultimately, in this respect, as between nations, Prof. Cairnes admits that an increase of money, where the conditions of production remain in other respects the same, must come to affect the prices of all commodities and services in an equal degree; "but before this result is attained, a period of time, longer or shorter according to the amount of the augmentation and the general circumstances of commerce, must elapse. In the present instance, the additions which are being

[1] "The rise in price has been most rapid in commodities produced in the gold countries; having in these, at a single bound, reached its utmost limit—the limit set by the cost of procuring gold. After commodities produced in the gold regions, the advance, I conceive, will proceed most rapidly in the productions of England and the United States; after these, at no great interval, in the productions of the continent of Europe; while the commodities the last to feel the effects of the new money, and which will advance most slowly under its influence, are the productions of India and China, and I may add, of tropical countries generally so far as these share, as regards their economic conditions, the general character of the former countries."—[P. 73.] This was written in 1858.

made to the monetary systems of the world are upon an enormous scale, and the disturbance effected in the relation of prices is proportionately great. Under such circumstances it is very possible that *the inequalities resulting may not find their correction throughout the whole period of progressive depreciation;* a period which even with our present facilities of production and distribution may easily extend over some *thirty or forty years.* During this transitionary term, the actions of the new gold on prices will not be uniform, but partial. Certain classes of commodities and services will be affected much more powerfully than others. Prices generally will rise, but with unequal steps."—[P. 56.]

An increased production of gold, argues Prof. Cairnes, operates to raise prices by a twofold process, first, directly, through the medium of an enlarged money-demand; secondly, indirectly, through curtailing the supply of articles which do not come within the range of the new demand.

The rise of wages in the industries which feel the force of the new demand will raise wages in those departments not so affected; but the prices of their products cannot advance proportionally; hence profits fall below the average, which contracts the production and the supply offered.

"An increased supply of money thus tends, by one mode of its operation, to raise prices in advance of wages, and thus to stimulate production; by another, to raise wages in advance of prices, and thus to check it; in both, however, to raise wages, and thus ultimately to render necessary, in order to the maintenance of profits, a general and permanent elevation of prices."[1]—[P. 60.]

---

[1] This is not inconsistent with Ricardo's doctrine that "high wages do not make high prices." That doctrine assumes the value of money to be constant.

In this view, Prof. Cairnes turns his attention to three points:

1. What is, and is likely to be, the direction of the new expenditure?

2. What are the facilities for extending the supply of the articles which feel the force of the new demand?

3. What is the term within which the production of articles which are left out of the new demand may be duly curtailed?

As to the first point, the new expenditure will naturally be determined by the habits and tastes of the persons into whose possession the new money comes, viz., in the first instance, the inhabitants of the gold countries, and secondly, those persons in other countries who can best supply the wants of the former class. "Speaking broadly, we may say that the persons who will chiefly benefit by the gold discoveries belong to the middle and lower ranks of society, in a large degree to the lowest rank, the class of unskilled laborers."—[P. 61.] What the principal objects of their expenditure are likely to be, does not require to be indicated.

As to the second point, the facilities for extending the supply will depend on two circumstances: (*a*) the degree in which machinery can be employed; (*b*) the degree in which the process of production is independent of natural agencies which require time for accomplishing their ends.[1] "The distinctions marked by these two conditions, it will be found, correspond pretty ac-

[1] Thus, the production of cotton throughout the world might conceivably be increased thirty or fifty per cent. in a single year, in obedience to a strong demand. It would take several years to increase the production of wool in the same degree. In the former case, it would only be necessary to sow a greater breadth of land; in the latter case, the increase of the flocks would require time.

curately with two other distinctions—with the distinction, viz., between raw and manufactured products; and, amongst the raw products, with that between those derived from the animal and those derived from the vegetable kingdom."—[P. 61.]

As to the third point: the supply of a commodity is not at once or easily contracted, on a falling off of demand, inasmuch as capital[1] is invested in the production and cannot disengage itself. "The difficulty of accomplishing this will generally be in proportion to the amount of fixed capital employed; and the principal form in which fixed capital exists is that of machinery. It is, therefore, in articles in the production of which machinery is extensively employed—that is to say, in the more highly finished manufactures—that the contraction of supply will be most difficult; and this, it will be observed, is also the kind of commodities for extending the supply of which the facilities are greatest. While, therefore, manufactured articles can never be very long in advance of the general movement of prices, they may, of all commodities, be the longest in arrear of it."—[P. 63.]

We have, perhaps, already sufficiently discussed the effects of a depreciation of money, in producing a diminution in the burden of permanent charges, rents, taxes, interest, etc.

---

[1] Prof. Cairnes gives much less weight here than he should do—less than he himself has given in his "Political Economy" (see his theory of "Non-Competing Groups," pp. 70–3)—to the consideration that labor, also, is committed to certain lines of production, and cannot soon or easily change its direction. In a degree, therefore, it submits to reductions of wages, which allow of prices being reduced without a corresponding diminution of profits, hence stimulating demand, and hence breaking the force of the impulse to contract production.

What, to follow out Prof. Cairnes's reasoning in a single direction only—for our space will allow no more—what will be the influence of the progressive depreciation of the precious metals, upon the condition of the working classes? M. Chevalier had held that the effects must be prejudicial, at least while the change should be in progress. "Experience shows," he declares, "that when provisions rise, wages are not necessarily raised in the same proportion." Prof. Cairnes, on the other hand, says of the working classes, "the general effect of the gold discoveries will be to alter the distribution of wealth in their favor, and, on the whole, to benefit them."—[P. 148.] The proposition that prices rise earlier and further than wages,[1] he regards as essentially unsound. If the prices of the laborers' provisions and clothing rise, it is because more money is spent upon them. "The rise in wages, in short, is (when it proceeds from abundance of money) the cause of the rise of the price of commodities." And here we find, in Prof. Cairnes's view, a certain occasion for an increased demand for money which will take up a portion of the new supply without involving a rise in prices. "As the production of gold continues, the proportion of the aggregate wealth of the world, which goes to the industrial classes, will increase; and, the field of credit contracting as we descend in the scale of society, the necessity for coin[2] will increase also."—[P. 131.]

This influence of the gold discoveries, in throwing

---

[1] We shall have occasion to consider this proposition when treating of inconvertible paper money.

[2] It was from the operation of this principle, according to this writer, that England between 1851 and 1860 absorbed into its retail circulation an addition to its gold money of not less than forty per cent. without anything like a commensurate advance of prices, the population not having increased ten per cent. meanwhile.

into the hands of the industrial classes an increased share of the purchasing power of the world, Prof. Cairnes regards as "the great redeeming incident of the gold discoveries. In almost every other aspect in which we contemplate the occurrence, it is fraught with inconvenience, hardship, and injustice, introducing uncertainty into mercantile dealings, disturbing contracts which were designed to be fixed, stimulating the spirit of commercial speculation, already too strong, and bringing unmerited loss upon classes[1] who have the strongest claims on our sympathy and whom, upon social grounds, it is most desirable to sustain."—[P. 152.] "That good will on the whole predominate, we believe; but let us not, on that account, close our eyes to the serious cost at which this preponderance of good will be obtained."—[P. 158.]

On the other hand, we have quoted the opinion of Mr. J. R. McCulloch, that while cases of individual hardship may arise, a progressive depreciation of money is, like a fall of rain after a long drouth, beneficial to incomparably the larger part of society, and is of great public and national advantage.

### CORN-RENTS.

The narrative given in this and the two preceding chapters has exposed the one failing of the precious

[1] The classes suffering by the depreciation of money are, according to this writer, first, those living on fixed incomes, including especially widows, orphans, and aged persons; and secondly, those "whose remuneration is determined more by custom than by competition, and this description includes a much larger number of persons than is commonly supposed," especially the members of the learned professions, civil officials, salaried servants, etc. On the other hand, the tax-payer gains, the lessee, the mortgagor, the client of the lawyer, the patient of the physician, etc., etc.

metals in their use as money. That weakness appears solely in the function of a standard for deferred payments.[1] As the medium of exchange, or the denominator of values, gold and silver have fully justified the preference bestowed upon them by the general consent of mankind in the earliest ages. No article that could be taken combines so many qualities fitting it for such a use.

Moreover, as a standard for deferred payments, within ordinary terms of commercial credit, the precious metals derive from their slow consumption in use and their absolute imperishableness in store, a stability which no other important article of commerce attains. From year to year these metals hold their way with great steadiness, while cotton, corn, coal, and most of the necessaries of life fluctuate from month to month, often within a wide range of prices.

When, however, contracts have to be made for long periods, as in the lease of lands and buildings, or in loans to governments or corporations, there is always the possibility, and, in view of recent developments, we must say the probability, that one or the other party will suffer loss through variations in the value of the precious metals. Not to speak of the great changes produced between 1570 and 1640 by the influx of silver from the mines of America, Prof. Jevons estimates that the value of gold fell, between 1789 and 1809, 46 per cent.; from 1809 to 1849 it rose 145 per cent.; while between 1849 and 1874 it fell again at least 20 per cent. Even if we allow largely for the insufficiency and inaccuracy of the data used in such computations, there

[1] The reader will recall Prof. Jevons's statement that the several Money-functions are not necessarily united in one substance.

would remain an unquestionable variation, of wide reach, within each of the periods indicated.

These extensive changes in the value of the precious metals have given rise to the question, whether something may not advantageously be substituted for them in payments protracted through considerable periods of time. To a certain limited extent such a substitute, where lands are to be leased, has been found in corn-rents. Locke advanced this idea in his paper on the "Value of Money." "Wheat in this part of the world, and that grain which is the constant general food of any other country, is the fittest measure to judge of the altered value of things, in any long tract of time." Mr. Horner, in his speech during the bullion debates, declared that "Bread-corn is the paramount and real standard of all values." "We are forced to admit," says Prof. Jevons, "that the statesmen of Queen Elizabeth were far-seeing when they passed the act which obliged the colleges of Oxford, Cambridge and Eton to lease their lands for corn-rents. The result has been to make those colleges far richer than they would otherwise have been, the rents and endowments expressed in money having sunk to a fraction of their ancient value."

### A TABULAR STANDARD FOR DEFERRED PAYMENTS.

Prof. Jevons, in his excellent work on Money, so frequently cited in this treatise, has re-opened the question, "whether the progress of economical and statistical science might not enable us to devise some better standard of value?" "We have seen," he says, "that the so-called double-standard system of money spreads the fluctuations of supply and demand of gold and silver over a large area, and maintains both metals more unchanged in value than they would otherwise be. Can we not conceive a multiple legal tender which would be still less liable to variation? We estimate the value of one hundred pounds by the quantities of corn, beef, potatoes, coal, timber, iron, tea, coffee, beer, and other principal commodities, which it will purchase from time to time; might we not invent a legal-tender note which should be convertible, not into any single commodity, but into an aggregate of small quantities of various commodities, the quantities and qualities of each being rigorously defined?"

Prof. Jevons sees that a bill-of-goods would be an impossible medium of exchange. "This scheme would therefore resolve itself into that which has long since been brought forward under the title of the Tabular Standard of Value." In other words, such a multiple legal tender would only be applied to correct the single failing of gold and silver as money, viz., in the function of a standard for deferred payments. After referring to the schemes proposed[1] by Messrs. Joseph Lowe (1822) and Poulett Scrope (1833), Prof. Jevons proceeds to say:—"Such schemes for a tabular or average standard of value appear to be perfectly sound and highly valuable in a theoretical point of view, and the practical difficulties are not of a serious character. To carry Lowe's

---

[1] There is a considerable body of literature on this point. Mr. Horton [Silver and Gold, p. 157] appends the following note by Dr Karl Walcker: "Further progress in this direction is merely a question of time. Count Soden, Roscher, and Schäffle have rightly recommended Mixed Rents, reckoned by the values of the precious metals, breadstuffs and cloths, and the writer, (Dr. Walcker) has proposed that the state should make obligations expressed in these terms. . . . Soden's idea is applicable only to taxes, salaries, state obligations, and perhaps for purchase-money of real estate, etc.'

and Scrope's plans into effect, a permanent government commission would have to be created, and endowed with a kind of judicial power. The officers of the department would collect the current prices of commodities in all the principal markets of the kingdom, and by a well-defined system of calculations would compute from those data the average variations in the purchasing power of gold. The decisions of the commission would be published monthly and payments would be adjusted in accordance with them."

The first thought on reading these words of Prof. Jevons is, that such a scheme would "never do for Yankees." Yet I am not sure that even the desultory and peremptory genius of our people would offer a fatal objection to a system which should place under special safeguards, like those proposed, the property of charitable institutions, trust-funds of whatever description, the estates of widows and of persons retired from business. Certainly, as Prof. Jevons says, "such a standard would add a wholly new degree of stability to social relations, securing the fixed income of individuals and public institutions from the depreciation which they have often suffered." But that this author's suggestion of the application of a tabular standard to the payment of debts of more than three months' standing, even ordinary commercial debts, would be practicable, I cannot believe. Commerce must do the best it can with the use of money and of credit expressed in terms of money. Business men must protect themselves, trusting to make good their losses by fresh efforts, or by a turn in values. They are in the way of doiug so. The only plea which would justify the erection of cumbrous machinery for determining the value of more or less permanent charges, in the case of the classes first referred to, is that they are not in the way of repairing losses; that the full effects of a depreciation of the standard for deferred payments fall upon them and remain without relief.

Nor would commerce tolerate such obstruction. It is true that, as Prof. Jevons claims,[1] purely speculative enterprises would be in a degree discouraged; but it is certain that legitimate enterprise would be hampered. It is true that bankruptcies would, to a certain extent, be avoided; but the same might be effected by any cause which should induce a slower rate of movement in production and trade. Nothing is more characteristic of the commercial spirit than the disposition to take the evil with the good, roughly to strike the average of gain and loss, to charge-off bad debts, looking always to the future and never regretting the past. This spirit leads, doubtless, into many errors; but it is the life of the world of commerce. For one, I cannot believe that merchants and manufacturers will ever submit to a mode of computation which would render it impossible to cast up rapidly and decisively, at any moment, the results of a venture; but would require every note given or taken in the course of business to be liquidated like a bankrupt's estate.

But in the case of those who have definitively retired from active life, carrying out with them all they will ever have to support old age and provide for their children; in the case of trustees and guardians, under a solemn responsibility in the care of estates, where loss is

---

[1] "Speculations based upon the frequent oscillations of prices which take place in the present state of commerce, would be to a certain extent discouraged. The calculations of merchants would be less frequently frustrated by causes beyond their own control, and many bankruptcies would be prevented."—[Money and the Mechanism of Exchange, p. 333.]

more to be dreaded than gain to be desired; in the case of institutions whose funds are sequestered for charitable uses from the stock of active capital, this objection does not lie against the scheme of a multiple legal tender, which might also, perhaps, be extended to the cases of loans by savings banks and of loans to governments and corporations.

## CHAPTER IX.

### COINAGE.

UNDER Coinage, as a title in the theory and history of money, we may properly, without reference to the etymology of the word, take account of all methods of determining, for easy popular recognition, the quantity and quality of individual portions of that which has been adopted into use as money. Some historical forms of money, however, have not required any such mode of determination, the divisions being natural, and the individual portions passing simply by tale. The shells and red feathers used in the islands of the Indian Ocean, the cattle and sheep used by the early Greeks and Romans, needed only to be counted.[1]

Coinage, in the sense here given it, embraces more than the operations of the modern mint. Historically the first achievement in this direction was the establishment of a customary or legal form to be given to individual portions of what was to serve as money. Thus the Abyssinians, who used rock salt[2] as money, had it cut

---

[1] Speaking of the early Mexicans, the historian Prescott says: "In their dealings it is singular that they should have had no knowledge of scales and weights. The quantity was determined by measure and number."—[Conquest of Mexico, ii, 140.]

[2] Poucet, in his "Voyage to Ethiopia," says: "They make use of rock salt for small money. It is as white as snow and as hard as a

into bricks of uniform dimensions, any considerable departure from which would be easily detected by the eye.

"The first species of metal money," says Mr. Knight,[1] "that was circulated by tale, and not by weight, of which we have any account, consisted of spikes, or small obelisks, of brass or iron, which were symbols of great sanctity and high authority."

"Six of these being as many as the hand could conveniently grasp, the word *obolus* and *drachma*, signifying spike and handful, continued, after the invention of coining, to be employed in expressing the respective values of two pieces of money, the one of which was worth six of the other."

Another early form of coinage, in the larger sense in which we here use the term, was that of Ring-money, which is reported to be still in actual use in Nubia,[2] and which once had circulation, not only throughout Egypt and Ethiopia, but as it would seem, in many distant countries. The disinterment in Ireland of large amounts of this money during the present century has been made use of by writers of a certain school as affording additional evidence connecting the Irish with the Phenicians. These rings, so called, were not always or generally welded; but were adapted to be connected in the form of a chain, which could thus be lengthened or shortened according to the financial condition of the owner.

---

rock. They dig it out of the mountain Softa, and carry it into the Emperor's magazines, where they form it into bars which they call amouli, or into half-bars, which they call courman. Each bar is a foot in length, and three inches in breadth and thickness."

[1] Enquiry into the Symbolical Language of Ancient Mythology.

[2] Address of Dr. John Lee, President, Numismatic Society of England, 1837–8.

Rings known in the trade as *Manillae*, have been, during this century, extensively manufactured at Birmingham (for a long time the seat of the counterfeiting enterprise of Great Britain), for export to the coast of Calabar, in shape closely resembling the ring-money found during the same period in Ireland, after an inhumation of centuries.

The Cash,[1] so called, of Cochin China and China, conforms somewhat to the same idea. It is described by Milburn, in his "Oriental Commerce," as composed chiefly of tutenage (defined by Webster as Chinese copper, an alloy of copper, zinc and nickel), 600 pieces making a quan. This is divided into 10 mace, of 60 "cash" each, the whole being strung together and divided by a knot at each mace. "There is nothing better," Milburn remarks, "and scarce anything else that will do to carry to Cochin China, than tutenage, which the king always engrosses to himself."—[P. 442.]

Another early form of coinage was found in the sealed bags of gold dust which passed without examination as to quantity or quality in exchange between persons of repute. The bags of money mentioned in the Scripture, in the episode of Naaman and Gehazi, may have been of this character. On the same principle, quills of gold-dust are mentioned by Prescott as in use among the early Mexicans, and the like are still current upon the coast of Africa.

Just when and where the later and now universal form of coinage, viz., the impress upon pieces of metal of signs expressive of their weight and fineness, first appeared, historians are not wholly agreed.

The invention has been claimed severally, for Erich-

---

[1] The most important *billon* in the world.—[Chevalier, La Monnaie, p. 768.]

thonius, the two-faced Janus, and Theseus, but these characters or their present legal representatives may well be content to relinquish the honor, having good reason to be more than satisfied if they escape with their historical existence from the rage of modern investigation.

To Pheidon, king of Argos, is generally attributed the first coinage of the modern form. He is reported to have stamped both copper and silver money in the Island of Ægina, in order to facilitate commerce; and upon the respectable authority of Mr. Grote[1] we may rest comfortably upon this as the true account of this great invention.

It is in their adaptation to coinage that the metals possess one of their most important advantages for use as money. Articles passing by tale will generally be found to vary not a little in quantity or quality, generating controversies which will do much to retard their circulation as money, and inducing the picking or selecting of the better specimens; but it is within the capabilities of modern art to make the quantity and quality of the metal contained in coins of the same mintage so nearly alike that no selfish interest could be served by making choice between any two of them that may be offered.

The metals, however, differ not a little among themselves in the ease and the completeness with which this result can be effected; and it is in this respect that silver and gold, especially the latter, exhibit their most marked adaptation to use as money. "Platinum," says Mr. Babbage,[2] "cannot be melted in our furnaces, and is chiefly valuable in commerce when in the shape of in-

---

[1] History of Greece, iii, 318.

[2] Economy of Manufactures, p. 121.

gots, from which it may be forged into useful forms. But when a piece of platinum is cut into two parts, it cannot easily be re-united except by means of a chemical process in which both parts are dissolved in an acid. Hence when platinum coin is too abundant, it cannot, like gold, be reduced into masses by melting, but must pass through an expensive process to render it useful." Notwithstanding this want of adaptation to the purposes of coinage, the Russian government attempted the circulation of platinum money in 1828, but after a conclusive experience, relinquished the effort in 1845.[1]

In all lands coinage has been one of the most cherished prerogatives of sovereignty. This, however, in England, at least, only extended to the coinage of gold and silver. Mr. Toumlin Smith, a high authority, cites the declaration of Lord Coke that the king of England "hath no prerogative in any other metal than gold and silver;"[2] and refers to Boyne's book on the "Tokens of the Seventeenth Century," for a list of nine thousand four hundred and sixty-six different sorts of copper coin,[3] issued with different devices and by different peo-

---

[1] An account of the platinum coinage of Russia is found in Chevalier's "La Monnaie," sect. vi, chap. 3.

[2] According to the decisions of Lord Coke, Sir Matthew Hale, and other jurists, money, to be covered by the king's prerogative, *must be of gold or silver.* "Money is that metal, be it gold or silver, which receives authority by the prince's impress to be current; for, as wax is not a seal without a print, so metal is not money without the impression."—[Coke's Littleton.]

[3] "By all that I can discover, the copper coins of Ireland for three hundred years past consisted of small pence and half-pence which particular men had license to coin, and were current only within certain towns and districts, according to the personal credit of the owner who uttered them, and was bound to receive them again."—[Swift, Drapier's letters.]

ple, these being but a part of those actually issued. Private issues of copper coin were indeed not prohibited until the Act of 57 George III (c. 46), and then not on the ground of prerogative, but for the public convenience.

No subjects, says Hallam,[1] ever enjoyed the right of coining silver in England without the royal stamp and superintendence.[2] "I do not," he adds, "extend this to *the fact,* for in the anarchy of Stephen's reign, both bishops and barons coined money for themselves."

In France the prerogative of the king was not seldom surrendered to the great vassals[3] through fear, or sold through cupidity.

Of India Dr. Hunter writes:[4]

"One of the most cherished insignia of sovereignty was the striking of coin; and little potentates who, in every other respect, acknowledged allegiance to Delhi, maintained their independent right of coining. As it was the last privilege to which fallen dynasties clung, so it was the first to which adventurers rising into power aspired. While the Mahrattas were still mountain robbers, they set up a mint; and in 1685 the East India Company, at a period when it had only a few houses and gardens in Bengal, intrigued for the dignity of striking its own coin."

---

[1] Middle Ages, i, 204.

[2] Mr. Jacob enumerates thirty-eight Mints in England in 1017, A.D. In the reign of Henry VI there were only eight; under Henry VIII but four. During and after the reign of Elizabeth, all coins were struck in London.

[3] Silver and even gold were coined by the Dukes of Brittany, so long as that fief continued to exist.

[4] Annals of Rural Bengal, p. 299.

In our further course I shall use the word coinage in its ordinary sense, as relating only to the operations of the mint, in the modern form of determining the quantity and quality of individual portions of the metals used as money.

The progress of the art of coinage was very slow, for the chemical and mechanical difficulties to be encountered were of the most serious nature.

At first coins were impressed[1] only upon one side.

---

[1] Mr. Knight, in his work on the "Symbolical Language of Ancient Mythology," says: "In examining the symbols in the remains of ancient art which have escaped the barbarism and the bigotry of the Middle Ages, we may sometimes find it difficult to distinguish between those compositions which are mere efforts of taste and fancy, and those which were emblems of what were thought divine truths. There is one class, however, the most numerous and important of all, which must have been designed and executed under the sanction of public authority, and, therefore, whatever meaning they contain must have been the meaning of nations and not the caprice of individuals.

"This is the class of *Coins;* the devices upon which were always held so strictly sacred that the most proud and powerful monarchs never ventured to put their portraits upon them until the practice of deifying sovereigns had enrolled them among the gods. Neither the kings of Persia, Macedonia, or Epirus, nor even the tyrants of Sicily ever took this liberty, the first portraits that we find upon money being those of the Egyptian and Syrian dynasties of Macedonian princes, whom the flattery of their subjects had raised to divine honors. The artists had, indeed, before found a way of gratifying the vanity of their patrons without offending their piety, which was by mixing their features with those of the deity whose image was to be impressed; an artifice which seems to have been practiced in the coins of several of the Macedonian kings previous to the custom of putting their portraits upon them.

"It is in a great degree owing to the sanctity of the devices that such numbers of very ancient coin have been preserved fresh and entire."

Milburn in his work on Oriental Commerce, already referred to, states that the "gall," a small piece of silver worth about fourpence, which forms the only native coin of Cochin China, has characters only upon one side. Manifestly, this incomplete form of coinage allowed the metal to be taken largely from the under side, and hence led to the extensive corruption of the money in circulation.

Even when, at a later period, the coin was protected on both its sides by the impressions of the mint, its proper area remained undefined, allowing the edges to be clipped to an extent which, without impairing the integrity of the central device, might abstract a quarter or a third of the metal originally contained. Mr. Seyd states[1] that the coin of Persia at present consists of rough and irregular pieces, so largely clipped that the Tomans, coins corresponding to the European ducat, usually pass by weight, and not by tale.

"Little skill and less taste," says Mr. Jacob, "were shown in the coinage of the Middle Ages." Time will not allow us to trace step by step the progress[2] in the art of coining, by which the rude pieces of an earlier

---

"Præterea in quibusdam nummis inscribitur nomen dei, vel alicujus sancti, et signum crucis; quod fuit inventum et antiquitus institutum in testimonium veritatis monetæ in materia et pondere. Si igitur Princeps sub ista inscriptione immutet materiam sive pondus, ipse videtur tacite mendacium et perjurium committere, et falsum testimonium perhibere, ac etiam praevaricator fieri illius præcepti legalis quo dicitur: *Non assumes nomen dei tui in vanum.*"—[N. Oresme, de origine, etc., Monetarum.]

[1] Bullion and Foreign Exchanges, p. 364.

[2] According to Sir James Steuart it was about the time of the Revolution that the custom of weighing the current money went into disuse in England, owing to the introduction of the wheel or fly-press.

age have been replaced by the exquisite productions of the modern mint. To this progress no nation has contributed more than the French. Two of the greatest inventions in the history of the art, the mill and the screw, and the steam coining-press, the world owes to that people.[1]

It is a just subject of pride to Americans that the Mint of the United States[2] is recognized, the world over,

[1] [Snowden on Coins, xv.] In the light of this fact Prof. Rogers's remark reads somewhat strangely. "I have been unable to find out any instance of mechanical genius in any other race but our own, except the solitary discovery of the carding-machine. This, beyond doubt a great invention, though it consists like all great inventions in a simple and obvious principle, was discovered by a Frenchman. . . . But I have found no other notable invention for saving human labor which is not the offspring of Anglo-Saxon thought."—[Historical Gleanings, i, 144.]

[2] An account of American Coinage will be found in articles by Mr. J. H. Hickok, in the "N. Y. Banker's Magazine" for October and November, 1861.

The first colonial Mint was established in Massachusetts in 1652, during the period of the Commonwealth, shillings and sixpences being issued in large amounts. After the Restoration further coinage was forbidden, as an invasion of the rights of the crown. It is stated that the Mint continued to coin under the original date, 1652. Virginia, by law, instituted a Mint in 1645, and Maryland in 1661; but both schemes proved futile. Some brass or copper pieces were struck, prior to the Revolution, in Carolina and Virginia. An attempt to extend the circulation of Wood's famous pence into the American Colonies failed, though specimens are found as far south as Carolina. During the Confederation the right of coining was vested in the individual states as well as in the federal government. By the constitution, Congress has sole power to regulate coinage, as well as to control the circulation of foreign moneys. The most important coinage laws of the United States are those of 1792, 1834, 1837, 1853 and 1873, all of which will be referred to in the course of these discussions.

as of highly exceptional authority. "There can be no doubt," says Mr. Seyd, "that the United States gold coin is, as a rule, superior to all others except that of Russia."[1]

Three gold coins, the Russian imperials, the French Napoleons, and the United States Eagles, are bought, without remelting, by the Bank of England.

On the other hand, Mr. Seyd takes a very unfavorable view of the British mint, as to both its mechanical arrangements and its official administration; and I note that Prof. Jevons[2] gives his sanction to Mr. Seyd's view.

"The British Mint still enjoys the Remedy of about 2½ per mille for weight and of about 3 per mille for fineness. This may have been all very well and equitable in olden times, when science had not yet attained its present high state of development: but the progress which has been made since then ought surely to entitle the public to demand that the Remedy should be restricted now within closer limits."—[Bullion and Foreign Exchanges, p. 556.]

A very striking admission, as it would seem to be, of this imperfection of the British mint operations, was until recently found in the refusal of the mint authorities to take cut[3] sovereigns by weight as standard gold; instead of which, the Bank of England paid only 77.6½*d.* per oz., or about four-ninths per cent. off the mint value (77.10½*d.*). Mr. Seyd also alleges that jewelers in Lon-

---

[1] The Russian half-imperial, 22 carats fine, which has *no remedy as to fineness*, Mr. Seyd regards as the most regular coin known to commerce; but I do not understand him as giving preference to the body of Russian gold coin over that of the United States.

[2] Money and the Mechanism of Exchange, pp. 120–1.

[3] That is, sovereigns which have been stamped as below the weight required for circulation.

don are accustomed to add six grains of fine gold to every oz. of standard[1] gold, in order to insure their products passing Goldsmith's Hall.

It is, not improbably, in consequence of Mr. Seyd's vigorous attack on the management of the Mint, in his book, published in 1868, that the authorities, as we learn from the fourth edition of Mr. Nicholson's work on the "Science of Exchanges," published in 1873, now receive light gold coin at 77.10½*d.* per oz. from the Bank of England, which pays the holder at the rate of 77.9*d.*, the same as for bullion.

The problem with which the mint has to deal is not mechanical merely, but also chemical.

To make a coin absolutely pure is perhaps possible, but it could be effected only by a great expenditure of labor. To bring gold or silver to a fineness of 995 or 996 parts in 1000 is easily accomplished by the refiner, but to exclude each of the remaining thousandths of impurity would require an amount of skill and time increasing as absolute purity were approached. Hence a certain toleration of impurity is required by practical considerations. But beyond this, it is seen that the addition of inferior metals has the effect to harden coin and thus diminish the loss by abrasion in use. To secure this desirable result, alloys in definite quantity are purposely introduced.

The earlier gold coins were generally finer than those of the present time. The Persian coin known as the Daric, from King Darius, was of a very high degree of

[1] *Fine* gold is the technical term for gold absolutely pure. *Standard* gold is gold mingled with alloy according to the legal standard of coinage, which in England is 11 parts fine gold to 1 of alloy while in the United States it is 9 parts fine gold to 1 of alloy.

purity, perhaps as great as could be attained by the artisans of that day; and it was in consequence of the reputation of this coin that the name "Daric" came in later times to be affixed to coins of any mintage which were exceptionally pure, just as, at a later period, the sovereigns of many countries coined Bezants, in imitation of the famous coin first so called because issued from Byzantium.

Egypt had for a long time no native coin, and the pieces celebrated for their purity under the name of Aryandics were of Persian mintage. The coins of the successors of Alexander in Egypt, contained 23 carats, 3 grains of gold, having but one grain of alloy. Bodin, as quoted by Pinkerton, informs us that the goldsmiths in Paris in assaying some gold coins of Vespasian, found in them no more than $\frac{1}{788}$ part of alloy.

"It does not appear," says Mr. Jacob, "that the same degree of purity was preserved in the silver coined by the ancients."

Just what degree of fineness will best accomplish the purpose of hardening the coin, while preserving a quality which will allow it to be kept clean and agreeable to sight and touch, is a somewhat disputed question.

The ratio most generally adopted in modern coinage, including that of the United States, is 9 : 1, yielding, that is, coins $\frac{9}{10}$ fine. The ratio adopted by the British Mint (covering the coinage of India) is 11 : 1, yielding coins $\frac{11}{12}$ fine. The Russian half-imperial is of this fineness, as are the gold coins of Brazil. The British Mint authorities strenuously insist on the ratio 11 : 1 as that best approved in use. Extensive experiments were conducted[1] between 1798 and 1802, under the most

---

[1] By Cavendish and Hatchett; see "Philosophical Transactions," 1803.

careful observation, and the result as it then appeared is thus stated by Mr. Jacob. "Our British standard gold[1] is proved by them to be less susceptible of loss by abrasion than that of any other of the several kingdoms of Europe, or than any that is coined in either Spanish or Portuguese America."—[P. 292.]

We may conclude with Chevalier[2] that the proportion of one-twelfth alloy is most efficacious, and that we owe the general adoption of the proportion of one-tenth to the general desire of the nations to promote decimal coinage.

As has already[3] been stated, in accounting for the more rapid abrasion of the earlier coins, the nature of the metals used in alloying gold and silver is of great consequence.

"If gold 22 parts fine in 24 were to have the alloy formed of a mixture of iron and tin, the loss by friction would be five times as great as it is with the alloy actually used in the British coinage. With alloy of copper and tin, the loss would be nearly four times as much." —[Jacob, p. 294.]

Secondly, it should be noted that the loss by abrasion depends, also, upon the surface exposed. The smaller the denomination of the coin, the larger, generally, the exposure. "Thus it appears by the English experiment of the officers of the English Mint in 1787, that of the silver coins then in circulation, the loss on crowns was,

---

[1] Gold coins were first minted in England 23 carats, 3½ grains fine. The Act of 18 Henry VIII introduced the new standard 22 : 2. From that time till 1663 both standards were used, under different denominations. Since 1663 all have been 22 : 2.—[J. R. McCulloch's Commercial Dictionary.]

[2] La Monnaie, p. 225.

[3] See p. 121.

disregarding fractions, about 3 per cent., on half-crowns about 10 per cent., on shillings 24 per cent., and on sixpences 38 per cent. And by another series of experiments made at the Mint in 1816, the loss on sovereigns, for the average of five years, was 0.726 per cent., and on half-sovereigns, 0.883 per cent. On half-crowns for the same average time, 2.28 per cent., on shillings 2.88 per cent., and on sixpences 3.26 per cent.

"Agreeably to the experiment made at the Mint of the United States, on the eagle, half-eagle and quarter-eagle, the loss they severally sustained in fifty years appeared to be in the proportion of 1, 2, 3, and that sustained by the dollar, half-dollar, quarter, dime and half-dime, respectively, 1, 2, $3\frac{1}{2}$, 6, and 10."[1]

For a similar reason, with coins of a given denomination, the thicker the coins the less the rate of loss by wear in use.

The alloy it needs to be observed is never taken into account in computing the worth of coin. It is only the pure metal which gives value in the computations of exchange; thus, the value of the copper used to alloy standard gold is less than $\frac{1}{11000}$, the value of copper used to alloy standard silver is less than $\frac{1}{750}$.[2] Not even if the largest amount of standard gold or silver were to be estimated for, would the copper be reckoned, that is, with 750 shillings we should not add one shilling for the value of the copper contained; with 11,000 sovereigns, we should not add one sovereign on a similar account.

Even with respect to the silver contained in the gold coinage, the inferior metal is not accounted of value. This has led, as is alleged, to a practice of sending

---

[1] Tucker on Money and Banks, p. 69.

[2] Seyd, Bullion and Foreign Exchanges, p. 176.

15*

British sovereigns to Paris, where the French refiners, working at lower rates than those of London, part the metals, remove the silver, supply an equal alloy of copper, and return the gold in ingots (still standard, 22:2) to England to be recoined into sovereigns. The sovereigns thus coined, says Mr. Jacob, are distinguished by their deeper color. On the other hand, in Australia, where refining is an even more expensive process than in England, the sovereigns frequently contain silver for their sole alloy, which gives them, says Mr. Seyd, a pale straw-colored appearance. Such coins are likely in time to fall into the hands of English or French refiners, who melt them up for the silver they contain.

But while gold must contain a very large proportion of silver to make it worth while to part the metals, a very small proportion of gold in silver, stated by Mr. Seyd[1] at 1 per mille, will repay the expenses of refining. Mr. Ward states that the silver coined in Mexico during the revolutionary period, subsequent to 1809, contained no inconsiderable proportion of gold, which, in the haste of mining and coining, had not been extracted. "Many millions of these dollars," he says, "in the course of circulation found their way to Europe, where the refiners of London and Paris, to their great gain, soon separated the gold from the silver. The dollars of that description have at length almost wholly disappeared; but their melting has added considerably to the stock of gold in Europe."

In those periods of history when frauds in coinage were extensively practiced, the exceptionally good reputation of any coin would naturally give it a circulation

---

[1] Bullion and Foreign Exchanges, p. 181.

in a degree irrespective of national boundaries.[1] The gold coins of the Eastern Empire known as Bezants had a wide acceptance over western Europe.

"But a small part of the English circulation between 800 and 1500," says Mr. Jacob, "was of domestic coinage." The agnels of St. Louis, which were 23½ carats fine, were brought back in great numbers from the conquests in France, and long found favor in the eyes of the English. Lord Lauderdale, in his "Depreciation Proved," notes the extensive circulation of Portuguese moidores in the western counties where they were indeed preferred to the national coin. The same writer states that not less than £1,400,000 in French louis d'or were, in a brief space, brought to the English Mint to be melted, in consequence of a proclamation forbidding them to be taken at more than 17 shillings.

In our own day we have seen the sovereign[2] attain a wide currency beyond the limits of Great Britain, though perhaps from its high value it has never commanded that almost boundless circulation which has made the Spanish dollar what Chevalier calls "an universal coin."[3]

---

[1] "From the year 1797 to 1806 all foreign coins, except 'Spanish milled dollars and parts thereof,' ceased to be a legal tender in the United States; yet during that period the gold coins of Great Britain, Portugal, and France, constituted a large part of the metallic currency of the United States." "In like manner, from 1809 to 1816, foreign gold coins were no part of the currency recognized by the law, yet no one who had them found any difficulty in passing them at the same rate as the current coins of the country, especially if they were such as the public were familiar with."—[Prof. Tucker, Money and Banks, pp. 94–5.]

[2] First coined in 1816.

[3] Speaking of China, M. Chevalier says: "A côte de l'idée bien acquise que les métaux précieux sont les marchandises et que les

pièces monnayées, par conséquent, ne doivent circuler que pour leur poids de fin, on y observe ce fait étrange que le métal argent qui y joue le plus grand rôle dans les transactions du commerce, soit reçu pour des valeurs fort différentes, par la seule raison de la forme, ou, pour parler plus exactement, de l'empreinte qu'il porte. Ainsi la piastre espagnole, la piastre à colonnes notamment, y est admise pour une valeur proportionnellement bien supérieure à celle d'autres monnaies tout aussi correctement fabriquées et à celle de l'argent en lingot."—[La Monnaie, p. 345.]

## CHAPTER X.

### SEIGNIORAGE.

THE expense of rendering metals into coin has given rise to one of the vexed questions of Political Economy, that of Seigniorage.

Shall the value of the coin be computed according to the market value of the metals in the shape of bullion; or shall the cost of mintage be added to the value of the metal taken for the coin? [1]

On the one hand, it is urged that gold and silver are worth more in coin than in bullion; that they serve an additional use, and thus give rise to a new demand; that, to fit them for this use, labor is required over and above what is necessary to raise the metal from the mine and bring it into a state of commercial purity; and that the cost of this labor should appear in the value of the product.

It is said that there is no more reason why gold in coin should not be valued higher than gold in bars, than

[1] "Justa autem et equa monete estimatio est, quando paulo minus auri vel argenti continet quam pro ipsa ematur: utpote quantum pro expensis dumtaxat monetariorum oportuerit deduci. Debet enim signum ipsi materie aliquam addere dignitatem."—[Copernicus, Monete Cudende Ratio.]

"Sicut ipsa moneta est communitatis, ita facienda est ad expensas communitatis."—[Oresme, de origine, etc., Monetarum.]

there would be for selling iron in plates, rivets and rods, at the price of iron in the pig; and that, if gold in coin costs more, and is worth more, than in ingots, those who want the coin, and not the entire community, should pay for it.

On this principle, many governments cut from the ingots brought to the mint enough of the metal to pay the charges of coinage.

Again it is urged that, in the absence of such a charge, a great waste of labor will result, of which no one will secure the benefit, through the unnecessary melting down of coin for export as bullion, or manufacture as plate.

If, it is said, the amount of coined money in any country becomes superabundant, the value, or purchasing power, of each portion thereof will be lowered, and hence a movement for its exportation will begin. But a seigniorage will put a distinct charge upon the exportation. If, for example, out of every 100 oz. of gold brought to the Mint the United States government were to reserve 1 oz. for the expenses of coinage, and give back only 99 oz. in the form of coin, the holder would not melt the coin for export unless the money of the country were so much in excess that the 99 oz. into which the coin could be melted would purchase more abroad (expenses of transportation included) than the coin which now represents the cost of 100 oz. of gold will purchase here. But if no seigniorage is charged, the exporter will indifferently ship coin or bullion; and vast amounts will be alternately coined and melted, at a constant expense, to the state, of machinery and labor, with no compensating advantage to any portion of the community. Thus free coinage becomes, in the language of Dudley North, "a perpetual motion found out, whereby to melt and coin, without ceasing, and so to feed goldsmiths and coiners at the public charge."[1] In the same way, manufacturers of jewelry and plate will, under free coinage, take coin and bullion indifferently for their purposes.[2] Economists have very generally been agreed in recommending that the cost of mintage be charged upon the coin; yet the most important commercial nation of the world exacts no seigniorage upon its gold, or principal, coin. Adam Smith attributes the English law of 1666 [18 Charles II. c. 5], establishing gratuitous coinage, to the prevailing notions respecting the relation of money to other forms of wealth, known as the Mercantile Theory;[3] and its continuance, to the influence of the Bank.

The English system, which has been adopted by Russia and was followed by the United States until 1853, is not, however, wholly without a defense. Looking, in the first instance, at the coinage of the amount actually required for domestic purposes, it is said that the use of money is of general public benefit, as much as the use of roads, and that the same policy which abolishes the toll-gate (by which those who actually travel upon the roads

---

[1] Dr. Adam Smith says: "The operations of the mint were, upon this account, somewhat like the web of Penelope: the work that was done in the day was undone in the night. The mint was employed, not so much in making daily additions to the coin, as in replacing the best part of it, which was daily melted down."

[2] In order to meet this difficulty, Prof. Storch, the Russian economist, proposes that a higher standard for gold and silver plate be established than for coins, so as to compel melters to refine, at an appreciable expense. "A. V.," the author of a tract addressed to Lord Godolphin, in 1696, anticipated this suggestion. "When the coyn hath alloy and not the household plate, etc., it is not so lyable to be melted down, for the charge and trouble for to separate it will much discourage the working it up." This suggestion is, of course, appropriate only in countries where there is a standard for plate, gold and silver ware, etc., established by law or custom.

[3] See pp. 44–8.

alone pay, and pay, too, exactly in the proportion in which they travel, which is, of course, right in theory), and substitutes therefor a service maintained at the expense of the general treasury, justifies and requires the making free this other great agent of commercial progress.

As to the objection that the removal of seigniorage causes great quantity of coin to be melted down for export unnecessarily, when some slight delay or trouble, not commercially appreciable, would suffice to send abroad bullion instead: it is answered, that the cost of coinage, with modern appliances, is at most but small.[1] Mr. Nicholson, by dividing the expenses of the British Mint for six months by the number of sovereigns coined during the year (assuming the Mint to be occupied the remaining six months in coining silver and bronze pieces) gets three farthings as the cost of coining a sovereign.[2] Moreover, as the Mint, with its machinery, officers and laborers, has to be maintained,[3] in any event, in any

[1] The cost, per cent. of value, in coining, is greater proportionately the smaller the denominations of the coin; and also greater the smaller the amount issued. According to Prof. Storch, the expense of coinage, per cent. of value, was, for gold coins as compared with silver coins, as follows:

| | | | | | | |
|---|---|---|---|---|---|---|
| France, | gold coins, | | 0.29; | silver coins, | | 1.50 |
| England, | " | " | 0.70; | " | " | 2.22 |
| Denmark, | " | " | —— | " | " | 2. |
| Russia, | " | " | 0.85; | " | " | 2.95 |

while in the latter country, the small coins of 25 copecks cost 3.47 per cent. and those of 10 copecks, 4.44 per cent. The variety of denominations adopted in the coinage also has to do with the expenses of the mint.

[2] Science of Exchanges, p. 101.

[3] "No mint can be kept constantly at work unless coining becomes a kind of manufactory for foreign commerce."—[Harris, Essay on Money and Coins.]

considerable country, the actual expense, to the state, of coining an additional amount may be small.

The country, then, it is argued, is compensated for the expense involved in an equality in the value of gold in coin and in bars, first, by the instantaneousness with which the export of gold follows the slightest accumulation in excess; and, secondly, by the fact that, with a coinage of undiminished value, the coins will often, perhaps generally, not be melted down when exported, but sent abroad in bags, and will either be returned shortly in the course of exchange, or, being admittedly worth their nominal value in bullion, a kind of qualified circulation, amounting indeed sometimes to a full and free circulation, will be given them in foreign countries. Such a circulation, it is claimed, will amount to an advertisement of the trade of the country conducting the coinage, which it can very well afford to pay for, as truly as a merchant can afford to pay for advertisements in a newspaper, or a circus-manager for having his fearful and wonderful pictures displayed along the streets.

Thus it is asserted, not without show of cause, that the free circulation of English sovereigns in Portugal,[1] which has been traditional since sovereigns were first coined, has been worth more than its cost to British trade. It will be remembered that the prime advantage anticipated from the coinage of the "trade dollar" by the Mint of the United States was the advertisement of our trade with China.

So much for seigniorage in the sense which we have thus far given to the word, as covering, that is, the expenses of coinage. But seigniorage may be made to have a wider application, and may come to include any

[1] And, by a sort of political sequence, in Brazil.

charge which the sovereign or the state, having the monopoly of coinage, shall be pleased to make. And this extent seigniorage has historically had in a degree, at times, which has dwarfed all consideration of the actual cost of performing the service.

So troublesome is it, in economical discussions, to be obliged to distinguish, continually, between the two sorts of seigniorage, that M. Chevalier has proposed to apply the term *brassage* to the charge for the actual expenses of coinage, leaving seigniorage to express the charges which are in the nature of a tax for the benefit of the sovereign or of the state.

The exercise of the larger right of seigniorage has been carried to great extremes. Ruding, the English antiquarian in the department of money, finds that, at one period in the reign of Edward IV, the seigniorage on gold was above thirteen per cent. In the thirty-seventh year of Henry VII it exceeded sixteen per cent. These, however, were exceptional instances. The average of the period eighteenth Edward III to fourth Edward IV was between three and four per cent. "The seigniorage on silver," says Jacob, "never seems to have attained the monstrous height to which that on gold had been carried in some few instances. It was, however, raised or lowered according to the King's greed or necessities."[1] The seigniorage exacted by John II of France rose at times, it is stated, to three-fifths, changing, however, says Le Blanc, almost every week and sometimes oftener.

It is in successive reductions, through the exercise of sovereign authority, of the quantity of fine gold and silver in the coin, that we find the explanation of the use of the word *pound* in English, and *livre* in French

---

[1] Inquiry into the Precious metals, p. 209.

coinage. The English pound was once an actual pound of silver; but a pound of standard silver is now coined, not into twenty, but into sixty-six shillings. The "pound Scots" had been reduced to one-thirty-sixth of its original value. Even the material of coins has been changed by the exercise of this same right of the sovereign. The florin was once a piece of gold; it is now a piece of silver; the Spanish maravedi was once a piece of gold; it is now a piece of copper.

Against seigniorage carried further than the cost of coinage, economists have, in general, raised a decided protest. "The limits beyond which a seigniorage cannot be advantageously extended," says Ricardo, "are the actual expenses incurred in manufacturing the coin."—[Reply to Bosanquet, p. 91.] The distinction is, however, very strongly drawn between a reduction in the quantity of pure metal in the coin, produced by the introduction of an increased proportion of alloy, and a reduction effected by diminishing the weight of the coin, preserving the customary fineness.[1] It is evident that the difference in the two cases is merely that, in the latter case, the change is advertised, if not by public proclamation, then, by each man's senses, for himself, and the community are enabled to adapt their commercial transactions to the new state of the coinage;[2] while the

[1] "The debasement of coin, in its proper sense, means a reduction of fineness. This has occurred only in one instance in our silver coinage; or rather, when our 3 cent coin was instituted, by the Act of March 3, 1851, it was ¾ (.750) fine and was afterwards, by act of March 3, 1853, raised to .900, the fineness of the larger coins."—[Letter of James Pollock, Director of the U. S. Mint, January 17, 1863.]

[2] "I have sometimes been surprised," says Mr. Hallam, "at the facility with which prices adjusted themselves to the quantity of

reduction of fineness has generally been in the nature of a fraud, to be concealed long after it had begun to work pernicious effects.

"The legend of the Maltese money," says Prof. Rogers, "ran—'*non æs sed fides*'—designating that the basis of the currency must be laid in the integrity of those who issue it. Yet hardly a European government fulfilled the duty, even if they understood and acknowledged it. But the kings of France were the principal offenders. They diminished the amount of silver in their coins. This is a temporary wrong, a remediable offense. But they debased it also, a far more serious and lasting evil. Philip the Fair was threatened with excommunication by Boniface the Eighth for this fraud, and was branded as long as time lasts by Dante for his offense. . . . .

"But the greatest offender in this particular was the unlucky John, the prisoner of Poitiers. . . . Owing to this king's practices—whom the romances called the Good—the value of the currency underwent seventy changes in ten years. John took an oath of his moneyers that they would keep his frauds a profound secret, especially from the merchants. . . . . To me the weakness of France, during the century 1340–1440, seems to be directly traceable to economical causes,[1] to the universal

---

silver contained in the current coin, in ages which appear too ignorant and too little commercial for the application of this mercantile principle. But the extensive dealings of the Jewish and Lombard usurers who had many debtors in all parts of the country would of itself introduce a knowledge that silver, not its stamp, was the measure of value."—[Middle Ages, iii, 348.]

[1] "In this way," says Mr. Kitchin, "Philip of Valois made ready to meet the dangers of the great Hundred Years' War, which would so soon break forth upon his shores."—[History of France, p. 394.]

"Parmi les gouvernements civilisés, celui de l'Espagne est le der-

distrust which these royal frauds induced. . . . Exactly similar results, though perhaps of a less serious kind, attended the frauds of Henry VIII, and the Protector Somerset."—[Hist. Gleanings, i, 95–7.]

What is the effect of Seigniorage on the purchasing power of coin, that is, on Prices?

Properly to answer this question will require our most careful reference to the principles we have already reached[1] respecting the relations of the volume of money to the prices of commodities; while a correct answer to the question here will afford us a key to the mysteries of inconvertible paper money. Let us trace Mr. Ricardo's views on this point.

Suppose, in a certain country, there are required, for the purposes of internal trade, 1,000,000 pieces, each containing 100 grains of fine gold. There are, then, 100,000,000 grains of fine gold in use as money; and a certain average level of prices is determined by the relation between this amount and the demand for money arising from the exchanges actually needing to be effected by the use of money.

Now, suppose the principle of seigniorage to be introduced; and the sovereign, out of every 100 grains brought to the mint, takes one grain for the actual cost of coinage, giving back, thus, 1,000,000 pieces of 99 grains each, and putting 1,000,000 grains into his own storehouse as treasure, or causing it to be manufactured into plate. There are now only 99,000,000 grains of

nier qui ait cru pouvoir clandestinement vicier les monnaies. C'est ainsi que la monnaie d'or, déjà altérée en 1772, fut mise, en 1786, à 875 millièmes. Le titre des monnaies espagnoles fabriquées dans le nouveau monde, était primitivement de 917 millièmes."—[M. Chevalier, La Monnaie, p 51.]

[1] See pp. 59–65.

fine gold in circulation; but the same number of pieces of the same mint-value.

Will each piece now purchase as much of other commodities as before, or less?

Mr. Ricardo answers, as much.[1] There is the same demand for pieces for the purposes of exchange; there is the same supply: the same price results.

How, then, can we say that money is the measure of value, and that, to measure value, we must have value, and that value is proportional to the labor expended?

I gave warning[2] that we should have to revise this view of the Money-function, and we are now getting a glimpse of the ground; but we shall so much better command the field from a point yet to be reached[3] that we need only make a note of the question here.

But suppose the sovereign proceeds further, and takes out 10 grains from every 100, putting 10,000,000 grains into his storehouse; and issuing 1,000,000 pieces containing 90 grains each, but of the same official denomination as before. Will the purchasing power of each piece be affected? Not at all, says Mr. Ricardo; there is the same demand for pieces to effect exchanges; the same supply: the value of each piece is therefore maintained, and the same rate of general prices results.

But let us take a step in a somewhat different direction, and suppose that the sovereign, instead of placing

---

[1] M. Chevalier apparently dissents. "Comme les espèces monnayées ne sont qu'une marchandise intermédiaire et ne passent qu' en cette qualité, les changements que les princes apportaient au poids ou au titre des monnaies entraînaient toujours, du moment qu'ils étaient connus, un changement pareil dans les prix."—[La Monnaie, 47.]

[2] See pp. 4–9.

[3] See pp. 280–90.

the 10,000,000 grains, which he has charged as seigniorage, in his treasury, coins them into pieces of ninety grains each, and issues them in purchase of supplies for his army or his household. Immediately we have a supply in excess of the demand, and depreciation results. The 90,000,000 grains, while coined into the same number of pieces of the same official denomination as the 100,000,000 had been, retained the same purchasing power; but when the 100,000,000 are coined into a larger number of pieces, the purchasing power of each piece falls at once.

This is Mr. Ricardo's argument in his "Reply to Bosanquet":

"There can," he asserts, "exist no depreciation of money, but from excess; *however debased a coinage may become*, it will preserve its mint value; that is to say, *it will pass in circulation for the intrinsic value of the bullion which it ought to contain*,[1] provided it be not in too great abundance."—[Pp. 94-5.]

Again: "While the state alone coins, there can be no limit to this charge of seigniorage, for by limiting the quantity of coin, it can be raised to any conceivable value."—[Political Economy, p. 212.] And still further: "On the same principle, namely, by a limitation of quantity, a debased coin would circulate at the value it should bear if it were of legal weight and fineness, and not at the value of the quantity of metal which it actually con-

[1] I must, in candor, confess myself wholly unable to offer an explanation of a remark made by the same writer, in his pamphlet on the "High Price of Bullion," that "if guineas were degraded, by clipping, to half their present value, every commodity, as well as land, would rise to double its present nominal value." There can be no doubt that the principle stated in the text contains Mr. Ricardo's settled view of the subject.

tained. In the history of the British coinage, we find accordingly that the currency was never depreciated in the same proportion that it was debased, the reason of which was, that it was never increased in quantity, in proportion to its diminished intrinsic value."—[*Ibid.*]

Mr. Ricardo offers the following illustrations of his principle from the history of English money:

"Our silver currency now (1811) passes at a value in currency above its bullion value, because, notwithstanding the profits obtained by the counterfeiter, it has not yet been supplied in sufficient abundance to affect its value."

"It is on this principle, too, that the fact must be accounted for, that the price of bullion previously to the recoinage in 1696,[1] did not rise so high as might have been expected from the then debased state of the currency: the quantity had not been increased in the same proportion as the quality had been debased."—[Reply to Bosanquet, p. 96.]

And again, he says of the period previous to 1797: 'The silver currency was, during a part of this period, very much debased, but it existed in a degree of scarcity, and, therefore, on the principle which I have before explained, it never sank in its current value."

Now what, according to Mr. Ricardo, would become of the coins thus in excess?

We have seen that upon his principle there was, in the case taken, a demand (from trade in its then existing conditions) for 1,000,000 pieces, of the mint-value of 100 grains of gold each; that the fact that the coins were pinched at the mint till they contained but 90 grains each, could not alter the purchasing power of the whole

---

[1] See pp. 209-12.

body of 1,000,000 pieces, which would "preserve its mint-value, that is to say, pass in circulation for the intrinsic value of the bullion which it *ought* to contain."

And Mr. Ricardo does not flinch from supposing a seigniorage of 50 per cent. with the same result: the 50,-000,000 grains spared by government accomplishing the same exchanges at the same prices, if coined into 1,000,-000 pieces of the mint value of 100 grains each, as twice the amount of gold had done. But, now that, with a seigniorage of 10 per cent., there are issued, not 1,000,-000, but 1,111,111, pieces of the mint value of 100 grains each, depreciation must result. The state of the world's commerce will not allow the commodities offered for money in that country to be exchanged, at prices corresponding with those of other countries, by means of a currency of the mint value of 111,111,100 grains.

Exportation is the sole resource. But which shall be exported? The whole body of coin has become depreciated: what is to determine which portions shall "leave their country for their country's good"?

We have supposed the coins to be all issued of a uniform weight of 90 grains of fine gold; but, in the nature of things, this uniformity cannot long continue. Some will pass into more active use than others, and hence will suffer more rapid abrasion. The criminal acts of the clipper and sweater will be necessarily exercised with great irregularity upon the circulating coin. Upon a body of money of unequal value, the principle known as

GRESHAM'S LAW

will at once begin to operate. This principle, called by the name of Sir Thomas Gresham, the founder of the

Royal Exchange of London, is that, of two sorts of money circulating together, the inferior will drive out and replace the better. Stated thus, without qualification, as it usually is, the proposition is not true. It is only when the body of money thus composed is in excess, that the better part begins to yield place and retire from circulation.

"It is a mistaken theory, therefore, to suppose that guineas of 5*dwt.* 8*gr.* cannot circulate with guineas of 5*dwt.*, or less. As they might be in such limited quantity that both the one and the other might actually pass in currency for a value equal to 5*dwt.* 10*gr.*, there would be no temptation to withdraw either from circulation, there would be a real profit in retaining them."[1]—[Ricardo, Reply to Bosanquet, pp. 95–6.]

When, however, the aggregate amount of the two or more sorts of money in circulation becomes excessive, that is, greater than the community's distributive share of the money of the world, the principle of Gresham's Law begins at once to operate, acting through the desire of

---

[1] It is in this way that we explain the phenomenon noted by Alexander Hamilton when he says in his "Report on the Mint": "The new Dollar has a currency in all payments in place of the old [which, he had stated, 'by successive diminutions of its weight and fineness, has sustained a depreciation of five per cent.'], with scarcely any attention to the difference between them;" and again he speaks of "the unequal values allowed in different parts of the union to coins of the same intrinsic worth."

Mr. Buchanan had neglected this consideration in his remarks on the money in use in the British American colonies, and Mr. Ricardo corrects him as follows: "Mr. Buchanan evidently thinks that the whole currency must necessarily be brought down to the level of the value of the debased pieces; but surely, by a diminution of the quantity of the currency, the whole that remains may be elevated to the value of the best pieces."—[Political Economy.]

men to pay their debts, or effect their purchases, with the least valuable commodity which will answer the requirements of exchange. By this means the heavier coins are selected[1] for exportation in payment of debts abroad, where only the actual weight of fine metal will determine their power in exchange, or for consumption in the arts, industrial or decorative, at home, where the denomination of the coin is of equally little account.

It is not to be understood that the mass of the people engage in this occupation of sifting the coin to get out the heavier pieces. It is the dealer, and especially the dealer in money,[2] who, with his scales always at hand and always adjusted, quickly detects the least difference in weight, letting the light coins go their way into circulation again, while those of full weight are quietly laid aside till wanted by the jeweler or the exporter.

We have said that, on Ricardo's principle, it does not matter whether the loss of the precious metal in the coin results from an external abrasion from year to year in circulation, or through the clipping or sweating[3] of the

---

[1] "*Picking* or *selecting* which some persons think to stigmatize under the affected name of *billonnage*, or *trébuchage*."—[Chevalier on Gold, Cobden's transl.]

[2] King John of France, when a prisoner in the hands of the English, employed, it is said, agents to pick the nobles of the first and second coinage, for transmission to France, and did quite a flourishing business in this way.

[3] Peculiarly an English crime: "La coupable industrie de la rognure semble avoir été pratiquée en Angleterre qu'ailleurs."—[Chevalier, La Monnaie, p. 81.]

Let us not, however, exclude the English colonies. The merchants of New York in a petition to Lord Cornbury complained as

coin, or from an original abstraction of a certain portion of the metal at the mint, whether for the expenses of coinage, or for the profit of the sovereign. In no case will depreciation result, unless the coin be supplied in excess.

We cannot too often repeat his words: "However debased a coinage may become, it will preserve its mint-value, that is to say, it will pass in circulation for the intrinsic value of the bullion which it ought to contain, provided it be not in too great abundance." There is observable in discussion an inveterate tendency to slip away from this doctrine, even on the part of those who in terms accept it in its fullness. This tendency is due, I apprehend, to the influence of the idea that money measures value as the yard-stick measures length, or the bushel, capacity. It is evident that, were the yard-stick or the bushel-measure to be treated as we have supposed the coin to be, that is, were the yard-stick to be shorn of three or four inches, or the bushel measure to have a false bottom inserted, we should not avoid disturbance of relations in buying and selling goods, simply by limiting the number of such yard-sticks and bushel-measures to the number of the unabridged articles previously in use.

This idea of money as a measure of value is going to give us a great deal of trouble till we finally settle it, as I hope we shall be able to do when we reach the discussion of Inconvertible Paper Money.

---

follows: "The people of Boston publicly and avowedly have practiced to clip and file all the small current money along the continent, to 25 per cent. loss, which practice and the unlawful profit coming thereby, did encourage enough to make it their business to carry it thither and return it again to us and our neighbors, where it passed for the same value as formerly."—[Documentary History of New York.]

But if the abstraction, under the name of seigniorage, of a portion of the precious metals which the coin formerly contained, whether that portion be one per cent., or ten, or fifty; whether it be to cover simply the cost of coining or to afford a revenue to the sovereign or the state, does not necessarily affect the purchasing power of the coin, why is not seigniorage in every way economically desirable?

It meets the charge of coinage, which otherwise falls upon the state; it may be used to form a sort of sinking-fund, against the expense of recoinage,[1] whenever that shall become necessary; it may even be used as a form of taxation, to bring a large revenue into the public treasury. Moreover, it enables a smaller amount of the precious metals to discharge the office of circulation, and thus allows a portion of the labor employed in mining to be directed to agriculture or mechanical industry.

In reply to these arguments it will suffice, at present, to say that we shall meet them all again in our discussion of Paper Money, and in a shape, too, where they can be more conveniently canvassed and more conclusively answered. "*The whole charge for Paper Money,*" says Mr. Ricardo, "*may be considered as Seigniorage.*"[2]

I have thus far made use of Mr. Ricardo's name in tracing the effects of seigniorage on the purchasing

---

[1] Prof. Jevons brings out this idea in his "Money and the Mechanism of Exchange." He shows that the British seigniorage of 9 per cent. or thereabouts, on silver coin, more than provides for the issue of fresh coins as those in circulation are returned, worn or clipped, to the Mint.—[Pp. 163–4.]

[2] Political Economy. In his "Reply to Bosanquet," he says: "A Bank-note may be considered as a piece of money on which the seigniorage is enormous; amounting to all its value."

power of coin, the reason being that it seems to me an important proviso needs to be made in the practical application of this doctrine to the actual coinage of any country at any time. Mr. Ricardo's conclusions are just, upon his assumption, not expressed, indeed, and this is where he scarcely did justice to his readers; but clearly carried along by Mr. Ricardo in his reasoning, viz., that the general knowledge, or the popular suspicion, of a reduction of the metal in the coin does not operate upon the public mind to interfere with its circulation.[1]

In other words, Mr. Ricardo's reasoning assumes that the demand for money is fixed in the state of production and trade, at the time, with the commercial agencies existing; that the people will use so much money, anyhow; and that the supply of money, that is, the number of money-pieces, or coins, of a given mint-value, has alone to do with the question whether depreciation shall result.

And it needs to be said that such a reduction in the quantity of metal in the coin may conceivably take place, nay, there is reason to believe, actually has taken place in not a few instances, with the full public knowledge of the fact, and yet without affecting the currency of the coin, and hence without affecting the demand for money.

But such is not necessarily, and there is reason to believe that it has not always been actually the case. Hence, when we speak of a debased coinage circulating without depreciation, if not in excess of the amount of

---

[1] Prof. Sumner gives countenance to the proposition, "the worse the currency, the more mobile it will be," provided it be uniformly bad.—[Hist. Am. Currency, p. 176.] It takes two to make a bargain. It is true that the worse the currency, the more anxious the holder is to pass it off; it is also true that every other person is, on that account, less willing to receive it.

money of full value which might circulate in the community at the time, it must be understood always with the proviso, that nothing in the public mind limits the circulation of such a debased coinage; for, should it be blown upon, should prejudice arise against it to such an extent that, rather than receive it, people will resort to barter, in spite of all its inconveniences, or to extended credit leading to the mutual cancellation of obligations,[1] then we should have a new condition; the demand for money would be diminished just so far; and an amount of coin not in excess of the amount of money of good repute which would circulate freely, might become redundant and hence depreciated.

Such a prejudice against the coin in circulation as is referred to, might be produced among the ignorant and unthinking by false reports concerning its weight or fineness, or by mere abuse of it from the press or from persons in high positions. Among the more intelligent classes, an apprehension of larger issues or of further debasement might lead to distrust and a reluctance to receive considerable amounts of it.

As was remarked[2] in our analysis of the Money-function: while barter is, in a large proportion of the exchanges of modern industrial society, impracticable, in respect to other large bodies of exchange operations, it is simply a question of a little inconvenience or risk, more or less, whether barter, or exchange through the medium of money, shall be resorted to. "In agriculture the world over, full payment in money is highly exceptional, where it is not wholly unknown. In England, the money wages in general far exceed the estimated

---

[1] See pp. 65–9.

[2] P. 21.

value of all the other forms of payments, and rarely constitute less than one-half the nominal wages. In Scotland, except in the neighborhood of large towns, payment in kind is very general, while in some parts of the Highlands little money passes at all between employer and employed. In Germany, the report of the recent Commission of the Agricultural Congress proves the custom of payments in kind to prevail in every province from East Prussia to Alsace. In France this custom prevails, to a greater or less extent, in all departments. In the United States, board to the unmarried laborer is perhaps the rule; while in the South, at least, the payment in kind generally includes the subsistence of the laborer and his family, and to a considerable extent, other necessaries of life."[1]

Now, it is obvious that in all branches of agriculture where the produce was suitable for the laborer's consumption, any degree of distrust of the coin in circulation might result in throwing the body of laborers and employers back in a greater degree upon the condition of barter. Many employers had reasoned that they would not be harassed by the small cares and troubled by the inevitable complaints attending the payment of wages in kind; they would market their crops and pay their workmen the stipulated wages in money, letting them feed, shelter, clothe, and otherwise provide for themselves. In this way the employers, while losing the possible profits of truck, would be relieved from a thousand annoyances and inconveniences; would no longer have to hear the good wives chatter about leaky roofs and broken windows, or their good men growl over undersized potatoes, thin cider, musty meal or green fire-

[1] Walker, The Wages Question, p. 20.

wood. At the same time, this willingness of the employers to dispense with payment in kind had doubtless been assisted by the growing uneasiness of the laborers and their readiness to revolt against truck, or at least to give preference to masters who paid in cash. But a distrust of the money which had been the ordinary medium of payments might send both the parties gladly back to barter. However strong the workman's educated dislike of truck, he might choose it rather than be robbed through a fraudulent money.

It was said that a return to barter might be effected in the case of all branches of agriculture where the produce was suitable for the laborer's use. In the case of the cotton crop, however, the produce of the plantation is not suitable, in its raw state, for personal consumption, and when made up it meets but one of his many wants. Even here, however, under such circumstances as we are contemplating, both masters and men would find it for their interest to come to the plan of paying and receiving wages, in a degree, at least, in articles necessary for subsistence. The employer might agree to furnish definite quantities of bacon, corn, and clothing for the laborer and his family, in return for definite amounts of work, and thus obviate the use of the distrusted medium. By thus making one person purveyor for large numbers, a great saving would be effected in the use of coin, for it is retail trade which especially demands the employment of money.

Moreover, the reputation and pecuniary responsibility of the employer would permit the extensive introduction of credit, resulting in the mutual cancellation of large amounts of obligations, which, in the ordinary course of trade, would have been separately settled, at their different dates of maturity, by the use of money. The planter, with his large capital and his growing crop as security, might purchase supplies wholesale, not only at lower rates, but on longer time, than his individual laborers could do. This would allow him to pay for his supplies by bills drawn on the consignees of his crop, and thus the necessity for the use of money be entirely obviated.

In the two ways thus described, a large portion of all the money ordinarily used in the payment of agricultural wages and kept in circulation between agricultural laborers and the small shop-keepers who supply their wants, might be released through the operation of a continued and increasing distrust or dislike of the coin, arising from a popular knowledge of its debasement, combined with the natural apprehension of further reductions in quality, so that an amount not in excess of what would be the volume of money of full value, might prove redundant.

The former of these methods of reducing the use of money could not be extensively applied in most branches of mechanical industry, inasmuch as the product would generally be found to be suited to few or none of the laborers' necessities; but the latter method might come largely into play just as soon as suspicion attached to the ordinary medium of exchange. Unquestionably, to anticipate somewhat, this was one of the reasons which explain the rapid depreciation of the Revolutionary paper money. Not only was the amount continually increasing, under the pressure of the financial necessities of Congress, but the use of it was decreasing, perhaps even more rapidly, as men learned, by the bitter experience of their losses, to make exchanges as far as possible in kind, and to ask and give accommodation in the matter of payment, so as to bring income and outgo together, and thus secure a mutual cancellation of obligations.

A greater or smaller use of money is often not a matter of necessity, but of convenience or even of pleasure or fancy.[1] If the circulating medium breaks down wholly or in part, the community resorts to barter or to credit, to a certain extent, with perhaps no loss whatever industrially, but only a slight increase of personal care and trouble. If these methods have to be carried further and applied to a larger volume of transactions to which they are less easily adapted, there may be an appreciable loss resulting from the hinderance of production and of exchange; but still, that loss, being definite, may be preferred to the losses apprehended from those of distrusted money.

In such a temper of the public mind, many dealers will act on the principle announced by Swift's Drapier: "For my own part, I am already resolved what to do. I have a pretty good shop of Irish stuffs and silks: and instead of taking Mr. Wood's bad copper, I intend to truck with my neighbors, the butchers, the bakers and brewers and the rest: *goods for goods.*"[2]

I have not intended, in what has been said, to disparage the importance of the Money-function; but only to show that, in any advanced state of industrial society, there is a margin, often a wide margin, of exchange transactions which may be occupied by barter or by money-sales, indifferently, so far as any actual industrial loss is involved, the use of money being ordinarily resorted to from the force of habit, or from considerations of convenience which do not go to the real capabilities of production; that there is a still larger body of ex-

[1] Prof. Jevons has a significant paragraph "O— .he Force of Habit in the Circulation of Money."—[Money, etc., p. 73–80.]

[2] Dean Swift's works. "Wood hath Liberty to offer his coin, and we have Law, Reason, Liberty and Necessity, to refuse it."

change transactions in respect to which the choice between barter or money-sales is a matter, not of necessity, but of convenience, within a degree which may allow the advantages of the latter method to be offset by evils experienced or apprehended from the use of a distrusted medium; and that, from these causes, as well as through an increased use of credit allowing the mutual cancellation of obligations, a body of debased coin, not in excess of the amount of money of full value which would, under the same industrial conditions, have circulated freely in the community, may become redundant and suffer depreciation.

It is not, however, let us repeat, at all in the nature of the case, that a debased coinage, even though the fact of debasement be publicly known, should depreciate, if not issued in excess. We freely take nickel five-cent pieces, the material of which is worth only about half a cent, or silver fifty-cent pieces, the material of which is worth even less than half-dollars in our irredeemable paper money, because we look confidently to have others take them from us in turn. In like manner, a community may continue to accept worn or clipped or debased sovereigns or eagles without hesitation, so long as the habit of receiving them suffers no shock, each man taking them, not at all for what is in them, but for what he can get by means of them.

## CHAPTER XI.

### RECOINAGE.

THE frequent allusions which have been made tc losses sustained by the coin from abrasion in circulation and from the evil arts of the clipper and the sweater, naturally introduce the subject of Recoinage.

The three great English recoinages to which I shall refer in illustration of the difficulties besetting a reformation of the coin of a country when it has become greatly and irregularly debased at the mint, or abraded in circulation, are those of 1560, 1696, and 1774.

In each of these instances, the volume of the coin had undoubtedly been increased above the quantity of money of full weight which would have circulated; though in the latter two cases at least, Mr. Ricardo asserts,[1] not proportionally to the debasement of quality. Of each instance it might be asserted that it was not so much the fact of the general debasement or deterioration of the coin, as the want of uniformity therein, which induced confusion in trade. Had all the shillings in King William's time been debased to groats, exchanges would have been effected with comparative ease and equity. It was because one shilling was worth twelve pence, another ten, another eight, and another only six, or even

---

[1] See p. 192.

four, that disputes arose at every payment. "It is surely," says Prof. Tucker,[1] "of far less inconvenience that there should be a disparity of value of the same coin at different periods, and these probably distant, than that there should be a disparity in similar coins circulating at the same time."

The first recoinage is thus described by Mr. Froude:

"In their first moments of serious leisure, immediately after the Scotch war, in September, 1560, the council determined, at all hazards, to call in the entire currency and supply its place with new coin of a pure and uniform standard. Prices of all kinds could then adjust themselves without further confusion.

"The first necessity was to ascertain the proportions of good and bad money which was in circulation. A public inquiry could not be ventured for fear of creating a panic, and the following rudely ingenious method was suggested as likely to give an approximation to the truth: 'Some witty person was to go among the butchers of London (and to them rather than to any other, because they retailed of their flesh to all manner of persons in effect, so that thereby of great likelihood came to their hands of all sorts of money of base coin) and to go to a good many of them—36 at least,—and after this manner, because they should not understand the meaning thereof, nor have no suspicion in that behalf, requiring all of them to put all the money that they should receive the next forenoon by itself, and likewise that in the afternoon by itself, and they should have other money for the same, promising every one of them a quart of wine for their labors because that there was a good wager laid whether they received more money in the afternoon; whereof nine

[1] Money and Banks, p. 99.

score pounds being received of the butchers after the manner aforesaid, being all put together, then all the shillings of three oz. fine and under, but not above, should be tried and called out, as well counterfeits after the same stamp and standard as others; and after the rest of the money might be perused and compared one with another.'

"Either by this or some other plan, the worst coin in circulation was found to be about a fourth of the whole, while the entire mass of base money of all standards was guessed roughly at £1,200,000. How to deal with it was the next question.

"Sir Thomas Stanley offered several schemes to the choice of the government.

"1. The testers, worse and better together, might be called down from sixpence to fourpence; a period might be fixed within which they must be brought to the mint, and paid for at that price. The £1,200,000 would be bought in for £800,000; the bullion which it contained being recoined and re-issued at 11 oz. fine would be worth £837,500; and the balance of £37,500 in favor of the government, together with the value of the alloy, would more than cover the expenses of the process. If the queen wished to make a better thing of it, the worst money might be sent to Ireland[1] as the general dirt-heap for the outcasting of England's vileness.

---

[1] "From 1296 to 1355, the coins of England and Scotland were of the same weight and purity; but at the last mentioned epoch the standard of Scotch money was, for the first time, sunk below that of England; and by successive degradations the value of Scotch money, at the union of the Crowns in 1600, was only a twelfth part of the value of the English money of the same denomination. It remained at this point till the union of the kingdoms canceled the separate coinage of Scotland. The gold and silver coins of Ireland have been for a considerable period the same as those of Great Britain; but

"2. The bad coin might be called in simply and paid for at the mint according to its bullion value, a percentage being allowed for the refining.

"3. If the queen would run the risk, she might relieve her subjects more completely by giving the full value of fourpence-halfpenny for the sixpence, three halfpence for the half-groat, and so on through the whole coinage, allowing three-quarters of the nominal value, and taking her chance—still with the help of Ireland—of escaping unharmed.

"Swiftness of action, resolution, and a sufficient number of men of probity to receive and pay for the moneys all over the country, were the great requisites. The people were expected to submit to the further loss without complaint, if they could purchase with it a certain return to security and order. Neither of Stanley's alternatives were accepted literally. The standard for Ireland had always been something under that of England. But the queen would not consent to inflict more suffering on that country than she could conveniently help. The Irish coin should share in the common restoration, and be brought back to its normal proportions. On the 27th of September the evils of an uneven and vitiated currency were explained by proclamation. The people were told that the queen would bear the cost of refining and recoining the public moneys, if they on their side would bear cheerfully their share of the loss; and they were invited to bring in and pay over to persons appointed to receive it in every market town the impure silver in their hands.

---

until 1825 they were nominally rated $8\frac{1}{3}$ per cent. higher. This difference of valuation, which was attended with considerable inconveniences, was put to an end by the Act 6 Geo. IV, c. 79, which assimilated the currency throughout the empire."—[J. R. McCulloch, Commercial Dictionary.]

"For the three better sorts of tester the Crown would pay the full value of fourpence-halfpenny and for the half-groats and pence in proportion. For the fourth and most debased kind, which was easily distinguishable, it would pay twopence-farthing. To stimulate the collection, a bounty of threepence was promised on every pound's worth of silver brought in. Refiners were sent for from Germany; the Mint at the Tower was set to work under Stanley and Sir Thomas Fleetwood, and in nine months the impure stream was washed clean, and a silver coinage of the present standard was circulating once more throughout the realm.

"Either a large fraction of the base money was not brought in, or the estimate of the quantity in circulation had been exaggerated. There was a balance in favor of the Crown of £95,135; but the cost of collection, the premiums and other collateral losses reduced the margin to £49,776 9*s.* 3*d.* £35,686 15*s.* 6*d.* was paid for the refining and reminting, and when the whole transaction was completed, Elizabeth was left with a balance in her favor of £14,079 13*s.* 9*d.*"—[History of England, vii, 467.]

The second great recoinage was that accomplished in the reign of William III, when Montague was at the head of the Treasury and Isaac Newton was Master of the Mint. This great political and financial event is familiar to every reader, through the picturesque description given by Macaulay in his 21st chapter. "In the autumn of 1695, it could hardly be said that the country possessed, for practical purposes, any measure of the value of commodities. It was a mere chance whether what was called a shilling, was really tenpence, sixpence or a groat."

The officers of the exchequer weighed 57,200 pounds of hammered money, which had recently been paid in. The weight ought to have been above 220,000 oz.; it proved to be under 114,000 oz. Three eminent London goldsmiths were invited to send a hundred pounds each in current silver, to be tried by the balance. Three hundred pounds ought to have weighed above 1200 oz. The actual weight proved to be 624 oz. It was found that a hundred pounds, which should have weighed above 400 oz., did actually weigh, at Bristol, 240 oz.; at Cambridge, 203; at Exeter 180; and at Oxford, 116.[1]

"It may be doubted," continues the eloquent historian, "whether all the misery which had been inflicted on the English nation in a quarter of a century by bad kings, bad ministers, bad parliaments, and bad judges, was equal to the misery caused in a single year by bad crowns and bad shillings. . . .

"The evil was felt daily and hourly, in almost every place, and by almost every class; in the dairy and on the threshing-floor; by the anvil and by the loom; on the billows of the ocean and in the depths of the mine.

"Nothing could be purchased without a dispute. Over every counter there was wrangling from morning to night. The workman and his employer had a quarrel as regularly as the Saturday came round. On a fair-day or a market-day the clamors, the reproaches, the taunts, the curses were incessant, and it was well if no booth was overturned and no head broken. No merchant would contract to deliver goods without making some stipulation about the quality of the coin in which he

[1] "A. V." in his letter to Lord Godolphin, gives the results of numerous trials made by him on the current coin. Macaulay appears to draw his figures from this source, though the correspondence is not complete.

was to be paid. Even men of business were often bewildered by the confusion into which all pecuniary transactions were thrown. The simple and the careless were pillaged without mercy by extortioners whose demands grew even more rapidly than the money shrank. The price of the necessaries of life, of shoes, of ale, of oatmeal, rose fast. The laborer found that the bit of metal, which, when he received it, was called a shilling, would hardly, when he wanted to purchase a pot of beer or a loaf of rye-bread, go as far as sixpence.

"Where artisans of more than usual intelligence were collected in great numbers, as in the dock-yard of Chatham, they were able to make their complaints heard and to obtain some redress; but the ignorant and helpless peasant was cruelly ground between one class which would give money only by tale, and another which would only take it by weight."[1]

It was to remove this evil, which had gone so far as to

---

[1] Dr. Hunter, in his admirable work "The Annals of Rural Bengal," has strikingly shown the suffering of the poorer classes through the use of an *irregularly debased* money. "The coinage, the refuse of twenty different dynasties and petty potentates, had been clipped, drilled, filed, scooped out, sweated, counterfeited and chahged from its original value, by every process of debasement devised by Hindu ingenuity during a space of four hundred years. The smallest coin could not change hands without an elaborate calculation as to the amount to be deducted from its nominal value. This calculation, it need hardly be said, was always in favor of the stronger party. The treasury officers exacted an ample discount from the landholders—a discount which, when Bengal passed under British rule, amounted to 3 per cent. after a coin had been in circulation a single year, and to 5 per cent. after the second year, although no actual depreciation had taken place. The landholder demanded a double allowance from the middleman, and the middleman extorted a quadruple allowance from the unhappy tiller of the soil. In a long, indignant letter on the illegal cesses under which the cultivator groaned, Mr. Keating

paralyze trade and threaten the stability of the kingdom, that the great recoinage was effected under the masterly administration of Newton. The loss on the clipped and worn pieces was borne by the nation, the deficiency, exclusive of the actual cost of recoinage, amounting, according to Mr. Bosanquet [Practical Observations, p. 37n], to £2,415,140.

Of the wild excitement or painfully suppressed anxiety with which, according to the temperaments of individuals, the nation awaited the result of this great experiment by which the whole coin of the realm was withdrawn and re-issued, the reader cannot have forgotten Macaulay's most impressive account.

In the recoinage of 1774[1] gold only was withdrawn, silver, being no longer the principal money, was allowed

---

singles out the 'batta,' or exchange on old rupees, as the most cruel because the least defined. No recognized standard existed by which to limit the rapacity of the treasury officers. The government held them responsible for remitting the net revenue in full, and left them to deduct such a proportion from each coin as they deemed sufficient to cover all risk of short weight. Moreover, so great was the variety of coin in use, that they claimed a further discretion as to what they would receive at all. Cowries (shells), copper coins of every denomination, lumps of copper without any denomination whatever, pieces of iron beaten up with brass, thirty-two different kinds of rupees, from the full sicca to the viziery, hardly more than half its value, pagodas of various weights, dollars of different standards of purity, gold mohurs worth from 25 to 32 shillings each, and a diversity of Asiatic and European coins whose very names are now forgotten. At some treasuries, cowries were taken; at others they were not. Some collectors accepted payment in gold; others refused it; others again could not make up their minds either way; and the miserable peasant never knew whether the coin for which he sold his crop would be of any use to him when he came to pay his rent."—[Pp. 293–5.]

[1] So called; Chalmers says it began August 1773 and ended in 1777.—[Considerations, etc., p. 92.]

to remain in its debased condition. Mr. Huskisson, in his Bullion pamphlet, states the average reduction of the gold coin, in 1773, at from four to five per cent.

The Act of 1696 brought out a very full discussion of the whole system of recoinage. When it is said that Montague, Somers, Isaac Newton, and John Locke participated in the high debate, it is needless to say that little has since been added to the philosophy of the subject.

Two issues are involved in a general recoinage. First, shall the ancient standard be restored? We shall see this question arising in 1819, in connection with the resumption of specie payments in England; and we find the same issue presented in our own day, after a suspension of sixteen years.

The argument against a return to "the ancient right standard," to use the proud phrase of the English statute, is not wholly a plea for repudiation.

It is urged in its behalf that, when the debasement of the coin has been long in progress, prices have adapted themselves, painfully and irregularly indeed, to the state of the coin; that contracts for goods, for rents, for interest, etc., have been based on existing prices; and that an abrupt return to the ancient standard will work great injustice to all debtors who will be obliged to meet their obligations in a money which has suddenly become more valuable. We shall have to meet this question again in connection with the Resumption Act of 1819.

In 1696 Mr. Lowndes, the Secretary to the Treasury, stood as the champion of the scheme[1] of lowering the

---

[1] He proposed that the pound of standard silver be coined into 77 instead of 62 shillings, which would have effected a reduction of nearly one-fourth.

standard to meet the condition of the money actually in circulation;[1] Locke as the champion of the ancient standard. Of the writings of this great philosopher on this occasion Macaulay remarks: "It may well be doubted whether, in any of his writings, even in those ingenious and deeply meditated chapters on language, which form perhaps the most valuable part of his 'Essay on the Human Understanding,' the force of his mind appears more conspicuously."

The second issue that arose in connection with the recoinage of 1696 was this: conceding the maintenance of the ancient standard, on whom should the loss by light coin fall?

On this point Prof. Thorold Rogers's objection to the plan adopted in 1696, must be deemed wholly insufficient:

"As a matter of abstract justice, it is clear that the act of coinage, being a service which the government does for the public, and being a certificate of the fineness[2] contained in the pieces issued, the Exchequer should not be called on to bear the loss of wear, still less, losses by fraud."—[Hist. Gleanings, i, 30.]

Now, to say that the government should not bear the cost of recoinage because it bears the cost of coinage: is not this much like saying that government should not repair roads because it has in the first instance to make them?

---

[1] In anticipation of the recoinage of 1774, Mr. Harris, in his very able essay on "Money and Coins," proposed to reduce the guinea to 20 shillings, to meet the average deterioration of the existing body of coin, which was estimated to be between 4 and 5 per cent.

[2] A singular slip; the stamp on the coin is a certificate both of the fineness and of *the weight*. This fact turns Prof. Rogers's argument against himself.

But there is a deeper objection to government throwing-off the cost of recoinage. It is that, while the service of which Prof. Rogers speaks was rendered to the public at large, the accidental present holder of the coin is made to pay the entire cost of that service from the period of issue, extending perhaps through a score of years.[1] Hundreds of persons have handled the coin and helped to abrade it: one alone, he in whose hands it happens to be found at the date of the proclamation, is made to suffer the entire loss.

But it is not on grounds of justice alone that most of the governments of Europe have adopted the principle that the charge of recoinage shall fall upon the public. Considerations of policy also require it. Great Britain, whose government still stands out against the principle, suffers from a steady deterioration of its coin, in consequence of the reluctance of holders to submit to loss[2] by bringing light sovereigns to the mint. The Bank of England and its branches, with a few Irish banks, alone comply with the requirement to cut light pieces. Other banks and dealers in money, as well as tradesmen generally, throw the coin back into circulation.

Prof. Jevons estimates[3] that, in 1868, there were

---

1 "The loss from natural abrasion," says Mr. Tooke, "should be repaid by the government, and not by the last holder, for the reason that it has occurred while the coins were performing the function of a circulating medium."

2 Mr. Nicholson states that in the three years ending March 31, 1872, gold coins to the nominal value of £1,975,716 were cut by the Bank; the loss sustained by the owners of the coin amounted to £25,415, being $\frac{1}{78}$ of the nominal value.—[Science of Exchanges, p. 99.]

3 Statistical Journal, xxxi, 433–4.

about 20,000,000 light sovereigns (out of a total of 64,-500,000, at the most, in circulation) and £5,600,000, in value, of light half-sovereigns, circulating in defiance of law. In some agricultural districts the proportion of light sovereigns rises to 44 per cent. The average deficiency in weight of the sovereigns is computed by Prof. Jevons at 0.53 per cent.; that of the half-sovereigns at more than twice as much.

## CHAPTER XII.

### THE CONCURRENT CIRCULATION OF TWO METALS.

In referring to the English coinage, it has been said that since 1666 no seigniorage has been exacted.

This assertion holds true, however, since 1816, only of the principal, or gold, money of the realm. On silver and bronze coin, the seigniorage charged by the British government is considerable.

"Standard silver," wrote Prof. Jevons in 1874, "can usually be bought by the mint for 5 shillings [gold] per standard ounce. It is issued to the public [in coin] at the rate of 5*s.* 6*d.* per oz., so that the government receives a seigniorage of at least 9 per cent. on the nominal value of the coin issued."

"The average coinage of silver at the English mint," he continues, "during the last ten years has been £546,580, upon which the seigniorage would be about £49,200 per annum. On the other hand, the Mint has to buy back worn silver coinage at its nominal value; and in recoining such money there is a loss, which, on the average of the last ten years (1864–73), has been £16,700, leaving a net annual profit of £32,500, no account being taken of the cost of the mint establishment."

"At present," he adds, "the price of silver is not above 4*s.* 10*d.* per oz., so that the seigniorage is about 12 per cent., and the profit on coining silver proportionately greater."—[Money and the Mechanism of Exchange, pp. 163–4.]

On the smaller coins of the kingdom a much larger profit, proportionately, is made by the government. "The bronze of which the pence are made is worth, according to Mr. Seyd, 10*d.* per troy pound, so that the metallic values of the coins are almost exactly one-fourth part of their nominal values."—[*Ibid.*, p. 110.] That is, the British penny contains one farthing's worth of metal.

The primary object of this seigniorage on silver and bronze coins, in England, is not the profit to be derived from the coinage: but the establishment of a "single standard"—in this case, gold; and the remitting of silver to the position of a subsidiary coinage, to be issued in arbitrary amounts by the government, and to be legal tender[1] only for strictly limited and inconsiderable sums. Money thus issued is called Billon (from the French) or Token-money. Even among the nations which assume to keep both gold and silver in circulation, the policy of making the smaller coins, even the smaller silver coins, of less than their nominal value, is now generally adopted.[2] Russia almost alone preserves the full actual metallic value of her silver coins, down to the smallest. Economically speaking, what is the relation of token-money to standard-money?

Only two points under this head require to be noted.

---

[1] In Great Britain silver coin is not a legal tender above 40 shillings; pence are a legal tender in payments to the amount of 1 shilling only; half-pence and farthings to the extent of 6 pence only.

[2] The Report of Mr. Göschen's Committee on the Depreciation of Silver (1876), and Mr. Ernest Seyd's treatise on "Bullion and Foreign Exchanges," contain full information respecting the *billon* of the world.

The first concerns the complaint that the debasement of the coin in which the wages of common labor are paid, is an injury to the working classes. For example, a laborer who is paid on Saturday twenty-two coined shillings for his week's work, in reality gets less than a sovereign's worth of silver; the girl who is nominally paid tenpence for her day's work in the mill gets only about a threepence worth of copper. Here, it is said, is a manifest injustice. The wealthy and well-to-do receive their incomes in the principal coin of the country which is of full weight and fineness; the poor are paid in coins which contain only a part, and perhaps only a small part, of the metal which would be worth the sum for which they are made a tender by law. This complaint, sometimes heard among laborers, was recently given a wider hearing through Colonel Tomline, a member of the British Parliament. The answer of Mr. Hubbard appears to be conclusive, so long as such billon or token-money is not issued in excess.

"It is quite true," says Mr. Hubbard, "that silver, rather than gold, is the medium through which the wages of the laboring classes are paid; but to show that the laboring classes are injured by the Mint regulations, it must be demonstrated that the shilling they now receive commands a smaller quantity of the necessaries of life than would a shilling coined as an integral measure of value. The shilling now circulating derives its purchasing power, not from the silver it contains, but from its being by law a twentieth part of a pound, —the golden standard. All prices, wholesale or retail, whether of a bullock or a beefsteak, of a quarter of wheat or a loaf of bread, are computed upon a gold valuation. The artisan's shilling is intrinsically the twenty-second part of a pound, his penny but the four hundred and eightieth part of a pound, but how do these facts affect his interest, if he can always, with twenty shillings or two hundred and forty pence, secure the value of a pound?"

But suppose billon or token-money to be issued in excess of the real requirements of trade, what will be the result? Depreciation of course; but how will this affect the poorer classes? how will it influence retail prices?

I do not see how such an excess of small coin can influence peculiarly the condition of the poorer classes, except through the operation of the principle expressed by Roscher, as quoted in the chapter on the Money-function. Were the members of the community economically on equal terms, all would suffer inconvenience, but all would suffer alike. If, for example, there were such a flood of shillings issued by the English Mint, that those who received them in trade found it difficult to get rid of them,[1] and it became necessary to submit to a discount, the tradesmen would, it is true, be compelled to charge the workman more for groceries, meats and vegetables, which were to be paid for with

---

[1] Dr. Hunter says of India: "Copper coins, when transferred in large quantities were, and are to the present day, sold; that is to say, they do not pass at their full denominational value, but at a lower rate, the proportion deducted depending on the locality, and the comparative demand for silver or copper coins. Indeed, the tendency of copper coins to accumulate in the district treasuries still forms a subject of frequent official correspondence, and a percentage is in some places allowed to the collectors of the assessed taxes—such as the municipal police—for converting the petty copper payments into rupees."—[Annals of Rural Bengal, p. 298.]

shillings; but on the other hand, the employer, being able to exchange at a premium the gold or bank-notes which he received from the sales of his goods, for shillings with which to pay his workmen, would be able to give an advance of wages to correspond. The whole community would doubtless suffer an impairment of industrial and commercial activity from such an obstruction; but rich and poor would share this loss alike.

If, however, the community were divided, as there is reason to believe every community is, into the economically weak and the economically strong, peculiar disadvantages might be experienced by certain classes. It is more than probable that, in the instance given, while the tradesmen would put up their prices promptly and perhaps further than was strictly necessary to make themselves good for the discount to which the shilling had become subject, the employer would advance wages tardily and partially.

What would be the effect on prices of a redundancy of token-money? Speaking of the effort of the Secretary of the United States Treasury to push out the so-called "fractional currency," Prof. Sumner says:[1] "In 1872 this issue was forced up to between $40,000,000 and $50,000,000, producing a redundancy and *enhancing retail prices.*" The suggestion is an interesting one. Is it possible that a redundancy of small money should produce any peculiar effect on retail prices? I see but two ways in which this can take place. First, retail prices would have to be advanced to the extent of any discount actually submitted to by the dealers in turning

[1] Hist. Am. Currency, p. 205.

the small-money which they had received from their customers into the large-money in which they were to pay the merchants and manufacturers from whom they purchased their goods. But was there in 1872 any discount on "fractional currency," ordinarily submitted to by retail dealers? I cannot learn that there was.

The only other way in which a redundancy of small-money could produce an enhancement of retail prices, specially, which occurs to me, is through aggravating what Prof. Cairnes characterizes as "the excessive friction" of retail trade.[1] The effect of an excess of small-money in this direction might easily be very considerable, increasing the disadvantage which the laboring classes always suffer, through poverty, ignorance and inertia, in the purchase of articles for domestic consumption.

### SINGLE OR DOUBLE STANDARD?

As to the expediency of the issue of bronze and copper coins, and even of the minor silver coins, with a real value below, it may be much below, the mint-price, there is no great difference of opinion among economists; but the policy adopted in Great Britain, by the Act of 1816, of restricting to one metal the coinage of full value and of unlimited legal tender, has been very warmly disputed.

---

[1] "Competition in retail markets," writes Prof. Cairnes, "is conducted under conditions which may be described as of greater friction than those which exist in wholesale trade."

Mr. Mill says: "Retail price, the price paid by the actual consumer, seems to feel slowly and imperfectly the effect of competition, and where competition does exist, it often, instead of lowering prices, merely divides the gain among a greater number of dealers."

We have now reached the ground of the controversy respecting a Single or a Double Standard for Deferred Payments: that controversy to which Prof. Jevons has applied the phrase, "The Battle of the Standards."

I need not say that this is the question in the whole field of political economy which at present awakens the greatest popular interest and commands the most strenuous exertions of professed economists. Unfortunately, prejudice and passion enter so largely into the controversy as to obscure the true issue in the public apprehension, and even not a little in the minds of the contestants. Invective has taken the place of investigation; and writers of repute set themselves about the work of refuting and holding up to ridicule statements which the representatives of the opposing party would not for a moment accept as embodying their views.

My only object here will be to set fairly forth, without prejudice, the real issue, and indicate the economical principles upon which it must be decided. I shall hope to place side by side the arguments of the two parties to the controversy in such a manner that either might accept the representation of its own views without qualification, much more, without challenge.

The position of the Mono-metallists, or the advocates of a Single Standard, may be given in the words of Mr. Nicholson:

"We cannot keep gold standard coins and silver standard coins in circulation side by side in any one country for a continuance, because the value of one metal when measured in the other is sure to fluctuate; and, as all standard coins are but so many stamped ingots of standard metal, people will always select the metal which costs them least when they have a payment to make; so that if more can be got for a given quantity of one metal in foreign countries than can be got for its legal equivalent in the other metal, supposing them to be circulating as stamped ingots side by side, the metal for which the most can be got will be exported, because of the two it is the cheapest mode of payment. For instance, if eleven rupees' worth of goods can be got in England for a sovereign, which is circulating side by side with rupees as ten in British India, the sovereign will be exported and the rupees will be kept in India.

"On the other hand, if one sovereign's worth of goods can be got in England for ten rupees, when rupees are circulating at the rate of eleven to one sovereign, side by side with sovereigns in India, the rupees will be exported and the sovereign will be kept in that country." —[Science of Exchanges, p. 107.]

The treatment of the two metals in the coinage of England is thus narrated by Mr. McCulloch. "From 1257[1] to 1664, the value of gold coins was regulated by proclamation, or, which is the same thing, it was ordered that the gold coins then current should be taken as equivalent to certain specified sums of silver. From 1664 down to 1717, the relation of gold to silver was not fixed by authority, and, silver being then the only legal tender, the value of gold coins fluctuated according to the fluctuations in the relative worth of the metals in the market. In 1717 the ancient practice was again re-

[1] "During the 13th Century," says Prof. Rogers, "and the earlier portion of the 14th, the English currency was entirely silver. Edward III coined gold in 1344. Macpherson, indeed, has given evidence of a gold coinage under Henry III, of the year 1257, but he acknowledges that the quantity must have been small, as the existence of this currency is gene ally unknown.' —[History of Agriculture and Prices, i, 173.]

sorted to; and it was fixed that the guinea should be taken as the equivalent of 21 shillings, and conversely.[1]

"In 1816, however, a new system was adopted in this country, it being then enacted (56 George III, c. 68,) that gold coins should be legal tender in all payments of more than 40 shillings. The pound of silver bullion that had previously been coined into 62 shillings was then also coined into 66 shillings, the additional four shillings being retained by government as a seigniorage or duty (amounting to $6\frac{14}{31}$ per cent.) upon the coinage. To prevent the silver coins from becoming redundant, government has retained the power to issue them in its own hands."—[Commercial Dictionary.]

From 1717 down to 1797, it is claimed that, while government sought to keep the two metals in concurrent circulation, at a fixed ratio, only one, that which was overrated in the coinage, was in fact the money of the kingdom. "During a long period previous to 1797, gold was so cheap, compared with silver, that it suited the Bank of England, and all other debtors, to purchase gold in the market, and not silver, for the purpose of carrying it to the Mint to be coined, as they could in that coined metal more cheaply discharge their debts."—[Ricardo, Political Economy.]

The experience of the United States with the two metals is thus given by Prof. Sumner:

"The coinage law under which coins were first struck in 1794 and 1795, fixed the ratio of gold to silver at one to fifteen [the silver dollar being 416 gr., 371.25 gr. pure and the gold dollar 27 gr., 24.75 gr. pure, the alloy counting for nothing]. The actual rate of gold to silver

---

[1] This is held to have overrated gold, compared with silver, $1\frac{1}{3}$ per cent.—[Liverpool on Coins.]

was at that time different in different countries;[1] but in England it was 15.2 to 1. Gold was, therefore. underrated in the coinage, and it was easier for a deotor to get silver to the amount of one dollar, than gold to the amount of one dollar. Silver accordingly became the real measure used and gold bore a premium." . . . "Of all the gold that came in and was coined, the Secretary of the Treasury said, 1836, that not over $1,000,000 remained in the country in 1834, 'and of that small amount only a very diminutive portion was in active circulation.'"

. . . . . . .

"By an act of June 28, 1834, the gold eagle was made to weigh 258 gr., standard, 899.225, that is, its pure contents were 232 gr. or 23.20 gr. to the dollar. Under this regulation silver was to gold as 16 : 1. This ratio was fixed upon in a blaze of exultation about the recent discoveries of gold in North Carolina, which, though known to exist since 1801, had only been developed since 1828, and extravagant hopes were entertained of finding 'a new Peru,' in the mountains of Georgia and the Carolinas. It was thought by some that it would 'encourage the miners' to overrate gold in the coinage.[2] In 1837, silver and gold were both made exactly nine-tenths fine; but the pure contents of the silver dollar remained the same as before, the gross weight being re-

---

[1] See p. 233.

[2] "Another consideration may be adduced in favor of the proposed reform of our gold coins. It seems to be well ascertained that the United States contain one of the most extensive deposits of gold that has yet been discovered. . . . It appears but just to afford to those employed in collecting that natural product, a certain, and the highest, home market of which it is susceptible."—[Gallatin, Considerations, etc., 1831; p. 64.]

duced to 412.5 gr. The gold dollar now contained 23.22 gr. fine.

"There were two different dollars after these changes as much as before. The silver dollar remained as before, but the gold dollar was now worth less than before. The gold dollar had formerly been worth, in the silver coinage, $1.038, taking the true ratio to be 15.6 : 1, which was asserted by the best authorities to be the true one at that time. The new gold dollar was worth, at the same ratio, in the same coin, 97.5 cts. As before no one would pay a debt with gold dollars, so now no one would pay with silver dollars. Silver went out of circulation and became the better metal to export, while for the same reasons gold became the better remittance this way. The only silver which could circulate here was that which was worn or clipped until it was not worth more than silver was rated at in our coinage. All the worn-down Spanish pillar-pieces came here, because they had a value here higher than anywhere else in the world. While the Mint was coining fine American pieces, scarcely one was to be seen in circulation. The people were obliged to use the smooth shillings, which produced a quarrel at almost every exchange, as to whether you could 'see the pillars,' until some one crossed them and they sank into unquestionable dimes. They were generally overrated at that."—[History of American Currency, pp. 104–110.]

In 1853 the United States, which had to that time followed the lead of England, imposed a seigniorage charge of one-half of one per cent. By the same act the government practically abandoned the attempt to keep the metals in circulation as equally the money of the land. The silver dollar had disappeared, owing to being underrated in the coinage, and the law of 1853 did not touch its legal rating, but the fractional coins were purposely made of less than their nominal value,[1] upon the principle of the English law of 1816; and became legal tender only for sums under $5. The silver was now coined by the government out of purchased metal, and not out of bullion brought by private parties to the Mint.

I have stated the position of the Mono-metallists in the language of Mr. Nicholson, and have illustrated it by the experience of England and the United States, as recited by Mr. McCulloch and Prof. Sumner.

Mr. Nicholson's position on this subject is the position of the English economists generally, scarcely more in the present than in the past, though they have not always been agreed as to the metal which should be selected to be the principal medium of exchange.

Locke and most of the earlier economists advocated silver[2]; of late the opinion of the English economists has been quite decidedly[3] the other way. It was Lord

---

[1] Half-dollar, 192 grains standard, $\frac{9}{10}$ fine.
Quarter-dollar, 96 " " " "

[2] The fact that Locke and the elder economists advocated the use of silver, has been made use of by Bi-metallists as favoring their cause. Properly considered, however, it has no such bearing. Silver has fallen so much in purchasing power since Locke's day, as to take from it much of the fitness it then had for use as the principal coin of the realm; while Locke's arguments against the possibility of a concurrent circulation of two metals have precisely the same validity when the preference is given to gold, in these days, as when silver seemed best fitted for unlimited legal tender.

[3] Subsequently to 1816, and prior to the outbreak of the present controversy, in 1867, Lord Ashburton was perhaps the most eminent advocate of a return to the double standard. The views of several English economists upon this question will be referred to in the course of our further discussion.

Liverpool, son of the author of the Letter on the Coins of the Realm, who led in the change which resulted as has been said, in 1816, in the definitive establishment of gold as the single standard for deferred payments and the reduction of silver money to the position of a subsidiary or token coinage.

It will be observed that the argument against the concurrent circulation of two metals upon equal terms turns upon the assumption that the relative values of gold and silver may be expected to vary from time to time.

Our first duty clearly is to inquire into the history of the variation in the comparative purchasing power of the two metals, from which results, of course, the price of each as expressed in terms of the other.

The point we have reached requires us to make a distinction not heretofore found necessary. Economists have been wont to make this distinction between Value and Price: Value is purchasing power—power in exchange; Price is the power to purchase money—it is the money-value of commodities. Money itself, then, while it has value (the value of a given amount of money being measured by the quantity of commodities it will purchase), has not price.[1] This is true so long as we think of money as one. But when we come to contemplate it as composed of two variable elements, it is evident that the price of either may be expressed in terms of the other. Hence, when we speak of the price of gold, we mean its silver-value; when we speak of the

[1] "On appelle prix d'une chose la quantité de numéraire qu'elle vaut, c'est a dire, sa valeur exprimée en numéraire. Chaque chose n'a qu'un prix, quoi qu'elle ait beaucoup de valeurs différentes, et toute chose a un prix, excepté le numéraire lui même."—[Cherbuliez Science Economique, i, 238.]

price of silver, we mean its gold-value. When we speak of the value of either gold or silver, we mean the power it has to purchase other commodities, including the one element of money besides itself.

I have already referred to a statement contained in a fragment of Agatharchidas, that silver was in very early times more valuable in Arabia than gold, in equal quantities of the two metals.[1] In our own day, three hundred years after the stream of silver began to pour from the opened sides of Potosi, the proportionate value of silver to gold[2] in Japan was as one to four. Throughout European history, however, we have no record of any approach of silver towards equal value, in equal quantities, with gold.

"In the reign of Darius, son of Hystaspes," says Mr. Duncan,[3] "gold was thirteen times as valuable as silver; in the time of Plato, twelve; and in that of the comic poet Menander, it was only ten. In the epoch of Julius Cæsar the ratio of gold to silver fell to nine for one."

In 1262 Prof. Rogers finds an account of two pur-

---

[1] "The learned researches of Boeckh, Letronne, Humboldt, Jacob and Dureau de la Malle. . . . They agree in the admission that originally the value of silver, in some countries, has equaled, if not exceeded, that of gold."—[Leon Faucher on the Production of the Precious Metals, Hankey's translation.]

[2] As represented respectively in the two coins, the Itzi Boo and the Cobang. "It followed naturally," says Mr. Seyd, "that the American and European traders, giving dollars for Itzi Boos, speedily exchanged the latter for gold Cobangs, drawing gold away from Japan, at an enormous profit to themselves. The Japanese, of course, soon became aware of this, and a revolution in their monetary valuation took place. The gold Cobang was, after a period during which its circulation was forbidden on pain of death, reduced to one-fourth of its previous size."—[Bullion and Foreign Exchanges, p. 373.]

[3] On Currency, p. 135.

chases of gold in England which average $9\frac{3}{5}:1$. In 1292, only thirty years later, the rate is $12\frac{1}{2}:1$.—[Hist. Agr. and Prices, i, 594–5.] Again: "The rate at which Edward III issued his florins in 1345, taking the six shillings, which they were declared to be worth by proclamation, at 1485 grains of pure silver, is exactly 13.75 : 1. If this ratio really represented the existing proportions between the two metals, it would point to a rise of about ten per cent. in the value of gold, in the course of fifty years."—[*Ibid.*] This remarkable rise we shall have occasion to refer to hereafter,[1] as of not a little significance. Standing alone, the fact of so great a rise in so short a time would seem to favor strongly the cause of the single standard, as showing how unreasonable is the expectation of anything like a permanent relation between gold and silver; but with the explanation which Prof. Rogers finds for this rise of gold, between 1262 and 1345, the case furnishes a very effective illustration to the advocates of the "double standard," or the Bi-metallists.

While the discovery of America took place in 1492, the great increase of the volume of the precious metals was, as we have seen, deferred till the conquest of Mexico in 1521, and even until the opening of the mines of Potosi in 1545. The bulk of the production of the Spanish American mines being in silver,[2] the fall in

[1] P. 251.

[2] Humboldt stated the quantity of silver taken from the American mines down to about the beginning of the present century, as 46 : 1 of gold. This would make the value of the silver produced as between 3 and 4 to 1. Why did not this disproportion of product cause a greater variation in the value of gold, in terms of silver, than from 10 or 12 to 15 or 16? Mr. Jacob offers in explanation what was doubtless one of the principal causes concerned: "The value of the silver produced since the discovery of America is three times that of gold; but the loss by wear on silver is four times that of gold."

purchasing power was unequally distributed between the two metals. As Adam Smith stated it, "both metals sank in their real value, or in the quantity of labor which they could purchase; but silver sank more than gold.'

M. Chevalier estimates the fall in the value of silver, from the discovery of America, as 6 : 1; that of gold 4 : 1. Prof. Cairnes is disposed to deem both these estimates excessive.—[Essays in Pol. Econ., p. 124.]

Prof. Leone Levi, in his "History of British Commerce," thus traces the effect of the silver discoveries of America upon the price of gold in the several countries of Europe:

"During the reign of Ferdinand and Isabella, viz., from 1474 to 1516, the relative value between gold and silver in Spain was as $1:10\frac{69}{612}$. In the year 1537, and during the reign of Charles V,[1] the relative value was fixed at $1:10\frac{371}{612}$; during the reign of Philip II it was established as $1:12\frac{143}{1224}$; during the reign of Philip III, as $1:13\frac{1}{3}$; during the reign of Charles II, as $1:15\frac{371}{2448}$; and finally on July 17, 1779, the relative value of the two metals was fixed at 1 : 16. In the year 1641, Louis XIII of France issued an edict which regulated the proportion between gold and silver at the French Mints, and this proportion was established at $1:13\frac{1}{2}$, with the view to conform in this respect to the regulations of foreign countries, where the proportions were as follows: in Germany as 1 : 12; in England, as $1:13\frac{1}{5}$; in the Netherlands, as $1:12\frac{1}{2}$; and in Spain, as $13\frac{1}{3}$. These regulations lasted about a century, when it became necessary again to alter them, and accordingly in the year 1724 an edict was issued by which the proportion be-

[1] Charles I of Spain.

tween gold and silver at the French Mint was fixed as 1:14½. At the time of this last edict the mint regulations of England established the proportions between gold and silver as 1 to about 15⅕, and they remained at the same footing until the new coinage. In 1780 the relative value between gold and silver was, at Amsterdam, as 1:14.885; in France, as 1:14.581; in Spain, as 1:15.636; at Venice, as 1:14.779; at Genoa, as 1:14.915; at Leghorn, as 1:14.510; in England, as 1:15.189, and at Hamburg, as 1:14.171. In the standard of British coinage at the present time 1 part of gold is worth 14½ of silver; in the French, 1 part of gold is equal to 15½ of silver, and in the countries where the silver standard prevails the proportion varies from 1:15½ to 15¾."—[P. 326.ⁿ]

The wide deviation between the standard of the present British coinage and that of France, is, as we have seen, due to the intention of the British Government to reduce silver to the grade of subsidiary or token coinage.

The discovery of the Californian and Australian gold mines,[1] between 1848 and 1851, led to expectations of

[1] "Speaking very broadly, silver was produced, as compared with gold, in the proportion of 3 to 1 during the earlier part of the century; the proportion fell to .68 to 1 in 1848; to .27 to 1 between 1852 and 1856; and between 1857 and 1875 it gradually rose to .68 to 1."—[Report of Mr. Göschen's Committee on the Depreciation of Silver (1876), p. v.]

Prof. Levi gives the following summary of the product of the mines in 1846 and 1852:

| | 1846. | | 1852. | |
|---|---|---|---|---|
| | GOLD. | SILVER. | GOLD. | SILVER. |
| North and South America, | £1,300,000 | £5,250,000 | £13,300,000 | £7,250,000 |
| Russia, | 3,500,000 | 1,250,000 | 3,500,000 | — |
| Europe, | — | — | — | 1,250,000 |
| Asia, Borneo and Africa, | 1,200,000 | — | 1,200,000 | — |
| Australia, | — | — | 12,000,000 | — |
| | £6,000,000 | £6,500,000 | £30,000,000 | £8,500,000 |

still further changes in the relation of the two metals. "At that time," says Prof. Cairnes, "according to all estimates on the subject, the stock of silver in existence was at least one-half greater than that of gold." These proportions were in twenty years to be reversed.

"Frightened, and not without reason," says Prof. Levi, "at the possible consequences, some countries, heretofore anxious to attract and retain gold in circulation even at great sacrifices, showed a feverish anxiety to banish it altogether. In July, 1850, Holland demonetized the gold ten florin piece and the Guillaume. Portugal prohibited any gold from having a current value except English sovereigns. Belgium demonetized its gold circulation. Russia prohibited the export of silver; and France alarmed, but less hasty, issued a commission to inquire into the matter."—[Hist. British Commerce, p. 336.]

It was in anticipation of a change so great as to amount to a practical confiscation of one-quarter, one-third, or even one-half, of all debts which had been contracted under the former proportions of gold and silver established in France by the law of the year XI (1803), that M. Chevalier wrote his treatise on the "Probable Fall in the Value of Gold," already referred to. The conclusions he reached were of the most alarming nature, and in his view, the situation required the instant action of the French government to prevent a social and industrial catastrophe.

The work of M. Chevalier appeared in 1857, when the production of gold had been proceeding in California nine years, in Australia six years. Yet though the rate of gold production had reached a point which would allow the whole yield (of gold) during the 356 years between 1492 and 1848 to be equaled in ten years, the actual effect upon the relation of the twc metals, and even upon the purchasing power of the whole mass of money, realized at the date of his essay, had been small.

How was this to be accounted for? M. Chevalier deemed the explanation to be this: The new gold had been absorbed by France, to replace the silver formerly in use which, when so replaced in the circulation of France, flowed away to India and the East in payment for the rapidly increasing purchases of oriental productions, teas, coffees, silk, spices, and drugs, to which a stimulus had been given both by the opening of the ports of China and Japan, and by the fact that the new money came first into the hands of the laboring classes, allowing them an unwonted indulgence in luxuries of this character. The explanation of M. Chevalier was not fanciful. The coinage of gold in France between 1850 and 1857 had been 2,749,693,490 francs, or £109,-987,735. In a word, and that M. Chevalier's, France had been the *parachute* which had retarded the fall in gold. That state of things, however, could not long continue. The silver of France would soon be replaced by gold; and the new supplies would soon result in a general and rapid depreciation, first, of the two metals in mass, and secondly, of silver as compared with gold.

In England, Prof. Cairnes, in the essays heretofore so frequently cited, and especially in that of 1860, in which he reviewed M. Chevalier's work, took the same view of the influence of France in retarding the fall;[1] but was inclined to think that the substitution of gold for silver in France was only a very striking example of a process

[1] "The fall in the value of gold has thus, up to the present time, been at once checked and concealed; checked by being substituted for silver, and concealed by being compared with it."

which had been in unobserved operation over a much wider area, and which would continue after the French movement should cease. In India, he noted, where there was an immense silver currency, the process had already begun and signs were not wanting that it would soon assume more important dimensions. "These considerations," he remarked, "do not apply to India alone; they are applicable, more or less extensively, to other countries where silver is the currency, and more particularly to China, where there is a large silver circulation, and where the habits of the people are, in many respects, similar to those of the people of Hindostan.

"For these reasons we cannot concur in the assumption that, when the movement in the French currency is concluded, the future action of the new gold must be concentrated upon the gold currencies of the world. We think that its effect will still continue to be shared, though probably in a less degree than heretofore, by the other precious metal, and that consequently, the fall in gold, though accelerated, will not proceed with that rapidity which M. Chevalier seems to anticipate." —[Essays in Political Economy, pp. 144–5.] Writing in 1872, Prof. Cairnes used the following language: "The writer can now claim the verdict of events in favor of the view which he here ventured to maintain against that taken by M. Chevalier. Indeed, the course of depreciation has been even less affected by the completion of the process of substituting gold for silver in the currency of France, than he anticipated. That process would seem to have been completed about the year 1861. . . . But he is not aware that any sensible change in the rapidity of the depreciation of gold can be traced to that period. . . . In point of fact, the price of silver has undergone little change over the whole of this period, and is now rather lower than when M. Chevalier wrote. This may be partly due to the increased production of silver in recent years, which would more or less counteract any tendency to an advance in its price; but I have no doubt that the principal cause is that assigned—the extensive substitution of gold for silver, not only in various currencies, in different countries, but in all those uses in which the two metals may be indifferently employed."—[145–6n.] The last sentence of Prof. Cairnes intimates another turn in the course of gold and silver production.

Whereas between 1852 and 1860 the annual yield of gold had ranged from 119 to 182.5 millions of dollars, the yield of silver being estimated at an average for the term of 40.5 millions, the annual yield of silver from 1864 to 1870 rose to about 50 millions, while the range of the gold product was between 113 and 121 millions; and for the period 1871 to 1875, the yield of silver rose from 61 to 71.5 millions, the gold product running down in 1872 to 101.5 millions, in 1874 to 90.5, and in 1875 to 81.5.[1]

It was no more than was to be expected from human nature, that the rapid reversal of the relative amounts of gold and silver yielded by the mines, in consequence of the discovery of the marvelous silver deposits of Nevada, and the continually increasing application of quicksilver in the treatment of silver ores,[2] while the

[1] See a paper on the "Causes of the Depreciation of Silver," by Baron Von Reinach, translated and published in the "Bankers' Magazine" (N. Y.), October, 1876.

[2] Owing to its affinity for other bodies, silver, unlike gold, is rarely found in its native state, but is obtained chiefly from ores. The cost of producing silver is, therefore, at all times greatly dependent on

gold mines of California and Australia were falling rapidly off in their production, should excite a panic such as followed the discoveries of 1848 and 1851, though, this time, it was a prospect of a decline in the value of silver which gave the alarm. The adoption of a single, gold standard by Germany added to the supply of silver pouring into the countries which still maintained the lower metals in coinage at a ratio supposed to approximate their respective market values; and the "Latin Union," constituted under the monetary convention of 1865, and consisting of France, Belgium, Switzerland and Italy,[1] were obliged in 1874 closely to limit their coinage of silver.

Meanwhile the United States had, in 1873, declared the silver dollar to be no longer legal tender in unlimited amount as before. Inasmuch, however, as few silver dollars had been in circulation after 1834 and as neither silver nor gold had been in use as money after the suspension of specie payments in 1862, this action of the United States, though having doubtless its moral effect, could not directly and presently influence the demand for silver.

The present is the general situation: Austria and Russia alone in Europe represent the single silver standard; and even Austria, since 1870, has been coining gold pieces of 8 and 4 florins, severally, in weight and fineness identical with the gold 20 and 10 franc

---

the state of the metallurgical arts and upon the plenty or scarcity with which quicksilver is produced for the processes of amalgamation. In mining gold, on the other hand, the problems are mainly mechanical.

[1] Greece has since acceded to the convention.

pieces; while by a decree of 1873, the gold pieces of the Latin Union are made current throughout the empire.

"Nevertheless," says Prof. Jevons, "the silver standard practically prevails over a large part of the world. The vast populations of India and China, Cochin China, the East Indian islands, portions of Africa and the West Indies, Central America and Mexico, have a currency mainly consisting of silver coins, either rupees, as in India, sycee bars, as in China, or silver dollars, as in many other places."—[Money and the Mechanism of Exchange, p. 148.]

The countries having the single gold standard are Great Britain and Ireland, the Australian colonies and New Zealand, with many of the minor possessions of the British Empire,[1] the German Empire, the Scandinavian Kingdoms, Portugal, Turkey, Egypt, the United States, Chili and Brazil. "Even Japan," says Prof. Jevons, "has imitated European nations, and introduced a gold coinage of 20, 10, 5, 2, and 1 *yen* pieces, the *yen* being only 3 per mille less in value than the American gold dollar. The new fractional money of Japan is to consist of 50, 20, 10 and 5 *sen* pieces in silver (the *sen* corresponding to a cent), and forming a token-money, at the fineness of eight parts in ten."

The double standard is nominally maintained in Europe[2] by France, Italy, Belgium and Switzerland, con-

---

[1] The currency of Canada, says Prof. Jevons, can hardly be classed at all, at present.

[2] Of Holland, Sir Edward Harris writes under date of April 12, 1876: "The whole question of the currency, especially that of the standard to be ultimately adopted in this country, is now under the consideration of the government."—[See Mr. Göschen's Report, p. 128.]

stituting the Latin Union, and by Spain, Greece and Roumania, and in the New World, by Peru, Ecuador and Grenada. Several of these, however, like Austria and Russia of the single silver standard, and the United States, Brazil and Turkey of the single gold standard countries, have at present an irredeemable paper money in circulation, so that they contribute little to the actual demand for either or both metals.

Upon a review of the situation thus disclosed, Prof. Jevons, whom I cite especially because he has been conspicuously fair towards the Bi-metallists, as they, indeed, recognize him to be,[1] concludes that the tendency towards the adoption of gold as the sole principal medium of exchange, is unmistakable.

"The gold standard has thus made great progress, and it will probably continue to progress. When the United States return to specie payments, they will certainly adopt gold; and Canada, whose currency can hardly be classed at all at present, must do the same. The Latin nations, having once abandoned the double standard, in practice, are not likely to return to it; and Austria must follow. An extensive monetary change is hardly to be expected in Russia. . . .

"Hence we arrive, it seems to me, at a broad, deep distinction. The highly civilized and advancing nations of Western Europe and North America, including, also, the rising states of Australasia, and some of the better second-rate states, such as Egypt, Brazil and Japan, will all have the gold standard. The silver standard, on the other hand, will probably long be maintained

[1] M. Wolowski writes: "On peut comparer la réserve et le ton dont il use quand il parle d'une question hérisée de graves difficultés avec le dogmatisme tranchant qui s'étale trop souvent chez nous."—[L'Or et L'Argent, p. 64.]

throughout the Russian Empire, and most parts of the vast continent of Asia; also in some parts of Africa and possibly in Mexico.

"Excluding, however, these minor and doubtful cases, Asia and Russia seem likely to uphold silver against the rest of the world adopting gold. In such a result there seems to be nothing to regret."

Prof. Jevons arrives thus at the conclusion that the double standard will be universally abandoned, and that the nations will divide as gold standard or silver standard nations,[1] the former comprising, perhaps we might say, those countries where a day's labor will purchase from ten grains upward of fine gold.

But on the other hand, we see going on all around us an active agitation for the remonetization of silver in the United States; while abroad, some of the ablest economists of France and Germany are writing actively in favor of the double standard, maintaining their cause with vigor and courage. The question is, therefore, not yet settled by general consent; and the policy of a double standard evidently has more vitality than two years ago was accorded it,[2] after the reverses it had suffered in Germany and the United States. The victory of the Mono-metallists had been largely through sur-

[1] "On ne voit douc pas de raison pour que, systématiquement, tous les peuples civilisés se mettent à répudier l'un des deux métaux précieux, et à réserver absolument l'attribution monétaire pour l'autre. Les diverses nations, ou pour mieux dire, *les différents groupes d'états*, pourront être conduits, par des raisons qui leur seront propres, les uns à préférer l'or, les autres à préférer l'argent."—[M. Chevalier, La Monnaie, p. 171.]

[2] "La question du double étalon est revenue. . . . A ma grande surprise, je l'ai vu renaître, plus vivace que jamais."—[Th. Mannequin, La Monnaie et Le Double Étalon.]

prise[1] and the uncertainty of their conquest brings to mind the wise words of Bacon: "Things will have their first or second agitation; if they be not tossed upon the arguments of counsel, they will be tossed upon the waves of fortune; and be full of inconstancy, doing and undoing, like the reeling of a drunken man."

---

[1] Especially in the United States. There is no evidence in support of the charge made by some Bi-metallists, that the legislation of 1873, demonetizing silver, was obtained by a parliamentary trick, or was inspired by sinister motives; but it certainly was not preceded by that thorough discussion, or accomplished with that general consent of the popular intelligence and will, which are desirable when changes in fundamental policy are to be made in a free country.

## CHAPTER XIII.

### "THE BATTLE OF THE STANDARDS."

THE question of a Single or Double Standard is really, like the question of Protection or of a National Bank, largely a political question. It is discussed as such, and I believe is likely to be decided as such, and that, too, in the way intimated by Prof. Jevons. I can entertain no doubt that the action of Germany in rejecting silver was largely influenced by political considerations on the part of her statesmen, and was rendered more acceptable to her people by the animosity felt towards France at the close of a desperate war. On the other hand, the very phrase, Latin Union, testifies to the strength of ethnical affinities[1] operating upon governments and people, in inducing concerted action in matters of monetary standards and coinage.

I cannot but think that the failure to distinguish between the political and the purely economical considerations which are concerned with this question, has been the cause of not a little of the confusion which has arisen in the discussion, as well as of the acerbity, one might almost say animosity, with which that discussion has been carried on. The examination of any question

---

[1] Herr Bamberger asserts that nothing prevents the other states of the Union from breaking away but a feeling of political dependence on France.

that has both political and economical bearings, is liable to degenerate in this way.

Confining ourselves wholly to the economical aspects of the question, and discharging ourselves, as far as we may, of all prepossessions on the subject, let us inquire what of economical truth there is in the position of the Bi-metallists. As the first step, we need to ask what determines the comparative purchasing power, and, through that, the terms of mutual exchange, of gold and silver: the price of silver in gold; the price of gold in silver.[1]

A notion sometimes coming to the surface in discussion is, that the ratio of values follows the ratio of quantities; that gold is, say, 15½ times as valuable as silver, because there are 15½ times as much silver as gold. This notion is cleverly hit-off by Adam Smith:

"The proportion between the quantities of gold and silver annually imported into Europe, according to Mr. Meggens's account, is as 1:22 nearly. . . . . . The great quantity of silver sent annually to the East Indies reduces, he supposes, the quantities of those metals which remain in Europe to the proportion of 1:14 or 15, the proportion of their values. The proportion between their values must necessarily, he seems to think, be the same as that between their quantities, and would therefore be as 1:22, were it not for this greater exportation of silver.

"But the ordinary proportion between the respective values of two commodities is not necessarily the same as that between the quantities of them which are commonly in the market.[2] The price of an ox, reckoned at

---

[1] See pp. 229–30.

[2] Dr. Smith goes on to remark that "the whole quantity of a cheap commodity brought to market is commonly not only greater, but

10 guineas, is about three-score times the price of a lamb, reckoned at 3*s.* 6*d.* It would be absurd, however, to infer from thence, that there are commonly in the markets three-score lambs for one ox."—[Wealth of Nations, i, 222.]

But, again it is said, it is the cost of production which determines value. This is the usual form of statement. If gold is to silver in value as $15\frac{1}{2} : 1$, we are carried at once to the conclusion that it costs $15\frac{1}{2}$ times as much to bring an ounce of gold to market, as to bring an ounce of silver.

But it is always and everywhere the relation of supply to demand that determines value. Cost of production only affects value by affecting the actual or potential supply. A lower cost of production allows, under given conditions, a larger supply to be marketed. A higher cost of production diminishes supply. This is the only way in which a change in the cost of production can influence existing values. In the act of exchange, it does not matter what a thing cost; the one question is, what would it cost to replace it. "Labor once spent," says Prof. Jevons, "has no influence on the future value of any article."—[Theory of Pol. Econ., p. 159.] This principle, which is of great consequence in respect to any commodity which is brought to market, is of exceptional importance in respect to the metals, especially silver and gold, and in a pre-eminent degree the latter, because of the fact, so often made use of, that the amount of any year's production must always bear a very small proportion to the total stock.

---

of greater value, than the whole quantity of a dear one. . . . There are so many more purchasers for the cheap than for the dear commodity, that not only a greater quantity of it, but a greater value, can commonly be disposed of."

But while the above holds true respecting the value of all commodities, the value of money is, in one respect, subject to a law of its own.

"The value of other things conforms," says Mr. Mill, "to the changes in the cost of production, without requiring as a condition that there should be any actual alteration of the supply: the potential alteration is sufficient; and, if there even be an actual alteration, it is but a temporary one, except in so far as the altered value may make a difference in the demand, and so require an increase or diminution of supply, as a consequence, not a cause, of the alteration in value. Now this is also true of gold and silver, considered as articles of expenditure for ornament and luxury; but it is not true of money.

"If the cost of production of gold were reduced one-fourth by the discovery of more fertile mines, it *might* happen that there would not be more of it bought for plate, gilding, or jewelry than before; and if so, though the value would fall, the quantity extracted from the mines for these purposes would be no greater than previously. Not so with the portion used as money: that portion could not fall in value one-fourth, unless actually increased one-fourth; for, at prices one-fourth higher, one-fourth more money would be required to make the accustomed purchases; and, if this were not forthcoming, some of the commodities would be without purchasers, and prices could not be kept up.

"Alterations, therefore, in the cost of production of the precious metals do not act upon the value of money except just in proportion as they increase or diminish its quantity, which cannot be said of any other commodity." —[J. S. Mill, Principles of Political Economy, III, ix, 3.]

One or two illustrations will show the importance of these principles in their application to the value of money. Suppose the cost of producing silver to rise suddenly, through the exhaustion of the better mines, from five shillings per oz. to twenty shillings. Silver would not, therefore, be worth twenty shillings. On the contrary, we should have the phenomenon noted by Mr. Jacob[1] respecting the period 480 to 680 A.D.: production would cease entirely, and, for the moment, silver would remain at five shillings. From year to year, however, the stock would be diminished by the wear of coin, by accidental loss, and by the consumption of the metal in the arts, so that, were the demand to remain the same, the value would slowly and steadily rise, as was the case from the fifth to the thirteenth century. The demand, however, probably would not remain the same. In spite of an increasing economy in the use of money, the growth of population and the extension of trade would doubtless afford continually larger occasions for the use of money; and by this increase of demand the value of silver would still further rise. Such a process might continue through centuries, the value of silver having no respect at any time to either the original cost of the production of the existing volume (say, five shillings per oz.), or to the cost of reproduction (say, twenty shillings), but steadily rising from five shillings towards twenty shillings, as the varying relation of supply to demand determined. We have seen that such a practical cessation of silver mining, leading to the progressive enhancement of the value of silver, through demand operating on a stock of metal cut off from all new supply but subject to unremitting wear and loss, has actually occurred in the history of Europe.

On the other hand, if we suppose the cost of produc-

---

[1] See p. 129.

tion to fall suddenly from five shillings per oz., to two, the value of silver would not in consequence fall to that point. Indeed, for the moment, it might stand at the old figures, as Mr. Mill has shown. A lower cost of production would of course encourage mining, would draw large bodies of labor and capital into this branch of industry, and the yield might in a few years be doubled, trebled or quadrupled; yet, owing to the large stock in existence, the stimulus afforded by the most extravagant profits could not for many years reduce the value of silver to a point corresponding to the cost of production.

The bearing of this principle on the question of the relative values of gold and silver is clearly seen. The question is often discussed, as if the value of either metal depended directly on the cost of production at the time; and, as it is evident that the cost of production must vary from a thousand circumstances, it is concluded that the value of each must fluctuate correspondingly, as to frequency and extent of movement. We have seen, however, that the influence of changes in the cost of production upon the value of money is indirect and distant, giving thus, not only a great steadiness to the value of either metal used as money, when compared with the body of commodities in the market, but also, by consequence, a great degree of permanence to the ratio between the metals themselves.

But, again, a certain additional degree of steadiness is given to the relation of the two metals by the fact that they are, in a considerable degree, interchangeable in their uses, both as money and in the arts.

"If," says Prof. Cairnes, "anything unfits one commodity for measuring the value of another, it is the circumstance that they may be both applied to common purposes. No one would think of measuring the fluctuations in wheat by comparing it with oats, because, both grains being employed for the same or similar purposes, any change in the value of one is sure to extend to the other. When, *e. g.*, the wheat crop is in excess, while the oat crop is an average one, it always happens that a portion of the consumption which, in ordinary years, falls upon oats, is thrown upon wheat;[1] the effect of which is at once to check the fall in the price of the more abundant grain, while, by diminishing the need for the other, it causes it to participate in the decline. The influence of the increased abundance of one commodity is thus distributed over both; the fall in price being less intense in degree, in proportion as it is wider in extent. Now this is precisely what is happening [1860] in the relations of gold and silver. The crop of gold has been unusually large; the increase in the supply has caused a fall in its value; the fall in its value has led to its being substituted for silver; a mass of silver has thus been disengaged from purposes which it was formerly employed to serve; and the result has been that both metals have fallen in value together, the depth of the fall being diminished as the surface over which it has taken place has been enlarged."—[Essays in Pol. Econ., p. 141.]

This interchangeability in the use of the two metals

[1] Mr. Tooke takes note of the great consumption of barley in 1838, involving a marked increase of price, in consequence of the short crop of wheat. There is, he says, no doubt that in the course of that year a great deal of barley, which would otherwise have been used for malting and distilling, was manufactured into flour, entering largely into consumption as bread.—[Hist. Prices, iii, 19.]

tells so strongly against the position of the Mono-metallists that we find them naturally, and doubtless in perfect candor, taking a rather disparaging view of the extent to which interchangeability, in fact, exists. Thus M. Chevalier, who admits[1] the principle involved, holds the relation of the two metals in consumption to be much less intimate than Prof. Cairnes regards them. Prof. Cairnes compares their relation to that between two different kinds of breadstuff, M. Chevalier making it no more intimate than that between bread and meat.

"The value of gold and that of silver depends, in fact, to a large extent upon circumstances peculiar to each of them, they being identical in this respect with iron or copper, bread or meat. It would doubtless be an exaggeration to say that they are absolutely independent of each other, for whenever two substances have a common use, the value of one exercises a certain influence upon that of the other; but between gold and silver this relation is not closer than that between corn and wine or between bread and meat. Now, who has ever maintained that so close a connection exists between these two products that, the price of one being given, that of the other can thereby be determined?"—[On Gold, Cobden's translation, p. 38.]

But while there may be dispute as to the degree in which one of the metals, gold and silver, is, in fact, replaced by the other, in consequence of changes in cost of production, there can be none as to the effect of such replacement, so far as it proceeds, upon the relative values of the two. In his "Theory of Political Economy," Prof. Jevons, under the title "The Equivalence of

[1] "Sans doute l'or et l'argent sont, dans une certaine mesure, solidaires et réagissent à ce titre l'un sur l'autre, à cause de l'emploi simultané qu'on en fait pour le monnayage."—[La Monnaie, p. 458.]

Commodities," says: "We must, in fact, treat beef and mutton as one commodity of two different strengths, just as gold at eighteen and twenty carats is hardly considered as two, but as one commodity, of which twenty parts of one are equivalent to eighteen of the other.

"It is upon this principle," he continues, "that we must explain, in harmony with Prof. Cairnes's view, the extraordinary permanence of the ratio of exchange of gold and silver. . . . That this fixedness of ratio does not depend upon the amount or cost of production, is proved by the very slight effect of the Australian and Californian gold discoveries. . . .

"The French currency law of the year XI [1803] establishes an artificial equation—utility of gold $= 15\frac{1}{2} \times$ utility of silver. It is probably not without some reason that M. Wolowski and other recent French economists attributed to this law of replacement an important effect in preventing disturbance in the relations of gold and silver."—[P. 129.]

We have now reached the point where we may appropriately consider Prof. Rogers's explanation of the great rise in the value of gold between 1262 and 1292 A. D.,[1] a rise which, standing by itself, appears a striking instance of the variability of the ratio between gold and silver; but for which the historian of English agriculture and prices alleges a cause which makes the incident tell strongly in favor of the position of the Bimetallists.

It will be recollected that Prof. Rogers found that in 1262 gold exchanged for silver at $9\frac{3}{5}$ for 1; and in 1292, at 12.5 for 1, in value, for equal weights.

"Such a discrepancy between the value of gold in the

---

[1] See p. 230.

two quotations, after an interval of only thirty years, is sufficiently surprising, and cannot, I think, be explained except by an increased adoption of gold on the Continent as a means of currency; for it will be clear that, just as a very great fall would take place in the value of existing stocks of gold, were this metal absolutely demonetized, so, *e converso*, a considerable rise would occur in its comparative value, if, in the economical history of any community, or rather of a large number of communities, gold were increasingly adopted as a measure of value and a means for carrying on commerce.

"I cannot," continues Prof. Rogers, "agree with the opinion[1] expressed by some economists, that the market value of gold will always be relative to its demand in the arts, unless, indeed, the term be extended so as to include the art of the moneyer. The price of gold must be relative to the aggregate of all demands for it, corrected by the cost of producing it. . . . Now, it appears that, at or about the conclusion of the thirteenth century, gold currencies became general in Italy. The Venetians, we are informed, coined gold ducats in the year 1285, and it is said that the weight and shape of these ducats were copied in Germany and Hungary. It appears, too, that the reputation of the gold coinage of Brescia and Florence commenced at about 1270 and 1290, respectively, and that it extended over all Italy, and even to the whole civilized world, in the next century. This extension of a gold currency was, no doubt, furthered by the migration of the Pope to Avignon, for the currency of the Curia is entirely gold. These causes, and the fact that France issued a gold currency as early, we are told, as the reign of St. Louis, are sufficient to

[1] The allusion is to Prof. Senior's view, cited on p. 43.

explain the rise in the relative value of gold to silver at the conclusion of the thirteenth century."

Of the further rise of gold (about 10 per cent.) between 1292 and 1345, Prof. Rogers remarks that it is "a rise which might occur as a consequence of the increased circulation of gold as a means of currency. Now, according to Muratori, it was in the first forty years of the fourteenth century that this gold currency was so generally extended."

The power thus shown to reside in fashion or law to affect the value of one of the metals, without reference to any change in the cost of production, by giving to it an increased use in coinage, tells, of course, in favor of the claims of the Bi-metallists; as does the unprecedentedly rapid decline of silver, after it was thrown out of its office as unlimited legal tender in Germany during the present decade.

Yet, in spite of the tendencies which have been noted towards keeping steady the demand and the supply of gold and silver, we have seen the fact of fluctuations in value from generation to generation, and even from year to year, sufficient to send now one, and now another, of the two metals out of circulation, in countries which, like France down to the present time, and the United States to 1873, and England to 1816, attempt to keep both in circulation at a fixed ratio of exchange. For purposes of economical reasoning we may assume all men to be actuated by the desire to make purchases or payments, whenever a chance is offered, with that commodity which it will cost the least effort and sacrifice to replace. What has the Bi-metallist to say to this?

The answer is that of the late M. Wolowski, the most

able and ingenious of the school of writers who advocate a concurrent circulation. Gold and silver have not, either in the mass or singly, preserved their value from age to age, or from year to year. The value of a pound of gold relatively to that of a pound of silver, has varied from time to time; as the value of a pound of gold and a pound of silver jointly to purchase commodities has varied. Such variations in purchasing power are in the very nature of exchange. Absolute steadiness in value cannot be attained. But to unite gold and silver in the office of money is to generate a compensatory action which shall not only tend to reduce the variations in their mutual relation, but shall give to the two, as a mass, a steadiness in comparison with the general body of commodities which neither[1] by itself could have. It is in this way that the Bi-metallist accounts for the remarkable fact that in several centuries down to 1873, gold and silver never diverged

[1] It has been somewhat hotly disputed whether gold or silver has, from the circumstances of its production, the greater likelihood of remaining constant in value. The Mono-metallists now strenuously claim this advantage for gold on account of its slow consumption; the Bi-metallists allege the production of silver to be the more stable, making much of the fact that gold is found largely in surface placers and accidental deposits, while silver is found in veins, and procured by systematic mining operations. On this point the admission of M. Chevalier, the foremost champion of the single standard must be regarded as important: "La plus grande fixité qu'il était assez à la mode, pendant le premier quart du dix-neuvième siècle, de représenter comme étant l'attribut spécial de' l'or, est éminemment problématique et on peut la considérer comme une fiction. On n'aperçoit aucune bonne raison pour affirmer que les circonstances, qui de temps en temps agissent sur la valeur des métaux pour la modifier, soient de nature à affecter l'un beaucoup plus que l'autre."—[La Monnaie, p. 171.]

far from the ratio of 15 : 1, even the Australian and Californian discoveries raising the gold price of silver less than five per cent., the permanent effect not exceeding one and a half per cent.

This claim of a compensatory, or equilibratory, action under the double standard, Prof. Jevons fully concedes.[1] "If silver," he says, "becomes more valuable than in the ratio of 1 : 15½ compared with gold, there arises at once a tendency to import gold into any country possessing the double standard, so that it may be coined there and exchanged for a legally equivalent weight of silver coin, to be exported again. This is not a matter of theory only, the process having gone on in France until the principal currency, which was mainly composed of silver in 1849, was, in 1860, almost wholly of gold. France absorbed the cheapened metal in vast quantities, and emitted the dearer metal, which must have had the effect of preventing gold from falling and silver from rising so much in value as they would otherwise have done. It is obvious that, if gold rose in value compared with silver, the action would be reversed; gold would be absorbed and silver liberated. At any moment the standard of value is doubtless one metal or the other, and not both; yet the fact that there is an alternation tends to make each vary much less than it would otherwise do. It cannot prevent both metals falling or rising in value compared with other commodities; but it can throw variations of supply and demand over a larger area, instead of leaving each metal to be affected merely by its own accidents.

"Imagine two reservoirs of water, each subject to in-

---

[1] M. Mannequin, in his tract "La Monnaie et le Double Étalon" (pp. 11–3), undertakes to demonstrate the futility of the compensatory action adduced by M. Wolowski.

dependent variations of supply and demand. In the absence of any connecting pipe, the level of the water in each reservoir will be subject to its own fluctuations only. But if we open a connection, the water in both will assume a certain mean level, and the effects of any excessive supply or demand will be distributed over the whole area of both reservoirs. The mass of the metals, gold and silver, circulating in Western Europe in late years, is exactly represented by the water in these reservoirs; and the connecting pipe is the law of the 7th Germinal, An XI, which enables one metal to take the place of the other as an unlimited legal tender."—[Money and the Mech. of Exch., pp. 139–40.]

"The German Economists," says M. Laveleye,[1] "have generally recognized the compensatory action of bi-metallic money, even those who are the partisans of the gold standard. We may, I think," he concludes, "consider it as demonstrated that money of two metals is less subject to fluctuations in value, within short intervals; and consequently, entails fewer changes of price, than money composed of one metal only, for precisely the same reason that a compensated pendulum made of steel and copper, is less subject to expansion than if it were made of a single metal."

And here we note that whatever may be decided respecting the comparative advantages of a standard, wholly and permanently of money of one metal, and an alternative standard, now of gold and now of silver, according to variations in value, M. Chevalier[2] and the

---

[1] Article translated by Hon. George Walker, and published in the N. Y. "Banker's Magazine," March, 1877.

[2] "Mais si les deux métaux sont étalons, il y aura double chance à courir, car aux variations de l'un, il faut ajouter les variations de l'autre."—[M. Chevalier, Procès-verbaux de la Commission Monétaire de 1867.]

English economists generally, are clearly wrong in asserting that the French system exposes the commercial community to the extreme fluctuations of both metals. On the contrary, it is manifest that, instead of prices following the extreme fluctuations of both metals, prices will always be governed by the course of that metal which, at the time, sinks below the legal ratio. The standard, as Prof. Jevons remarks, always follows the metal that falls.

Hence, as M. Wolowski[1] insists, the variations of value under the alternative standard are more frequent, perhaps, but are necessarily reduced in extent; instead of violent fluctuations, we have gentle oscillations about a fixed line. On this point M. Wolowski has the complete concurrence of Prof. Jevons in England and of the Germans Roscher and Rau. But some of the advocates of bi-metallic money go even further, and claim that it is practicable, by a convention of the principal commercial nations on the plan of the Latin Union, to establish a legal ratio between gold and silver which shall

---

[1] "On prétend que les changements sont plus grands quand on emploie deux métaux pour monnaie, au lieu d'un, car, dit-on, on subit alors les variations des deux métaux. On oublie que *ces variations, au lieu de s'ajouter et de grossir en se cumulant, se modèrent, au contraire, et se compensent.* Ce qui serait plus vrai, ce serait de dire qu'avec des deux métaux les variations peuvent être plus fréquentes, mais qu'elles se trouvent forcément beaucoup plus faibles, en se rapprochant d'une stabilité parfaite, autant que la possibilité matérielle le permet tandis qu'avec un seul métal, les *écarts* deviendraient peut-être un peu plus rares, mais ils se produiraient d'une façon plus vive, en risquant d'altérer l'expression des transactions conclues pour un terme quelque peu éloigné. La *stabilité* des engagement ne pourrait qu'y perdre."—[M. Wolowski, L'Or et L'Argent, p. 49.]

have absolute stability, the two[1] metals forming what M. Cernuschi calls electron, and both thus remaining in circulation at the same time within the same field.

The following is M. Cernuschi's theory stated in his own words:

"The abundant metal is the least demanded. Its tendency is to be depreciated, while the scarcer metal becomes dearer. But it is evident that, if to increased production we can continue to oppose increased demand, and to decreased production, decreased demand, we shall maintain the equilibrium and things will remain unchanged. This is precisely what we propose to do. For the demand, which, without the adoption of the tariff of 15½ would be directed to the metal which is scarce, would, if the tariff were anywhere in force, be directed to the metal that is abundant. For, if the bimetallic law permits each and every one to pay his debts at will, in gold or silver, every one must see that the dealers in money will neglect the metal which is hard to find, and will seek for that which is plentiful, to have it coined. Moreover the scarce metal, if it is not in demand, will not rise in price, and the abundant metal, if active demand springs up, cannot fall."—[Banker's Magazine, N. Y., Nov., 1876.]

M. Cernuschi has advocated his theory with abundance of wit and ingenuity; but it may fairly be questioned whether he has not, on the whole, prejudiced it in public estimation by the extent of his claim for the power of law over value.

---

[1] If two, why not ten? Sure enough: M. Cernuschi is nothing daunted by the suggestion. Find him the metals and he will engage to put them at work, harnessed together at ratios fixed by law: "Que n'avous-nous la fortune de posséder *dix* métaux monétaires! Les variations dans la valeur de la monnaie seraient presque impossibles."—[Or et Argent, p. 60.]

Economists have been too much disposed to treat slightingly the agency of law in determining the demand for, or the supply of, articles of commerce. Thus, Mr. Ricardo almost invariably refers to laws prohibiting the melting down of coin, or the export of bullion, as if they were absolutely nugatory. Mr. Mill, however, finds himself compelled to say: "The effects of the prohibition cannot have been so entirely insignificant as it has been supposed to be by writers on the subject. The facts adduced by Mr. Fullarton show that it required a greater percentage of difference in the value between coin and bullion than has commonly been imagined, to bring the coin to the melting-pot."

But while law can do something, in the way of affecting values, it cannot do everything; and what it can do is rather by way of directing or diverting economic forces, than of squarely opposing their current. The impotence of government when it sets itself to controvert urgent human interests, has been clearly shown in innumerable instances. We shall soon be called to contemplate the strongest governments the world has ever known, completely baffled in their efforts to give currency to their legal-tender notes, when issued greatly in excess, no brutality of punishment proving sufficient to deter the subject in the pursuit of gain from evading, or, if he must, defying, the requirements of the law.

Hence, when the bi-metallist claims for the law force enough to establish any permanent ratio of exchange, whatever, between gold and silver, were it 4:1 or 1:1, he exposes his cause to unnecessary prejudice.

The Austrian economist, Hertzka, thus attacks this position, using M. Cernuschi's name:

"Whether now Cernuschi believes that it costs, and

must always cost, just fifteen and a half times as much to produce gold as to produce silver, or not, we cannot determine. At any rate, he knows that for the cost of producing one pound of gold, several pounds of silver can be produced. What happens then, when the law decrees that one pound of gold shall exchange for one pound of silver? Cernuschi understands perfectly that the value of the circulating medium depends on the demands of business and the amount of money. He knows and makes use of the fact in arguing for his electron, that if the demands of business remain the same, the purchasing power of the stock of money in the country, or in the world, remains the same. He knows, therefore, that the ten thousand million dollars stock of the precious metals in the western world must possess the same purchasing power as now, if the ratio of value between the two metals which constitute it were altered. Now this ten thousand million dollars stock of the precious metals is made up of seventeen million pounds of gold for two-thirds of the value, and one hundred and eighty million pounds silver for one-third of the value. Hereafter, therefore, if the bi-metallic electron were made out of this stock there would be one hundred and ninty-seven million pounds of it, worth just what the whole is now; that is, each pound of it would be worth fifty dollars. Bringing the two metals to an equality of value, therefore (ratio 1:1), would have the effect of more than doubling the value of silver, and reducing gold to less than one-seventh the value which it now has on the market. What would be the effect on production? The silver miners would see their returns more than doubled. Mines which formerly did not pay, would now pay richly. New capital would flow into silver mining, and it would only depend on the extent of the known mines and the amount of disposable capital whether the silver product would rise to four hundred, five hundred, two thousand or three thousand million dollars per annum. The contrary effect would be felt upon gold. Since it is not possible to support seven laborers with the product which one laborer now gets from a gold mine, the gold mines would be abandoned, and the production of gold would cease entirely, unless there might be some mines so rich that one-seventh of their present yield would be remunerative to the labor and capital they employ.

"Inasmuch as there are now one hundred and eighty million pounds of silver and seventeen million pounds of gold, that is to say, gold is far rarer than silver, we cannot assume that mankind will at once esteem gold and silver in every respect equal because a law of bimetalism may so ordain. There will probably still be human beings who will prefer rings, bracelets, chains and vessels of gold more highly than similar objects of silver. As things are now, people put up with silver for many purposes because gold is so much dearer. When bi-metalism establishes equality between the two metals, many people will carry all their silver plate to the mint and have all their articles of luxury made of gold obtained for it, ounce for ounce. We must doubt whether the seventeen million pounds of gold now in the Occident would suffice for this exchange. There are probably fifty million pounds of silver plate in existence, and unless the present taste of the human race could suddenly be changed, people would present a demand for gold, at the rate of 1:1, in order to get gold plate of the same size and weight as their present silver plate without greater cost, which would at once exhaust the whole stock, in coin or other forms. This danger is the greater since the Asiatic peoples, who now possess far more silver than gold, might be tempted by the ratio of 1:1 to exchange their silver ornaments for gold. They would prefer gold, although the Bi-metallists should assure them that it was worth no more than silver. The demand for gold would indeed increase, from the fact above mentioned, that the gold mines would be unworked, while the production of silver would be prosecuted with nearly threefold vigor. Gold is consumed slowly but surely, and there are arts which consume it. Some might therefore fear lest gold should disappear from the earth, and might hasten to buy it with silver. The universal bi-metallic system thus pushed to an extreme could not sustain itself for a day, or an hour, or a second."—[Währung und Handel: chapters translated and published in the "N. Y. Evening Post," 1877.]

The demonstration is complete; but I am not satisfied that Mr. Hertzka and his American translator are on equally firm ground when they argue that the extreme case of 1:1 affords a test of the bi-metallic theory, and that, if it be found to fail here, it would fail on any ratio assumed.

If it is a question of the power of law to hold the metals in concurrent circulation against admitted tendencies to divergence, it cannot be a matter of indifference what the strength of those tendencies shall be. To drive a horse and a locomotive together, would probably result in killing the horse without helping-on the locomotive. But *it does not follow from the failure to produce effective co-operation between agents so diverse, that two horses of somewhat unequal power cannot be harnessed and driven together*, not only without injury to either, but with a distinct gain in industrial force.

There never were two horses of precisely the same rate and style of movement; yet horses are driven in span. The bi-metallic theory proposes to harness two metals of somewhat diverse tendencies value-wards, and to drive them together. The success of the undertaking will probably depend on the strength of the impulse to divergence, as compared with the strength of the carriage, of the harness and of the driver's hand.

Let us take a case: During 1870, the average market ratio of silver to gold was 1:15.57; during 1871, 1:15.58. Now suppose that, while the true market ratio was 1:15.57, this had been established as the legal ratio in the coinage of all civilized nations; and that immediately thereafter, there had begun to operate upon the supply of, or the demand for, one or the other of the metals, the forces, which did, in fact, between 1870 and 1871, bring about the ratio 1:15.58. Would the fact of a fixed legal rating so widely adopted be sufficient to restrain that movement towards a change in the market rating?

I cannot see any reason to say no, when it is considered that, at any given time, debts to the amount of thousands of millions of dollars are outstanding; while debts to the amount of hundreds of millions are arriving at maturity every year and every month. Just so soon and just so surely as silver, for instance, tended to become cheaper, from causes affecting the supply, would the desire of every debtor to pay with the cheaper metal operate upon the demand for that metal, bringing it back towards the legal rating.

Let it be freely granted that value is determined in the relation between demand and supply. The position of the Bi-metallists is that government can influence the demand for gold and silver and hence influence the r value, through its power to make either or both a legal tender in the payment of debts. Only in this way, however, as I apprehend the matter; at least I do not see how the establishment of a fixed legal ratio is to operate against the tendency towards divergence, so far as the body of current purchases are concerned.

When Hertzka's translator, after giving his demonstration of the impossibility of keeping gold and silver in concurrent circulation at a ratio far wide of the market ratio, say 1:1, draws the conclusion that: "In whatever degree the legally fixed ratio should differ from the market ratio, in that degree the results described would follow;" and again: "All this holds true, according to its measure, of any other legal ratio than 1:1, if it were not the true ratio of the market," he overlooks the important principle stated by Mr. Mill, that, in efforts towards certain ends, "small means do not merely produce small effects; they produce no effects at all."

I have assumed, for purposes of illustration, the causes operating to produce a change in the market rate to be slight. Thus, I compared the years 1870 and 1871, when the ratios were respectively 1:15.57 and 1:15.58. It is reasonably certain that in such a condition, the fixing of the former ratio universally, by law, would not have diminished by one ounce the amount of gold brought into existence in 1871; first, because, with capital and labor committed to the production of gold, so slight a reduction in the profits or wages of the occupation would not close a single mine or contract its operations; and secondly, because in a degree the production of silver involves the production of gold,[1] and *vice versa*. But the efficiency

[1] Pliny called attention to the fact that, in his day, gold and silver were invariably found together, though in varying proportions

of such a measure as that proposed would not necessarily be limited to a condition where the causes operating on the supply tended to bring about a divergence so slight as that indicated. It is entirely reasonable to suppose that a tendency to a very considerable divergence, operating through a considerable period of time, might be restrained by the force of law making either metal, indifferently, tender in payment of debts. Even if we are not prepared to assent to Mr. Horton's assertion[1] that "Wolowski's position would stand the shock of a second Siberia, Australia, California, or all combined," we may rationally believe that the consent of the leading commercial nations[2] in establishing a ratio of exchange between gold and silver would operate with sufficient force upon the demand for that which might tend to become the cheaper, to preserve an equality, in spite

"In every species of gold," he said, "there is a proportion of silver; in some one-tenth, in others one-ninth, in others one-eighth."

Many persons speak of the wonderful silver mines of Nevada who are not aware that a very large proportion of the value of the metal extracted is in gold. The production of the Comstock Lode is stated to be about 45 per cent. in gold and 55 per cent. in silver.—[See Report of Mr. Göschen's Committee, Q. 478–88; Chevalier, La Monnaie, pp. 362–4; Seyd's Bullion and Foreign Exchanges, pp. 136–7.]

[1] Silver and Gold, 144.

[2] "En 1803, on a évalué le taux du *prix du change* entre l'or et l'argent dans la proportion de 1 à 15 et demi; malgré les variations énormes de la production des métaux précieux, ce rapport est encore celui qui se pratique sur le marché libre en 1868. Ajoutez à la solidarité naturelle qui unit les deux métaux appelés à se combiner, dans le même office, la solidarité légale qui résultera de l'adoption commune, dans tous les États Civilisés, du même taux de *change* entre les deux monnaies, et les légères oscillations auxquelles la valeur relative de l'or et de l'argent a été sujette depuis soixante-cinq ans, deviendront plus rares and plus restreintes encore."—[M. Wolowski, L'Or et L'Argent, p. 31.]

of the discovery of many new fields of production, in spite of many inventions in the mechanical and metallurgical processes involved in raising the metals and bringing them to market, and in spite of wide and lasting changes in the demand for either metal for use in the industrial and decorative arts.

The extensive fall in the value of silver since 1873, which is often referred to as proving the unfitness of silver to be joined with gold in the office of money, appears to me to show most strikingly the power of legislation in keeping the two metals together. If gold and silver actually held a course through three centuries so nearly parallel; yet, when silver was demonetized by the United States and Germany, and the Latin Union ceased to coin silver in unrestricted amount, the price of gold, expressed in terms of silver, mounted upwards in four years from 15.63 to 17.77, rising momentarily even to 20.17: these two facts taken in connection would seem to afford a very strong proof of the effects of their interchangeable use as money,[1] in keeping their market values together. As Mr. Bagehot said in September, 1876: "The cardinal present novelty is, that silver and gold are, in relation to one another, simply ordinary commod-

---

[1] That the changes in the comparative purchasing power of the two metals between 1873 and 1876 were wholly or mainly due to changes in supply, or to changes in demand disconnected from the acts of governments dealing with the legal relations of gold and silver, I really cannot conceive any intelligent and candid man as now maintaining. That it was so held in perfectly good faith, for a year or two after the demonetization, I do not doubt.

"Qu'on suppose les Français prenant tout à coup le vin en aversion, se portant à admirer les peuples adonnés à la bière et voulant les imiter: il est certain que le vin se déprécièrait et que le prix de la bière s'élèverait." —[H. Cernuschi, Or et Argent, p. 9.]

ities. Until now they have not been so. A very great part of the world adhered to the bi-metallic system, which made both gold and silver legal tender; which established a fixed relation between them. In consequence, whenever the values of the two metals altered, these countries acted as equalizing machines. They took the metal which fell; they sold the metal which rose, and thus the relative value of the two was kept at its old point. But now this curious mechanism is broken up. There is no great country now really acting on this system. The Latin Union, it is true, adhere to the name; but they have abandoned the thing. As they do not allow silver to be coined except in limited quantities, they have no longer an equalizing action. They no longer receive the depreciated, and part with the appreciated, metal; and therefore the two metals are now exchanged for one another, just as other commodities. *The gold price of silver is now like the gold price of tin, for the first time in history, without artificial regulation, and free from the manipulations of government.*"[1]

But while the Bi-metallists assert the concurrent circulation of the two metals to be good as a permanent policy, inasmuch as it limits the extent of the variations in the value of money, they have an argument of perhaps even greater force, one certainly which appeals more strongly to the popular mind, in the consideration that, both metals having been so widely in use under fixed ratios, the disestablishment of silver and its reduction to the rank of mere merchandise must suddenly and largely diminish the supply of money

[1] The Economist, Sept. 2, 1876.

available for the payment of debts and permanent charges of all sorts, private or national, contracted under a money of both metals. We have already, in Chapter IV, dwelt very fully on the economical effects of an increase in the Money-supply, inciting to a temporary activity in production, as well as diminishing the burden of obligations derived from the past, in favor generally of the industrial classes. The object of the Bi-metallists—at least of the European Bi-metallists[1]—is not so much to favor the debtor class by diminishing the weight of debts, as to prevent those debts being artificially increased by a diminution in the stock of money, through the demonetization of one of the precious metals.

"It may be safely asserted," says Mr. Laveleye, "that the demonetization of silver is a great injustice, since it modifies all contracts to the detriment of those whose interests are most worthy to be considered,[2] viz., the debtors."

We have already dwelt so fully on the consequences of a reduction in the Money-supply of the world, that it is only necessary to point out the relation of the subject to the question of the so-called single or double

[1] I say the European Bi-metallists, because it is not to be concealed that the party here is largely re-inforced from the ranks of the inflationists and repudiationists of the political struggles of 1868, 1874, and 1876. It is a misfortune of the present position of those who disinterestedly advocate bi-metalism in the United States, that they have such associates. The fact, however, furnishes no just cause for misrepresenting their views.

[2] "Laveleye is, indeed, right," remarks Hertzka, "so far as he makes the point that the debtors are, in general, the active producers, while the creditors, whether for large or small amounts, are in general passive consumers."—[N. Y. Evening Post's translation.] On this point, see pp. 89–94.

standard. Mr. Seyd estimates[1] that the stock of gold and silver now current as coin, or existing as bullion, is 6,750 millions of dollars, of which 3,250 millions is in silver. Assuming that 700 millions of silver would remain in use after the adoption of the single gold standard by the nations commonly known as civilized, Mr. Seyd reaches the result that the Money-supply would be reduced 38 per cent. by the demonetization of silver. "The total production of both metals," says Mr. Laveleye, "has remained stationary during the past nine years, and in the last two years it has rather declined. Is this, then, the time to prohibit the use of one of these metals?"

It was the argument from the effects of a diminution of the Money-supply which mainly determined the mind of Hamilton, with whom Jefferson and Gallatin concurred, in favor of the concurrent use of the two metals.

"Upon the whole, it seems to be most advisable, as has been observed, not to attach the unit exclusively to either of the metals: because this cannot be done effectually without destroying the office and character of one of them as money, and reducing it to the situation of a mere merchandise. . . . To annul the use of either of the metals as money is to abridge the quantity of circulating medium, and is liable to all the objections which arise from a comparison of the benefits of a full with the evils of a scanty circulation."—[A. Hamilton, Report on the Mint.]

These objections are not of less force than in Mr. Hamilton's day. On the contrary, they have acquired greater importance with the vast extension of imperial,

---

[1] N. Y. Banker's Magazine, April, 1877.

national, state, and municipal indebtedness which has characterized the present century. Whatever makes it harder to pay the war debts of the world, and the obligations contracted for purposes of public display or public convenience, works great injury to all productive interests, discourages enterprise, and breeds pauperism.[1] This is not a consideration to be put out of sight because of the greater convenience and simplicity of operation which the Mono-metallists think they find in the use of gold as the sole money of commerce. I do not say that no considerations could outweigh this increase of the burden of existing debts. I agree with Mr. Horton,[2] that it is a practical question, in which advantages and disadvantages should be fairly balanced; and, that this may be done, it is very desirable that the question should be discussed without excitement or prejudice.

The question is also largely a political one. The concurrence of the Latin Union, Germany, Great Britain and the United States would, I do not question, establish a bi-metallic money on a durable basis, subject to change only in the event of developments of a revolutionary nature, not to be anticipated, in the production of the precious metals. But the very mention of such a condition shows how largely the question is political.

---

[1] "La suppression de l'argent amènerait une revolution véritable. L'or, appelé à régir seule le marché universel, augmenterait de valeur dans une progression rapide et constante, qui porterait atteinte à la foi des contrats, et qui aggraverait la situation de tous les débiteurs, à commencer par l'Etat."—[M. Wolowski, L'Or et L'Argent, p. 29.]

[2] "It is a purely practical question whether substantial unity with bi-metallic money is more for the interest of the world, than mathematical and metrical unity with the adoption of the single gold standard."—[Silver and Gold, p. 143.]

What is the likelihood of Great Britain retracing the course in which she has persisted since 1816? Small as is the likelihood of that being done, I should be disposed to believe it far more probable than that Germany would rescind her recent action, acknowledge before French economists her error, and join her late enemy in a monetary convention to put gold and silver on the basis which Napoleon established. But all these are political considerations which have no place in an economical treatise.

# PART II.

# INCONVERTIBLE PAPER MONEY

## CHAPTER XIV.

### THE THEORY OF INCONVERTIBLE PAPER MONEY.

It has been rather the fashion with political economists to refuse the name Money to any medium of exchange which is not "a material recompense or equivalent."[1] It is, however, fairly to be questioned whether anything is hereby gained in scientific precision, or for the popular understanding of the subject. For myself, I can see no valid objection to the scientific acceptance of the popular term, Paper Money. The presence of the word paper so far qualifies and explains the word money,[2] as to show that a material recompense or equivalent is not meant. No one is likely to be misled by the use of the term; nor am I confident that this use of the term does not conform to the highest conception of the Money-function. Certainly, the word Currency has proved a most disastrous substitute, inducing infinite

[1] "La monnaie n'est donc point un signe; c'est un corps, une substance précieuse; je ne saurais trop le redire, c'est, en même temps, une mesure commune des valeurs, et un équivalent."—[M. Chevalier, La Monnaie, p. 56.] "Cet attribut d'équivalent est essentiel à la monnaie."—[*Ibid.*]

[2] Whether we should speak of anything which is not a material recompense or equivalent, as Money, without the qualifying word, paper, is a question which we can best discuss when we come to speak of convertible paper money, *i. e.*, bank-notes.

confusion and contradiction. By the word Inconvertible, in this connection, is meant that the paper, whatever it promises and however it is guaranteed, is not, in fact, whatever be the fiction of law, subject to conversion, on the demand of the holder, into metallic money.

While some political economists, as has been said, deny the propriety of applying, with or without qualification, the word money to any medium of exchange which is not a material recompense or equivalent, others admit the use of the word as applied to paper resting upon authority, that is, to the issues of government, but not as applied to paper resting upon confidence, that is, to the issues of banks. The distinction is thus expressed by Mr. Huskisson: "Paper resting upon confidence is what I have described as circulating credit, and consists in engagements for the payment on demand of any specific sums of money, which engagements, from a general trust in the issuers of such paper, they are enabled to substitute for money in the transactions of the community. Paper resting upon authority[1] is what, in common language, is called paper money, and consists in engagements issued and circulated under the sanction and by the intermediate intervention of the public power of the state. Paper, such as alone used to be current in Great Britain before the restriction on the Bank, was strictly circulating credit. The paper current in Austria, Russia, etc., is properly denominated paper money." —[Depreciation of the Currency, p. 3.]

Inconvertible Paper Money is often discussed as if it

---

[1] Prof. Storch makes the same distinction: "On reserve le nom de papier-monnaie à des billets que le souverain ordonne de recevoir en payement à la place du numéraire métallique."

*Billets de banque*, Prof. Storch characterizes as *billets de confiance*.

resulted from a degeneration of convertible paper money. But this has not been the case historically in the greater number of instances where Inconvertible Paper Money has come into existence. It appears to me, moreover, that we get a much better view of the nature and operations of such money by taking up the inquiry close upon our analysis of the effects of seigniorage upon price.[1]

Several expressions of Mr. Ricardo have already been quoted to the effect that a bank-note may be regarded as a coin upon which the seigniorage is enormous, extending to its whole nominal amount. While some exception might possibly be taken to this statement regarding a bank-note,[2] there can be none to its application to government paper. We said that, by Mr. Ricardo's reasoning, a seigniorage of 10 per cent., or even of 50 per cent., on coin would not alter the purchasing power of each piece, provided only the pieces were not supplied in excess of the amount of money of full value which would circulate as the community's distributive share of the world's stock of money.

No more, if we suppose the seigniorage to be carried out to 100 per cent., and instead of debased coin, pieces of paper to be issued, costing so little in their production that, for purposes of economical reasoning, we may say they cost nothing, would the purchasing power of each piece be diminished, provided the pieces were not issued in excess. Upon this point there is substantial unity among economists.[3]

---

[1] See pp. 190–7.

[2] Because of the reserves of coin necessary to keep up a bank-note circulation, which must, in any philosophical view be regarded as entering into *the cost* of the bank-notes so circulated.

[3] Mr. Tooke states that depreciation is not a necessary consequence of inconvertibility.

"It is on this principle," says Mr. Ricardo, "that paper money circulates. The whole charge for paper money may be considered as seigniorage. Though it has no intrinsic value, yet by limiting its quantity its value in exchange is as great as an equal denomination of coin, or of bullion in that coin. . . . On these principles it will be seen that it is not necessary that paper money should be payable in specie to secure its value: it is only necessary that its quantity should be regulated according to the value of the metal which is declared to be the standard. If the standard were gold of a given weight and fineness, paper might be increased with every fall in the value of gold, or, which is the same thing in its effects, with every rise in the price of goods.

"Dr. Smith," he continues, "appears to have forgotten his own principle in his argument on Colony Currency.[1]

---

Mr. James Wilson remarks that if inconvertible paper be kept somewhat below the amount of the currency required, "there is no reason whatever why such notes should suffer depreciation."—[Capital, Currency and Banking, p. 42.]

"Experience," says Prof. Price, "has proved that it need not of necessity suffer any depreciation of value."—[Principles of Currency, p. 156.]

"La valeur de ce papier, résultant uniquement de l'usage auquel il sert, est limitée par cet usage même. Si les émissions etaient médiocres, le papier-monnaie pourrait valoir autant que la monnaie métallique."—[M. Courcelle-Seneuil, Opérations de Banque, p. 370.]

[1] Prof. Sumner appears to have followed Dr. Smith in his criticism of the notes of the Land Bank of Massachusetts. "A note for $1 payable twenty years hence in gold, without interest, when interest is 3 per cent., is worth 55 cents; or, if interest is 6 per cent., 31 cents."—[Hist. Am. Currency, p. 29.] This is to look on these notes as an investment, and not as, what they were intended to be, money circulating from hand to hand. In the same vein, Mr. Horton says of the greenbacks, "Present payment in silver is more desirable than future payment in gold."—[Silver and Gold, p. 61.] That does not appear. Indeed, the market quotations contradict the statement.

Instead of ascribing the depreciation of that paper to its too great abundance, he asks whether, allowing the colony security to be perfectly good, a hundred pounds, payable fifteen years hence, would be equally valuable with a hundred pounds to be paid immediately. I answer yes, if it be not too abundant."—[Pol. Econ.]

This statement needs, however, to be carefully guarded by the proviso which was offered [1] in respect to a debased coinage, viz., that the popular distrust or dislike of the money be not excited [2] to the extent of driving the people down to barter, in which case an amount of money, whether of paper or of debased coin, not in excess of the amount of a money of full value which would freely circulate, may become redundant, whereupon depreciation will follow.

This proviso, which is often wholly neglected [3] in discussions respecting Inconvertible Paper Money, is of capital importance.

It has been said that historically we do not find that Inconvertible Paper Money has usually originated in a degeneration of paper money which was once convertible. We may have occasion to note instances of the latter kind when we come to speak of convertible paper

---

[1] See pp. 197–204.

[2] This is not at all a matter of course. "Discredit," says Mr. Tooke, "is not an essential element in variations of the value of an inconvertible paper."—[History of Prices, 1839–47, 177.]

[3] Thus Prof. Price writes: "The public has a certain *definite* want for notes to use in the daily operations of buying and selling" [Principles of Currency, p. 156.]; and in the immediate connection adds: "It is plain that the prohibition to pay the notes can make no difference in the extent of the use which exists for the notes; so far as this reaches, it is immaterial whether the notes will, or will not, be paid on demand."—[P. 157.]

money [Part III]; but for the present let us consider only those in which governments, generally to meet the exigencies of state, most frequently in war, but also, in not a few instances, for purposes of peaceful expenditure, and sometimes with the avowed object of furnishing a plentiful and cheap medium of exchange, have put forth paper money, having the quality of legal tender in payment of debts between man and man, and generally receivable at the treasury[1] in payment of taxes and other obligations from the citizen, or subject, to the state, without any provision being made for the conversion of such paper money into the coin of the country.

Can Inconvertible Paper Money measure values?

We have reached a point which requires us to go back to the analysis of the Money-function [Chapter I]. At the time, warning was given[2] that the necessity might arise for re-opening the question as to a measure of value. Inasmuch as primitive money, constituting as it does a material equivalent or recompense, possesses value in itself (according to the usual significance of that phrase), the notion has arisen and has become almost universal, that money serves as a measure of value, as yard-sticks and bushel-measures serve respectively as measures of length and of capacity.[3] On the first

---

[1] "Note the effect produced upon the circulation of the paper money of China by the government refusing to receive it in payment of taxes."—[P. 303, note.]

[2] Pp. 9–10.

[3] Un instrument de mesure, à moins d'impossibilité absolue, ce qui n'arrive pas pour la monnaie, doit être de même nature que la chose qu'il sert à mesurer; il doit être *long* si cette chose est longue, *pesant* si elle est pesante, *capable* si elle est capable, etc., etc., comme le

occasion when we had to meet this notion, we put it over as not essential to be considered in dealing with metallic money of full value.

Again, when, after dealing with metallic money of full value, we came to deal with the subject of seigniorage, and to contemplate a debased coinage in circulation, the question instinctively arose,[1] how such money could possibly measure values? and this time, again, the discussion was postponed.

We must now fairly meet the issue and settle it, if we are to have any peace in the further course of our inquiry into the principles of money. Fairly to start with the question, let us take up again the statements of the economists whom we quoted on this subject in our first chapter.

"At what rate," writes Prof. Jevons, "is any exchange to be made? . . . . *How much beef for how much flax, or how much of any one commodity for a given quantity of another?* In a state of barter the price-current list would be a most complicated document, for each commodity would have to be quoted in terms of every other commodity, or else complicated rule-of-three sums would become necessary. . . . . All such trouble is avoided, if any one commodity be chosen and its ratio

---

mètre, comme le gramme, comme le litre, qui sont respectivement long, pesant et capable. La monnaie est dans le même cas; c'est ce qui fait dire aux économistes qu'elle doit être une marchandise, c'est-a-dire, une richesse, puisque les marchandises sont des richesses. Mais la richesse qui est caractérisée à la fois par le travail et utilité, deux choses subordonnées aux circonstances si variables de la production et de la consommation, est essentiellement variable; variable par conséquent doit être l'instrument qui sert à la mesurer."—[Th. Mannequin, La Monnaie et la Double Étalon.]

[1] See p. 190.

of exchange with each other commodity be quoted. . . The chosen commodity becomes a *common denominator*, or *common measure of value*, in terms of which we estimate the values of all other goods, so that their values become capable of the most easy comparison."—[Money and the Mech. of Ex., pp. 5–6.]

And Prof. Rogers says: "A little reflection will show that some measure of value must needs be adopted in all societies whose condition is superior to mere barbarism. . . . . Even if money were not a physical object, it would still be necessary as a symbol or calculus. *We need some common measure of value, as we need measures of length and capacity.*"—[Pol. Econ., p. 22.]

And Mr. Mill writes of the inconveniences of barter: "The first and most obvious would be the want of a *common measure of values* of different sorts. If a tailor had only coats and wanted to buy bread or a horse, it would be very troublesome to ascertain *how much bread he ought to obtain for a coat, or how many coats he should give for a horse.* The calculation must be recommenced on different data every time he bartered his coats for a different kind of article, and there could be no current price or regular quotations of value. Whereas now each thing has a current price in money, and he gets over all difficulties by reckoning his coat at £4 or £5, and a four pound loaf at 6*d.* or 7*d.*"—[III, 7, 1.]

I have already remarked upon the confusion which prevails in the statements of these writers respecting this function of money, as shown more conspicuously in the extended passages quoted in Chapter I. These economists, eminent for their general correctness of thinking and accuracy of expression, have here, after showing the desirableness of a "common denominator" (Jevons), "a unit of calculation" (Mill), "a symbol or calculus" (Rogers), at once concluded that one of the functions—in the view of Prof. Bowen[1] the most important function—of money is to serve as a measure of value. And clearly, as Prof. Bowen states, if money is to measure value, it must itself possess value, as that which measures length or capacity possesses length or capacity.[2]

That a common denominator is not necessarily a measure has been shown.[3] But let us look further into the matter.

In examining the text-books on the subject of Money, it is noticeable that in almost all the illustrations given of primitive exchange, one person of a trade is assumed to be dealing with a single member of another trade; and the writer directs the attention of his readers solely to these two parties to the exchange actually effected.

---

[1] "We can do without money as a medium of exchange, and can even barter commodities for other commodities without the use of any medium. But we cannot do without money as a common standard or measure of value."

[2] "*A measure must be homogeneous with the thing measured; as that which measures length or capacity must itself possess length or capacity, so that which measures value must have value in itself.*"—[Prof Bowen, Pol. Econ., p. 293.]

Un objet destiné à être mesure de valeur doit nécessairement avoir une valeur lui-même.—[Art. Argent, Répertoire Générale d'Économie, Sandelin.]

"How was the tailor to discover how many loaves he ought to get for his coat, or the mason to learn how much brickwork he was to make for the garment?" . . . "It [money] supplied the indispensable convenience of a measure of value; it provided the means for learning the comparative worth of every commodity. *This comparative worth is measured by identically the same process as that by which the length or weight of anything is ascertained.*"—[Price, Principles of Currency, pp. 39–40.]

[3] See pp. 7–10.

It is *the* hatter, *the* baker, *the* tailor. But is not this to render a correct analysis impossible, by the very conditions of the case? Is not Competition of the essence of trade, at least in that state of industrial society in which money appears? I deal, indeed, with but one tailor, or hatter, or baker, in any single transaction; but it is because there are two tailors, two hatters, two bakers, or three, or five, or more, than I am able to answer Prof. Jevons's question, how much of any one commodity for a given quantity of another? Mr. Mill asks, how much bread *ought* the tailor to obtain for a coat; how many coats *should* he give for a horse? The answer is, he *ought* to get as much bread as any one baker, having, at the time and in his place, more need for a coat than any other baker of the town or the neighboring towns, will give him for the coat he has to sell; he *should* give as many coats for a horse as he finds he has to do, after numerous owners of horses, having severally visited numerous tailors, have come, each for himself, to the decision how many coats, at the lowest, such a horse as the tailor wants to buy, is worth.

Now, is any *common measure of value* needed for the purpose of the above-contemplated exchanges?

The statement that money is needed as a measure of value in exchange, is based upon the notion, of the genesis of which it would be difficult to give an account, that each person, having in hand something from which he is willing to part, and having in view many things, which, in differing degrees, he wishes to obtain, can more easily determine the amount of labor involved in the production of the one article—money, than he can successively determine the amount of labor involved in the production of the various articles which he may, now and then, here and there, desire to obtain with the proceeds of his industry; while each other producer in turn is able to compare the amount of labor in his own product with that contained in a given quantity of this one article—money—which thus becomes the common measure of value for all commodities. The prices (*i. e.*, the values, in terms of money,) of all articles, being thus commonly measured, become mutually comparable.

If the term, common measure of value, has any significance, it is this:[1] no less: no more.

This is not, however, even in theory, the process by which the relative values of articles brought to market are determined. The rates at which articles shall be respectively exchanged are reached through the relations of supply to demand. When the economist says that, as a rule, equal amounts of labor are exchanged against each other in trade, he means no more than that, if, in the existing relations of supply to demand, the products of labor in one occupation fail to command the products of an equal amount of labor in another occupation, labor and capital will pass from the occupation whose products are at a disadvantage in exchange, into the occupation whose products have the advantage in exchange, until the equilibrium is restored. It is only when laborers find that, by working at one occupation, they get for themselves fewer of the comforts, luxuries, and necessaries of life than they would by working in another occupation, that transfer of labor takes place, and the supply of the products of the former occupation is diminished till their price rises to a point which allows wages to be paid equal to those received by laborers elsewhere. Now, money, as the common denomi-

---

[1] "The cost price of the goods is compared with the cost price of the gold."—[Prof. Price, Principles of Currency, p. 159.]

nator of values, allows the laborer with great ease and accuracy to determine whether he is receiving less or more of articles to eat, and drink, and wear, than his neighbor Brown, who works at another trade. He would find it very difficult to make an exact comparison between the supplies, of all sorts, coming in the course of a day, a week, a year, into his own house and into Brown's, respectively: but if he learns that Brown receives $1.25 a day, while he receives only $1.20, he knows at once that Brown's occupation is the more remunerative, and in just what degree.

But we must get rid decisively of all remnants of the notion that things exchange on a basis of equality because they have cost equal amounts of labor. The proposition already quoted from Prof. Jevons, "Labor once spent has *no influence* on the future value of any article," applies throughout the whole length and breadth of exchange. Products often exchange for only half what they cost; they often exchange for twice what they cost. It is simply a question of the demand for an article and the supply of it. The cost of production only comes in as influencing the supply. The past cost of production has regulated the present supply; the present cost of production will regulate the future supply.

If this be so where goods are exchanged for goods, it is not the less so where goods are exchanged for money. An ounce of silver buys a bushel of wheat not at all because each has cost a day's labor. The silver may have been dug out at Laurium, more than two thousand years ago, at the cost of labor necessary to produce twelve bushels of wheat. The wheat itself may sell for one-half as much more than last year, for no other reason than that two nations in Europe have fallen to cutting throats. It is simply a question of supply and demand.

Present cost of production—days' labor—only enters to affect the supply hereafter.

But the further to show the fallacy of this notion, let us for a moment suppose that in barter the amounts of labor involved in the production of commodities are really measured against each other, and that this measurement serves as the basis of exchange; that it is in this way we get an answer to Prof. Price's question, how the tailor is to discover how many loaves he ought to get for his coat; or the mason to learn how much brick-work he is to make for the garment? Could we find any article which would less advantageously answer the requirements of a common measure of value than the present money of the world, gold and silver? In the first place, we have the fact that, owing to the special conditions governing the production of these metals, taken in connection with the peculiar principle which regulates the purchasing power of money, the value of gold or silver may be hundreds of years behind the cost of production or scores of years in advance of it.[1] In the second place, we may fairly say that men in general know less about the conditions, as to cost of production, under which gold and silver are brought to market, than they do about the corresponding conditions under which nineteen-twentieths, if not ninety-nine hundredths, of the articles they deal in are produced. Almost any man may know something personally, or form, second-hand, some sort of an idea, of the cost of producing wheat, or cattle, or clothes, or chairs. How few things does he buy of whose respective costs of production he knows so little as he does regarding that of gold or silver! A man has an almost indefinitely better opportunity to compare the

---

[1] See pp. 246–8.

amount of labor involved in the production of the commodity he has to sell, with that involved in the production of spices in the islands of the Indian Ocean, than he has to make the same comparison with respect to gold, raised, as it chiefly is, in regions not only remote but comparatively inaccessible, yielding irregularly and spasmodically, the industry shifting its seats and suffering changes of condition, not only from generation to generation, but from year to year.

I apprehend that this notion of money serving as a common measure of value is wholly fanciful; indeed the very phrase seems to indicate a misconception. Value is a relation. Relations may be expressed, but not measured. You cannot measure the relation of a mile to a furlong: you express it as 8:1.

But how can anything perform the office of a common denominator in exchange, unless it possesses what Prof. Bowen calls "intrinsic value;" unless, in Chevalier's phrase, it constitutes a material equivalent or recompense? With a view to answering this question, let us take, not a debased coinage, containing but a part of the silver or gold it purports to contain, nor a paper money consisting of the notes of banks which promise to pay coin on demand, and which hold a certain amount of coin for that purpose, but a paper money costing as nearly nothing as may be,[1] but limited by restrictions, natural or legal, to a definite amount. Let, for example, these be nothing but curiously colored bits of paper with a government stamp upon them which it is felony

[1] The principle *de minimis non curatur* holds true in economics as in law.

to imitate. No redemption of these need be promised by the government. Like some of the paper money of our early colonial days, they may simply bear the inscription, five dollars, five shillings, or what not.

Now let it for once be granted that a demand is created for this paper by a law making it legal tender, at certain rates, for debts contracted, or by the offer of the government to receive it for taxes,[1] or by a general conviction that it "will do" for a medium of exchange. These are no unreasonable suppositions. A score of such moneys are, as we shall see, in existence to-day, circulating freely throughout large communities. No matter how it came about that currency was first given to these colored bits of paper, we assume them in circulation, men being willing to take them for what they have to sell, knowing that with them they can obtain what they wish to buy.

A demand for these bits of paper being once created, every barrel of flour, every cow and calf, every pair of boots, brought into market will be offered for them, the desire and effort of each possessor of these commodities being to get the most pieces he can for his stock, while it is the desire and effort of each possessor of the paper to get for a given number of pieces the greatest number of bushels of wheat, the best, if not the largest, pair of boots, the choicest cow or calf, which can be had. Is it not evident that this would result in establishing exchanging-proportions between the different commodities in the market? Every holder of the paper money would be willing to give more pieces for a cow than for a calf, for a cow in good condition than for a lean one; and

[1] "A prince may give a certain value to money, by receiving it in taxes."—[Adam Smith.]

thus the commodities would speedily become differentiated, at first coarsely and rudely; then more and more nicely and exactly. The same number of pieces might at first be given for a load of wheat as for a milch cow; but, in that case, of the many farmers who had both cows and wheat, and knew the comparative cost and trouble of raising them, many would bring loads of wheat and few would drive cows to market, till the holders of the paper would begin to bid more pieces for cows and fewer for loads of wheat, and *the prices* of the two would assume proportions closely corresponding to their respective costs of production.

## IDEAL MONEY.

I suppose it was an apprehension of this use of money as a common denominator, to express and record relations in exchange,[1] which lay beneath the doctrine of "Ideal Money," advocated in England by many writers down through the discussions attending the Bullion Report and the resumption act of 1819, giving rise to the famous controversy on the question, "What is a pound?"

The economist of highest repute who has been claimed by the more recent advocates of "ideal money" as the champion of their cause, was Sir James Steuart.

"His work," says Lord Lauderdale, "has been copi-

[1] "Whether the terms, crown, livre, pound sterling, etc., are not to be considered as exponents or denominations? And whether gold, silver and paper are not tickets or counters for reckoning, recording or transferring such denominations? Whether, the denominations being retained, *although the bullion were gone*, things might not nevertheless be rated, bought and sold, industry promoted, and a circulation of commerce maintained?"—[Bishop Berkeley's Querist, Nos. 25 and 26, A.D. 1710.]

ously quoted as affording authority for this strange and unintelligible doctrine of the advantage of conducting the circulation of a country by abstract currencies, representing imaginary denominative values."[1]—[Depreciation Proved, p. 70.]

"So far," however, asserts Lord Lauderdale, "is it from being true that Sir James Steuart sanctions the opinion that the circulation of a country can be conducted by paper representing no metallic currency, and enjoying no denominative value, that those who are really acquainted with his writings must consider such a representation as a gross perversion of his doctrine, for he distinctly states that 'some intrinsic value or other must be found out to form the basis of paper money, for without that, it is impossible to fix any standard worth for denominations contained in the paper.'"—[*Ibid.*, p. 73.]

I venture to think that Lord Lauderdale and the advocates of an ideal money are both right and both wrong respecting Sir James Steuart's views. The fact is, this able writer not only contended for the theoretical possibility of conducting exchanges by means of an ideal money, or a money not embodied in material form, but held that there were certain marked advantages[2] herein.

---

[1] "The idea of a currency without a specific standard was, I believe, first advanced by Sir James Steuart . . . directly at variance with the general principles he endeavors to establish."—[Ricardo's Proposals, p. 14.]

[2] "The advantages found in putting an intrinsic value into that substance which performs the functions of money-of-account is compensated by the instability of that intrinsic value, and the advantage obtained by *the stability of paper or symbolical money* is compensated by the defect it commonly has of not being at all times susceptible of realization into solid property, or intrinsic value." Sir James in-

If the writers who have stumbled over Sir James Steuart's seemingly contradictory expressions would recall the circumstances under which his treatise was written, that is, prior to the recoinage of 1774, when the current coin was so debased that a guinea might contain an amount of gold 10, 20, or even 30 per cent. below the mint standard, and hence the question, What is a pound?[1] became a practical and serious one, they would find less difficulty in understanding his distinction between money-of-account and money-coin.

Briefly, Sir James held that when an article of so-called intrinsic worth, such, *e. g.*, as gold, is taken at once as the standard and the actual means of deferred payments, the creditor is liable to wrong from one or both of two causes:

First, the ounce of gold may, from influences affecting the production of that metal, come to represent a much smaller expenditure of labor than when the contract was made. The possible range of such an effect is seen in tracing the history of the production of the precious metals.—[Chap. 4–7.]

---

stances the habit of trade among the savages upon the African coast of Angola, "where there is no real money known.' The inhabitants there reckon by *macoutes*, and in some places this denomination is subdivided into decimals, called pieces. One maconte is equal to ten pieces. This is just a scale of equal parts for estimating the trucks they make." Lord Lauderdale, in his "Depreciation Proved," says that the macoutes were pieces of net-work used by the natives as a covering, perhaps against insects. There are, however, few writers who have not, with Sir James Steuart, followed the statements of travelers that the maconte is a mere name or symbol. It figures in a score of treatises, from Montesquieu to Mill, as an illustration of ideal money.

[1] "The disorder of the English coin has rendered the standard of a pound sterling quite uncertain. To say that it is 1718.7 grains of fine silver, is quite *ideal*."—[Pol. Economy, Book III, part ii, ch. 8.]

Second, irrespective of and additional to this, the coin in which the creditor shall be paid may actually embody a smaller amount of the metal than was in contemplation at the time the contract was made, owing to continued abrasion in use, or to further debasement at the mint. Not only may the average value of the coin be thus reduced; but the corruption and debasement of the coin may proceed very irregularly. Here are two sovereigns and two shillings, one of each kind of coin badly worn; one fresh. The heavy shilling which is nominally $\frac{1}{20}$ part of a sovereign, may be $\frac{1}{15}$ part of the light sovereign. The light shilling may be only $\frac{1}{25}$ part of the heavy sovereign. In such a coinage, what is a sovereign? what is a shilling? and what is the relation of a shilling to a sovereign? The actual range historically of such an effect may be seen by reference to Chap. II.

Now Sir James Steuart's position on both these points is incontrovertible. All coined money is subject to variations, it may be important variations, on these several accounts.[1]

Moved by these considerations Sir James, in his "Political Economy," advocated the adoption of a money of account which should be distinct from the actual coin of the country.

"The value of commodities depending upon a general combination of circumstances relative to themselves and to the fancies of men, their value ought to be considered as changing only with respect to one another; consequently, anything which troubles or perplexes the as-

---

[1] It is, of course, conceivable that the two effects should in a degree neutralize each other. The changes in gold production tending to make the coin more valuable, might coincide with abrasion, etc., tending to make the coin less valuable.

certaining those changes of proportion by the means of a general, determinate and invariable scale, must be hurtful to trade and a clog upon alienation." . . .

"Money, which I call of account, is no more than an arbitrary scale of equal parts, invented for measuring the respective values of things vendible. Money-of-account, therefore, is quite a different thing from Money-coin. . . . Money, strictly and philosophically speaking, is an ideal scale of equal parts." . . .

Just what the writer means by a money-of-account will best be seen by Dr. Hunter's description of the monetary system which Sir James, as the adviser of the East India Company, caused to be introduced into India in consequence of the general corruption of the coin.

"The actual coin at any single mint could not be selected as the standard, for no mint could be trusted, *and whatever could be handled was sure to be falsified. An ideal coin was accordingly invented*, by which all rupees might be valued, and one of the Company's earliest and soundest financial advisers has left on record the process:

"'When a sum of rupees is brought to a shroff (banker or money-changer), he examines them piece by piece, ranges them according to their fineness, then by their weight. Then he allows for the different legal battas (deductions) upon siccas and sunats; and, this done, he values in gross by *the current rupee* what the whole quantity is worth. The *rupee current*, therefore, is the only coin fixed by which coin is at present valued: and the reason is, because *it is not a coin itself, and therefore can never be falsified or worn.*' "[1]—[Rural Bengal, p. 300.]

---

[1] The quotation is from Sir James Steuart's work on the Coin of Bengal, addressed to the East India Company. Among the regulations proposed by Sir James is the following:

Now by such a system as Sir James Steuart caused to be introduced into India, the scheme of a "determinate and invariable scale" for the expression of value is realized. Under such a system in England, the shilling would always be the twentieth part of a pound and be twelve times the penny. It will be observed, however, that this does not obviate the use of the metals: of a material medium of exchange. It merely makes the coin merchandise, bought and sold according to this "scale." Of course, this impedes the freedom and the fullness of circulation, and thus we may say that Sir James's scheme assists money to perform its function as a denominator of values, at the expense of its efficiency as a medium of exchange. Whether this would be desirable or not in any given situation, would depend upon the general condition of the circulating coin. With a coinage in such a condition as Macaulay describes, writing of England in 1696,[1] and as Dr. Hunter describes as existing in India[2] down to a more recent date, commerce would doubtless be facilitated by the authoritative announcement of a standard by which coins, in all considerable transactions, should be bought and sold by test and weight. If this retarded their circulation, it would make at least a tardy justice possible between man and man.

---

"The Company, therefore, having resolved to put an end to all confusion in future, do for this purpose determine that the rupee current shall be the standard money of Bengal; and that, in order to preserve it merely as a standard, consisting of a determinate quantity of fine silver, they hereby *forbid the making of any current coin of the exact value*, or which shall ever carry the denomination of a rupee current, to the end that this *denomination of money* may at no time be subject to the inaccuracy of coinage or of wearing in circulation."

[1] See pp. 209–11.

[2] See pp. 211–2.

We have said that a money of account for registering values, as determined by the state of the market, and for measuring the obligations of debtors, does not necessarily dispense with the "material equivalent or recompense," as a medium of exchange. "Although moneys of account," says Kelly's Cambist, "be not represented by real coins,[1] yet their intrinsic value may be determined by their known relations or proportions to certain coins." A money of account of such a character is, therefore, not properly an ideal money merely because it refers to a non-existent coin.

During the discussions in Great Britain attending the Bullion Report and the Act of 1819, the kingdom being then in a state of suspension, plans for an Ideal Money altogether irrespective of metal were urged with not a little persistency. A few quotations from the pamphlets of Messrs. Gloucester Wilson and Perceval Eliot will serve sufficiently to give an idea of the nature and extent of their claim for a money without material embodiment:

"Mediums of currency are all properly, in so far as they have any real import, personifications of abstract value.

"What is called the equivalency of some of them,

---

[1] "What is the reason why no nations that I know keep their accounts by any specific coin? Neither the pound sterling, nor the livre, nor the German florin, nor the Flemish schilling, nor the Spanish piastre, ducat, or maravedi, nor the Portugal re, nor, in short, the rupee current in Bengal, are real and specific coins."—[Steuart, Coin of Bengal, p. 12.]

Since this was written, the pound sterling has been coined under the name of the sovereign.

whether imaginary or even truly real, is, as far as it interferes with their abstract character as measures, a mere remaining leaven of savage barter.

"Their greater or less grossness of personification shows the skill to which we have arrived in laying our vessel near the wind."—[Gloucester Wilson, Defense of Abstract Currencies, p. 93.]

It appears to be Mr. Wilson's idea that currency, like saints, can only be perfected when completely rid of the flesh.

"Gold is, as it were, the vernacular tongue of currency; we speak it perhaps more glibly than we do any other; but it by no means follows, nor is it indeed true, that we construe it so grammatically as we do the acquired language of paper."—[*Ibid.*]

"The gold is no more essential to the guinea than the brass or ivory of the ruler is to its inches."—[P. 44.] "Paper, as the mere abstract expression of value, is more likely to be uniform in value than gold."—[P. 48.]. "The abstract idea of a pound will be far more uniform in value than any fixed quantity of gold or silver."—[P. 49.]

"I am told by the realists that an *inch* is a sensible object, because it can be shown me on brass and ivory rulers. . . . Even this slight personification exposes our degrees to error: Nature mocks all such endeavors to bind her sensible objects in strict subjection to the mind's abstractions. We may change brass and ivory for platina: still she contracts and dilates the best material we can select, at her caprice or pleasure, and sends us back for any fixed criterion to what we are thus idly deserting, our own pure abstract idea of inches. . . . Measures are all in their nature purely abstract."—[Pp. 116–7.]

25*

Mr. Perceval Eliot adopts the following line of argument: "Whatever in itself possesses an embodied form and an intrinsic value, must, as a material commodity, be subject to variation, under the universal principle of the relative proportions of product and demand. And, paradoxical as it may seem in theory, it is nevertheless most incontrovertibly true in practice, that it is the very attribute of intrinsicality which necessarily imposes the quality of variation. It is the ideal money only which admits of invariable value, because it is not formed of substantial and therefore variable materials."[1] —[Observations on the Fallacy of the Supposed Depreciation of Paper.]

It is scarcely worth while to separate the parts of truth and error in these paragraphs.

We have seen that a paper money, expressing simply the will of the sovereign, or accepted, irrespective of any intrinsic worth, by the general consent of the people, may serve as a medium of exchange, and, if confined within the limits of money of gold or silver, may remain without necessary depreciation.

We have seen, moreover, that, though destitute of value, in the sense of the economists, such money will serve to express and record the relative values, the comparative purchasing power, of commodities.

And the writers quoted are undoubtedly right in urging that the affixing of such a scale to any material commodity, like gold, must result in something less than perfect justice in deferred payments, through the depreciation or appreciation of the metal due to changes occurring meantime in the cost of production, if not also

[1] "It is submitted," says Lord Lauderdale, "to the refined ingenuity of this gentleman's mind, that an immaterial army would also have the advantage of being invulnerable."

to the deterioration or debasement of the specific portion, or portions, of that commodity which the debtor is to pay and the creditor to receive. That the wrong done to one or the other party to long contracts may be not slight, but serious, and at times even ruinous, will be admitted by all who are familiar with the history of money and of the production of the precious metals.

If, then, a money, consisting of colored bits of paper, of a cost so small as to be inappreciable, may serve as a medium of exchange, and may register the comparative purchasing power of commodities, and thus perform the function ordinarily spoken of as *measuring values*, and may even act as a standard for deferred payments, to fix the obligations of debtors—why should not such money be adopted by all civilized communities, and the vast amount of wealth and labor now expended in raising gold and silver from the mines be applied to occupations more immediately productive of health, comfort and happiness to mankind? This question may perhaps be more intelligently answered after a rapid glance at the history of Inconvertible Paper Money. But, first, let us note one characteristic of this money, a knowledge of which is necessary to an understanding of its history.

It has been said that, while Inconvertible Paper Money has, in certain instances, resulted from the degeneration of paper money originally convertible, yet, that, for the present, we would confine ourselves to the consideration of those alone which have been put forth by government, as an act of authority, the circulation of the paper being primarily due to, or at least largely dependent on, the force of law.

It follows, pretty much as of course from the statement made, that such paper has no circulation beyond the territory over which the authority of the issuing government extends. *Limited circulation*, non-exportability—then, may be regarded as of the essence of this money. Indeed, this has been, by not a few, regarded as one of its crowning excellencies. John Law claimed for his paper money, that no nation could draw it away from France.

"Let it be remembered," said the Continental Congress in their address to the people September 13, 1779, "that paper money is the only kind of money which cannot 'make wings unto itself and fly away.' It remains with us; it is ever ready and at hand for the purposes of commerce or taxes, and every industrious man can find it."

Mr. Duncan says of the political economy of his school: "It affirms that every independent state is entitled to issue legal tender for its own internal purposes, in discharge of private debts and public taxes, within its own realm; such legal tender not possessing intrinsic value, but only a conventional value derived from the authority of the state which calls it into existence. . .

"Thus secure of being always kept within the realm of the state which created it, this legal tender would be the special monetary instrument by which all fiscal obligations and mercantile liabilities would be discharged at home."—[On Currency, p. 28.]

Mr. Wells in his tract, "Robinson Crusoe's Money," makes the following citations to the same effect:

"Beyond the sea, in foreign lands, it [the greenback] is fortunately not money; but when have we had such a long and unbroken career of prosperity in business as since we adopted this non-exportable currency?"—[Hon. W. D. Kelley, Ho. Reps., 1870.]

"Does or does not our duty to ourselves and the world at large demand that we maintain permanently a non-exportable currency? . . . The affirmative of this question is also in perfect harmony with the practice and experience of leading nations and in harmony with the teachings of sound economic science."—[H. C. Carey—letter to Hon. M. W. Field, Sept., 1875.]

This fact of non-exportability brings us face to face with the vital characteristic of an inconvertible currency, viz., that its amount is not subject to regulation by the law which, as we have seen, distributes the metallic money of the world, among the several nations and communities, according to the requirements of their trade.

We have seen that if the amount of the precious metals in any country becomes excessive, that is, reaches a height which, with the number of exchanges now requiring to be effected by the use of money, will not allow the commodities of that country to be exchanged at prices on a level (making due allowance for all the charges of transportation) with those of other countries, a movement at once begins for the importation of commodities and the exportation of gold or silver, which tends to restore the equilibrium.

With the money we are now contemplating, however, no such security against redundancy and consequent depreciation exists. "If," say the authors of the Bullion Report, "the issue is of inconvertible paper, prices will rise. The progress may be as indefinite as the range of speculation and adventure in a great commercial country."

## CHAPTER XV.

### ILLUSTRATIONS OF INCONVERTIBLE PAPER MONEY.

We have perhaps gone far enough in the theory of the subject, to make it profitable to take up the history of Inconvertible Paper Money, after which we shall return to consider more attentively the relations of this form of money to the industrial welfare of the community.

In looking about for illustrations of the natural course of Inconvertible Paper Money, we are offered an unfortunately large number of instances to pick from. M. Wolowski notes that[1] Poland alone of European nations preserved itself from this evil down to the time of its final subjugation; while centuries[2] before France, Spain

[1] Les Finances de la Russia, p. 148. Prince Adam Wiszniewski, in his "Histoire de la Banque de Saint Georges de Gênes," says: "Si la Pologne avait eu, en 1792, une banque bien constituée, elle eût mis sur pied cent mille hommes, qui auraient sauvé son indépendance," etc., etc.—[P. xxix.] This is, however, rather a cry of grief from a patriotic Pole, than a sober statement of the financial and military possibilities of the situation in 1792.

[2] Col. Yule says: "The issue of paper money in China is at least as old as the beginning of the 9th Century. In 1160, the system had gone to such excess that government paper, equivalent in nominal value to 43,000,000 ounces of silver, had been issued in six years; and there were local notes besides, so that the empire was flooded with rapidly depreciating paper."—[The Book of Ser Marco Polo, i, 381[n].]

or Sweden had tasted the sweets of paper money, Marco Polo, in visiting China, found in circulation a money made of the inner bark of the mulberry tree, the pieces having value according to their size. These notes were issued "with as much solemnity and authority as if they were of pure gold or silver."[1] The Persians had paper money in 1294. The notes were direct imitations of the Chinese. Even the Chinese characters appeared as part of the device. The Chinese name *chao* was applied to them. "Expensive preparations were made for this object; offices called *Chao-Khanahs* were erected in the principal cities of the provinces, and a numerous staff appointed to carry out the details."[2] After two or three days of enforced circulation the markets were closed, the people rose, the officials were murdered, and the project was abandoned. Col. Yule informs us that the

---

[1] "And the Kaan causes every year to be made such a vast quantity of this money, which costs him nothing, that it must equal all the treasure in the world. With these pieces of paper, made as I have described, he causes all payments on his own account to be made; and he makes them to pass current universally over all his kingdoms, provinces and territories, and whithersoever his power and sovereignty extends. And nobody, however important he may think himself, dares to refuse them on pain of death. And, indeed, everybody takes them readily, for wheresoever a person may go throughout the Great Kaan's dominions, he shall find these pieces of paper current, and shall be able to transact all sales and purchases of goods by means of them just as well as if they were coins of pure gold."—[Chap. xxiv.]

Col. Yule attributes the downfall of the system to the refusal of the Ming dynasty to receive the paper in payment at the treasury, requiring coin from the people, while paying out paper in disbursements on government account. In 1448, the *chao* of 1000 cash was worth but 3. After 1455, there is no mention of it in Chinese history.

[2] Col. Yule's Notes to Marco Polo, ch. xxiv.

Japanese, also, had a paper currency in the fourteenth century; but he offers no details respecting it.

In illustration of the tendencies of Inconvertible Paper Money, we select, as most instructive, as well as historically most important, the paper money of our own colonial period and of the Revolutionary War, the assignats of France, the notes of the Bank of England during the period of the so-called Restriction, 1797–1819. The episode in French history associated with the name of John Law, 1717–21, is dwelt upon by most writers on money; but I am disposed to think there is sufficient show of truth in Mr. Duncan's plea[1] that the miseries of 1720–1 were the result of downright swindling on the part of the Regent Orleans and his rascally associates, in which Law became, by more or less of compulsion, the tool, to make it inexpedient to select this out of the many instances offered to illustrate the natural course of Inconvertible Paper Money. We shall do better to take instances where issues were made in undoubted good faith, and where, consequently, the results may with more confidence be traced to inherent tendencies.

The colonial period of American history offers examples of inconvertible paper issues in great variety. We find here the three usual forms of paper: that issued on landed security;[2] that based on taxes; and that representing the pure credit or authority of the government.

---

[1] On Currency, pp. 72–3.

[2] The reader will please bear in mind the definition given [p. 276] of Inconvertible Paper Money. It is paper money not, in fact, subject to conversion into metallic money on the demand of the holder.

We have paper issued to meet the current annual exigencies of the treasury, corresponding to the Exchequer Bills of England; paper issued for war expenses; paper issued, of choice, for the professed purpose of affording a circulating medium; and paper issued as a loan for the promotion of industry. No field could be richer in all known varieties.

### THE PAPER MONEY OF THE COLONIAL PERIOD.

In the early days of settlement great complaints arose of the scarcity of the circulating medium. Sir Walter Scott's comparison of Great Britain to the image in Belshazzar's dream: the money of London, the head, being of fine gold; the circulation of the fertile provinces of England, like the breasts and arms of the image, of silver; that of the southern parts of Scotland, of brass and copper; while the Highlands and the remoter parts must needs be content with iron and clay, would require a new term to be introduced to express the condition of the colonies on the shores of North America.

Hence we find the colonists in the South resorting, as has been stated, to tobacco and rice as a medium of exchange, while those of New England made use of corn and cattle in large transactions, and, in smaller exchanges, of "wampum" made of black and white beads, or parts of shells, the black (inclining to blue, and often so denominated) of the quohoag, the white of the periwinkle.[1] Bullets were for a time resorted to as small change below a shilling.

Notwithstanding the scarcity of general capital, and the especial scarcity of metallic money, owing to the slow

[1] "The stem or stock of the periwinkle, when all the shell is broken off," explains Roger Williams.

growth of foreign trade among a people having everything to create for themselves, some silver came into the colonies, as the result of exchanges with the West Indies, and small amounts were brought over by immigrants from Europe. This money the colonists sought to detain by declaring it of legal value superior to its mint value at the place of coinage. Thus the money of the provinces came to be of less value than sterling.[1]

By these acts the colonists deliberately cut themselves off from the monetary circulation of the world.[2] "The impossibility of maintaining a metallic currency, in a state of colonial dependence," says Mr. Bancroft, "was assumed as undeniable."—[Hist. U. S., iii, 387.]

Was this action necessary? If there was room for choice, was it wise?

"The attempt of our forefathers," says Dr. Bronson,

---

[1] "The pound has four different values in the United States," says Prof. Tucker. "In New England, Virginia, Kentucky, Tennessee, Ohio, Indiana and Mississippi the pound is $3⅓, and the dollar, 6*s.*

| | | |
|---|---|---|
| In New York and North Carolina, | $2\frac{1}{2}$, " " " | 8*s.* |
| In Pennsylvania, N. Jersey and Del., | $2\frac{2}{3}$, " " " | 7*s.* 6*d.* |
| In South Carolina and Georgia, | $4\frac{2}{7}$, " " " | 4*s.* 8*d.*" |

I think Prof. Tucker is in error as to the value of the shilling in Ohio.

In his "Notes on Virginia," Jefferson writes: "How it has happened that, in this as well as the other American States, the nominal value of coin was made to differ from what it was in the country we had left, and to differ among ourselves, too, I am not able to say with certainty."—[Query xxi.]

[2] In the report of a Committee of the R. I. Assembly, in 1749, the following proposition is enunciated as the basis of the colony's action respecting money:

"This will always be the case with infant countries that do not raise so much as they consume; either to have no money, or if they have it, it must be worse than that of their richer neighbors, to compel it to stay with them."

"to get along without the currency of the old world was unwise and unprofitable. The unwieldy and inconvenient substitutes they adopted were practically expensive, costing more, there is reason to believe, than good hard money. By fixing the prices of the selected commodities very much above the specie rates, they made them, as far as could be done by legislation, the exclusive currency, threw out of use the coin in the country, destroyed the market for it among themselves, and drove it to other lands. . . . They were poor indeed; their surplus earnings were small, but they had a surplus nevertheless; hence their need of money. They had all along a trade (quite limited for the first few years) with England, Manhadoes (New York) and the West Indies. At first they shipped peltry, fish and lumber; and afterwards, pipe staves, hoops, beef, pork, peas, fat cattle, horses, etc., and brought back manufactured goods, sugar, molasses, cotton, wool, bills of exchange, silver and rum. They would have brought more silver and less rum and other merchandise, had the first been in greater request at home. . . . Had the colonists withheld opposing legislation and rejected substitutes, commerce would have supplied them with all the coin they needed (which was but little), in spite of themselves."—[Connecticut Currency, p. 9.]

In the same view, Prof. Sumner remarks: "No sound economist can hesitate how to decide this question. The losses occasioned by a bad currency far exceed the gains from imported commodities. The history of the United States from the landing of Winthrop to to-day, is a reiterated proof of it."—[History, American Currency, p. 6.]

Notwithstanding the complaints of the scarcity of money and the shifts to which the settlers were reduced for a medium of exchange, the first issues of paper money were those of Massachusetts, which grew out of the disastrous expedition against the French in Canada, in 1690. The bills of Massachusetts were issued in payment to the soldiers of the expedition, and were at first at a considerable discount, "at least one-third," says Mr Felt.[1] The colony sought, however, to hedge around their credit by calling in a portion of the issues, promising early redemption of the remainder, and making the bills receivable for taxes at the treasury, at a premium of five per cent. These measures proved sufficient, and the paper remained at par for nearly twenty years.

The ice having been broken under the stress of war, paper money continued to be issued, from time to time in anticipation of annual taxes; but the amounts so issued were not excessive. A second expedition against Canada was contemplated in 1709, and in preparation for it, extensive issues were made. £30,000 new and £10,000 old bills were put out in 1709. In 1711, the expedition, equally disastrous with that of 1690, took place, and £10,000 more paper was issued.

New Hampshire, Rhode Island, Connecticut, New York and New Jersey, joined in the expedition and followed the example of Massachusetts in emitting "bills of credit." "I believe," says Dr. Bronson, "the paper money of Massachusetts emitted before Connecticut had bills of her own, did not circulate in the latter colony."—[Conn. Curr., p. 29.]

Connecticut copied the provision of Massachusetts making the bills receivable at the treasury at a premium of five per cent. Neither this paper nor that of the other colonies was made legal tender in private payments; but in 1718, to encourage the currency of the bills, it was enacted by Connecticut that a debtor who

[1] Massachusetts Currency, pp. 50–1.

should tender payment in the bills of the colony should not be liable to have execution levied on his estate or person, or be imprisoned upon any recovery of judgments granted against him. It was the same subterfuge to which the Parliament resorted during the Restriction period. To save the honor of the British name, the Bank of England notes were not made a legal tender; but all remedy was taken away from the creditor, if the notes were tendered.

The Connecticut money, through being issued only for the expenses of government, and not upon loan, and being provided for, in a degree, by special taxes, appears to have maintained a comparatively good reputation. Thus, the author of the tract entitled "Currencies of the British Plantations in America," written in the interest of the British merchants who suffered by the depreciation of the colonial paper, states that Connecticut "emitted bills only for the present necessary charges of government, upon funds of taxes, until, 1733, having granted a charter for trade and commerce to a society in New London, this society manufactured some bills of their own; but this currency being soon at a stand-still, the government was obliged, in justice to the possessors, to emit £50,000 upon loan, to enable those concerned in the society to pay off the society's bills in colony bills."

Rhode Island, on the contrary, receives severe treatment at the hands of this writer. "A handful of people," he says, "admitting of no instructions from the king, Council, or Board of Trade and Plantations, have lately made a very profitable branch of trade and commerce by negotiating their own paper money in various shapes." And the author notes the "promiscuous currency, in the four governments of New England," of the paper emissions of each and every colony, by which "the king's instructions to the commissioned governments are evaded by the popular charter governments, rendering them of no effect."

We have seen Massachusetts first (1690), and afterwards (1709–11) the other New England colonies, with New York and New Jersey, drawn into issues by the disastrous expeditions against Canada which followed the English Revolution of 1688. The taste for paper money once acquired, the colonists were not disposed to go back to the rude currencies of wampum and bullets, corn and cattle, or even the scanty circulation of accidental dollars from the West Indies. Issues of paper followed fast one upon another, in spite of efforts to restrain them made by the Crown, which was moved thereto by the clamors of British merchants, who found their profits seriously impaired by the uncertain character of the colonial money.

But it deserves to be noted as a most instructive fact, that redundancy and depreciation came primarily not so much from increasing emissions as from withdrawing the safeguards thrown around the bills at their issue, extending the time for which they were to circulate, failing to impose and collect the taxes which had been voted for their redemption, or even re-issuing bills which had been redeemed and brought into the Treasury for cancellation. By every such device the people of the colonies sought to deceive themselves and the Crown as to the real nature and extent of their issues. Prof. Sumner[1] attributes to the chafing of the colonists under the restriction and final prohibition of paper money by the Crown, much of the force which the Revolutionary movement acquired later in the century.

---

[1] History of American Currency, p. 30.

Of all the New England colonies, Connecticut, as has been intimated, managed her earlier emissions with most caution and judgment. At the first, and indeed generally, her issues were made wholly for government expenses, and not upon loans to promote industry. Habitually, too, the redemption of the bills was specially provided for by the assignment of taxes.

"In the earlier legislation of Connecticut," says Dr. Bronson, "the same law which authorized the emission of bills of credit, levied a tax, payable within a certain period, to sink the whole issue, together with the five per cent. advance. At first this period was one and two years, then six years, then eight, nine, twelve, and again eight years. After the close of the war, in 1713, the time was frequently shortened. I discover no instance in which this tax was neglected. The same principle of providing by taxation for all bills put in circulation was observed so far as can be ascertained, with regard to the re-issues. . . . I know not whether these taxes were all gathered in accordance with the original intention. As they were levied in gross sums and required additional legislation for their apportionment, according to lists, very possibly they were not. But I have met with no law, till after the Revolution, for their postponement, in the manner which was common in Massachusetts."—[Connecticut Currency, p. 37.]

We may not unfairly suppose that the fact that Connecticut had a charter to lose made her more mindful than her sisters of the proclamation of Anne (1704), fixing the value of money in the colonies, the Act of Parliament of 1707, and the instructions to colonial governors in 1720.

Perhaps, also, we may conjecture with the historian that the good reputation of Connecticut in this matter was due in part to the circumstance that, in making up the statutes of the colony for publication, all laws ordering paper issues were oddly enough overlooked,[1] and that the Assembly had no representative of the king present to report these doings.

But the common circulation of the paper of the New England colonies had before long the effect to deprive the people of Connecticut[2] of much of the benefit of their prudence and self-restraint in issue, and ultimately made them careless of their credit.

The course of depreciation is thus stated by Dr. Bronson:

| | | | | | | |
|---|---|---|---|---|---|---|
| 1710 | 1 oz. | silver plate | was worth | 8 | shillings | in paper. |
| 1721 | " | " | " | 12 | " | " |
| 1724 | " | " | " | 15 | " | " |
| 1729 | " | " | " | 18 | " | " |
| 1739 | " | " | " | 26 | " | " |

In May 1740, it required 28 shillings in paper to buy an ounce of silver, and Connecticut undertook the work of reformation. £30,000 in "new-tenor"[3] bills were to

---

[1] Bronson, Connecticut Currency, pp. 44–5.

[2] October, 1719, the bills of other colonies were recognized. The regular taxes of that session might be paid "in bills of credit of this colony, with the usual advance [5 per cent.], or in the true bills, with four signers [the larger bills], of the Province of the Massachusetts Bay, or in the true bills of New York, Rhode Island or New Hampshire, without any advance upon them." Later, this recognition of the New Hampshire and Rhode Island issues had to be withdrawn.

[3] The good people of New England borrowed this device. "The Mongols," says Col. Yule, "commenced their issues of paper money long before they had transferred the seat of their government to China. Kublai made such an issue in the first year of his reign (1260), and continued to issue notes copiously to the end. In 1287 he put out a complete new currency, one note of which was to exchange against *five* of the previous series of equal nominal value!"

be issued, of which £8,000 should be devoted to canceling the depreciated "old-tenor" bills, the remainder to be loaned out on mortgage. These bills were made a legal tender, but this clause was repealed upon an intimation from the Board of Trade.

The threatening attitude of the royal government in 1740 appears to have checked the emissions of paper money for four years; but the outbreak of the war with France led to enormous issues between 1744 and 1746, amounting to £131,000.

"These last emissions" says Dr. Bronson "broke the camel's back. . . . An ounce of silver which, in 1739, could be bought for 28 shillings in paper, and in 1744 32 shillings, cost, in 1749, 55 or 60 shillings. Trade was embarrassed and the utmost confusion prevailed. No safe estimate could be made as to the future, and credit was almost at an end. No man could safely enter into a contract which was to be discharged in money at a subsequent date. Prudence and sagacity in the management of business were without their customary reward."

"The new issues," he continues, "called new-tenor, instead of benefiting the currency and preventing depreciation, had a disastrous effect. They damaged the old emissions, produced new complications, introduced more confusion, and sunk rapidly in value. A break-

---

The italics and punctuation-marks are Col. Yule's. Had he been familiar with the early history of New England, he never would have wasted a good exclamation-point in that way. "In both issues," continues Col. Yule, "the paper money was, in official valuation, only equivalent to half its nominal value in silver." The Carolinians issued paper at a tenth its nominal value in silver. Col. Yule says, "the paper money was called chao." The American colonies made chaos of it.

down through their agency became necessary. In the expectation, however, that they would fare better in the general wreck, they did not sink so low as the old emissions. They came finally to be worth in the proportion of 1:3.5. . . . They were never used as the ordinary medium of exchange. Accounts were kept and payments made as, previously, in old-tenor. If new-tenor bills were employed in a business transaction, they were converted by multiplication into old-tenor."—[Conn. Curr. 65–6.]

In 1751, Parliament, moved by the representations of the British merchants, passed a law applying to His Majesty's colonies of Rhode Island, Connecticut, Massachusetts and New Hampshire, declaring that it should not be lawful for the governors of these colonies to give assent to any act whereby bills of credit should be created or issued, under any pretense, or whereby said bills should be re-issued, or the time set for their redemption extended. Such acts were to be void, and any representative of the Crown who should fail of his duty therein, was to be dismissed from office.

Acts creating bills for the expenses of the current year, not to run over two years, were excepted from the operation of this act; nor was the law to extend to paper issued in extraordinary emergencies, as in case of invasion; provided a fund should be established for sinking the same within five years, but such bills were in no case to be constituted a legal tender.

Connecticut made some feeble and hesitating efforts to comply with this law, as to the redemption of her bills, giving one oz. of silver for 58*s.* 8*d.* in paper, or at the rate of 1*s.* for 8*s.* 10*d.* The notes of Rhode Island were put under the ban, and large amounts of bills received at the Treasury in payment of taxes were burned

Before, however, the entire outstanding issues could be canceled, war with France broke out in 1755, and the remaining bills sank to 88 shillings per oz.

This extreme discredit proved the way out of the embarrassments of trade. Accounts began to be kept in "proclamation money;" the necessities of the war were provided for by the issue of notes running from two to five years, bearing interest at 5 per cent. per annum, which were paid out to the public creditors "as their value should be at the time." Taxes were imposed sufficient to sink the notes at maturity. "The notes," says Dr. Bronson,[1] "seem to have all been paid at maturity or before. I find no evidence that those which had once reached the treasury were ever re-issued." "Strictly speaking, they do not appear to have constituted a part of the currency." "During all this period, coin was the standard of value, contracts were made and debts paid in it, or its equivalent. Government bills, like ordinary commodities, were converted into it, before their value could be stated."

"Under the circumstances," continues this judicious writer, "it is not surprising that the government credit was preserved and the par value of its paper maintained. The experiment proved how much better, more profitable and more honorable, it was to raise money in the ordinary way, paying what it was worth, than to attempt it by the fraudulent, interest-saving method previously resorted to."

This, however, did not close the experience of colonial Connecticut with paper money. Between October, 1771, and October, 1774, £39,000 in bills of credit, bearing no interest, running two years, were issued for the expenses

[1] Connecticut Currency, pp. 82–3.

of government, seasonable and sufficient taxes being provided for their redemption. "Twenty-five years had elapsed since bills of this kind had been emitted. They introduced a new paper-money era; but as they did not exceed the sum required by the trade of the colony, and were not interfered with by the notes of the adjoining governments, they did not depreciate."[1]

Such was the condition of Connecticut at the outbreak of the Revolution.

We have traced somewhat at length the colonial experience of Connecticut in the matter of paper money, the issues of that colony being generally confined to occasions of public necessity.

Turning to Rhode Island, we find a colony in which the issue of bills of credit, arising out of similar exigencies, created an appetite for paper money which, by indulgence, grew to an overmastering passion, of the force of which we could have no more striking indication than the fact that the unwillingness of that State to submit its right of independent issue was the principal, if not the sole, cause of Rhode Island's absence from the Constitutional Convention of 1787, which devised the subsisting Union of the States.

As the history of Connecticut currency has been written by Dr. Bronson, that of Rhode Island has been written by Mr. Potter. It will not be necessary to enter greatly into detail in following the course of paper-money inflation in this colony. There is a beautiful simplicity about the Rhode Island issues which conduces to brevity of description. The characteristic dif-

[1] Bronson, p. 84.

ference between them and the Connecticut emissions is that they were generally of choice, and for the expressed object of advancing trade and promoting manufactures.

"An important distinction," says Mr. Potter, "is here to be noticed, between bills emitted for the supply of the treasury, which emissions were generally in small sums, as occasion required, and a Bank, which was an emission generally of a large sum, not for the exigencies of government, but to be loaned out, at interest, to the people, on mortgage security, for a term of years."

The use of the word Bank in the colonial days was peculiar. With us the word signifies an institution for conducting the functions of deposit, of exchange, and of discount, with generally a building of its own, and with permanent officials. A Bank in Rhode Island or Massachusetts was simply a batch of paper money.

The first emissions of Rhode Island were in 1710, aggregating £7,000, in sums from £5 down to 2 shillings. In 1715, £30,000 was issued (£5 to 1 shilling), which, with £10,000 more the same year, became known as the First Bank. The bills were loaned for ten years, at 5 per cent. interest, on mortgage of real estate. In 1721 came another Bank, of £40,000, five years loan, interest payable in hemp or flax, the reason for the emission being, in addition to the alleged scarcity of specie, the expediency of encouraging the growth of these staples.

In 1728, under pressure from the colony's debtors, the time of payment for previous loans was extended,[1]

[1] "New claimants who desired to come under this shower of wealth clamored for new banks on the ground of 'justice' and 'equality.' All who had received loans joined as a compact body in favor of further issues. All new issues to others depreciated the currency and enabled them to pay back more easily. However, they did not in many cases pay at all, either principal or interest

and a Third Bank, of £40,000, was emitted, this time on account of the decay of trade and commerce—and small wonder! In 1731 and 1733 came other Banks, the latter for £100,000."

"The emissions of paper money," says Mr. Potter, "were generally opposed by the merchants and business men, and the more intelligent part of the community. They were generally advocated by the multitude who were indebted and distressed in pecuniary circumstances, as a measure of relief. It was an easy way of paying old debts. . . . Pretenses were never wanting. The colony was in debt, the fort was out of repair, or a new jail[1] or court-house was to be built. And when the specie had been driven away by the increase of paper money, the 'scarcity of silver' was a fresh excuse for further issues."

Of the interest of the emission of 1731, a bounty was established on flax, hemp, whale oil, whalebone, and codfish. Of the interest of the Bank of 1733, as that of 1721, half was to be divided ratably among the towns.

From this time forward, paper money became the principal subject of political controversy. "Governors

---

Having accumulated large arrears, they decamped, and when process issued could not be found. The mortgaged estates were found entangled in inextricable confusion. The legislatures, composed largely of men in the system, would allow no extreme measures. Foreclosures were rare, and did not pay for the trouble and excitement they caused."—[Sumner, Hist. Am. Currency, p. 21.]

[1] The Pennsylvania issue of April 10, 1775, was for the purpose of erecting a jail in Philadelphia. It bore on the reverse a picture of that building, known as the Walnut Street Prison. Mr. Phillips says: "These notes are commonly but incorrectly believed to represent the Independence Hall."

"North Carolina issued paper to build a palace for the governor. A similar project was started in New Jersey."—[Sumner, p. 39.]

were elected and turned out, as the different interests happened to prevail." The debtor party needed only to come into power once in ten or five years, to secure the privilege of paying their creditors off at pretty much any rate they might choose to fix, as convenient and agreeable to themselves.

In 1738 a Bank of £100,000 was issued with new provisions for securing the interest of the mortgages, of which the colony had thus far been largely defrauded. In 1740, for fitting out a privateer against the Spaniards, £20,000 were issued. These bills were declared to be equivalent to a certain amount of silver. The rates at which they passed in circulation showed the inefficacy of mere assertion. Now began the denominations of *Old and New-tenor*, which we noted in the history of Connecticut. In 1741 the Assembly made 6*s.* 9*d.* of the new-tenor equal to 27 shillings of the old. In 1749, a Committee of the General Assembly presented the following as the condition of the paper money issues:

| | | |
|---|---|---|
| Outstanding of the Bank of | 1728, - - | £8,000 |
| | 1731, - - | 12,000 |
| | 1733, - - | 40,000 |
| | 1738, - - | 90,000 |
| | 1740, | 20,000 |
| | 1743, - - | 40,000 |
| | | £210,000 |

This in addition to bills issued to supply the treasury; mostly in 1746-7—£110,444.

This, for a colony no larger than Rhode Island, might seem sufficient to promote manufactures and encourage trade, but it was not, and in 1751 the Ninth Bank was issued, this time for £25,000, but *on new plates.* A great deal was hoped for from this circumstance. The issue was for giving bounty on flax, woolen manufactures and the fisheries. The bills were to be made equal to silver at 6*s.* 9*d.* per oz.; which was to be equal to 13*s.* 6*d.* new-tenor, or 54 shillings old-tenor.

But why pursue the narrative? The colony, under the complete domination of the debtor party, had continued its issues to the almost total destruction of trade and industry. In 1763, the war with France being concluded, Parliament re-enacted the prohibition of colonial acts for issuing paper money; and a scale of depreciation was fixed by the courts for the settlement of debts. It put the Spanish milled dollar at the rate of £7 in old-tenor notes. September 1764, old-tenor bills were ordered to be received in payment of a tax, at $23\frac{1}{3}:1$ of lawful money. February, 1769, 6 shillings lawful money were ordered to be reckoned equal to £8 old-tenor. By act of 1770, the old-tenor notes were to be exchanged at this rate and no longer allowed to circulate.

Massachusetts had led the way in the emission of paper money in 1690. The history of the issues of this colony has been written by Mr. Felt. These took both forms described, that of issues for the current expenditures of government, or for extraordinary war expenses, and that of Banks, or loans to the public, for the promotion of the shipping, fishing, or manufacturing interests. The following table shows the depreciation of the paper money:[1]

| | |
|---|---|
| 1706, Exchange on London | 135 |
| 1713, " " " | 150 |
| 1716, " " " | 175 |
| 1717, " " " | 225 |

[1] Sumner, pp. 35–6.

| | |
|---|---|
| 1722, Exchange on London | 270 |
| 1728, " " " | 340 |
| 1730, " " " | 380 |
| 1737, " " " | 500 |
| 1741, " " " | 550 |
| 1749, " " " | 1100 |

The rapid rise between 1741 and 1749 had been due to the large issues involved in the successful expedition against Louisburg. Now, however, Massachusetts led the way towards a restoration of commercial values, though not without that repudiation in which, as history teaches, excessive issues almost invariably result. Parliament voted to ransom Louisburg from the colonies. The sum coming to Massachusetts was £138,649 sterling, which, at 11 : 1, would nearly cancel the paper. Under the enlightened and energetic lead of Hutchinson, the colony was brought to ask that its share of the repayment be shipped in silver and copper coins, to be used, as far as they would go, in canceling the bills of credit.

"The silver," says Prof. Sumner, "was sent over and exchanged.[1] Prices were adjusted to this new measure, and silver remained in circulation when it no longer had a meaner rival. The 'shock' which was apprehended did not occur. The only shock was to Rhode Island and New Hampshire, who found their trade transferred to the 'silver colony,' and their paper suddenly and heavily depreciated. The West India trade of Massachusetts had been largely done through Newport. It was now transferred to Salem and Boston."

[1] The amount redeemed was £1,792,236 5*s.* 1*d.* "For years," says Mr. Felt, "petitions continued to be laid before the legislature, that parcels of them discovered in old desks, bottoms of leather chairs, and other private places of deposit, might be allowed and exchanged."—[Massachusetts Currency, p. 131.]

But though Massachusetts thus, by a resolute effort, rid herself of the incubus upon her trade and industry, treasury-certificates, bearing interest, were systematically issued, without prejudice to the public interests, until the outbreak of the Revolution.

It has been stated that New York and New Jersey, joining with the New England colonies in the second expedition against Canada, had followed the lead of Massachusetts in issuing paper money. Of the issues of New York the author of the tract, "Currencies of the British Plantations in America," writing in 1740, states that they were originally issued in 1709, bearing interest, but that this was taken off in 1710, "upon pretense that it occasioned them to be hoarded up as bonds, and did frustrate their currency."

Of the Jersey paper money the same writer remarks: "The Jersey bills keep their credit better than those of Pennsylvania and New York, for these two reasons: First, New York bills not being current in Pennsylvania, and Pennsylvania bills not current in New York, but Jersey bills current in both, all payments between New York and Pennsylvania are made in Jersey bills. Second, *In the Jerseys, failure of the loan-payments at the day appointed is confessing judgment,* and thereafter only 30 days' redemption of mortgage is allowed."

The history of the New Jersey paper money has been written by Mr. Henry Phillips, Jr.

Of all the colonies issuing paper money, none deserves more attention from the student of political economy than Pennsylvania.

"In our colony of Pennsylvania," wrote David Hume to the Abbé Morellet, "the land itself, which is the chief commodity, is coined and passed into circulation.'

The phrase of Hume appears earlier in the tract of Benjamin Franklin [1] (then a young man of twenty-three years), published in 1729, entitled "A Modest Enquiry into the Nature and Necessity of a Paper Currency." "For as bills issued upon money security," wrote the youthful philosopher, "are money, so bills issued upon land are in effect *coined land*." [2]

The paper-monëy loan-system of Pennsylvania was as follows: The trustees of the loan-office were to lend out the bills of the colony upon real security of at least double the value, for a term of sixteen years, to be repaid in yearly installments, with interest. Thus, one-sixteenth of the principal was to be yearly paid back. The interest was applied to the public services. The principal was, for the first ten years, to be let out again to fresh borrowers. The new borrowers, from year to year, were to have the money for only the remaining part of the term of sixteen years, repaying by fewer and proportionately larger installments. During the last six years of the sixteen, the sums paid in were not to be reloaned, but the notes burned, so that the whole might be called in, and the accounts completely settled at the end of the term. Of this system, Governor Pownall

[1] Prof. Sumner says: "The great philosopher was not unbiased in his judgment."—[P. 19ⁿ.] Franklin, in his autobiography, gives the following account of his interest in the emissions: "My friends there, who considered that I had been of some service, thought fit to reward me by employing me in printing the money; a very profitable job, and a great help to me."

[2] The following play upon words occurs in the correspondence of Wm. Short and Gouverneur Morris: "There is a plan for paper money now before the Assembly. . . . Some insist on calling it *papier terre*, and the idea was near passing."—[Wm. Short to G. Morris, Sept. 12, 1790, Paris.] Mr. Morris replies: "*Apropos* of this currency, this *papier terre*, I could tell them of a country where there is a *papier terre*, now *mort et enterré*."

wrote: "I will venture to say that there never was a wiser or a better measure, never one better calculated to serve the uses of an increasing country; that there never was a measure more steadily or more faithfully pursued for forty years together, than the loan-office in Pennsylvania."

In spite of Governor Pownall's panegyric, however, what with increased loans and the extension of the terms of repayment, this system, the perfection of what Mr. McLeod[1] calls *Lawism*, viz., the basing of currency upon land, was not found incompatible with a depreciation represented by the rise of exchange on London, first to 160:100, and later, in 1748, to 180 or 190.[2]

When the paper money of Pennsylvania was, with that of the other colonies, outlawed by the act of Parliament of 1763, Dr. Franklin wrote a pamphlet protesting against the act.

"In Maryland," says the writer of the tract so frequently quoted, "silver continued at proclamation value until 1734, with a considerable concomitant truck-trade as a medium, viz., tobacco. They then emitted £90,600 sterling in bills, which, though payable to the possessors in sterling, well secured, the sum being too large, and the periods too long, viz., partial payments of fifteen years period each, exchange immediately rose from 35 to 100 and 150 per cent."

The history of Virginia paper money has been written by Mr. Phillips. That history, through the colonial period, is brief and comparatively barren. No bills of credit existed in Virginia before the old French War. In 1755 an issue of £20,000 was authorized to meet the

---

[1] Economical Philosophy, ii, 338.

[2] Sumner, p. 36.

expenses of the Braddock expedition. The notes were to bear interest at five per cent.; were lawful tender in payment of debts, and the penalty of death was denounced for altering or counterfeiting them. In the same year a further issue of £40,000 was made to discharge the bounties proposed by the government for killing or capturing hostile Indians, £30 being offered for each scalp. Frequent issues took place between 1755 and 1775, but we have little information respecting the degree of depreciation which resulted.

The issues of North Carolina were so much out of proportion to the requirements of the colony's trade, that exchange on London rose in 1740 to 1400:100.

A full account of the paper money of South Carolina, is given by Dr. Ramsay in his history of that colony and State. The first emission of paper took place in connection with the expedition against St. Augustine in 1702, being for £8,000. In 1712, a Land Bank was established; the issue was for £52,000, the interest and one-twelfth of the principal to be repaid annually. A fourth emission took place in 1716, in connection with the war against the Yamasses.

In 1736 the provincial House of Commons carried their point, an increase of paper money, against the King's Council; and an emission of £210,000 took place, to be loaned at 8 per cent.

Dr. Ramsay records[1] the powerful and dignified protest offered by Arthur Middleton and other opponents of this measure; and notes it as remarkable that the struggles over the emission of 1736, and in particular this protest, were not referred to in the Revolutionary debates over paper money.

---

[1] History of South Carolina, ii, 93.

"In the interval a new race had sprung up who had no personal knowledge of them. Tradition was obscure, history was silent. Newspapers gave no information. Old official records were seldom examined or referred to. From these causes the Carolinians of 1776 had little advantage from the knowledge of what their fathers had done in 1736 or 1719."

Under the effects of these emissions, exchange on London had risen by 1740 to 800 : 100.

The author of the tract on the "Currencies of the British Plantations" charges bad faith against the South Carolinians of this time. "Their legislatures have been most notoriously guilty of breach of public faith in not canceling their bills." Writing in 1740, he declares that there were then outstanding about £250,000 in province bills, whereof above £100,000 were "without fund or period." "The whole amount issued in bills of credit by provincial South Carolina," says Dr. Ramsay, "in the sixty-eight years which intervened between the first and last emissions of paper, was £605,000, of which more than two-thirds were secured by mortgaged property."

## THE PAPER MONEY OF THE REVOLUTION.

Of the emissions of Paper Money during the Revolutionary period of our history, we have accounts from a great variety of sources. Inasmuch as those authorized by the Continental Congress were made under a single and constant impulse, viz., the overwhelming financial necessities of the new government, engaged in a desperate struggle for existence, the facts can be briefly stated.

The question has sometimes been raised by economists whether issues of Inconvertible Paper Money are ever really necessary, even in time of war. However this question might be decided with reference to ordinary governments, the situation of the Continental Congress must be admitted to have been highly exceptional. In only a qualified sense was it a government at all. It had no coercive power. It could not levy taxes. Even its moral authority over the constituent States was very slight. Its requisitions for money, its recommendations of policy, were treated with neglect, if not with open contempt. The States, with one or two honorable exceptions, hardly made a show of doing their duty by the government of the Confederation. There are few more distressing chapters in history than that which records the delinquency of the States which had pledged life, fortune and sacred honor to the cause of American independence.

The first emission of Continental bills of credit was ordered in June, 1775, the amount being $2,000,000; in July $1,000,000 was ordered; in Novembei, $3,000,000. During 1776 the emissions amounted to $19,000,000.

"The United States," says Dr. Ramsay, "for a considerable time derived as much benefit from this paper creation of their own, though without any established funds for its support or redemption, as would have resulted to them from the free gift of as many Mexican dollars. . . . But there was a point, both in time and quantity, beyond which this congressional alchemy ceased to operate. That time was about eighteen months from the date of their first issue; and that quantity about $20,000,000."—[History of the United States, ii, 308–9.]

Whether or not Dr. Ramsay has correctly estimated the amount of Continental bills which might have circulated without depreciation, no room was left for doubt by the close of 1776 that the limit had been passed.

Depreciation, that unmistakable sign of excess, had already proceeded so far that the bills stood at 50 per cent. discount.

The worst feature of the situation was that the States, despite remonstrance and entreaty, continued also to emit bills of credit. The Continental Congress could not tax the people; the States would not. In most of the States scarcely an effort was made from first to last to meet the charge of the war manfully by assessment and contribution.[1] With a public morality deeply perverted by the colonial experience of paper money, with the false start of 1775–6, and with the apprehension on the part of each that its neighbors would take advantage of any forbearance it might exercise to fill the channels of circulation with their bills, the States fell without a struggle into the wretched policy of constantly increasing issues of constantly depreciating paper. Mr. Shuckers gives the following table of the State issues. [It will be noted that in some States, from lack of the requisite data, the total issues are not distributed among the several years of the war.]

---

[1] The following, from the observations on the finances of the United States, addressed by Congress to the French Minister, contains a frank acknowledgment of the unwillingness to resort to taxation to meet the expenses of the war:

"America having *never been much taxed, nor for a continued length of time,* being without fixed government, and contending against what was once the lawful authority, had no funds to support the war; and *the contest being upon the very question of taxation,* the levying of imposts, unless from the last necessity, would have been madness. To borrow from individuals without any visible means of repaying them, while the loss was certain from ill success, was visionary. A measure, therefore, *which had been early adopted, and thence became familiar to the people,* was pursued. This was the issuing of paper notes representing specie, for the redemption of which the public faith was pledged."

| | 1775. | 1776. | 1777. | 1778. | 1779. | 1780. | 1781. | 1783. | Totals. |
|---|---|---|---|---|---|---|---|---|---|
| Massachusetts, | —— | —— | —— | —— | —— | —— | —— | —— | $3,868,000 |
| Rhode Island, | $200,000 | $300,000 | $15,000 | —— | $133,000 | $66,000 | —— | —— | 714,600 |
| Connecticut, | 500,000 | 366,300 | 17,500 | —— | —— | 632,700 | —— | —— | 1,516,500 |
| New York, | 112,500 | 637,500 | —— | —— | —— | —— | $411,250 | —— | 1,161,250 |
| New Jersey, | —— | 133,000 | —— | —— | —— | 600,000 | 800,000 | $85,000 | 1,618,000 |
| Pennsylvania, | 420,000 | 227,000 | 532,000 | —— | —— | 1,516,000 | 1,330,000 | 300,000 | 4,325,000 |
| Delaware, | 80,000 | —— | 66,500 | —— | —— | —— | —— | —— | 146,500 |
| Maryland, | 535,000 | 415,000 | —— | —— | —— | —— | —— | —— | 950,000 |
| Virginia, | 875,000 | 1,500,000 | 2,700,000 | $2,700,000 | 2,500,000 | 30,666,000 | 87,500,000 | —— | 128,441,000 |
| North Carolina, | —— | —— | —— | 2,125,000 | 1,250,000 | 3,600,000 | 26,250,000 | 100,000 | 33,325,000 |
| South Carolina, | —— | —— | —— | —— | —— | —— | —— | —— | 33,458,926 |
| | | | | | | | | | $209,524,776 |
| Congress, | —— | —— | —— | —— | —— | —— | —— | —— | 241,552,380 |
| Total issues authorized, | | | | | | | | | $451,077,156 |

"It seems to be pretty clear," says Mr. Shuckers, "that the issues of continental bills of credit were materially in excess of the emissions authorized by Congress."—[Finances, etc., of the Revolution, p. 110.]

In the face of a premium on silver of more than 100 per cent., Congress resolved that the nominal value of gold and silver had been raised, just as in England, during the Bullion Controversy, the government declared that the bank-note had not fallen, but the guinea had risen, in value. Efforts were made to suppress the tell-tale premium; and those were denounced as enemies of liberty who recognized a specie price, as distinguished from a paper price, of commodities. In spite of all, however, the depreciation went on through 1777, as the emissions continued. The authorized issues of the year were $13,000,000. The situation was now complicated by the fact that the British authorities began to disseminate counterfeits of the Continental money, as they subsequently did in respect to the assignats of revolutionary France. Extensive counterfeiting also went on at home. And still we find the States disregarding the entreaties of Congress to undertake in earnest the taxation of their citizens, in place of a resort to further issues. More attention was paid to the recommendation by Congress, in November, 1777, of laws to limit prices, and to authorize supplies to be seized in the hands of "forestallers" and "engrossers." Many of the States passed stringent laws to repress the premium on silver and to restrain speculators from forestalling and engrossing the market with a view to secure the anticipated rise of prices due to continued inflation. Public meetings were held to denounce speculation, and mob-law was not infrequently resorted to against the holders of goods, with the same popular applause which had greeted the destruction of the stamped paper in 1765. All such measures, however, were powerless to keep up the credit[1] of the Continental paper. As prices rose, the necessities of the government increased. The emissions authorized during 1778 amounted to $63,500,000.

In December of that year Congress, in a public address, indignantly repelled the insinuation that the bills of credit would be allowed to sink in the hands of the holders, and in the September following issued a second address of the same purport.

"We should pay an ill compliment to the understanding and honor of every true American, were we to adduce many arguments to show the baseness or bad policy of violating our national faith, or omitting to pursue the measures necessary to preserve it. A bankrupt, faithless republic would be a novelty in the political world, and appear among reputable nations like a common prostitute among chaste and respectable matrons. . . . Apprised of these consequences, knowing the value of national character and impressed with a due sense of the immutable laws of justice and honor, it is impossible that America should think without horror of such an execrable deed."[2]

The emissions of 1779 amounted to $140,000,000, of the coin value, according to Mr. Jefferson, of $7,329,278.

The course of depreciation during the year was as follows:

---

[1] Napoleon was wont to say, "Tout peut se rétablir." It may be so, but, as M. Thiers observes, there is nothing which it is so difficult to restore as the reputation of paper money.

[2] "That the money should finally sink, or that it should be redeemed by a scale of depreciation, were events neither foreseen nor expected by the bulk of the people.—[Ramsay, Hist. of South Carolina, ii, 98.]

| | | | |
|---|---|---|---|
| Jan. 14, - - | 8 : 1 | June 4 and 17, | 20 : 1 |
| Feb. 3 and 12, | 10 : 1 | Sept. 17, | 24 : 1 |
| April 2, - - | 17 : 1 | Oct, 14, - - | 30 : 1 |
| May 5, - - | 24 : 1 | Nov. 17 and 29, | 38.5 : 1 |

On the 18th of March, 1780, Congress swallowed all its brave words about public faith and the honor of republics, and authorized silver to be received for paper at the rate of 1 : 40. All bills brought in were to be destroyed. Certificates not to exceed in nominal value one-twentieth of the bills thus destroyed were to be reissued, redeemable in specie after six years, bearing interest at five per cent. Funds were to be established by the individual States for their redemption, the faith of the United States being pledged as an additional security. Six-tenths of these bills were to be delivered to the States, in due proportions; four-tenths to be reserved for the use of Congress.

Such was the end of the "Continental Currency." The new certificates never acquired to any considerable extent the character of money, and soon sank to one-eighth their nominal value, so that the account of a holder of $320 in Continental paper money be thus stated: $\$320 \times \frac{1}{40} = \$8$ in certificates. $\$8$ at $.125 = \$1$ in silver.

So poorly was the security offered by Congress esteemed by the people that the greater part of the original issue was not brought in for redemption in the new certificates.[1] "It continued," says Mr. Jefferson, "to

[1] "88 millions, received into the State Treasuries (at the close of the war) in payment of taxes at the rate of 40 for 1, had been replaced by bills of the "new-tenor," to the amount of $4,400,000, bearing interest at 6 per cent. Massachusetts, New York and Rhode Island had thus taken up and redeemed their entire quota of the old paper. Connecticut, Delaware, the Carolinas and Georgia had

circulate and to depreciate till the end of 1780, when it had fallen to 75 : 1, and the money circulated from the French army[1] being, by that time, sensible in all the States north of the Potomac, the paper ceased its circulation altogether in those States. In Virginia and North Carolina it continued a year longer, within which time it fell to 1000 : 1, and then expired, as it had done in the other States, without a single groan." Or, as Dr. Ramsay more poetically expresses it, "Like an aged man, expiring by the decays of nature, without a sign or a groan, it gently fell asleep in the hands of its last possessors."

Of the effects produced upon society and industry by paper money thus rapidly depreciating, it cannot be necessary to enter into an analysis. "The property of the inhabitants," says Dr. Ramsay, "in a considerable degree changed its owners. Many opulent persons, of ancient families, were ruined by selling paternal estates for a depreciating paper currency, which, in a few weeks would not replace half of the real property in exchange for which it was obtained. Many bold adventurers made fortunes in a short time by running in debt beyond their abilities. Prudence ceased to be a virtue and rashness usurped its place. The warm friends of America, who never despaired of their country, and who cheerfully risked their property in its support, lost their

---

taken up none; the remaining States had taken up and replaced but a part of their quota."—[Hildreth, Hist. U. S., ii, 446.]

[1] Not only the silver brought over by the French, but that disbursed by the British troops within their lines, served to fill the void in the circulation, so soon as the paper money was got out of the way.

property, while the timid who looked forward to the re-establishment of British government, not only saved their former possessions, but often increased them."—[History of South Carolina, ii 98.]

On every hand breaches of trust and violations of commercial honor were committed under the stress of a terrible temptation, even, and perhaps especially, by those who had been most honored and trusted. In the language of Mr. Justice Story, the tender and maximum laws "entailed the most enormous evils on the country, and introduced a system of fraud, chicanery and profligacy which destroyed all private confidence and all industry and enterprise."

"Time and industry," writes Dr. Ramsay, "soon repaired the losses of property which the citizens sustained during the war, but both for a long time failed in effacing the taint which was then communicated to their principles."

It was the experience here recited which impressed our fathers with their horror of paper money, and which led to a prohibition of its issue by the States, under the Constitution.[1]

Says Mr. Madison in the "Federalist": "The extension of the prohibition to bills of credit must give pleasure to every citizen in proportion to his love of justice, and his knowledge of the true springs of public prosperity. The loss which America has sustained since the peace [1783] from the pestilent effects of paper money on the necessary confidence between man and man; on the necessary confidence in the public councils; on the in-

[1] In the interval between the close of the war and the adoption of the constitution, several States fell back upon paper money. Rhode Island, which had been the worst offender as a colony maintained the same reputation as a State.

dustry and morals of the people, and on the character of republican government, constitutes an enormous debt against the States chargeable with this ill-advised measure."

## CHAPTER XVI.

### ILLUSTRATIONS OF INCONVERTIBLE PAPER MONEY. REVOLUTIONARY FRANCE: ENGLAND UNDER THE RESTRICTION.

THE experience of France in the matter of paper money is most instructive. Our space will only serve to trace the course of the revolutionary issues.

The financial embarrassments of the government in 1789 were extreme. Many taxes had ceased to be productive; the confiscated estates not only yielded no revenue but caused a large expense, and, as a measure of resource, the finance committee of the Assembly reported in favor of issues based upon the confiscated lands.[1] But the bitter experience of France through the Mississippi schemes of John Law, 1719–21, made the Assembly and the nation hesitate. Dr. Ramsay notes that the debates in the South Carolina Legislature over the paper money of 1736 were not alluded to in the discussions concerning the revolutionary issues forty years later. But the lapse of seventy years had not effaced the recollections of the miseries of France under the Regent.

Necker, the Minister, stood firm in his opposition to the issue of paper money, even as a measure of resource;

[1] "L'idée des assignats remonte à 1787."—[J. Garnier, Traité de Finances, p. 408.]

but the steady pressure of fiscal exigencies, together with the influence of the fervid orators of the Assembly, gained a continually increasing support to the proposition of the committee. Nor were there wanting those who argued that the change of times and circumstances had altered the conditions of a paper issue so far as to make that safe and beneficial under the republic which, under the Regent, had spread misery and disaster over France. "Paper money," argued Martineau, before the Assembly, "paper money under a despotism is dangerous. It favors corruption: but, in a nation constitutionally governed, which itself takes care of its own notes, which determines their number and their use, that danger no longer exists."

"It was constantly urged, and with a great show of force," says President White, "that, if any nation could safely issue paper money, France was now that nation; that she was fully warned by a severe experience; that she was now a constitutional government, controlled by an enlightened, patriotic people; not, as in the days of the former issue of paper money, an absolute monarchy controlled by politicians and adventurers; that she was able to secure every franc of her paper money by a virtual mortgage of a landed domain of vastly greater value than the entire issue; that, with men like Bailly, Mirabeau, and Necker at her head, she could not commit the financial mistakes and crimes from which France had suffered when at the head stood John Law, and the Regent, and Cardinal Dubois."[1]

Surely there is something of a family resemblance between these arguments and the pleas we have heard in the United States during the last sixteen years. Pain-

[1] Paper Money Inflation in France.

fully instructive it is to note how feeble a subterfuge suffices to break the force of political experience, under the temptations of immediate interest or the stress of rising passion.

But, while the issue of paper based on the public domain was urged as a measure of resource, and with much artful apology for the confessed violation of economical principles, the leaders of the Assembly were secretly actuated by a political purpose, viz., by widely distributing the titles to the confiscated lands (for such the paper money in effect was) to commit the thrifty middle class of France to the principles and measures of the revolution.[1] In a recent review of President White's pamphlet, just quoted, Mr. Dillaye has sought to show that it was the political vice of the situation, the revolutionary and sacrilegious origin of the title to the domain pledged for the payment of the paper, and not any economical vice in the paper itself, as a form of money, which was mainly concerned in the subsequent depreciation and discredit of the assignats.

Oratory, the force of fiscal necessities, the half-confessed political design, prevailed at last over the warnings of experience; and a decree passed the Assembly authorizing an issue of notes to the value of four hundred million francs, on the security of the public lands. To emphasize this security the title of *assignats* was applied to the paper. This issue also bore interest and

---

[1] This reason was boldly avowed by Mirabeau: "Partout où se placera un assignat-monnaie, là sûrement reposera avec lui un vœu secret pour le crédit des assignats, un désir de leur solidité; . . . partout où se trouvera un porteur d'assignats, vous compterez un défenseur nécessaire de vos mesures, un créancier intéressé à vos succès."

purported to be payable at sight, though none in fact were ever paid.[1]

Mirabeau, who had declared paper money to be the nursery of tyranny, corruption and delusion, a veritable orgy of authority in delirium, now threw himself with all the force of his passionate nature into the contest on the side of the assignats. It is in vain, he declared, to assimilate assignats, secured on the solid basis of these domains, to an ordinary paper money having forced circulation. They represent real property, the most secure of all possessions, the soil on which we tread.[2]

The issue was made; the assignats went into circulation; and soon came the inevitable demand for more. Now appeared, as subsequently in the case of the United States legal tenders in 1862, that the real battle had been made over the first emission. Talleyrand, indeed, who had advocated the former, opposed the later issue, and with his accustomed sagacity struck the vital point of the controversy: You can, he said, arrange it so that the people shall be forced to take a thousand francs in paper for a thousand francs in specie; but you never can arrange it so that the people shall be obliged to give a thousand francs in specie for a thousand francs in paper. In that fact is imbedded the entire question, and on account of that fact the whole system fails.[3] But Talleyrand was to learn that the genius he had aided to invoke was not to be conjured by either phrases or ideas. Necker, too, still prophesied of evil; but the spirit of the Assembly had risen with the first emission, which no manifest evils had followed, and for a time the ghost of John Law was laid.

---

[1] J. Garnier, Traité de Finances, p. 409.

[2] White, Paper Money Inflation in France.

[3] White, p. 21.

The advocates of the assignats took a bold and aggressive tone. Mirabeau declared that the precious metals were at the best employed only in the secondary arts. The paper money proposed was to represent the first and most real property, the sole source of production, the land itself. "Paper money, we are told, will become superabundant. Of what paper do you speak? If of a paper without a solid basis, undoubtedly; if of one based on the firm foundation of landed property, never. . . . There cannot be a greater error than the fear, so generally prevalent, as to the overissue of assignats. It is thus alone you will clear off your debts, pay your troops, advance the revolution. *Re-absorbed progressively in the purchase of the national domains, this paper money can never become redundant*, any more than the humidity of the atmosphere can become excessive, which descends in rills, finds the river, and is at length lost in the mighty ocean."

The decree for a further issue of eight hundred millions passed, September, 1790. Though the opponents of the issue had lost heart and voice, they still polled 423 votes against 508. To conciliate a minority still so large, contraction was provided for by requiring that the paper when paid into the Treasury should be burned, and the decree contained a solemn declaration that in no case should the amount exceed twelve hundred millions. June 19, 1791, the Assembly, against feeble resistance, violated this pledge and authorized a further issue of six hundred millions.

Under the operation of Gresham's Law,[1] specie now began to disappear from circulation. In vain were those who hoarded coin denounced as enemies of liberty. The

---

[1] See p. 193.

revolutionary government could confiscate estates, but, as we have seen, was powerless to maintain their former value. It could issue assignats, and make them legal tender; but, as Talleyrand had warned the Assembly while it could force a man to receive a thousand francs in paper for a thousand francs which he had lent in specie, it could not oblige him to give a thousand francs of specie still in his possession for a thousand francs, or ten thousand francs, in paper, unless it was for his interest to do so.

But the statesmen and journalists of France would not even acknowledge that it was the prompting of self-interest which detained the specie from circulation and made it flow out of the kingdom. It was the work of the enemies of France, of English and Bourbon emissaries, seeking the overthrow of liberty, which produced the increasing discredit of the paper money and the growing scarcity of gold and silver.

And now came the collapse of French industry. "What the bigotry of Louis XIV and the shiftlessness of Louis XV could not do in nearly a century, was accomplished by this tampering with the currency in a few months. Everything that tariffs and custom-houses could do was done. Still the great manufactories of Normandy were closed; those of the rest of the kingdom speedily followed, and vast numbers of workmen, in all parts of the country, were thrown out of employment. . . . In the spring of 1791 no one knew whether a piece of paper money, representing 100 francs, would, a month later, have a purchasing power of 100 francs, or 90 francs, or 80, or 60. The result was that capitalists declined to embark their means in business. Enterprise received a mortal blow. Demand for labor was still further diminished. The business of France dwindled into a mere living from hand to mouth. This state of things, too, while it bore heavily against the interests of the moneyed classes, was still more ruinous to those in more moderate, and most of all to those in straitened, circumstances. With the masses of the people the purchase of every article of supply became a speculation, a speculation in which the professional speculator had an immense advantage over the buyer. Says the most brilliant of apologists for French Revolutionary statesmanship, 'Commerce was dead, betting took its place.'"[1]

Soon we observe the spectacle, familiar in the colonial assemblies of America, of the debtor class invading the legislature with their impudent demand for fresh issues, the further to scale down debts. A new issue was made of three hundred millions. To appease the opposition of the minority, to quiet the apprehensions of the people and to put a stop to the depreciation, it was declared that the actual circulation should never be allowed to exceed sixteen hundred millions. "What this promise was worth," says President White, "may be judged from the fact that, not only had the declaration made hardly a year before, limiting the amount in circulation to twelve hundred millions, been violated; but the declaration made hardly a month before, in which the Assembly had as solemnly limited the amount in circulation to fourteen hundred millions, had also been repudiated." In a word the pledge of the Assembly had become worth just as much as a drunkard's promises, and no more. In February, 1792, assignats had been more than 30 per cent. below par. During the spring and summer came two more issues of three hundred millions each. In December an official statement was put forth that thirty-four hundred millions had been issued,

[1] White, pp. 30–4.

of which six hundred had been burned, leaving twenty-eight hundred millions in circulation.

And here appeared a fresh basis for issues. The paper money had been put forth on the security of the confiscated estates of the Church. The seizure of the lands of the emigrant nobles, as the enemies of France, offered a larger ground for these issues, which Mirabeau had assured the nation could never become excessive. Still, as the assignats poured from the treasury in increasing volume, the cry of the scarcity of the circulating medium grew louder. Soon that cry gave way to another, not unfamiliar in the same connection. "Bread or Blood" riots took place in the streets; stores and shops were plundered by famished wretches; the government was driven by sheer stress of violence to feed the capital.[1] The government service itself was scarcely to be maintained, for the wholesale resignations of officials, driven out by the depreciation of the money in which their salaries were paid.

In logical order came the next resort of baffled power. Maximum laws were enacted, as has been related of the American Revolutionary government, with only the effect still further to diminish supplies of food and fuel, as producers withheld the goods for which they were forbidden to take a price which would enable them to replace their stock. The inhabitants of the cities of France were put on an allowance of food, like sailors drifting at sea in open boats. Still the depreciation of this money, based unshakably on "the only real property, the sole source of production, the soil on which we tread," went on. Against the Premium on Silver, the revolutionary government which had struck down

[1] "To supply five armies and a vast Capital, with the mere power of issuing assignats."—[Thiers, The Consulate and the Empire.]

Church and State, which had confiscated one-third and more of the real property of France, and was strong enough to send every morning tumbril-loads of freshly convicted Frenchmen—peasants, priests, and nobles—to the guillotine, directed its utmost force. By law of April 11, 1793, the purchase of specie was forbidden under penalty of six years in irons. In August, a law prohibited the sale of assignats below their nominal value, on penalty of twenty years in chains. Soon came another law, punishing with death investments of capital in foreign countries.

Towards the end of 1794 there had been issued 7,000 millions in assignats; by May, 1795, 10,000 millions; by the end of July, 16,000 millions; by the beginning of 1796, 45,000 millions, of which 36,000 millions were in actual circulation.[1]

---

[1] White, pp. 53–4.

"Sans compter le papier-monnaie que les insurgés de la Vendée, et de la Bretagne mirent en circulation."—[Garnier.]

Mr. Dillaye, in a recent pamphlet, has attacked this statement, which is found in a hundred works of reputation. His sole authority appears to be Louis Blanc. I do not profess to have investigated the subject; but nothing which Mr. Dillaye adduces strikes me as sufficient to throw doubt on the accepted figures of the issues for 1795–6.

M. Joseph Garnier, in his "Traité de Finances" [p. 408], gives the following itemized statement from a work of M. Ramel, former Minister of Finance: The numbers represent millions of francs.

| | |
|---|---|
| Assignats créés par l'assemblée constituante (lois des 21 Déc., 1789, 17 Avril, 1790, 19 Juin, 1790), - - | 1,800 |
| Assignats créés par l'assemblée législative, - - - | 900 |
| " " directement par la Convention, - - | 7,278 |
| " " par les Comités autorisés, } " " par le Directoire, } - - | 33,603 |
| | 45,581 |

M. Bresson gives a total differing by only two or three millions.

M. Bresson gives the following table of depreciation:[1] 24 livres in coin were worth in assignats

| | | | |
|---|---|---|---|
| April 1, 1795, | 238 | October 1, 1795, | 1,205 |
| May " " | 299 | Nov. " " | 2,588 |
| June " " | 439 | Dec. " " | 3,575 |
| July " " | 808 | January 1, 1796, | 4,658 |
| Aug " " | 807 | Feb. " " | 5,337 |
| Sept " " | 1,101 | | |

At the last, "an assignat professing to be worth 100 francs was commonly exchanged for 5 sous 6 deniers: in other words, a paper note professing to be worth £4 sterling passed current for less than 3*d.* in money."[2]

The downward course of the assignats had unquestionably been accelerated by the extensive counterfeiting of the paper in Belgium, Switzerland, and England. There is reason to believe that the government of the latter country directly encouraged this discreditable enterprise, as it had done the counterfeiting of the Continental money during the American Revolution. So completely had the country, to all appearances, been drained of its specie, that, when General Bonaparte set out, early in 1796, to take command in Italy, he carried with him in his carriage the "military chest" of his army, containing 2,000 gold louis, which were all the authorities could place at his disposal to carry on war in a foreign land. M. Bresson says there is still extant an order-of-the-day, signed by Berthier, announcing that each general officer would receive four louis to fit him out for the campaign.

Now appears that last resort of finance under a depreciating paper: an issue under new names and new

---

[1] Hist. Financière de la France, ii, 225.

[2] Twiss, Progress of Political Economy, p. 263.

devices. We have seen this in the history of Connecticut, giving rise to the distinction of "new-tenor" and "old-tenor"; and we have seen that much importance was attached in Rhode Island to the consideration that the new paper should be issued on plates virgin of previous impressions. In Massachusetts, by 1747, this financial expedient had been so often resorted to, that the paper money of the colony had to be distinguished as old-tenor, middle-tenor, and new-tenor, the latter being further divided as new-tenor-first and new-tenor-second.[1]

In the desperate extremity to which the revolutionary government was reduced in 1796, it had resort to a similar expedient. *Territorial Mandates* were ordered to be issued for assignats at 30 : 1, the mandates to be directly exchangeable for land, at the will of the holder, on demand. Eight hundred millions were to be used in canceling the assignats; the remainder to be applied to the exigencies of the government. For a brief time after the first limited emission, the mandates rose as high as 80 per cent. of their nominal value; but soon additional issues sent them down even more rapidly than the assignats had fallen.[2] Soon they were worth but $\frac{1}{1000}$ part of their nominal value. As one mandate was worth 30 assignats, remarks Mr. McLeod, the latter might be reckoned at $\frac{1}{30000}$.

This course was run and finished[3] before the 1st July, 1796, at which date the whole system was demolished.

---

[1] Sumner, p. 31.

[2] "Frappé de mort dès sa naissance."—[Bresson.]

[3] Bresson [ii, 222–3] states that a third kind of paper called *Rescriptions métalliques*, was created by the Directory; but that the career of this paper was so brief that there was not even time to engrave the plates for it.

A new decree authorized every man to transact business in the money and on the terms he chose. Mandates were only to be taken at their market value, which was published every day from the Treasury.

"No sooner," says Mr. McLeod,[1] "was this great blow struck at the paper currency, of making it pass at its current value, than specie immediately re-appeared in circulation.[2] Immense hoards came forth from their hiding places; goods and commodities of all sorts being very cheap, from the anxiety of their owners to possess money, caused immense sums to be imported from foreign countries. The exchanges immediately turned in favor of France, and in a short time a metallic currency was permanently restored. *And during all the terrific wars of Napoleon the metallic standard was always maintained at full value.*"

## ENGLAND UNDER THE RESTRICTION.

The sentence last quoted from Mr. McLeod, connects the experience of France, in the matter of Inconvertible Paper Money, with that of England.

In 1793 the two countries became at war. Besides the coin of the realm, which was variously estimated from 22.5 millions [Tooke] upwards, the money of Great Britain, excluding Ireland, consisted of notes issued by the Bank of England, by the country banks—some hundreds in number—not, as they largely are now, joint-stock banks, but often small traders, and by the Scotch banks, few and strong.

---

[1] Economical Philosophy, ii, 353.

[2] M. Thiers states that considerable amounts of specie had appeared in circulation, especially Spanish piastres in the southern provinces, even during the currency of the mandates.

The Lords' Committee of 1819 estimated the circulation of the kingdom as follows:

| | |
|---|---|
| Coin, - - - - - - - | £25,000,000 |
| Bank of England, - - - - - | 10,500,000 |
| Country Notes and Scottish, - - | 7,000,000 |
| Total, - - - - - - | £42,500,000 |

The war continued for three years without the suspension of specie payments, or, apparently, any serious apprehensions of such a result. At least, suspension was not regarded as a necessary concomitant of a state of war. In 1796, however, the government borrowed heavily of the Bank of England[1] for war expenses; and, to the great dissatisfaction of the directors, postponed or refused the promised repayments. The Bank, reduced to extremity, began to contract its circulation. At this juncture came a rumor of French invasion, and the news of an actual, though, as it turned out, accidental appearance of the enemy off the coast. A run on the country banks ensued, which caused them to make heavy demands on the Bank of England. So far, the narrative belongs to the history of Convertible Paper Money.

By the 27th of February the specie reserve of the Bank was reduced to £1,000,000, when an Order in Council forbade the Bank to pay further in specie till the will of Parliament should be made known. In May Parliament passed an act restraining the Bank from specie payments,[2] the Bank being placed in the attitude

[1] "It was owing to the too intimate connection between the Bank and Government that the restriction became necessary; it is to that cause, too, that we owe its continuance."—[Ricardo, High Price of Bullion.]

[2] The bank could only issue cash for sums under 20 shillings But if any person lodged specie in the bank, he might be repaid to the extent of three-quarters the sum lodged, if it exceeded £500

of desiring to pay specie but not being permitted; and this so-called Restriction was continued from time to time by various acts, the Bank in the earlier portions of the period professing its readiness to resume specie payments, should the public interest allow.

Two questions arise respecting the suspension. Was it inevitable, when and as it occurred? Would it eventually have become so, had it been for a time averted?

Upon the first point we have the high authority of Mr. Tooke and Mr. Ricardo, in giving a negative answer.

Mr. Tooke says: "I do not think that the suspension of cash payments was, at that time, of absolute necessity. I have never entertained the least question but that, if the Bank had continued to pay and to suppress its notes as it issued treasure, the crisis would have been got over."

Mr. Ricardo: "If the Bank had continued paying in cash, probably the panic would have subsided before the coin had been exhausted."

On the second question the weight of opinion, outside the professed economists, inclines perhaps to the ultimate necessity of suspending cash payments during a severe and protracted war. This way of looking at the subject has probably been strongly confirmed in the mind of the present generation by the easy collapse of the United States in 1862 and of France in 1870.

Sir Archibald Alison has left the strongest assertions of the necessity of the act of 1797. "No one can doubt that it was in the great extension of the currency, which took place from 1797 to 1810, that the resources were mainly found which provided both for the long-continued efforts with which the war was attended, and the gigantic expenditure of its later years.—[History of Europe.]

"Vain," he remarks elsewhere, "would have been the numerous advantages, physical and political, which Great Britain enjoyed during the contest, if a fortunate combination of circumstances, joined to uncommon wisdom on the part of its government, had not established a system of currency in the heart of the empire adequate to the wants of its immense dependencies, capable of expansion at will, according to the necessities of the times, and not liable to be drawn off at particular periods by the balances of trade or the military necessities of foreign states. . . . The vast and imperious demand for the precious metals, and especially gold, for the use and maintenance of the immense armies contending on the Continent, of necessity drained away nearly the whole of the precious metals from the country at the very time when they were most required for the support of domestic credit, or the cost of warlike establishments. When such a drain for specie set in from foreign parts, certain ruin must have ensued if the empire had possessed no resources within itself to supply the place of the precious metals which were taken away."

On the other hand, Prof. Sumner has said respecting the alleged necessity for suspension: "Political Economy emphatically declares that it never can be necessary."—[Hist. Am. Currency, p. 202]; and Prof. Newcomb, in his "Financial History of the United States," 1861–5, has made a very strong and suggestive argument on the same side.[1] Nor can we put out of sight

[1] "The military power of a nation is measured by the amount of industry which it can divert into the channels of war." . . . That amount "is not increased by the possession of any sort of money." ["The latter only facilitates the diversion by making it easier to measure each man's share of the public burden."] . . .

the fact that all the wars of Napoleon were conducted, on his side, without the use of paper money. Perhaps we may fairly say that the question is one of Finance rather than of pure Political Economy; that is, a question in which the statesman must take counsel of the economist, but always with respect to distinctly political considerations.

But though England thus entered upon a career of inconvertible paper, the prudence and firmness of the Bank management during the first eleven or twelve years prevented any considerable increase of issues over the amount of metallic money which would have circulated in the kingdom. It was indeed alleged and commonly believed between 1797 and 1808, that the notes of the Bank were largely in excess. The disturbance of commercial relations and the effects of war taxation had produced such fluctuations in markets, and had carried the prices of certain articles to such an extravagant height, as almost necessarily to create the belief referred to. But in the most memorable economico-statistical investigation ever undertaken, Mr. Thomas Tooke showed the opinion to be erroneous. His grand result was, that, during the first twelve years of the suspension, the exchanges were as favorable as they had been on an average of ninety-six years, or of any ten consecutive years preceding 1797.

In 1809, however, appeared a wide divergence between the mint price of gold[1] and its market price in

"It depends upon and is measured by what the nation is able to produce over and above what is necessary for its subsistence." . . . "Gold is a sinew of war in no higher sense than quicksilver or platinum, or anything else for which we can obtain munitions of war."

[1] The attempt of Parliament to restrain by law the melting and exportation of gold and silver coins, led to an absurd complication,

Bank of England notes. The mint price of an ounce of standard gold being £3 17*s.* 10½*d*, the market price had risen in 1811 to £4 4*s.* 6*d.*, in 1812 to £4 15*s.* 6*d.*, in 1813 to £5 1*s.*, and in 1814 to £5 4*s.*

The perturbations of exchange and of prices in the first years of the century had aroused the attention of thoughtful publicists in England. In 1800 Mr. Boyd addressed a letter to Mr. Pitt, ascribing the whole of the fall in the exchanges and the rise in the price of provisions to excessive issues of the Bank of England. This drew forth a reply from Sir Francis Baring. In 1802 Mr. Henry Thornton published his treatise on "Paper Credit," from which extracts have already been made. In 1803 Lord King published his "Thoughts on the Bank of England Restriction," a work of which Prof. Senior wrote in 1846: "It contains so full and, in the main, so true an exposition of the theory of paper money, that, after more than forty years of discussion, there is little to add to it or to correct." The doctrine known as "Lord King's doctrine" is thus stated by Mr. McLeod [Economical Philosophy, ii, 303]:

"The rise of the paper price of bullion above the mint price, and a continuous state of the foreign exchanges below the limits of the real exchange, are the proof and the measure of the depreciation of an inconvertible paper currency."

In 1809, the divergence between the mint and the

---

which is thus stated by Mr. Huskisson in his pamphlet on the "Depreciation of the Currency":

"The state of the law therefore, is this: The possessor of a heavy guinea, which is intrinsically worth about 24*s.* 6*d.* in bank paper, who should exchange it for more than 21*s.* of that paper, would be liable to fine and imprisonment. The more fortunate possessor of a light guinea is entitled by law to exchange it for what it will fetch, which would be about 24*s.* 3*d.*"

market price of bullion rapidly increasing, Mr. David Ricardo published his memorable pamphlet on the "High Price of Bullion." The doctrines of this pamphlet being attacked by Mr. Charles Bosanquet, Mr. Ricardo published a reply, which remains the masterpiece of this great economist.

In 1810 the subject was brought to the attention of Parliament, and a committee known as the Bullion Committee was appointed. Mr. Horner was chairman and Messrs. Huskisson and Thornton were among the members. The report was rendered in June, 1810. The doctrines of the report were nearly those of Mr. Ricardo.[1]

[1] Mr. Joplin, in his "Analysis and History of the Currency Question," asserts that Mr. Ricardo felt himself ill-treated, in that credit for his ideas was not given him by the Committee. Mr. Joplin goes so far as to invent the term *Hornerizing* as expressive of the borrowing of ideas without permission and without acknowledgment. Mr. Ricardo may have had the feeling attributed to him; but the charge of seeking to build up reputation out of other men's brains is not one which can justly be brought against Francis Horner.' In his letter to J. A. Murray, Mr. Horner makes the following frank admissions:

"I can let you into the secret, however, that the Report is in truth very clumsily and prolixly drawn, stating nothing but very old doctrines on the subject it treats of, and stating them in a more imperfect form than they have frequently appeared in before. It is a motley composition by Huskisson, Thornton and myself, each having written parts, which are tacked together without any care to give them a uniform style, or a very exact connection. One great merit the Report, however, possesses; that it declares in very plain and pointed terms both the true doctrine, and the existence of a great evil growing out of the neglect of that doctrine." In a subsequent letter to Jeffrey, July 16, 1810, he seems to admit that the authorship of the doctrines of the Report should be more publicly known "I will do a short article for you, this time, to do justice to Mr. Ricardo and Mr. Mushet, who called the public attention to this very important subject at the end of last year."—[ii, 51.]

The report of the Bullion Committee led to a war of pamphlets which is wholly without parallel in the history of economical literature.[1] The doctrines of the report were defended by Mr. Ricardo and Mr. Huskisson. They were attacked by two schools of writers, who differed among themselves almost as widely as they differed from the bullionists. They were, first, the authorities and friends of the Bank of England (including the government), who denied the existence of any increase of circulation; or indeed that the issues of the Bank required any regulation not implied in good banking. Second, the advocates of paper-money inflation. It is to the thorough discussion of the money question between 1809 and 1811 that we owe one of the greatest advances of economical science.

The practical recommendation of the Bullion Committee had been that the Bank should be required to resume cash payments within two years. This provision formed the last of a series of sixteen resolutions moved by Mr. Horner, in the House of Commons, May 6, 1811. A counter-set of three resolutions was moved by Mr. Vansittart, the third being the memorable one, food for unending laughter: "That the promissory notes of the Bank of England have hitherto been, and are at this time held to be, equivalent to the legal coin of the realm." This in the face of the fact that British gold coin was selling at a premium of nearly 20 per cent. in Bank of England notes!

The bullionists were beaten, and the House adopted, 151 to 75, Mr. Vansittart's resolutions, even to the last. Against the resolution of Mr. Horner for speedy resumption, the government triumphed 180 to 45.

---

[1] The fullest collection of Bullion pamphlets in this country, so far as I am aware, is in the valuable Watkinson library of Hartford.

During this year Lord King issued a circular to his tenants, demanding payment of his rents in specie or its equivalent. For this act Lord King was vehemently denounced as unpatriotic, and an act was passed by Parliament, known as Lord Stanhope's Act, making it an offense to buy or sell guineas at more than their denominative value in the notes of the Bank of England. Lord King's object in making this demand upon his tenants was to bring about a *gold price* and a *paper price* for rents and commodities within the kingdom, as a means of strongly attracting public attention to the fact of depreciation, and securing a general interest in the resumption of specie payments.[1]

But though the bullionists were beaten in the immediate parliamentary struggle, the principles of the Report won their way to the general conviction of the public mind of England, and the actual resumption, ten years later, was accomplished under their leadership.

The war closed in 1815. The average paper price of gold which had stood at £5 4*s.* per ounce in 1814, sank to £4 13*s.* 6*d.*, where it remained through 1816.[2]

---

[1] In view of the abuse heaped upon Lord King, it is interesting to find the philosopher Locke, who took so prominent a part in the reform of the coinage in 1696 [see p. 213], writing to his friend Clarke, in May, 1695: "I shall, I think, in the beginning of July have some money paid me in, and perhaps some sooner. Pray tell me whether I cannot refuse clipped money; for I take it not to be the lawful coin of England, and I know not why I should receive half the value I lent, instead of the whole."—[Fox Bourne's Life of Locke, ii, 325.]

[2] This was the year, it will be remembered, in which, under Lord Liverpool's leadership, England adopted the single gold standard, remitting silver to the office of subsidiary coin.—[See p. 225.]

In 1817 the premium encountered a further fall, until for the time there occurred what Mr. Tooke called "a spontaneous re-adjustment of the value between gold and paper to a perfect equality."—[Hist. Prices, ii, 60.]

At this point the directors of the Bank undertook voluntarily the redemption of their one and two-pound notes, dated prior to January 1, 1816. Under this offer as Mr. Francis states,[1] scarcely any demand was made on the Bank coffers, the amount of cash paid out for the redemption of these notes, held principally by the poorer classes, not exceeding £1,000,000. In October of the same year the directors, encouraged by the results of this partial experiment, announced that they would pay gold for their notes of all denominations issued prior to January 1, 1817. From this position the Bank was obliged to recede. A demand for gold set in which resulted in draining away over £5,000,000, and, on the report of Mr. Peel, the House, in two nights, passed a bill restraining further payment.

Thus, though the vessel had drifted in to land, and had fairly touched the shore, it was borne away by a counter-current and carried out again to sea.

What was the cause of the advance of the gold premium, after the partial resumption of 1817?

Mr. Francis, adopting the Bank view, says the bullion operators stepped in as soon as payment of large notes was offered and took off the gold. But what made it for the interest of the dealers in bullion to take gold away? The exchanges were unfavorable. But why, persist the bullionists, were the exchanges unfavorable?

Prof. Sumner thus summarizes the bullionist argu-

---

[1] History of the Bank of England, i, 316.

ments: "The balance of imports and exports never can move the exchanges either above or below par more than just enough to start a movement of bullion. On a specie system, any outflow of bullion would bring down prices and immediately make a remittance of goods more profitable than one of bullion, and if the exportation of bullion was artificially continued (as for instance to pay the expenses of a foreign war), it would reduce prices until a counter-current would set in and restore the former relative distribution all the world over. If all nations used specie, or even paper and specie in only due proportion, it would be as impossible for one nation to be drained of specie, as for New York harbor to be drained of water by the tide, and on the same supposition, it would be as absurd for the Secretary of the Treasury or a committee of Congress to regulate the currency, as for the same powers to see to it that New York harbor gets its fair share of water, on every tide. . . . . If, therefore, there is an outflow of gold, serious and long continued, accompanied by an unfavorable exchange, it is a sign that there is an inferior currency behind the gold which is displacing it.

"The surplus of imports of goods above the exports of goods is nothing but the return payment for this export of gold, and is not a cause, but a consequence. If, finally, we want to turn this tide and produce an influx, there is only one way to do it, and that is simply to remove the inferior currency. As for waiting for the balance of trade to turn and bring gold into a country which has a depreciated paper currency, one might as well take his stand at the foot of a hill and wait for it to change into a declivity before climbing it."—[Hist. Am. Currency, pp. 264–5.]

This is the familiar doctrine of Ricardo. I have said

that the general truth of the doctrine cannot be questioned, though some qualification of its severity may at times require to be made in application to particular cases.[1]

Consistently with the above views, the bullionists should allege that the re-appearance of the premium in 1818 was due to an increased issue of bank-notes, and so indeed they do.[2] Mr. Tooke, however, declares that the restoration of the value of the bank-note during the first six months of 1817 had coincided with an enlargement of the Bank issues, as compared with any previous period: he attributes the disturbance at the close of 1817 and throughout 1818 to the large loans negotiated in England for the French and Russian governments.—[Hist. of Prices, ii, 52; 60–1.]

However it came about, the year 1818 brought a severe commercial crisis and numerous failures occurred, compelling the attention of Parliament to the subject of the Restriction. Each House appointed a committee which conducted a separate investigation. Against strong opposition from "the City," where the effects of an effort towards resumption were greatly dreaded, and in spite of the remonstrances of the Bank, the House of Commons committee reported a bill based on the doctrines of the Bullion Report of 1810.

"This memorable bill," says Mr. Francis, "provides that, from the first of February to the first of October, the Bank shall deliver on demand gold of standard fine-

---

[1] How, for example, would Prof. Sumner explain the recent influx of gold into the United States, which has "a depreciated paper currency"?

[2] "Adhering to the doctrine that the issues could not affect the exchanges, it [the Bank] continued to expand the circulation while paying out gold."—[Sumner, Hist. Am. Currency, p. 285.]

ness, not less than 60 oz., in exchange for bank-notes at £4 1*s*. per oz. From the first of October, 1820, to the first of October, 1821, the same plan to be adopted; but the gold to be at the rate of £3 19*s*. 6*d*. per oz. From the first of May, 1821, to the first of May, 1823, the mint price of gold of £3 17*s*. 10½*d*. per oz. to be the rate, with the adoption of the same plan; and from the first of May, 1823, the notes to be paid in the gold coin of the empire if required. . . . They were permitted also the option of paying in specie on or after the first of May, 1822. By the same Act the laws which restrained the exportation of gold and silver coin, or prohibited it from being melted, were repealed."—[Hist. of the Bank of England, i, 325.]

The debate on the bill brought out two questions, besides the more general one of the expediency of attempting to secure resumption by legislation, instead of waiting for "a spontaneous re-adjustment," like that of 1817, which might become permanent, or, as the American phrase is, "growing up to the currency."

The first question was, shall the ancient standard be restored? This is the same question which we saw arising at the recoinages of 1696 and 1774. For twenty years specie payments had been suspended: during the latter portion of this term prices had been greatly raised by excessive issues. The government had contracted debts amounting to many hundred millions of pounds, representing loans for war purposes, made in money whose purchasing power was reduced by the causes indicated. Private indebtedness, commercial and industrial, to an enormous amount had also been incurred. Should the money of the realm now be restored to its full value, and creditors thus be enabled to exact in coin the full nominal amount of loans made in, or of sales at prices predicated upon, the depreciated money?[1]

The other question followed naturally upon the first What was the degree of depreciation of the Bank of England note?

Mr. Ricardo and the bullionists were bound to hold that the depreciation was measured[2] by the premium on gold, which at this time had sunk to 3 per cent.; and these figures became a sort of catch-word in the debates on the Act of 1819, and in the fierce discussions over the wisdom and justice of that Act which extended through the fifteen years next succeeding. The question whether, in a country having an Inconvertible Paper Money, the premium on gold measures the depreciation, may be deferred to the next chapter. It is enough here that this was the theory of the upholders of the Resumption Act of 1819, and it was probably through their confident assertions that the depreciation of the Bank of England notes was very slight that they were

---

[1] "One of the most fatal effects of that suspension is the great and unavoidable distress which attends a return to a specie currency, particularly when the suspension has been of long continuance. While this lasts, the loss falls on the creditors; but new contracts are daily made, founded on the existing state of the currency; and should the suspension continue twenty years, as was the case in England, as almost all the contracts in force and not yet executed, at the time when specie payments are resumed, must have been made when the currency was depreciated, the obligation to discharge them in specie is contrary to equity, falls on the debtors, who are always the part of the community less able to bear the burden, and proves more calamitous than the suspension had been."—[A. Gallatin, Considerations, etc., pp. 37–8.]

[2] "The effect produced by the depreciation has been most accurately defined, and amounts to the difference between the market and the mint price of gold."—[Ricardo, Reply to Bosanquet.]

able to carry that measure, which they accomplished under the championship of Mr., afterwards Sir, Robert Peel, who had opposed Mr. Horner's resolutions, and who frankly admitted that he went into Committee with a very different opinion from that he at present entertained. The debate, in breadth and force of argument, fell much below that of 1811.

After the passage of Peel's Act, whether in consequence of it or not, the premium on gold fell even faster than was necessary to meet the successive requirements of the law. In February, 1819, gold had been worth £4 1*s.* 6*d.* In February, 1820, it sold at £3 19*s.* 11*d.* In February, 1821, it was worth only the mint price £3 17*s.* 10½*d.*, and on May 1, 1821, in advance of the date fixed, the Bank, on its own instance, under permission of Parliament, resumed cash payment. Thus closed what Lord Overstone has called "the dark age of Currency."

The effects of Peel's Act have been the subject of vehement controversy. To this law, primarily, was attributed by one party the long succession of commercial disasters, producing deep and settled industrial distress, which followed the peace. The reduction in the world's supply of the precious metals through this period, due to the Spanish-American revolutions, was not so fully apprehended by the popular mind; but the restriction upon the issues of the Bank of England, and the obligation to pay in gold debts contracted under Inconvertible Paper Money, were of a nature to compel the attention of the least thoughtful. It is not at all surprising that the commercial and industrial misfortunes of the succeeding period were laid at the door of the Act of 1819.

Whatever may have been the logical effect of Mr. Ricardo's declaration,[1] that the depreciation of the Bank of England notes was but three per cent., the public mind had followed it out to a conclusion that the effect of resumption on prices would be slight. When, therefore, the most extensive disturbances in trade followed resumption, and the prices of the most important articles fell through many degrees, bringing to distress, if not to ruin, large manufacturing and agricultural interests, it was natural enough that the distress should be charged to the Act of 1819. The theory of that Act, it was alleged, had been wrong. Mr. Ricardo had been egregiously mistaken[2] in saying that the depreciation was but three per cent. The depreciation had been 30, 40, or even 50 per cent.; and the enforced resumption had aggravated to this extent the burden of all fixed charges, private and public, including the enormous debt with which England had issued from the twenty-two years' struggle. Of all who took a part in the controversy over the wisdom and justice of the Act of 1819, its ablest and boldest assailant was

[1] "If," says Mr. Tooke [History of Prices, ii, 117], "it had been an object with the legislature, when the state of the currency was brought before it in 1819, to maintain the prices which had been the consequence of scarcity and speculation, no means were open to it but to degrade the standard *by between* 30 *and* 50 *per cent.* at a time when, by the ordinary tests of the price of gold and the exchanges, the utmost depreciation of the paper did not exceed between 3 *and* 5 *per cent.*"

[2] It is a favorite assertion with writers on this side the question, that Mr. Ricardo subsequently recanted his opinions as to the extent of the depreciation, and admitted his error. See Sir James Graham, "Corn and Currency," pp. 39, 40, 43; William Ward "Commercial Legislation of 1846" (quoted by Duncan on Currency, p 116) Thomas Attwood, "The Scotch Banker," pp. 14, 22, 24.

Sir James Graham. His tract, "Corn and Currency," published in 1826, contains an unmeasured denunciation of that measure.

"Whether we regard private debts or public burdens, the effects of the measure of 1819 have been to enact, that for every less sum owing a greater shall be paid; prices falling, but pecuniary engagements remaining undiminished, the farmer has no profit, the landlord no rent, the manufacturer no customer, the laborer no employment; a revolution of property and a derangement of the whole frame of society must necessarily ensue. . . . It has conferred on the fund-holder a benefit to the extent of the depreciation of the money which he advanced; in many cases this is equal to 35 per cent. But this rise of the fundlord is affected by ruin of the landlord. Estates which have been held from generation to generation in the same family are rapidly changing owners; and, as the country gentleman retires, the fund-holder advances. . . . Amidst the ruin of the farmer and the manufacturer, the distress of landlords, and the insurrections of a populace without bread and without employment, one class flourished and was triumphant: the annuitant and the tax-eater rejoiced in the increased value of money; in the sacrifice of productive industry to unproductive wealth, in the victory of the drones over the bees." Sir James Graham appealed to the example of France and the United States at the close of the preceding century, in support of the justice and expediency of a reduction of the standard to meet the facts of the circulation.

"In the example of France we find retributive justice; in the example of America, prospective wisdom: but in vain shall we seek to discover the slightest vestige of either virtue in the British enactments of 1797 and 1819. *Here* by law we depreciated the currency, and, by a solemn resolution of the House of Commons,[1] denied the fact of depreciation. *Here* by law we raised the value of money, and, instead of avowing our purpose and preparing for its effects, we mystified the intention and were blind to the result."

But, while the opponents of the act of 1819 indulged in the very extravagance of vituperation, Mr. Tooke[2] has undertaken to demonstrate that that measure was, in fact, absolutely nugatory, causes, commercial and financial, operating independently of it to bring about resumption without reference to the law, and, as we have seen, in advance of its requirements.

"If, then," says Mr. Tooke, "Peel's Bill was thus inoperative and therefore innocent of all the evils which have been so abundantly, and with so much superfluous eloquence, laid to its charge, it may be asked, what was the merit of the bill, and what was the ground of the importance attached to it by its promoters? . . . The merit of the measure was, as it has since turned out, independent of the event. That merit consisted in the sanction which it afforded to the principle that the Bank has the power, by the regulation of its issues, to preserve the value of its paper on a level with that of gold; and the importance attached to it by its promoters is fully justified by the consideration that, at the time when it was under discussion, there was fair ground for contemplating circumstances under which the compulsory clauses of the act would come into operation."—[Hist. of Prices, ii, 108–9.]

It might well be thought that the history of the Bank

---

[1] Mr. Vansittart's, quoted on p. 354.

[2] See his letter to Lord Grenville 1829.

Restriction more properly belongs in a later department of our inquiry, inasmuch as the notes of the Bank were never, in any sense, government paper, and hence their inconvertibility from 1797 to 1821 might be regarded as resulting from the degeneration of a convertible paper money. But, as the government took the initiative in the suspension, and as the question whether the Bank should resume specie payments (which, for a time, the directors professed to be not only able and willing, but desirous, to do,) was always treated as a question of government policy, the account of the great English suspension has been introduced here.

### OTHER EXAMPLES.

England presents the last example of a great commercial nation, after a long period of suspension, freeing itself from the evils of inconvertible paper, and re-adopting the money of the world. France, Russia, Austria, Italy, and the United States, of the more important countries of the globe, with a number of smaller states, have, at various times, lapsed into this condition, and still remain under irredeemable paper money, though in France and the United States the government has pledged itself to an early resumption, and the premium on gold has approached a minimum.

In France the Revolution of February caused the government in 1848 to authorize the Bank of France to suspend specie payments. So closely, however, were the issues limited that the notes of the Bank were not depreciated beyond 2 or 3 per cent., and this only for a brief period. M. Wolowski states[1] that this forced circulation lasted only about four months.

[1] La Question des Banques, p. 258.

The occurrence of the war with Germany in 1870 caused a suspension by the Bank, which has lasted to the present time; but during all this period the condition of her circulation has constituted a triumph of sound finance. Although irredeemable, her paper has never been allowed, at any moment, to become greatly in excess. The premium in gold has never gone above 1.5 per cent. and, during the greater portion of the period, has been 5, 4, or even less, per mille. "The failure of the French armies," wrote the late Mr. Bagehot, in November, 1874, "has not been more striking than the success of French banking." This is the country which we saw run such a mad career, under the leadership of her orators, but now, under the guidance of statesmen and economists, offers the world a model of cautious, conservative, honorable finance.

The Russian paper money dates back to 1768, when a sort of assignats, to the amount of 40,000,000 roubles, were put in circulation, in direct payments by the government, on the commencement of the war with Turkey. "The manifesto accompanying the issue of this paper," says Mr. Tooke,[1] "left it in doubt whether the payment to bearer was to be in copper or silver; and, according to Storch, opinions were still divided when he wrote in 1815." "The *agio*," says Mr. Tooke, "in favor of silver varied only from 1 to 3 per cent. in that interval, while there was an *agio* of 1:5 per cent. in favor of paper against copper."

In 1787, however, a sudden addition was made of 60,000,000 roubles, accompanied by a pledge that no more should be issued; but a series of exhausting wars with

[1] Hist. of Prices, ii, 67. For Russian paper money see also, i, 140–1; ii, 209–16.

Sweden, Turkey, Poland, Persia, and France, caused a successive increase of the paper till, in 1810, the amount outstanding was computed at 577,000,000. The premium on silver[1] had risen to 400. During the progress of the depreciation, the customs-dues were paid in paper, the rates in silver, as fixed by law, being converted into paper rates, according to the premium ruling at the time. In 1839 the emperor, by a manifesto, ordained the adoption of cash payments, by making the paper rouble in circulation payable in silver on demand, in the proportion of $3\frac{1}{2}:1$.

The aggressive enterprises of Russia have since involved her in new financial embarrassments, and at the outbreak of the present war gold stood at 12 to 16 per cent. premium at St. Petersburg. Mr. Seyd[2] offers the following significant remark respecting the Russian paper money: "As regards the rouble notes in circulation in the Russian Empire, it is stated that the imperial government itself is not aware of the actual totals issued, and has thus lost control over its liabilities in reference to the same; moreover, a large quantity of successfully forged notes is in circulation, which the authorities hesitate to suppress, fearing a further disturbance of credit. If this be true, we may soon hear of something more serious than a mere farther depreciation of Russian paper money."

---

[1] Mr. Tooke notes as a curious fact, that the value of Russian paper money increased coincidently with the invasion of the French armies in 1812, insomuch that the exchange for the rouble, which a few months before had been 14*d.*, rose, by the time the French reached Moscow, to 24*d.*—[Hist. of Prices, i, 140.] Mr. Tooke attributes this singular phenomenon to the fear that the export of Russian produce would be cut off by the French, leading to the disposition to buy largely in advance, at almost any rate.

[2] Bullion and Foreign Exchanges, pp. 52–3.

Paper money has long been the curse of Austria,[1] but the present epoch of inconvertible paper began in 1848 through the revolutionary movements of that year. The existing government-issues amount to about one hundred and fifty millions of dollars, American money, circulating equally in both divisions of the empire.[2] The fluctuations of the gold premium in Austria have been very considerable, very largely depending, as it would seem, on political events.

"Twice already," says Herr Max Wirth,[3] "in 1859 and 1866, efforts have been made to return to hard money; but on both occasions they were frustrated by impending wars." In the latter year the exigencies of the war with Prussia drew the empire into a condition of almost hopeless insolvency. In May, 1866, there were in circulation notes amounting to fifty-four millions of dollars of American money: by the end of the year

---

[1] "La papier monnaie est, depuis la fin du siècle dernier, à la suite de la guerre de Sept Ans, l'ulcère de l'Autriche."—[J. Garnier, Traité de Finances, p. 411.]

[2] During the complications with Hungary in 1861, a suit was brought in the English Court of Chancery [the Emperor of Austria *vs.* Day and Kossuth] to compel the defendants to deliver up to be canceled 23 tons weight of paper money, to the value of over 100 million florins, engraved by order of the exile Kossuth, and purporting to be the notes of the Hungarian nation. The Court decided that it could not interfere to prevent a revolution in the Austro-Hungarian Empire, or on account of any alleged hostility to the political rights of the plaintiff as sovereign of Hungary; but that the intended introduction of the notes into Hungary constituted a damage to the property of the plaintiff as sovereign, and to the property of his subjects, whom he had a right to represent in an English court. The Court ordered the money to be reduced to paper pulp, and then returned to the defendants.

[3] International Review, May–June, 1876.

these had been increased to $100,000,000. The highest point was reached in May, 1873, when the issues stood at $170,000,000.

The forced circulation of paper in Italy is of more recent date; but the issues have been rapidly increased, and a corresponding depreciation, from 12 to 20 per cent., has resulted. In Spain, says Mr. Seyd, "the state of things is so uncertain that the relative value between paper money and metallic money can no longer be fixed with any degree of accuracy." Turkey, besides a medley of debased coin, has notes of the Imperial Ottoman Bank, practically irredeemable, circulating at a varying discount.

Most of the states of Central and South America sustain paper money in circulation, at a discount ranging upwards to 399 parts in 400.[1]

The present paper money of the United States was first issued in 1862, in the amount of $150,000,000, as *a measure of resource*, the recognized alternative being the selling of government bonds below par in gold. The choice was admittedly in the power of the government;[2] but

[1] The paper money of the Argentine Republic, at the last quotation I have observed, was at 96 per cent. discount. The Republic of Hayti recently had 300,000,000 piastres of paper money. The rate of exchange was authoritatively fixed at 300 paper dollars for one of coin. The Report of the United States Commissioners to San Domingo, in 1871, showed that the latest issue of paper was at 10 to 20 per cent. discount. "Credit notes," so called, an earlier issue, were received by the government at the rate, fixed by decree, of one dollar silver for 30 dollars paper—96⅔ per cent. discount. "Treasury notes," so called, a still earlier issue, were received at the rate of one dollar silver, to 400 dollars paper—99¾ per cent. discount.

[2] The author of the bill declared "its great object" to be ' to prevent all forcing of the government to sell its bonds in the market to the highest bidder for coin."—[Speech of February 19.]

the Committee of Ways and Means, through their chosen spokesman, Mr. E. G. Spaulding, "objected to any and every form of 'shinning' by government through Wall or State Streets, to begin with; objected to the knocking down of government stocks to seventy-five or sixty cents on the dollar, . . . and finished with firmly refusing to assent to any scheme which should permit a speculation by brokers, bankers, and others in the government securities."[1] Such absolute silliness takes the whole narrative out of the domain of serious history, and transfers Mr. Spaulding to the comic stage. When men speaking for the legislature of thirty millions of people can think of preventing speculation in stocks, declare a forced circulation of paper preferable to the sale of six per cent. bonds below par in gold by a government at war for its very existence, and talk about vindicating the power and dignity of the government,[2] by

---

[1] This is language used by the "New York Tribune" in its account of Mr. Spaulding's position in the interview between the Secretary of the Treasury, the Committee on Ways and Means of the House of Representatives and the Bank Committees of the principal cities, in January, 1862. As Mr. Spaulding adopts the language without qualification in his History of the Legal-tender Act of 1862, it may fairly be taken as expressive of his views.

[2] "But, sir, knowing the power of money, and the disposition there is among men to use it for the acquisition of greater gain, I am unwilling that this government, with all its immense power and resources, should be left in the hands of any class of men, bankers or money-lenders, however respectable and patriotic they may be. *The government is much stronger than any of them. Its capital is much greater. It has control of all the bankers' money, and all the brokers' money*, and all the property of the thirty millions of people under its jurisdiction. Why, then, should it go into Wall Street, State Street, Chestnut Street, or any other street, begging for money? . . . I prefer to assert the power and dignity of the government by the issue of its own notes."—[Mr. Spaulding's speech of January 28.]

the passage of a legal-tender act, what but financial folly in action can be expected?

Mr. Spaulding's language was not only not rebuked by the Congress which, in this supreme crisis of the national destiny, was to make choice of "ways and means" for conducting a mighty war, it was far exceeded in debate, not by a furious and desperate minority driven to the wall, but by the leaders of the House, the chairmen of important committees, occupying positions which in England, France, or Germany would be filled by men profoundly versed in public right, in constitutional law, and in finance.

Sneers and flings at "brokers and hawkers on 'change," "huckstering capitalists," "money-shavers," "harpies," "jobbers and money-changers," abounded in all the debates on the legal-tender bill introduced by the Committee. And so, "in the vigor of a nation not yet taxed a single dollar for the cost of this war,"[1] the Congress of the United States chose to inaugurate a period of forced circulation, rather than sell its six per cent. bonds below par, though at the time the ordinary rate of commercial interest in most of the towns and cities of the land exceeded six per cent.[2] What loss of wealth, not to be computed except by thousands of millions; what injury to national reputation and to private character, were involved in this measure!

None of the pleas which might be urged to excuse the Continental Congress for resorting to the issue of irre-

---

[1] Speech of Hon. J. S. Morrill.

[2] Mr. Spaulding states that the 7–30 notes could not at this time be paid out from the Treasury except at a discount of two per cent. This was a sufficient reason for forced circulation! He was, however, good enough to say: "When money can be obtained at par on six per cent. bonds, I would prefer to have that done to the issuing *a very large amount* of legal-tender notes."

deemable paper, can be offered in behalf of the Congress of 1862. The Continental Congress had no coercive authority, no powers of taxation, not even over foreign goods arriving at the ports of the country. It could obtain funds only by the contributions of the several States, which were free to grant or to withhold what was asked. Moreover, the people of almost every State had been debauched by the effects of their colonial issues, shrinking from the very thought of taxation, and resorting with fatal facility to the manufacture of paper money.

The Congress of the United States in 1862 had ample powers; it could lay its taxes directly upon the trades and occupations of the people, and upon every form of wealth, in every stage of production or exchange, excepting upon domestic goods in act of exportation. The people of the United States were not backward. They were prepared to bear the burdens of the war, not only with a noble patience, but with cheerfulness; and in fact, during the later years of the war and for years after, they did submit without complaining to as clumsy and irritating a system of taxation as has been devised in recent times. There was no failure anywhere, except in the leaders of Congress.

All, however, did not fail alike in this emergency. The little State of Vermont offered, through Representative[1] Morrill and Senator Collamore, a most manly resistance to the passage of the Act. Nor can much be added to or taken from Mr. Owen Lovejoy's financial programme: "I would issue interest-bearing bonds of the United States, and go into the markets and borrow money, and pay the obligations of the government. This would be honest, business-like, and, in the end,

[1] Now Senator.

economical." Messrs. Horton and Roscoe Conkling in the House, and Messrs. Fessenden and Sumner in the Senate, also showed an enlightened appreciation of financial principles.

The legal-tender bill became law February 25, 1862, and it was here seen, as before in France, that the real battle had been fought upon the first issue. Although the Chairman of the Committee had stated that, in his judgment, the $150,000,000 provided for by the Act was a maximum, on the 11th of July following Congress authorized another issue[1] of $150,000,000, and on the 3d of March, 1863, still another issue of equal amount. In the summer of 1864, the premium on gold having risen, in consequence of excessive issues, to 150 per cent., Congress passed an Act, June 30, declaring that the total amount of United States notes should at no time exceed $400,000,000,[2] "and such additional sum, not exceeding $50,000,000, as may be temporarily required for the redemption of temporary loans." Meanwhile the National Banking System had been established and was somewhat slowly going into operation, issuing notes which were redeemable in legal tenders, and hence a direct addition to the Inconvertible Paper Money of the

---

[1] March 17, 1862, demand notes, issued prior to the Legal-tender Act, to the amount of about $60,000,000, were made legal tender to the same extent as the notes authorized by the Act of February 25.

[2] Prof. Sumner finds in the $400,000,000 restriction a marked characteristic of our paper money system. It is, he says, "redundant, but fixed in amount." This he terms a peculiar feature, "unprecedented, so far as I have been able to learn, in the history of paper money."—[Hist. Am. Currency, p. 214.] We may suppose that Prof. Sumner finds the peculiarity of our present situation, not in the fact that a limit is set by law to the amount of paper, but in the fact that the limit so set has been maintained.

country. The following table exhibits the course of the premium on gold during the first five years of forced circulation:

*Table of Highest and Lowest Premium Rates of Gold, by Months, January,* 1862, *to December*, 1866.

| | 1862 | | 1863 | | 1864 | | 1865 | | 1866 | |
|---|---|---|---|---|---|---|---|---|---|---|
| | L | H | L | H | L | H | L | H | L | H |
| January, | 0 | 5 | 34 | 60¾ | 51½ | 60 | 97½ | 134½ | 36¾ | 44⅝ |
| February, | 2⅛ | 4¾ | 53 | 72½ | 57⅛ | 61 | 96⅜ | 116¾ | 35⅞ | 41¼ |
| March, | 1⅛ | 2½ | 39 | 71¾ | 59 | 69¾ | 48⅛ | 101 | 25 | 36½ |
| April, | 1½ | 2¼ | 46 | 59 | 66¼ | 87 | 44 | 60 | 25 | 29½ |
| May, | 2⅛ | 4⅛ | 43½ | 55 | 68 | 90 | 28⅝ | 45¼ | 25½ | 41½ |
| June, | 3½ | 9½ | 40½ | 48⅞ | 89 | 151 | 35¾ | 47⅝ | 37⅝ | 67¾ |
| July, | 9 | 20⅛ | 23¼ | 45 | 122 | 185 | 38 | 46½ | 48¼ | 55¾ |
| August, | 12½ | 16¼ | 22⅛ | 29¾ | 131½ | 162 | 40⅛ | 45⅝ | 46½ | 52¼ |
| September, | 16½ | 24 | 27 | 43⅛ | 85 | 155 | 42⅝ | 45 | 44 | 46¾ |
| October, | 22 | 37 | 40⅜ | 56¾ | 89 | 129 | 44 | 49 | 45⅝ | 54⅜ |
| November, | 29 | 33¼ | 43 | 54 | 109 | 160 | 45½ | 48¾ | 37½ | 48⅝ |
| December, | 30 | 34 | 47 | 52¾ | 111 | 144 | 44½ | 46¾ | 31¼ | 41¾ |

Only one manful effort has been made since the conclusion of the war to rid the nation of the irredeemable paper money brought into existence by the ill-advised legislation of February, 1862. Under the administration of the Treasury Department by Mr. McCulloch, a reduction of the amount of outstanding legal-tender notes was systematically undertaken; but, before this necessary work had proceeded far enough to accomplish any important results, the pain and terror of the country under the wholesome stringency of the discount market and the puncturing of inflated prices led to the repeal, in January, 1868, of the Act of December 18, 1865,[1] which had authorized the retirement of legal tenders.

[1] The utter lack of consequence in the financial legislation of Congress is seen in the history of this bill. It was originally passed

Prof. Sumner notes[1] that the turning-point at which the contraction of the legal-tender notes met the expansion of the national bank-note circulation was at the date of the repeal of the Act of 1865. By Mr. McCulloch's withdrawal of paper, the legal tenders had been reduced to $356,000,000, while the national bank issues stood at $294,000,000.

It is not within the scope of this work to propose or discuss schemes for the resumption of specie payments. The hard experience of four years of prostrate industry and collapsed credit has brought the nation to the point where the market value and the legal rating of United States notes closely approach each other. The exhausted swimmer thus borne in towards the shore may again be carried out to sea with a turn of the tide. A single manful effort would suffice to re-establish our national credit, and place industry on a sound basis. On the other hand, delay and evasion now may render vain all the suffering of the past four years. There has never been wanting for the achievement of specie payments more than the public virtue among the people strongly to desire it, the moderate intelligence among our rulers to choose the simple means that are pointed out by all experience, and the courage, in both people and rulers, to bear for a brief time the pain of the surgery and the cautery which alone can bring healing.

---

with only six dissenting voices in the House of Representatives; yet as soon as it began to produce its normal and necessary results, such as any man of plain sense would have anticipated, the Act was rescinded. What but confusion and disaster can be expected where laws concerning fundamental policy are thus heedlessly enacted and repealed?

[1] Hist. Am. Currency, p. 212.

## CHAPTER XVII.

### THE THEORY OF INCONVERTIBLE PAPER MONEY, CONCLUDED.

THE principles of money, as they have been stated in the progress of our inquiry, and the experience recited in the two preceding chapters, appear to justify the following conclusions:

1. A paper money, of mere convention, having no "intrinsic value" in the sense in which that phrase is commonly used, may become the general medium of exchange in any community, being freely received by all having goods to sell, in the confidence that it will, in due course, be taken by others. This acceptance of a paper money may become so general and complete that, for a time at least, it cannot be distinguished from the acceptance of the precious metals.

2. Given the fact of a general desire on the part of producers for one article of uniform quality which is susceptible of easy division, we have fulfilled all the requirements of a common denominator in exchange. The effort of every dealer to obtain as much as possible of this one article for each and every part of his stock; the aim of every producer to bring to market the product requiring least labor which will command a given quantity of this article in exchange, these must result in ranging all commodities, according to the cost of replacing them, upon a scale of value, the degrees of

which shall be expressed in terms of this one article. This, as we have seen, a money of mere convention is competent to effect.

3. Such money, so long as its popular acceptance continues, performs the office of a standard for deferred payments, well or ill, according as its amount is regulated. We have seen how inadequately, at times, the precious metals have discharged this money-function. The advocate of inconvertible paper, or "ideal" money, does not, therefore, admit the mere fact of depreciation, or the existence of a premium on gold and silver, to be proof of the failure of such money to perform its office. It may, the rather, be proof that gold and silver have failed, in part, to discharge their function as a standard for deferred payments. In the phrase of the anti-bullionists of 1810–9, it may be, not that paper has fallen, but that gold and silver have risen. The object of a standard for deferred payments being to secure the payment, at the maturity of obligations, of substantially the same purchasing power that was in contemplation of the parties at the formation of the contract, it is conceivable that a paper money might be so regulated as to preserve a more uniform value, from generation to generation, than the precious metals have maintained during any considerable period of the world's history. We have seen[1] that that is the weak point of the precious metals in their use as money.

4. Such a money, being released from all natural conditions of production, with whatever advantages, actual or theoretical, may be found in that fact, becomes subject to purely arbitrary regulation as to its amount. We have seen that, while the production of gold and

---

[1] See pp. 157–9.

silver is subject to great changes, it yet requires a term of years, often considerable, to influence greatly the value of the existing supply; and that, whatever the stock at any period, there is a force constantly operating to distribute it according to the occasion each country and each community may have for its use, preserving thus its value uniform[1] the world over.

Inconvertible Paper Money, however, may be increased indefinitely at will. It costs twice as much labor to raise two thousand ounces of gold from the mine as to raise one thousand ounces. It costs no more to print a thousand two-dollar bills, or ten-dollar bills, than to print a thousand one-dollar bills. We saw the assignats of France mount by two or three milliards a month, between May, 1795, and January, 1796. Nor does any force operate to distribute an excess of issues throughout the commercial world. Limited circulation is the essential characteristic of Inconvertible Paper Money.

The possibilities of evil, therefore, which lie in the abuse of the power of issuing such money, are almost infinitely greater than those which inhere in a metallic circulation.

5. The danger of overissue is one which never ceases to threaten an Inconvertible Paper Money.[2] The path winds even along the verge of a precipice. Vigilance must never be relaxed. The prudence and self-restraint of years count for nothing, or count for but little, against

---

[1] The cost of transportation being taken into the account.

[2] "Après un délai plus ou moins bref, le papier-monnaie a toujours subi une dépréciation. A cette règle je ne connais qu'une exception, celle du papier-monnaie émis par le royaume de Prusse, où l'attention la plus scrupuleuse a été apportée à ce que l'émission restât très-bornée."—[Chevalier, La Monnaie, p. 675.]

any new onset of popular passion, or in the face of a sudden exigency of the government. From this danger a people receiving into circulation an Inconvertible Paper Money can never escape. A single weak or reckless administration, one day of commercial panic, a mere rumor of invasion, may hurl trade and production down the abyss.

"The emitting of paper money by the authority of the Constitution," said Mr. Hamilton, in his "Report on the Bank," "is wisely prohibited to the individual States by the national Constitution: and the spirit of that prohibition ought not to be disregarded by the government of the United States. Though paper emissions, under general authority, might have some advantages not applicable, and be free from some of the disadvantages which are applicable, to the like emissions by the States separately: yet they are of a nature so liable to abuse, and, it may even be affirmed, so certain of being abused, that the wisdom of the government will be shown in never trusting itself with the use of so seducing and dangerous an expedient. . . . In great and trying emergencies there is almost a moral certainty of its becoming mischievous. The stamping of paper is an operation so much easier than the levying of taxes, that a government, in the practice of paper emissions, would rarely fail in any such emergency to indulge itself too far in the employment of this resource."[1]

6. Not only does the danger of overissue never cease to menace a community having such money in circulation, but the moment an overissue in fact occurs, the impulse to excess acquires violence by indulgence. The reason is obvious. To metallic money the formula of supply and demand applies. Demand creates supply: supply satisfies demand. If metallic money is brought

in excess into any country, it runs off. Paper money cannot run off. It makes a swamp wherever it is poured out. There is no outlet for such money. When in excess, prices rise, and may rise indefinitely without being corrected by international commerce. Consequently the government which has issued paper money as a measure of resource soon finds its necessities increasing. It has to purchase services and supplies at higher rates. Soon speculation sets in; "forestalling" and "engrossing" begin to operate on the stock of the necessaries of life, and prices rise more and more rapidly.

President White thus remarks upon the second issue of assignats in Revolutionary France: "In this comparative ease of a new issue is seen the action of a law in finance as certain as the action of a similar law in natural philosophy. If a natural body be allowed to fall from a height, in obedience to gravitation, its velocity is accelerated, by a well-known law in physics, in a constantly increasing ratio: so in issues of irredeemable currency, in obedience to the theories or interests of a legislative body, or of the people at large, there is a natural law of rapidly increasing issue and depreciation.[1] . . . . Nearly all Frenchmen now became desperate optimists, declaring that inflation is prosperity.

[1] "Une inévitable fatalité pousse les gouvernements qui en font usage vers l'abus; car le papier-monnaie est toujours créé dans des moments de crise où les ressources ordinaires sont insuffisantes et un premier excès dans l'émission du papier, rendu nécessaire par des dépenses excessives, amène la dépréciation qui entraîne une diminution correspondante du produit des impôts; cela oblige le gouvernement à de nouvelles émissions pour augmenter ses ressources en compensant le déficit de recette, et ainsi de suite jusqu'à ce que la valeur du papier-monnaie soit tombée à zéro, ce qui correspond à la banqueroute universelle."—[Ch. le Hardy de Beaulieu.]

Throughout France there came temporary good feeling. The nation was becoming fairly inebriated with paper money. The good feeling was that of a drunkard after his draught; and it is to be noted, as a simple historical fact, corresponding to a physiological fact, that, as the draughts of paper money came faster, the periods of succeeding good feeling grew shorter."

It will have been observed that the instances among those given in Chapters XV and XVI, where continence in issue was most conspicuously exhibited, were those of the Bank of England during the Restriction, and the Bank of France in 1848, and again from 1871 to the present time. No one, I think, can question that the prudence and self-restraint here shown were due to the fact that, in the case of neither Bank, did the issues inure directly to the benefit of the government, whatever the exigencies of state.[1]

"Real money," said Edmund Burke, "can hardly ever multiply too much in any country, because it will always, as it increases, be a certain sign of the increase of trade, of which it is the measure, and, consequently, of the soundness and vigor of the whole body. But this paper money may and does increase without any increase of trade, nay often, when trade greatly declines,

[1] One of the most amusing things to be found in that eminently amusing serial, the "Congressional Globe," is the remark of Mr. J. B. Alley, of Massachusetts, in his speech in favor of the Legal-tender Act of 1862: "*There can be no more issues than the real necessities of the government require. The government cannot make issues, like the banks, for profit. Its issues must necessarily be limited to its absolute wants.*" There is every reason to believe that the issues of the Continental Congress and the French Revolutionary Assembly were limited to the absolute wants of the government, and, in fact, fell considerably short of supplying those wants.

for it is *not the measure of the trade of the nation, but of the necessity of its government, and it is absurd and must be ruinous, that the same course which naturally exhausts the wealth of a nation, should likewise be the only productive cause of money.*"

"There has never been a government yet," says Prof Perry, in his "Elements of Political Economy," "of the many which have issued irredeemable paper, which had the wisdom and firmness to resist for any great length of time the strong temptation to overissues. . . . . When once the press is set at work, it must work on with livelier speed; because just in the ratio of the depreciation is the greater amount required."

7. It must not be thought that where the excess of inconvertible paper is small, the effects on trade and production are therefore slight. In no degree whatever can the money of any commercial community depart from the money in which international balances are discharged, without inducing obstruction and creating apprehensions to which modern trade, with its highly developed and sensitive organization, will not subject itself, or will do so only on the payment of a heavy fine on the part of the community offending.

"The circulating medium of a commercial community," said Mr. Webster, in his speech on the Bank Bill of 1815, "must be that which is also the circulating medium of other commercial communities, or must be capable of being converted into that medium without loss. It must be able, not only to pass in payments and receipts among individuals of the same society and nation, but to adjust and discharge the balance of exchanges between different nations."

We have seen with what sagacity the Management of the Bank of France since 1871 have succeeded in preventing any considerable discount upon their notes when exchanged for gold. Yet Mr. Bagehot, in his work, "Lombard Street," remarks: "The note of the Bank of France has not, indeed, been depreciated enough to disorder ordinary transactions. *But any depreciation, however small, even the liability to depreciation, without its reality, is enough to disorder exchange transactions.* They are calculated to such an extremity of fineness that the change of a decimal may be fatal, and may turn a profit into a loss. Accordingly London has become the sole great settling-house of exchange transactions in Europe, instead of being, as formerly, one of two."

8. When, however, an Inconvertible Paper Money is issued in marked excess, and hence becomes depreciated and fluctuating, the most disastrous consequences, industrially and socially, must ensue.[1]

*A depreciated paper money is always a fluctuating money.* This is so for two reasons: (*a*) The demand for money in any community undergoes a continual variation. This is seen in the almost perpetual bullion-movement to and from countries having a metallic or a convertible paper money. The volume of money never stands at a mean. It is in incessant motion, like the waters of the sea, now rising, now falling, on every shore. It is only by the freedom of this movement that steadiness in values is obtained. An Inconvertible Paper Money, however, as we have seen, has no outlet through foreign trade, and fluctuation in its value is therefore inevitable. (*b*) The

---

[1] "Quanquam innumere pestes sunt quibus regna, principatus et respublice decrescere solent, hæc tamen quatuor (meo judicio) potissime sunt: discordia, mortalitas, terre sterilitas et monete vilitas."—[Copernicus, Monete Cudende Ratio.]

fact of depreciation creates a prejudice against this form of money which impairs its circulation, as has been previously noted,[1] but, in doing this, acts very irregularly, according to popular rumor, the issue of battles, the prospects of alliances, the results of elections. The operation of causes like these can clearly be seen in the table of the depreciation of the United States legal tender, 1862–6, which appears on p. 374. M. Courcelle-Seneuil has noted that the market price of the paper money of the Revolution was nearly as much affected by political events as by the extent of the issues.[2]

A money of inconvertible paper being thus at once depreciated, as compared with specie, and fluctuating in its power to purchase commodities in general, becomes a grievous tax upon production; while if it gives to trade for a time excessive profits at the expense of consumers, only does so by making exchange highly speculative, putting all the sober virtues at a disadvantage, generating wasteful habits of transacting business, and in the result dividing the increased profits among a larger number of shops and stands.

It is, however, upon the condition of the laboring classes that a fluctuating paper money works its worst effects.

"The very man of all others," said Mr. Webster, "who has the deepest interest in a sound currency, and who suffers most by mischievous legislation in money matters, is the man who earns his daily bread by his daily toil. A depreciated currency, sudden changes of prices, paper money falling between morning and noon, and falling still lower between noon and night, these

---

[1] See p. 279.

[2] Opérations de Banque, p. 372.

things constitute the very harvest time of speculators, and of the whole race of those who are at once idle and crafty. . . . . But the laboring man, what can he hoard? Preying on nobody he becomes the prey of all."

And on another occasion the same great statesman said: "A disordered currency is one of the greatest political evils. It undermines the virtues necessary for the support of the social system and encourages propensities destructive to its happiness.[1] It wars against industry, frugality and economy, and it fosters the evil spirits of extravagance and speculation. Of all the contrivances for cheating the laboring classes of mankind, none has been more effectual than that which deludes them with paper money. This is the most effectual of inventions to fertilize the rich man's fields by the sweat of the poor man's brow.

"Ordinary tyranny, oppression, excessive taxation, these bear lightly on the happiness of the mass of the community, compared with fraudulent currencies and the robberies committed by a depreciated paper."

Of the exceptional disadvantages which the laborer experiences through the use of a fluctuating paper money, I may perhaps offer here the explanation I have given in another place:[2] In the competition which the laborer has incessantly to maintain, both with his employer and his fellow-laborers, his interest will not come to him, he must go to it, and to do so he must be able to identify it and locate it with precision and assur-

---

[1] Under date of October 25, 1810, M. Montalivet, Napoleon's Minister of the Interior, writes to the prefects:

"La papier-monnaie est considerée par l'Empereur comme le plus grand fléau des nations, et comme étant au moins au moral, ce que la peste est au physique."

[2] The Wages Question.

ance. With bad money in circulation, the laborer, in making his demand on his employer for wages, must follow blindly around after prices, guided only by a general sense of the inadequacy of what he is at present receiving. Acting without intelligence, it is a matter of course that his interests are in some degree sacrificed.

It was in view of this inability of the laboring classes, through poverty, ignorance, and inertia, to meet sudden and violent changes of condition, that Mr. Mill assigned to "Custom" in economics the same beneficent function which it has performed in government, as "the most powerful protector of the weak against the strong." Usage, habit, constitute a barrier which in a degree preserves the economically weak from the hustlings and jostlings of the market-place, and gives them room to stand. A fluctuating paper money breaks down this barrier and involves all classes in a furious and incessant struggle, in which the feeblest are sure to go down and be trampled on.

But it is not alone in competition with the employer that the laborer is put at a disadvantage. If it is difficult for him to secure the adjustment of his wages to the varying cost of living, much more difficult is it for him to hold his own in the contest with the retail dealer. He expends his earnings in hundreds of small purchases. If those earnings come to him in depreciated paper, and are to be expended in commodities at inflated prices, how can he tell what he ought to pay per pound, per bushel, or per yard? He knows nothing about the conditions of the production of the articles he purchases, and has no longer a traditional price to guide him. Formerly, if an article of domestic consumption rose, he was in the mood to resist the advance. He disputed the higher price; he alleged the customary price; he held off buying; he inquired elsewhere. With a community in this temper, retail prices will not be wantonly advanced; nothing less than a substantial reason will succeed in establishing a new price, and that new price will be kept down to something like the necessity of the case.

With bad money, however, this hold of the retail buyer upon customary price is broken. The laborer loses his reckoning. When prices go up, he cannot judge where they should stop. After finding advance upon advance established, in spite of his questioning and complaints, he becomes discouraged. He pays without dispute whatever the shop-keeper demands. Then it is the retail dealer gathers his largest profits and works his worst extortions.

But one question remains under this department of our subject: Does the premium on gold in a country having Inconvertible Paper Money measure the depreciation? This is perhaps the most difficult question in the theory of Money.

"There is for me, I confess," says Prof. Price, "a certain obscurity as to the law which regulates the depreciation of inconvertible notes."

On the one hand, it is difficult to see how, in any degree of consistency with Mr. Ricardo's law of the distribution of the precious metals, it should be otherwise than that the premium on gold measures the depreciation of the paper. On the other, it seems almost impossible, in the face of facts, to accept the doctrine as applied to England, 1819–21, or to the United States, 1865–8. All the statistical tables, showing the prices of commodities, which are accessible, seem to prove that the power of the paper to purchase commodities in general was, in the instances referred to, much further diminished than its power to purchase gold.

Mr. Mathias Attwood, the leader of the "Birmingham," or Inflation School, in England, 1823 to 1832, thus undertook to explain the matter:

"In a rise of prices occasioned by the exclusive use of paper money, the great demand for bullion, that for circulation, ceases at once. The bullion market then receives supplies from the quarter whence previously its principal demand originated. In the same manner, when a metal standard is again resorted to, a new demand for gold at once takes place, precisely at that moment when, in consequence of a contraction of the general demand for money, a reduced demand exists for all other commodities. Gold bullion, consequently, is, of all commodities, the last and the least to rise in a general rise of prices occasioned by the depreciation of paper money, and the last and the least to fall in a general fall of prices occasioned by the restoration of that depreciation."

The former part of this paragraph is true, and would serve to explain a temporary divergence extending through a few months following the act of suspension, or of resumption; but it is difficult to see how, upon accepted principles, this failure of gold to follow other commodities, in either the general rise or the general fall, could be protracted through a period of years. We may readily admit that gold rises last, but why, in the long run, least? After time has been given for the readjustment, through the ordinary operations of trade, why does not gold, if it remains below its value in the country having a depreciated currency, flow abroad where its power in exchange is greater?

One item, indeed, we find, which accounts, in a certain degree, for the failure of gold to rise in price correspondently to other commodities, under Inconvertible Paper Money. The former demand for gold was made up of the occasions for its use in all commercial countries, including that which has now discarded it. The use of it in that country being abandoned, the total demand is so far diminished, and until the supply has been reduced by the very gradual process of consumption, the value of each portion must fall. But this cause would, at the most, be sufficient to produce only a small part of the effect to be accounted for in the cases immediately under consideration.

An explanation, somewhat similar to Mr. Attwood's, was offered by Mr. J. S. Ropes, in a paper published in the proceedings of the "American Social Science Association."—[Vol. V.]

"Gold has been practically deprived of its chief function in the community, and, like all other commodities under similar circumstances, its exchangeable value has been greatly depreciated. We may illustrate this by the supposition that our government had been able and willing to make and strictly enforce a law prohibiting the use of wheat, in any form, for food. Can any one doubt that in such a case the price of flour would be greatly depressed, and that it would depend chiefly upon the demand in foreign countries for whatever exchangeable value it might retain."

What Mr. Ropes here adduces is true, and would be sufficient to account for a divergence such as we are inquiring about, extending through a certain period of re-adjustment. If, to take his illustration, government were to prohibit the use of wheat for food in the United States, the price here of flour would doubtless be greatly depressed for a time, until the existing stock had been shipped to a better market, or had moulded in store. But why should wheat thereafter be produced at all, except at prices corresponding, (expenses of transportation being considered) to those ruling abroad?

So of gold; the fact that the United States, in 1862, discarded the use of gold coin as the general money of commerce, retaining it for specific uses only, viz., in payments at the Treasury, inwards for customs-dues, outwards for interest on the public debt, afforded a reason for a lowering of the purchasing power of gold here sufficient to drive a portion of the existing supply abroad. It also afforded a reason for a permanent depression in the purchasing power of gold, the world over, so far as might be involved in a reduction of the general demand for gold through the cessation of the United States' demand for it. But beyond this, it is difficult to see any virtue in the explanation offered. Why should this action of the United States government, in 1862, diminish the purchasing power of gold in Boston or New York, in 1865, or 1873?

There certainly appears to be an effect on prices, in countries having a depreciated paper money, not accounted for by the premium on gold. The belief seems to be quite general among intelligent persons, many of them familiar with the principles of economics, that the premium on gold does not measure the advance of general prices. Fully agreeing with Prof. Price as to the obscurity which still rests on this subject, I can only suggest, first, that the time required for the international re-adjustment of the precious metals, after any disturbance of supply and demand, may be longer, much longer, than it has been commonly believed to be, the friction and inertia of trade extending that re-adjustment over considerable intervals, and giving to the local values of gold and silver a degree of persistency attributed to them by few economical writers; secondly, that the statistics of prices, which we have to use in the investigation of this subject, are not fairly representative of the whole body of commodities and services to be exchanged through the use of money, and thus, that while the prices of the commodities ordinarily taken for the purposes of this comparison are enhanced considerably above the price of gold, in paper, other large bodies of commodities and services, not easily to be embraced in such computations, have experienced a less considerable rise, tending to establish an average of general prices approximating the price of gold.

# PART III.

## CONVERTIBLE PAPER MONEY.

# CHAPTER XVIII.

## THE THEORY OF CONVERTIBLE PAPER MONEY.

We saw, in opening the subject of Inconvertible Paper Money, that objection exists on the part of many, perhaps most, economists to the use of the word Money except in connection with "a material recompense or equivalent"—gold, silver or copper, or grains and seeds, or living money,—articles having, as the phrase is, value in themselves, independently of convention.

It would at first seem that this objection would have less force in application to paper convertible at pleasure into coin. But on the contrary, we noted that Mr. Huskisson and Prof. Storch, who admit the use of the term, paper money, as applied to irredeemable government issues, reprehend its use in reference to paper issued by bankers, promissory of coin and convertible at the pleasure of the holder. In this these economists are generally followed by recent writers. Hence the wide adoption of the word Currency,[1] which Mr. Mc-

[1] "La langue anglaise a un mot générique qui embrasse la monnaie, le billet de banque, le papier-monnaie, ou assignat, non convertible en espèces, le chèque et toute autre espèce de titres qu'on peut mettre dans la circulation et qu'accepte plus ou moins le commun des hommes; c'est le mot de *Currency*. Notre langue n'en offre pas l'équivalent parfait."—[Chevalier, La Monnaie, p. 64.]

Leod denounces as a "Yankeeism," though he seems to think that the term has passed into too general use to be now extruded on either philological or national grounds.

On the same side, Mr. Tooke cites Johnson's Dictionary—"Money: metals coined for the purposes of commerce;" and proceeds to remark: "In no instance, I believe, will it be found that Mr. Locke, or Mr. Harris, or even the first Lord Liverpool, included promissory notes issued by banks and returnable to the issuers, at the will of the holder, in exchange for coin, in their use of the word Money. . . . The Bullion Report of 1810 affords no sanction to such a use of the word."[1]—[Hist. of Prices, ii, 155.]

It would be wrong to say that definitions are of small account in the treatment of economical questions, yet, as was remarked in connection with our discussion of Inconvertible Paper, I see no harm in the use of the term paper money. It has venerable sanction, for Adam Smith uses it. It can create no false apprehensions, for the adjective, or component word, paper, does not allow it to be conceived that a material equivalent or recompense is intended.

Moreover, it appears to me, I confess, that the usual

---

[1] The French writers, MM. Jos. Garnier and Courcelle-Sencuil, make a distinction between paper money and money of paper. By the former term they embrace government issues, resting upon authority; by the latter, bank-notes, resting upon confidence:

"Les billets de banque, payable à vue et au porteur, sont de la monnaie de papier; ils ne sont point du papier-monnaie. On a réservé ce nom à des titres sur lesquels le gouvernement qui les émet ou qui autorise leur émission, n'a stipulé aucune promesse de remboursement, ou n'a stipulé que des promesses auxquelles il a manqué." —[Courcelle-Seneuil, Opérations de Banque, p. 370.]

objection to the word Money, as applied, even without qualification, to paper, fails to note a point of vital importance in the connection. It is said that the bank-note is a form of credit.[1] But do we not here overlook the distinction between the relation of the buyer to the seller, where the bank-note is employed, and the relation of the holder of the note to its issuer? As between the buyer and the seller, a bank-note is money, if it is accepted in final payment of goods, or discharge of debts, without recourse to the person from whom it is received. As between the holder and the issuer, it remains a form of credit, and is required to be redeemed upon demand, in specie. Is it, however, the relation of the holder to the issuer, or the relation of the buyer to the seller, which determines the influence the note shall have upon prices? Clearly, the latter. And it is the influence of the bank-note on prices with which we are concerned. The question of final payment, as between the holder and the issuer, is a *banking* question. So long as the paper passes from hand to hand and is accepted, whether with or without force of law, by the creditor in final discharge of debts, or by the seller in full payment for goods, without further resort, in theory or in practice, to the buyer or the debtor, I am disposed to think it must be deemed to be money. It may be good money. It may be bad money. But in its universal acceptability, however obtained; in the fact of its general currency as a medium of exchange, we have the single condition of money realized. This was the position of Col. Torrens in his work on the English Bank Act of 1844. The

---

[1] Thus Prof. Price says that bank-notes "stand on a level with the entries in a shop-keeper's books. They are matters of account—debts whose payment is deferred."—[Principles of Currency, p. 178.]

same view of the bank-note was taken by M. Wolowski in his work, "La Question des Banques," and by Mr. Nicholson in his work, "The Science of Exchanges."[1]

A bank-note, so long as its currency remains, serves as the medium of exchange: it serves as the standard for deferred payments, precisely as the piece of gold which it replaces in circulation: and if anything serves as a common measure of value,[2] it is the paper that does so, and not the thing promised by the paper.[3] For these reasons I see no objection to the use of the word Money, as applied to bank-notes or convertible paper.

But it is said, if bank-notes are money, why are not checks money?

Simply because checks are a form of credit, both between the holder and the issuer and between the buyer and the seller; while, between the buyer and the seller, the bank-note, as has been remarked, is, in effect, final

---

[1] "Nous croyons que si l'on tient compte des résultats pratiques, on reconnaîtra combien la distinction établie, en principe, entre la monnaie et le billet, s'efface dans la circulation. . . . S'il n'est pas une monnaie dans la rigueur scientifique du terme, il en a tous les attributs."—[Wolowski.]

"Bank-notes, or transferable promises to pay coin to bearer on demand, circulating side by side with coin in endless succession; liquidating debts like coin, and which, when in circulation, all business people are, as it were, compelled to take, are absolutely money." —[Nicholson.]

[2] On this point, see pp. 4–9; 280–90.

[3] This was the argument of Lord Mansfield: "Bank-notes are not, like bills of exchange, mere securities or documents for debts, nor are so esteemed, but are treated as money in the ordinary course and transaction of business, by the general consent of mankind; and on payment of them, whenever a receipt is requred, the receipts are always given as for money, and not as for securities or notes.' —[1 Burrows, 452–7.]

payment. Now, it is not the relation of holder and issuer, but of buyer and seller, with which we have to do in the theory of Money.

I say the bank-note is, in effect, final payment, as between buyer and seller. In the English law, the receiver of a bank-note has a limited resort to the person from whom he takes it, in case the bank should fail before it had been in his (the receiver's) power to present it for payment. "This responsibility, however," says Mr. McCulloch, "seldom exceeds a couple of hours, and can hardly, in any case, exceed a couple of days. *In practice it is never resorted to,* and every one is thus encouraged, reckoning on the facility of passing it to another, to accept bank-paper, 'even though he should doubt the ultimate solvency of the issuer.'"[1]

This characterization by Mr. McCulloch appeals for its correctness to the observation of the reader. We take bank-notes with no other scrutiny, at the most, than to satisfy ourselves that they are not counterfeit. We never think of going at once with them, or sending them by an agent, to the place of issue, to demand the coin, in order that, if payment should be refused, we may have recourse to the persons from whom we received them; and, though the responsibility of the person passing the note expires within two or three hours, or, at most, within two or three days,[2] we hold the note for days or weeks, according to our occasions for expenditure, and, in probably ninety-nine cases out of a

[1] Mr. McCulloch here quotes Thornton on Paper Credit.

[2] Indeed it has been decided in several States of the American Union that the acceptance of bank-notes constitutes a sufficient payment, even though the bank be insolvent at the time, provided the tender was made by the debtor or purchaser in good faith.

hundred, we should be wholly unable to tell from whom we received any particular bill.[1]

In this view, the bank-note, while it remains a form of credit, as between the holder and the issuer, effects final payments between the buyer and seller, and is thus money.[2]

A check, on the other hand, is, as a rule, received on the credit of the person who draws it; has a circulation closely limited by personal or business acquaintance; passes generally by successive indorsements; its history appears[3] upon its face and upon its back; and it thus remains a form of credit, not only between the bank and the drawer, but between buyer and seller, in all the transactions in which it is employed.

The above distinction fairly leads to the remark that *Circulation, in the monetary sense, is a matter of degree.*[4]

---

[1] Mr. Francis speaks of a note coming in to the Bank of England which had been out for about a century and a quarter.

[2] "Anything which freely circulates from hand to hand, as a common acceptable medium of exchange, in any country is, in such country, money, even though it ceases to be such, or to possess any value, in passing into another country. In a word, an article is determined to be money, *by reason of the performance by it of certain functions, without regard to its form or substance.*"—[Appleton's Cyclopædia.]

[3] M. Rossi, though preserving a distinction between bank-notes and money, recognizes as of great importance the fact that bank-notes leave no trace of their movement from hand to hand. Thus, in his Report of 1840 to the Chamber of Peers, he says:

"Ils se distinguent de tout autre billet en ce que le porteur, quel qu'ait été le nombre des intermédiaires, n'a de recours que contre la Banque, et qu'il ne reste pas même de trace légale des nombreuses transmissions qui peuvent s'être opérées."

[4] M. Chevalier has justly remarked: "Lors qu'on traitera de pays différents, il sera rationnel et opportun de classer dans la *currency*, pour quelques-uns, des titres qui, par rapport à d'autres, ne sauraient

Bank-notes, from the ill repute of the issuers, might conceivably become of such slow, difficult and limited currency, as to fall out of the category of money, that is, men might come to accept them only as subject to the responsibility of the persons tendering them, and might carefully observe the legal conditions of enforcing that responsibility, keeping a record of persons, places and times, carrying the matter on their minds, and giving up other occupation in order to present the notes promptly, within the days or hours necessary to get to the place of issue. In such a condition of the public mind, bank-notes would not be money. On the other hand, checks might be so drawn and authenticated as to pass in circulation so rapidly, with such wide acceptance, with so little of resort, as to become practically money. The same test should be applied to Bills of Exchange, which are asserted by Mr. Fullarton and others to be money in the same sense as bank-notes. Mr. Fullarton cites the habit of Lancashire and the West Riding of York, and some other manufacturing districts of England, where bills of exchange were employed during a long series of years, to the almost total exclusion of bank-notes, the bills being drawn for all sums down to £5.

Mr. McCulloch's criticism of this claim is in the main just. "Bills are almost all drawn payable at some distant period, and those into whose hands they come, if they be not in want of money, prefer retaining them in their possession, in order to get the interest that accrues upon them. But the principal distinction between notes and bills is, that every individual, in passing a bill to

---

être présentés comme dignes de cet honneur, et investis de cette prérogative. En un mot, la classification dans la *currency* est un fait relatif, et sujet à conditions, et non pas un fait absolu et général."—[La Monnaie, p. 669.]

another, has to indorse it, and by doing so makes himself responsible for its payment. 'A bill circulates,' says Mr. Thornton, 'in consequence chiefly of the confidence placed by each receiver of it in the last indorser, his own correspondent in trade, whereas the circulation of a bank-note is owing rather to the circumstance of the name of the issuer being so well known as to give it an universal credit.' It is clear, therefore, that a great deal more consideration is always required, and may be fairly presumed to be given, before any one accepts a bill of exchange in payment, than before he accepts a bank-note. The note is payable on the instant, without deduction—the bill not until some future period; the note may be passed to another without incurring any risk or responsibility, whereas every fresh issuer of the bill makes himself responsible for its value. Notes form the currency of all classes, not only of those who are, but also of those who are not engaged in business, as women, children, laborers, etc., who in most instances are without the power to refuse them, and without the means of forming any correct conclusion as to the solvency of the issuers.[1] Bills, on the other hand, pass only, with very few exceptions, among persons engaged in business, who are fully aware of the risk they run in taking them."

And yet I should not wish to say that if bills of exchange were made for small amounts, and their currency facilitated by exceptional provisions, so that the public became familiarized with their use, they might not acquire, here and there, now and then, a degree of facility

---

[1] The German economist, Hartwig Fertz, as quoted by M. Wolowski, dwells particularly on this feature of the case, that persons taking bank-notes do not, and in fact cannot, verify their value.

in circulation, and an indifference to the question of recourse, which would give them the quality of money.

Indeed there is something, it appears to me, in Mr. Tooke's claim that the larger Bank of England notes are not money, in the sense in which the smaller ones are. The difference between a large and a small note, as to the length of time for which they severally remain out, the freedom with which they are taken, and the number of transactions in which they are used, is very marked.

The life of a bank-note[1] in days, says Prof. Levi, may be taken to have been as follows:

| | £5 | £10 | £20–100 | £200–500 | £1000 |
|---|---|---|---|---|---|
| 1844 | 105 | 87 | 38 | 14 | 12 |
| 1871 | 79 | 64 | 26 | 8 | 9 |

—[Hist. Br. Commerce, p. 481.]

It is best, perhaps, to treat all bank-notes as money for purposes of economical reasoning, yet we should not fail to recognize the consideration that, just as the same amount of money will perform a greater number of exchanges in the same time in one country than in another, so, within the same country or district, the same amount of bank-notes of one denomination may perform a much greater work in exchange than would an oqual amount in other denominations.

Adam Smith has shown the importance of this distinction. "The circulation of every country, may," he says, "be considered as divided into two different branches, the circulation of the dealers with one another,

---

[1] "The Bank of England never re-issues its notes. As they come in they are laid aside and kept seven years, and then burned. The whole number is not destroyed together, but at different times, and as many are burned as correspond with the new notes issued."—[Hankey on Banking, p. 62.]

and the circulation between the dealers and the consumers. Though the same pieces of money, whether paper or metal, may be employed sometimes in the one circulation, and sometimes in the other, yet, as both are constantly going on at the same time, each requires a certain stock of money of one kind or another to carry it on.

"Paper money may be so regulated as either to confine itself very much to the circulation between the different dealers, or to extend itself likewise to a great part of that between the dealers and the consumers. Where no bank-notes are circulated under ten pounds value, as in London, paper money confines itself very much to the circulation between the dealers. When a ten pound bank-note comes into the hands of a consumer, he is generally obliged to change it at the first shop where he has occasion to purchase five shillings' worth of goods, so that it often returns into the hands of a dealer before the consumer has spent the fortieth part of the money. Where bank-notes are issued for so small sums as twenty shillings, as in Scotland, paper money extends itself to a considerable part of the circulation between dealers and consumers."—[Wealth of Nations, i, 323.]

Upon these paragraphs, Mr. Tooke remarks: "Adam Smith is the first, I believe, who pointed out the distinction between bank-notes of the lower denominations, which served chiefly for the purposes of retail trade, and the higher, which were in use principally between dealers and dealers.[1] *The higher ones do not circulate*

[1] Mr. Hubbard, Governor of the Bank of England, 1853–5, testified before the Committee of 1857, that within the five years preceding, an addition of £2,000,000 had been made to the circulation of £5 and £10 notes, and an equal diminution had taken place in £50 to £1000 notes, the aggregate issues remaining unchanged but the purchasing power being increased by the substitution.

*now, even among dealers*, excepting cattle-dealers and horse-dealers, having been superseded by a general use of banking accommodations, and consequently by checks and book credits."—[History of Prices, 1839–47, p. 159.]

Not only have bills of exchange and checks been held by many writers to be money in the same sense as bank-notes, but bank deposits have been embraced in the same category,[1] on the ground that they are used to discharge debts and purchase commodities, and that they thus perform the functions of money. But nothing can perform the functions of money which is not money, for, as we have seen, an article is determined to be money solely by reason of its performance of certain functions. Money is that which passes from hand to hand in final discharge of debts and full payment for goods. The bank-deposit system allows the mutual cancellation of vast bodies of indebtedness which would, without this agency, require the intervention of an actual medium of exchange; but deposits are not such a medium. In a word, deposits, like every other form of credit, save the use of money; they do not perform the functions of money. *Money is that Money does.*

There seems to be little reason to question that Exchequer Bills, as they are called in England, or Treasury Notes, as they have been known in the United States, being acknowledgments of the Exchequer, or Treasury, which are received in payment of taxes, may, if issued in small sums, serve as money, passing from

---

[1] This view is maintained by Mr. Condy Raguet (Currency and Banking, pp. 191–4), and Prof. Amasa Walker (Science of Wealth, pp. 151–4). The opposite view is taken by Mr. Tooke (History of Prices, i, 152–3n, ii, 337–8n, iii, 123–4, 256), Mr. Nicholson (Science of Exchanges, pp. 41–2), and Lord Overstone (Tracts, etc., pp. 199, 200, 343.)

hand to hand, making payments and discharging debts, fully and finally, without recourse. In the reign of William III, considerable amounts of exchequer bills were issued as low as £5 and £10, "which," says Dr. Drake, "answered the necessities of commerce, among the meaner people, for the necessaries of life." "These bills," he adds, "passed in payment as so many counters." When, however, as is more commonly the case, treasury notes or exchequer bills bear interest, that fact, in a considerable degree, retards their circulation. As the weight of interest accumulates towards maturity, they gradually sink out of circulation, dropping to the level of ordinary investments yielding interest. Such notes or bills, when in large denominations, are commonly not money at all.

Perhaps already some reader has exclaimed impatiently, what is the effect of these distinctions but to render any conclusive definition of money impossible? If bills of exchange or checks may, here and there, now and then, become money; if bank-notes, on the other hand, may, in possible circumstances, fall out of the category of money, how are we ever to know what money is and what is money? Would it not be better to say that gold and silver are money and that nothing else is: and adopt some other term for those forms of paper which are substituted for gold and silver in trade?

But we do not get rid of the difficulty of saying, in any given case, just what is money and what is not money, if we contemplate gold and silver alone. On the contrary, a money of the precious metals only must always be subject to two peculiar deductions of large but indefinite extent. In the first place, gold and silver are being continually taken in exchange for other commodities where they are not received as money. In such exchanges gold or silver, even if in coin, is not money. It becomes, notwithstanding the impress of the mint, an article of ordinary merchandise, accepted, not with a view to being soon parted with, on the same terms and in the same form in which it was received, but that it may pass at once into consumption, perhaps as the material of elaborate manufacture. In the second place, of the gold or silver money of a country a large but always unknown share is in hoards or reserves, neither paying debts nor making purchases, and hence not money.

Indeed, the question, money or not money, is, in respect to anything that could be taken, wholly a question of degree—the degree of the extent and facility of its use in exchange. We say that money is any commodity which attains such a measure of popular acceptability that men habitually receive it for what they have to sell, knowing that it will in due time, that is, at any time, command in exchange what they may wish to buy. As we have seen, two commodities may be used as money at the same time; or one may be working its way into general currency, while another, the heretofore recognized medium, is losing its popular acceptance. At any given moment it might be impossible to say which was in the greater degree the money of the community; it might be difficult, at another moment, to say whether either was money or not. These considerations, however, while going far to impair the authority of all statistics of monetary circulation, do not cast the slightest doubt on the nature of the Money-function or its importance, or render it impossible to reason respecting it with accuracy and assurance.

The impatience of economic definitions which allow of exceptions is very widely manifested, appearing in many treatises, even those of great merit. M. Chevalier exhibits it in the discussion of the very subject on which we have dwelt at such length, viz., the question whether bank-notes are money.[1] Yet many of the most important distinctions in political economy are those drawn between classes of commodities, of services, or of persons, where yet individuals cannot with assurance be identified as belonging to either class. Prof. Cairnes has well stated this condition of economic definition:

"In controversies about definitions, nothing is more common than to meet objections founded on the assumption that the attribute on which a definition turns ought to be one which does not admit of degrees. This being assumed, the objector goes on to show that the facts or objects placed within the boundary line of some definition to which objection is taken, cannot, in their extreme instances, be clearly discriminated from those which lie without. Some equivocal example is then taken, and the framer of the definition is challenged to say in which category it is to be placed. Now it seems to me that an objection of this kind ignores the inevitable conditions under which a scientific nomenclature is constructed, alike in political economy and in all the positive sciences. In such sciences, nomenclature, and therefore definition, is based on classification, and to admit of degrees is the character of all natural facts. . . . It is, therefore,

[1] "Les personnes qui veulent que le billet de banque soit de la monnaie, n'ont jamais pu *tracer une ligne de démarcation qui fût nette* entre le billet de banque et la lettre-de-change, ou le billet-à-ordre. Si l'on dit que le billet de banque passe de main en main sans endossement, on peut répondre que les lettres-de-change *en blanc* sont dans le même cas," etc., etc.—[La Monnaie, p. 59.]

no valid objection to a classification, nor consequently, to the definition founded upon it, that instances may be found which fall, or seem to fall, on our lines of demarkation. This is inevitable in the nature of things. But this notwithstanding, the classification, and therefore the definition, is a good one, if, in those instances which do *not* fall on the line, the distinctions marked by the definition are such as it is important to mark."—[Character and Logical Method of Pol. Economy.]

The motive for the issue of Convertible Paper Money is twofold: first, the greater convenience of paper as compared with gold, and in a still higher degree as compared with silver.[1]

A thousand sovereigns weigh upwards of twenty-one pounds troy; silver of the same value, fifteen or sixteen times as much. Such an amount of metallic treasure would not only be exceedingly cumbersome, but its presence could hardly escape observation, inviting not only to robbery but to graver violence.

The second motive for the issue of Convertible Paper Money is its greater cheapness (*i. e.*, to the issuer), since it has been ascertained that a much larger amount of paper can be kept in circulation than is held of specie for redemption; and the issuer of the paper derives a

[1] In his recent letter on the silver question, Mr. Wells has dwelt sportively on the cumbrousness of silver, at its present purchasing power, as an argument against the rehabilitation of that metal as unlimited legal tender concurrently with gold. "The wheelbarrow, in fact, will become the essential, and possibly the fashionable, portemonnaie for all who purpose to engage in any considerable moneyed transactions." The sufficient answer to Mr. Wells's objection is that the bank-note has been in use two hundred years.

profit from the interest on all notes loaned, above the coin and bullion in his possession.

It is commonly said that paper money thus issued *represents* specie, but we shall do well to decline, with Mr. Tooke [Hist. of Prices, iii, 224], and Prof. Price, to admit a term so vague and misleading. "I cannot," says the latter, "accept the word 'represent' in currency, for I can never understand its meaning. It has no definite meaning for me, nor, as far as I can perceive, for any one else."—[Principles of Currency, p. 69.]

Were a paper money to be based upon the full amount of specie needed for its redemption entire, the question whether it would be more or less expensive to the community, as a whole, would depend upon the ratio between the loss of coin by abrasion in use, and the expense of putting out and keeping out paper promissory of coin. It might be that, in a given state of the arts of coinage, on the one hand, and of engraving, paper-manufacturing, and printing, on the other, the cost of replacing gold by paper would be an expensive one. At another time, the charge of issuing notes might be much below the value of the metal lost from year to year by abrasion; and hence, the country as a whole, would be a gainer by the substitution of paper for the full amount of coin held for redemption.

Looking, however, to the interest of any private issuing body, it will appear that the cost of maintaining such a circulation would be greater by the whole expense of engraving, printing, and issuing the paper. But with a reserve of coin and bullion, such as the experience of modern banking has ascertained to be sufficient to meet all demands reasonably to be anticipated, the profit to the issuing body may be very considerable.

"The gold and silver money," wrote Adam Smith,

"which circulates in any country may very properly be compared to a highway, which, while it circulates and carries to market all the grass and corn of the country, produces itself not a single pile of either. The judicious operations of banking, by providing, if I may be allowed so violent a metaphor, a sort of wagon-way through the air, enable the country to convert, as it were, a great part of its highways into good pastures and cornfields, and thereby to increase very considerably the annual produce of its land and labor. The commerce and industry of the country, however, it must be acknowledged, though they may be somewhat augmented, cannot be altogether so secure when they are thus, as it were, suspended upon the Dædalian wings of paper money, as when they travel about upon the solid ground of gold and silver."—[Wealth of Nations, i, 321.]

The closing sentence quoted from Dr. Smith intimates a contingency to which Convertible Paper Money is always, in a greater or less degree, subject, namely, a "run" upon the banks for the redemption of their notes, which shall exhaust their reserves of specie. Icarus, it will be recollected, set out with Dædalus on his flight through the air, but, by soaring too near the sun, which, after the manner of Lord Bacon, we may conjecture to represent the fierce blaze of competition, his wings of wax were melted, so that he fell out of the aerial highway and was drowned in the waters which bear his name. Nor is disaster possible merely. Miscarriages enough have occurred on these "wagon-ways through the air," in the brief history of the United States, to give a name to every bay and cape upon our coast.

Yet though the issue of bank-notes on a partial basis of specie, under the doctrine of chances, is always, in the nature of the case, at a certain risk, this does not constitute a fatal objection to paper-money banking, if it be otherwise desirable. Men and communities rightly take the necessary risk of collisions and boiler explosions for the sake of the saving in time and the gain in power which they derive from the use of steam-cars and steamboats.[1] So it might be with disasters to which, from the fault of managers or through causes that could neither be controlled nor anticipated, paper-money banking should be found subject.

Just what proportion between notes and specie-reserves will, in the balancing of gain against loss, leave the largest net result in favor of such a system, is a purely banking question. Lord Overstone, a very conservative writer, who will often be quoted in the remaining pages of this work, regards one-third bullion as sufficient even in a country where communication is so apt and quick as in England [Tracts, pp. 455–6]. This is the proportion actually taken in many countries of Europe, as the legal[2] minimum reserve. It is clear, however, that the conditions of issue must differ so widely, from time to time, and place to place, as to make it impossible to apply the same rule to all banks with any benefit.

A bank whose notes circulate among a rural popula-

---

[1] Wolowski, La Question des Banques, p. 385.

[2] Of the rule of one-third specie, M. Wolowski writes: "Si la Banque a été imprudente dans les émissions, la précaution est insuffisante; si, au contraire, la Banque est prudemment et loyalement administrée, la réserve métallique, du tiers ne tarde pas à paraaître excessive, comme condition absolue. L'observation et l'expérience peuvent apprendre, non sous forme de règle générale, mais pour chaque place de commerce et pour chaque banque, selon la nature et le mouvement des affaires, quelle doit être la réserve métallique combinée avec la rentrée des créances."—[La Question des Banques p. 202.]

tion, going twenty or fifty miles in all directions from the place of issue, where intelligence of disaster would make its way slowly, where panic would be impossible, from the mere lack of contiguity, and where the expense of presenting a small note at the bank-counter might equal or exceed its value, is in a very different position from one whose notes are mainly held in the city where they are issued. Here the whole population can be brought into the streets by the stroke of a bell; intelligence of evil spreads rapidly, and the contagion of panic acts with terrific force.

The question of specie-reserve is, however, as has been said, purely a banking question, with which in the theory of Convertible Paper Money we have little or nothing to do. The banks of a country might have reserves of two-thirds, or four-fifths their issues, putting them beyond all reasonable apprehension of a failure to redeem their notes on demand; and yet it would be an open question, whether they might not issue notes in excess, and thus subject the community to the effects of inflation. In a word, the question of the reserve is a question as to what is good for the banks and the actual holders of their notes. Beyond this is the question, what is good for the community.

Bank-notes, in the modern sense, were first issued in Sweden. The bank which, in 1668, became the Bank of Sweden, was first founded by Palmstruck, in 1656. The first note was issued in 1658,[1] nearly forty years before the Bank of England was chartered.

The Bank of England, until 1759, issued no notes of less value than £20.[2] The practice of issuing bank-notes

[1] Palgrave, Notes on Banking, p. 87.

[2] Francis, Hist. Bank of England, i, 172.

as the ordinary money of circulation began in Scotland long before it did in England, the Bank of Scotland issuing £1 notes as early as 1704. Sir Henry Parnell and Mr. Thornton assign the close of the war of the American Revolution as the date when the first considerable extension of paper-money banking in England took place.

We have seen that superior convenience and comparative cheapness are claimed for Convertible Paper Money. By some writers a third advantage is alleged, respecting which, however, wide difference of opinion exists.

Prof. Price, in his work on the "Principles of Currency," so often quoted in these pages, gives at considerable length, and with general approval, a letter of Mr. Charles Gairdner, manager of the Union Bank of Glasgow, who alleges concerning bank paper money, that "it confers a third advantage, in respect that the amount of money in circulation in any country being a fluctuating quantity, an increase or diminution in the amount of paper money in circulation may take place without disturbing the stock of coin which forms the reserve."

Mr. Patterson, author of a work entitled "The Science of Finance," writes: "The grand value of a note circulation nowadays, at least in this country where the economy of banking is so fully developed, consists, not so much in the extent to which it economizes specie, as in its power of ready expansibility, by which it can be made to neutralize the ever recurring fluctuations in the supply of specie, or in the monetary requirements of the community.

"The amount of these fluctuations is comparatively trivial, and they are exceedingly transient. Nevertheless, if any obstacle prevent the expansion of the note circulation at such times, the effects are tremendous. Not only trade, but the banking system itself, is liable to be pulled to the ground."—[P. 37.]

On the other hand, as opposed to those who hold that one of the advantages of paper money is that it forms a medium more "elastic" than metallic money, are two schools of writers, one of which holds, with Mr. Tooke in his later works, not only that elasticity is not desirable, but that, in the very nature of the case, it cannot exist; the second, which holds, with Mr. Tooke in his earlier works, and with Lord Overstone, that such capability of expansion exists in Convertible Paper Money, but is eminently undesirable, and indeed forms the great drawback to the motives of superior convenience and cheapness, in the issue of such money.[1]

In the question thus disputed, as to the expansibility of bank circulation over and above, or otherwise than, the expansibility of metallic money, lies the whole philosophy of Convertible Paper Money.

If the writers of the one school are correct, and such money cannot expand or contract otherwise than as metallic money would in the same circumstances, the problem is a very simple one. Nothing but good banking is needed to give the people good money.

---

[1] I have elsewhere [see p. 191] confessed my inability to reconcile with Mr. Ricardo's often repeated opinions as to the effects of seigniorage on prices, a sentence from his "High Price of Bullion." I have now to admit that I am wholly without an explanation of the following sentence in Mr. Ricardo's "Proposals for an Economical and Secure Currency": "Amongst the advantages of a paper over a metallic circulation, may be reckoned as not the least, the facility with which it may be altered in quantity as the wants of commerce and temporary circumstances may require, enabling the desirable object of keeping money at a uniform value to be, as far as it is practicable, securely and cheaply attained."

On the other hand, if such issues are subject to expansion and contraction otherwise than as metallic money, those who hold with Lord Overstone find the necessity of rigidly guarding the power of issue and subjecting it to regulations not such merely as are prescribed by correct banking principles, but such also as are required for the protection of the community against bad money, as the result of undue expansion or contraction.

And, first, a word and a word only, as to the desirableness of the so-called "elasticity" of a Convertible Paper Money.

We have seen that elasticity is also predicated of Inconvertible Paper Money by its advocates and admirers, but upon examination we found that there is no elasticity whatever in such a money, in the sense of its giving under pressure, to resume its shape after pressure is withdrawn. There is no more elasticity in a circulating medium composed of inconvertible notes, than there is in a lump of dough, which may be pulled out to any length, at least until it breaks apart, but never flies back when the distending force is withdrawn.

But is there elasticity, in any proper sense, in a Convertible Paper Money? Those who demand that money shall be "elastic," mean by this that there shall be more of it at one time than at another. Is this elasticity? A rubber band is elastic, but there is no more of it at one time than at another. It will cover more ground at one time than at another but it only does so by becoming thinner. There will be more of it, in any one place, at one time than at another, but, for this reason, there is less of it in some other place. There is no more rubber when the band is stretched, than there was before. Now, elasticity in this, the true sense, belongs eminently to metallic money. No class of commodities known to men, yield more quickly under pressure, or react more promptly. If an exceptional demand arises anywhere, gold or silver responds with an alacrity which would be unattainable by any article not possessing great value for its bulk, and not, at the same time, that article in which the values of all commodities are expressed for purposes of exchange. But while, in obedience to economical impulses, however slight, there may be more of such money in any one place, at one time than at another, the total amount is not, on that account, increased. There is less at the same time in some other place, or in all other places. This fact is essential to create that tension which shall make it certain that, when the exceptional demand in the first indicated place shall cease, the volume of money will be promptly and accurately redistributed, according to the prevailing conditions of international commerce.

With a Convertible Paper Money, however, no such assurance exists. Enlarged local demand is not met by a supply drawn from the general reservoir, to be returned again after the exigency is over to the common circulation, but by issues of local origin and local acceptance.

But it is said, trade everywhere needs more money at one season of the year than at another, and, as the amount of metallic money can be no greater in spring than in autumn, in summer than in winter, paper issues come in to meet the larger demands of the busier seasons, to which the precious metals are incapable of responding. It is unquestionably true that more exchanges require to be effected by the use of money at one season of the year, in any given place or within any given occupation, than at other seasons, but to the claim hereupon made that the amount of money should be susceptible of increase by local issues, three things are objected.

First. The periodical occasions for a larger use of money, on the part of different trades and different localities, go far to offset each other. The busy time of the manufacturer is not necessarily the busy time of the agriculturist; lumber and cotton are not moved to market in the same season. In the same way trade reaches its height in different sections and countries at different periods of the year, so that money may be doing its work this month in France, return next month to England to meet the demands of Lancashire, and go two weeks later to Glasgow, in the usual November drain northward, to satisfy the wants of the iron trade of Scotland.

Secondly. It does not follow from the fact that more exchanges are to be effected by the use of money, that more actual pounds or dollars are requisite. Money, as we have seen, is a quantity of two dimensions, the number of pieces of gold, or silver, or paper, and their rate of movement.[1] A scarcity of money will first make itself felt in an increased activity of what is on hand. Each piece will accomplish more payments in the same time. A rising rate of interest makes the use of money worth more, and hence it will not be allowed to remain so long idle in the pocket or the drawer. If the merchant or the manufacturer has to pay eight per cent., in place of six, for discounts, he will calculate his outgoings and incomings more closely, in order to reduce the average

---

[1] "Whether sixpence twice paid be not as good as a shilling once paid?"—[Bishop Berkeley's Querist, No. 478.]

amount lying in his till. He will deposit more promptly to secure the higher interest; he will take more pains in collecting sums due from his customers, with whom the money might otherwise have tarried a day or a week longer.

Thirdly. While there is a tendency, in a normal condition of production and trade, to a greater demand for money at one period than at another, a certain stringency at such times is desirable as exerting a wholesome repression upon speculative movement. The present industrial and commercial organization of the world powerfully tends to gather production into great waves with corresponding intervals of depression—overproduction succeeded surely by stagnation. This cannot be wholly prevented. A certain waste of energy, which always results from fitful exertions, must be accepted as among the economical conditions of this age. But it is utterly undesirable that the tendency should be quickened and strengthened by the facility of issues of local origin and circulation.

Passing now from the views of those who, with Mr. Patterson, hold that facility of increase in a Convertible Paper Money, any other in kind or degree than subsists in money of gold or silver, is both practicable and desirable, let us fix our attention on the two schools which agree in regarding any action of such money varying from the action of metallic money, under the same conditions, as eminently undesirable, but differ as to the possibility of such a divergence.

First, as to the undesirableness of divergence: "A mixed currency of coin and convertible paper," says Mr. Wilson, "ought to conform to the action of a purely metallic currency."

"A currency when composed of bank-notes and coin," says Mr. Nicholson, "ought to be made by law to fluctuate in its amount exactly as a currency composed of coin only would have fluctuated under similar circumstances."

"We are willing," said Mr. Tooke, "to consider a metallic currency as the type of that to which our mixed circulation of coin and paper ought to conform."

"I consider," said Mr. George Warde Norman, "a metallic currency to be the most perfect currency, except so far as respects inconvenience, in some respects, and cost. In everything else a metallic currency is the most perfect, and should be looked upon as the type of all other currencies."

What, asks Lord Overstone, "is the test of mismanagement of the circulation? I presume the answer will not be disputed. Fluctuations of the amount of paper issues not corresponding to those of bullion."—[Tracts, etc., p. 168.]

"The sole duty," he declares, "to be performed in regulating a paper currency is to make its amount vary as the amount of a currency exclusively metallic would vary under the same circumstances."—[*Ibid.*, p. 36, cf. pp. 27, 58, 73, 115, 168, 172, 189, 191, 362.]

These are the expressions of writers of both schools, and it will be seen that neither school yields to the other in the completeness and emphasis with which it asserts that a Convertible Paper Money should conform precisely, in all its operations, to the movement of metallic money.

"But, further," says Mr. Tooke,[1] "we contend that it has so conformed and must so conform, while the paper is strictly convertible."

---

[1] History of Prices, 1839–47, p. 218.

It is on this point that we see joined the issue which divides the two schools of economists known respectively by the titles, The Currency Principle and the Banking Principle.

## CHAPTER XIX.

### THE CURRENCY PRINCIPLE VS. THE BANKING PRINCIPLE.

HAVING seen how closely the two schools agree in holding it to be a desideratum that Convertible Paper Money shall operate in all cases precisely as metallic money would do, we now note how widely they diverge on the question of the practicability of an action in the one form of money different from what would occur, under similar circumstances, in the other.

"An expanded or inflated currency of bank-notes," says Prof. Price,[1] "is an absurdity, nothing better than pure nonsense." And again, "A convertible paper money encounters a most solid and objective obstacle to excess."

"We hold it," says Mr. Wilson,[2] "as an incontrovertible fact, that there can be no variation whatever in the quantities, values, or general action of a currency purely metallic, or of one composed of coin and convertible paper; and that the principle of convertibility alone is a perfect guarantee that, in all cases and in every re-

---

[1] Principles of Currency, p. 110. Of his predecessors in the department of Money, Prof. Price writes: "Mr. Tooke discerned the true answer. Mr. Mill, with some little wavering, and a few others, have seen the light."—[*Ibid.*]

[2] Capital, Currency and Banking, p. 66, cf. 82.

spect, the one currency would strictly conform with the other."

Prominent also among writers of this school was Mr. Fullarton, the author of a work of exceeding ability on the "Regulation of Currencies."

"I contend," says Mr. Fullarton, "that there not only ought to be such correspondence, but that there always is; that, wherever the convertibility of paper is perfect and secured from all delay or impediment, the coin of full standard value in weight and fineness, and the traffic in the metal, whether coined or uncoined, absolutely free and unrestricted, there the bank issues, if left to themselves, must necessarily fluctuate in conformity to the principles which govern the supply of the standard metal."[1]

Conspicuous among the English economists who maintained "the Currency Theory," so called,[2] that is, who held to the practicability of a divergent action of the two forms of money, and to the consequent necessity of regulating issues upon principles different from, or additional to, mere banking principles, was Lord Overstone, once Samuel Jones Loyd, an eminent banker, and a writer of marked originality and power. Alluding to

[1] "Lorsqu'on étudie avec attention les principes de la circulation monétaire, que nous venons d'exposer, on demeure convaincu qu'une ou plusieurs banques de circulation opérant sur un marché, et ne commettant pas de fautes dans leurs escomptes, ne peuvent jamais émettre trop de billets, quels que soient leurs efforts dans ce but, parce que leurs émissions ont une limite naturelle et nécessaire."—[Courcelle-Seneuil, Op. de Banq., p. 207–8.]

[2] "We are not aware," says Mr. Wilson, "of any reason for this appellation to the doctrine; but we use it as a well-known distinction."—[Capital, Currency and Banking, p. 61ª.]

the former consent of economists as to the similar action of the two forms of money in all cases, Lord Overstone wrote in 1840: "It is now discovered that there is a liability to excessive issues of paper, even while that paper is convertible at will."[1] This proposition Lord Overstone maintained during his life with great assiduity and much ingenuity. It was to the failure of the government properly to regulate the amount of paper money in England (consisting of Bank of England and country notes) prior to 1844, so as to enforce upon it an action conforming precisely to what the action of metallic money would have been, that Lord Overstone attributed the disasters "of the four great drains"[2] between 1824 and 1840; and when the act of 1844, based upon the principles advocated by him, if not, as generally believed,[3] designed and proposed by him, established

---

[1] Tracts, p. 138.

[2] The drain terminating in the crisis of 1825, the drain which continued from the year 1830 to the year 1832, the third drain, which began in the end of the year 1833, and terminated in the year 1836, and the last drain, which began in 1838 and ended in the autumn of 1839.

Mr. Tooke, on the other hand, denied that there was any disturbance whatever, of either banking or mercantile credit, in 1832. The effects of 1836, he asserted, were confined to the American and East Indian trade. He asseverates that there was not any crisis in 1839, any failures, or any difficulty in obtaining discounts. "The whole of the phenomena of that year are resolvable into a moderately increased rate of interest, during a very short interval, and an uneasiness in the minds of the public at the unsafe position in which the Bank had, by want of foresight, suffered itself to be placed."—[Hist. of Prices, 1839–47, pp. 263–270.] He makes the only real crises of English financial history prior to 1850 to be those of 1792–3, 1810–1 1825 and 1847.

[3] Lord Overstone disclaimed all credit for the Act. "I never exchanged one word upon the subject of the Act with Sir Robert Peel.

the paper circulation upon principles which, in his opinion,[1] secured its action in exact conformity to that of metallic money, Lord Overstone found in the subsequent financial disasters of England only the natural results of commercial misconduct in speculation and overtrading, which were inevitable in the constitution of things and would have occurred equally under any form of circulation.

With Lord Overstone were Mr. George Warde Norman and Col. Torrens, while Sir Robert Peel, adopting their views, carried through Parliament the Act which now regulates the circulation of the Bank of England and of the other banks of the United Kingdom.

But perhaps we may say that the ablest defense of the Currency Principle is to be found in the earlier works of Mr. Thomas Tooke, the same writer who afterwards came to be recognized as the leader of the opposing school. We find these views in the first edition of his great work on Prices, published in 1823, and in his tract on the "State of the Currency," published in 1826. From these earlier works of Mr. Tooke I shall frequently quote in the further discussion of this most difficult subject, not at all in the spirit of citing a man against himself, or with any view to break the force of his later utterances; but simply because I find his statements of the Currency Principle, at the time he

---

. . . By the Act of 1819, Sir Robert Peel placed the monetary system of this country upon an honest foundation, and he was exposed to great obloquy for having so done. By the Act of 1844, he has obtained ample and efficient security that this honest foundation of our monetary system shall be effectually and permanently maintained."

[1] For the general development of Lord Overstone's views, see "Hardcastle on Banks," pp. 177–8 cf. pp. 203, 209.

held it, to be more satisfactory than those of any other writer. This is, of course, to accord great importance to Mr. Tooke's subsequent recantation of this theory and his long opposition to it; and yet I am disposed to think that the historian of English prices was nearer the truth in his earlier than in his later works.

It was about 1840 that Mr. Tooke, through a new edition of the first two volumes of his work on Prices, finally parted company with the advocates of the Currency Principle, and for the first time announced the views which he afterwards consistently maintained. Mr. Tooke quotes[1] and accepts Mr. Fullarton's account of his progress in the theory of Money:

"At the time of that publication in 1823, Mr. Tooke's mind appears to have been strongly imbued with the prevailing notions that prices are liable to rise and fall with the increase or diminution of the amount of bank-notes in circulation; that banks have it in their power to increase at pleasure the quantity of paper money; and that the efflux and influx of gold are to be regulated by regulating the issues of the banks.

"He adhered to these doctrines after he had refuted them by his discoveries, and seems to have parted with them at last only by degrees and with reluctance, under the pressure of his growing convictions."

In speaking, then, of the early works of Mr. Tooke, I refer to those in which he maintained the so-called Currency Principle; and in speaking of his later works, to those in which he maintained what in opposition is called the Banking Principle.

The reasons given by the writers who support the

---

[1] History of Prices, 1839–47, pp. xi–xii.

Banking Principle, for denying the possibility of the inflation of Convertible Paper Money, are two:

First, that the additional notes, requisite for inflation, cannot be got out.

Second, that, if once out, they would not stay out.

Thus Mr. Wilson says: "A currency 'augmented without any corresponding augmentation of internal trade' [Horner] implies a quantity of notes retained in circulation, at the will of the issuers, which the public do not require. Now, the public do not receive notes from a banker without paying interest for their use; and, however low that may be, they will take no more than they absolutely require—nor do they retain notes in their possession beyond what the convenience of trade requires; and, therefore, if issued in excess of that quantity, and if convertible, a portion would instantly be returned upon the issuers."

Mr. Wilson insists that, throughout the entire operation of issue, banks are wholly passive, giving out just what the community require, and no more, or, as Prof. Price expresses it, serve as "mere shops for the sale of tools." "The prices of commodities," says Mr. Tooke, "do not depend upon the quantity of money, . . . but, on the contrary, the amount of the circulating medium is the consequence of prices."

The first reason does not seem to me entitled to much respect. It reads very much like the old catch in the logic books, by which it was proven that a thing cannot move. A thing, if it move at all, must move either where it is or where it is not. It cannot move *where it is not*. It cannot *move* where it is. Therefore it cannot move at all. And yet we know that objects move. And, as Mr. Ricardo says, the argument by which it is sought to demonstrate that bank-notes cannot be issued in excess of the amount of metallic money, would also suffice to prove that not an ounce of the silver of Potosi, or of the gold of California, could have got into circulation.

"Let us suppose all the countries of Europe to carry on their circulation by means of the precious metals, and that each were at the same moment to establish a bank on the same principles as the Bank of England. Could they, or could they not, each add to the metallic circulation a certain portion of paper? and could they, or could they not, permanently maintain that paper in circulation? If they could, the question is at an end; an addition might, then, be made to a circulation already sufficient, without occasioning the notes to return to the bank in payment of bills due.

"If it is said they could not, then I appeal to experience, and ask for some explanation of the manner in which bank-notes were originally called into existence and how they are permanently kept in circulation. . .

"If the principle advanced by the bank directors be correct, not a bank-note could ever have been permanently kept in circulation, *nor would the discovery of the mines of America have added one guinea to the circulation of England. The additional gold would, according to this system, have found a circulation already adequate and in which no more could be admitted.*"—[Ricardo, Reply to Bosanquet.]

The question of *keeping out* Convertible Paper Money in excess, is a wholly distinct question; and the argument of the advocates of the Banking Principle, at this point, is entitled to more respectful and careful treatment.

A metallic money, if it becomes excessive, is reduced by exportation.

A Convertible Paper Money, if it becomes in excess, cannot be exported, in its present shape; but may be reduced by the return of the notes to the issuer, with a demand for gold for exportation.

An Inconvertible Paper Money can be reduced neither by direct exportation nor by return to the issuer.

The question at issue is whether, in the case of a Convertible Paper Money, the reduction takes place with the certainty and celerity required to avoid the consequences of inflation.

It is claimed by the advocates of the Banking Principle, that there is a Law of Reflux which constitutes an ample security against inflation.

Before proceeding to argue this question, let it be said that it is admitted generally by writers of this school, that the convertibility of the notes must be immediate and unconditional, in order to secure the full working of the principle. "A paper money," says Adam Smith, "consisting in bank-notes, issued by people of undoubted credit, payable upon demand without any condition, and in fact always readily paid as soon as presented, is in every respect equal in value to gold and silver money. . . .

"It would be otherwise, indeed, with a paper money consisting in promissory notes, of which the immediate payment depended, in any respect, either upon the good will of those who issued them, or upon a condition which the holder of the notes might not always have it in his power to fulfill, or of which the payment was not exigible till after a certain number of years, and which in the mean time bore no interest." . . .

"Some years ago the different banking companies of Scotland were in the practice of inserting into their bank-notes what they called an optional clause, by which they promised payment to the bearer, either as soon as the note should be presented, or, in the option of the directors, six months after such presentment, together with legal interest for the said six months." Advantage, says Dr. Smith, was often taken of this by directors to induce note-holders to take, cash down, a part of what they wanted.—[Wealth of Nations, i, 326.]

Given a paper money immediately and unconditionally convertible, "the reflux," says Mr. Tooke, "takes place chiefly in two ways; by payment of the redundant amount to a banker on a deposit account, or by the return of notes in discharge of securities on which advances have been made. A third way is that of a return of the notes to the issuing bank by a demand for coin. The last seems, in the view of the currency theory, to be the only way by which a redundancy, arising from the unlimited power of issue, which they assume to exist, admits of being corrected, in a convertible state of the paper; it is certainly the one least in use."—[Hist. of Prices, 1839-47, p. 185.]

The paragraph here quoted requires us to note a distinction which did not emerge until comparatively late in the discussion. How, ask the advocates of the Banking Principle, can a convertible currency be maintained in excess? If we say that the paper is issued in excess, we assert that it is depreciated. If depreciated, a premium on gold will arise, the faintest beginnings of which will be sufficient to bring the paper back to the bank, to secure the profit arising from the premium.

But, answer Mr. Norman and Lord Overstone, when we say that Convertible Paper Money is issued in excess, we do not mean that paper is depreciated in comparison with gold. We assert that *the whole money of the country paper and gold, undistinguishably, is depreciated in compar-*

*ison with the money of other countries.* We do not assert that such an effect can be produced to an indefinite extent, or maintained for an indefinite period. We admit that such a depreciation of the whole body of the money of a country—its lower "local value"—must sò encourage imports and so discourage exports, as ultimately to bring the volume back to the level of a purely metallic money. But we assert that the inflation may proceed so far and be maintained so long, as to originate evils of the most momentous character in the production and trade of a country. We also assert, that when the reaction sets in, it is likely to be so sudden and so violent as not only to bring the volume of money back to the proper level, but for a time to carry it even below that level, which fact will, of itself, become a new cause of industrial and commercial distress and loss.

Such was the position of the Currency School. Convertibility is a security against permanent excess of the currency, and fixes a limit beyond which irregularity cannot be carried; but the principle comes into operation only through the medium of prices. This had been Mr. Tooke's own view, in his pamphlet of 1826. "It not unfrequently requires an interval of some length, before the commodities which are interchangeable with other countries are affected by an excess in circulation, in such a degree as to produce the effect of increased import and diminished export."—[P. 90.]

"It is very true," said Mr. Norman in his work on "Currency and Banking," "that convertible paper cannot permanently be depreciated; that it must at length become equivalent to the specie it represents; but, under certain circumstances, the adjustment may be long deferred."

"Mere convertibility of the paper," said Mr. Henry

Drummond,[1] "is sufficient to prevent its ultimate depreciation, and to make the currency right itself. . . . But mere convertibility is not sufficient to prevent ruinous vacillations, ebbs and flows, to an immense extent. . . . The mere convertibility of paper cannot check depreciation until it has proceeded great lengths."[2]

It needs to be borne in mind that the advocates of the Currency Principle do not generally assert that the banks can force their notes into circulation, irrespective of the condition of trade; nor do they generally claim that the speculative impulses which allow inflation to take place are due, primarily or principally, to redundancy of money. "Fluctuations in the amount of the currency," said Lord Overstone,[3] "are seldom if ever the original and exciting cause of fluctuations in prices and in the state of trade. The buoyant and sanguine character of the human mind; miscalculations as to the relative extent of supply and demand; fluctuations of the seasons; changes of taste and fashion; legislative enactments and political events; excitement or depression in the condition of other countries connected with us by active trading intercourse; an endless variety of casualties acting upon those sympathies by which masses of men are often urged into a state of excitement or depression; these, all or some of them, are generally the original exciting causes of those variations in the state of trade to which the report refers. The manage-

[1] Elementary Propositions respecting the Currency.

[2] The doctrine that paper money is liable to be issued in excess, has been strongly supported by Ph. Geyer in his work, "Theorie und Praxis des Zettelbankwesens." Not a few of the German economists incline to the same view.

[3] Tracts, etc., p. 167.

ment of the currency is a subordinate agent; it seldom originates, but it may and often does exert a considerable influence in restraining or augmenting the violence of commercial oscillations."

"When speculation is once on foot," wrote Mr. Tooke in 1826, "with a circulation of the expansive nature of ours, the rise of any one article may not only be in a ratio far greater than the occasion really calls for, but, by increasing the aggregate of the circulating medium, may cause indirectly a rise in other commodities."—[State of the Currency, p. 45.]

Again, writing of English trade in 1824: "This increase of the circulation at the present time, when the urgent necessity of a reduction of the issues, or, at any rate, of a limitation of them, was so strongly indicated, could not fail of promoting, though it had not excited, the tendency which then existed to extravagance of speculation. . . . The Bank had not kindled the fire, but, instead of attempting to stop the progress of the flames, it supplied fuel for maintaining and extending the conflagration."—[Hist. of Prices, ii, 178.]

And of the final consequences of such inflation, he says: "The factitious increase of a medium of paper and credit, raising the prices of commodities and of the public funds above the level which the metallic basis of the currency can support, must be succeeded, not only by a destruction of all that artificial medium, but by a temporary contraction of the circulation below the level from which that enlargement took place."—[State of the Currency, p. 63–4.]

It will be observed that Mr. Tooke, in these sentences, quoted from his earlier works, asserts that inflation (beyond the limits of metallic money) only takes place when a tendency to speculation, otherwise induced, already exists.

"In the absence of inducement from the state of the markets to speculate in goods, if extra notes were issued, they would either have returned in the shape of deposits into the hands of the Bank, or have remained inert in the drawers of bankers."—[Hist. of Prices, ii, 64.]

I confess that to my mind there appears no more difficulty in believing that the commercial community will take up and hold more money when agitated by a speculative impulse and flushed with expectation of extraordinary gains,[1] than in believing that water will retain more of a certain salt in solution when heated than when cold. "The public," says Mr. Wilson, "do not receive notes from a banker without paying interest for their use, and, however low that may be, they will take no more than they absolutely require." But is it true that men are always equally solicitous to save on their interest account? always equally careful in expenditure? Surely not. At one time the man of business is mainly intent on saving, seeking not so much to enhance his gross profits, which, in the state of trade, he may know is impracticable, as to economize in his outgoings. These are ordinary times, dull times, when opportunities for exceptional gains do not present themselves. At another time, the man of business gives his thought, his effort, his care, more to gaining than to saving; he is ready to spend liberally, it may be lavishly, because

[1] "In most countries, but especially in England, there is at all times a profusion of enterprises to be undertaken; of experiments to be tried; of schemes to be worked out; of improvements to be made; of ingenious men to be set up with capital; of trades already profitable to be made more so by vast extensions."—[Wm. Newmarch, The New Supplies of Gold, p. 71.]

he sees, or thinks he sees, opportunities to make exceptionally high profits on his ventures. These are good times, flush times. At such a period, men do not scrutinize the contents of their tills, or the entries in their deposit-books, to see if they can contrive to reduce their dead stock or their interest account.

Again, though speculation and overtrading do not usually originate in an excess of money, the fact that they find in circulation a medium which can be rapidly increased at will, without cost, and which will thus respond without strain, so to speak, to the rising demands of trade, surely must enable speculation and overtrading to proceed faster and further than would be practicable if the money needed to support the higher prices had to be called in from foreign countries, and actual solid value given in exchange for it. When, therefore, Mr. Wilson asserts that the public do not "retain notes in their possession beyond what the convenience of trade requires," the advocate of the Currency Principle rejoins that the higher prices resulting from a general speculative movement of trade actually require more money; and hence that the public will retain the additional amount of notes in circulation, paying for their use, for the same reason which led them to retain, and pay for the use of the notes previously in circulation.

It is manifest that, if banks have the ability in times of speculative impulse thus to increase their issues, or if there is in trade, without any conscious purpose on the part of bank managers, a tendency to call out paper money from the banks more rapidly or more extensively than metallic money would, under the same circumstances, have been called in from other countries, this movement will necessarily be assisted by

### COMPETITION AMONG ISSUERS.

"The paper issues of this country," wrote Lord Overstone in 1840, "are . . . competing issues,[1] each endeavoring to encroach upon the other, and to appropriate to itself, at the expense of its competitors, a larger proportion of the whole circulation of the country. . . . Hence it arises that an expansion by one issuer may very naturally lead to a corresponding expansion by the other issuers. Such is the legitimate result of competitive action."[2]

In the same view, Mr. McCulloch says of the country banks of England prior to 1844: "Being a very numerous body, comprising several hundred establishments, scattered over all parts of the country, each is impressed with the well-founded conviction that all he could do in the way of contraction would be next to imperceptible, and no one ever thinks of attempting it so long as he is satisfied of the stability of those with whom he deals. On the contrary, every banker knows, were he to withdraw a portion of his issues, that some of his competitors would most likely embrace the opportunity of filling up

[1] Prof. Jevons finds "an evident flaw" in the position of those writers who hold that it is impossible to overissue convertible paper money. "When prices," he says, "are at a certain level and trade in a quiescent state, a single banker is, no doubt, unable to put into circulation more than a certain quantity of bank-notes. He cannot produce a greater effect upon the whole currency than a single purchaser can, by his sales or purchases, produce upon the market for corn or cotton. But a number of bankers, all trying to issue additional notes, resemble a number of merchants offering to sell corn for future delivery; and the value of gold will be affected, as the price of corn certainly is."—[Money and the Mechanism of Exchange pp. 314–5.]

[2] Tracts, pp. 97–8, cf. pp. 115, 122–3.

up the vacuum so created, and that consequently he should lose a portion of his business, without in any degree lessening the amount of paper afloat. Hence, in nineteen out of twenty cases, the country banks go on increasing their aggregate issues long after the exchange has been notoriously against the country; and when at last they are compelled, because of the altered state of things in the metropolis, to pull up, the chances are ten to one that the contraction is carried to an improper extent."—[Notes to Smith's Wealth of Nations.]

In consonance with their general views, the advocates of the Currency Principle hold to the necessity of closely restricting the power of issue,[1] while the advocates of the Banking Principle cannot admit this to be necessary.

"Rival issuers," said Lord Overstone, "equal in power and unlimited in number, on the one hand,—a single issuer, limited in his franchise but invested with plenary power for the discharge of them, on the other hand—are the respective principles."—[Tracts, etc., p. 117.]

Indeed, as the advocates of the Banking Principle hold that Convertible Paper Money cannot be issued in excess, they are bound to hold a high degree of competition in issues to be desirable. Individual issuers, writes Prof. Price,[2] "are proved by experience to cover

---

[1] "We do not want an abundant supply of cheap promissory paper."—[Sir Robert Peel.]

[2] While Prof. Price asserts that the principles of money have nothing to do with the question whether there shall be one issuer or many, this being a matter "of pure detail, of time and place, of local circumstances and habits" [p. 152], he admits that, *as a branch of banking*, the power of issue is so liable to abuse as properly to become the subject of regulation by the State.

"It may be perfectly reasonable for the law to say that no man

the land far more speedily and more effectually than the notes of a central institution."—[Principles of Currency, p. 153.]

The question of holding the power of issue under strict control, or of breaking it up [*fractionnement du privilége d'émission*] among many institutions, with the result of competition in issues, has also divided the economical opinion of France, where the monopoly of the Bank of France[1] makes the question a very practical one. MM. Chevalier, Coquelin and Courcelle Seneuil,[2]

---

shall be allowed to incur so vast a debt to the public, to an immense aggregate of individuals, all accepting these debts as a matter of course, almost without any choice in the matter, unless he gives some security for repayment."

"The individual efforts of each private person for himself are insufficient to procure the safety which is indispensable for him and the rest of the world. The state must be summoned to do what it alone can perform."

Mr. Tooke, even in his later writings, strongly asserted the necessity of a government regulation of issues, as a branch of banking. "I agree," he says, "with a writer in one of the American papers, who observes that free trade in banking is synonymous with free trade in swindling." . . . "The claims of right to such freedom of action in banking ought to be strenuously resisted. They do not rest in any manner on grounds analogous to the claims of freedom of competition in production. . . . The issue of paper substitutes for coin is no branch of productive industry. It is a matter for regulation by the State with a view to general convenience, and comes within the province of police."—[Hist. of Prices, iii, 206–7.]

[1] This monopoly was threatened, curiously enough, as an incident to the annexation of Savoy, after the Italo-Franco-Austrian war The Bank of Savoy, having rights of issues while that province belonged to Italy, claimed to retain those rights after annexation, which would have substituted an unintentional *duopoly* for the previously existing *monopoly*.

[2] "Soit qu'une seule banque jouisse du privilége exclusif d'émettre des billets, soit que plusieurs banques, stimulées par la concurrence

with whom are perhaps the majority of well-known writers, have advocated competition in issues, deeming the American system the most desirable for imitation. M. Wolowski, with whom are MM. Rossi and Léon Faucher, has defended the restrictive and regulative principles of the English system.

### SMALL NOTE ISSUES.

Besides the question of competition in issues, still another, that of small notes, entered prominently into the discussions respecting Convertible Paper Money in England, prior to the Act of 1844. In 1826, Mr. Tooke had written:

"There is one part of that circulation which ought not, upon any footing, or with any modification, to be any longer tolerated. I mean the notes under £5. These are, in every point of view, a most objectionable medium of exchange. *They offer greater facilities for being issued in excess than notes of a higher denomination; and they almost invariably exclude specie entirely from the districts where they pass current.* . . .

"It is quite idle to contend that the lower classes have the option of refusing to take the country notes. Practically, in the great majority of instances, they have not and cannot have any such option."

The public sentiment of England was set strongly against small notes by the experience of 1825, which Mr. Tooke had in mind when writing the above paragraph; and, as is well known, small notes are excluded from the circulation of the kingdom. The same objec-

---

essayent de forcer les émissions, le résultat est exactement le même; il est impossible de dépasser le chiffre fixé par les besoins du service des échanges."—[Op. de Banque, p. 200.]

tion to small notes has been exhibited by economical writers generally on this side the Atlantic.

On the other hand, Prof. Price sees no reason, so far as the principles of currency are concerned, why small notes should not issue without restraint; and declares that "one-pound notes are a glory to Scotland at this very hour."—[Principles of Currency, p. 154.] Mr. Wilson, in his work on "Currency and Banking," makes a plea for the issue of one-pound notes by the Bank of England, declaring that the money of the kingdom would be greatly economized thereby. The prejudice against one-pound notes, he asserts, arose during the Suspension; but should in reason have equally applied to five-pound notes. The strictly economical arguments of those who advocate the suppression of small notes are three: first, as stated by Mr. Tooke in the paragraph cited, that they are more liable to be issued in excess than larger notes, being at best but imperfectly convertible [*i. e.*, the holders being, through ignorance, through poverty, or through distance, unable in fact to present them for redemption]. It was probably due to this cause that when the Bank of England, in 1817, as previously recited [see p. 356], offered to redeem in coin its one-pound and two-pound notes, a small demand was made upon its coffers, while an offer to redeem the larger notes brought in such a mass of paper for redemption as compelled the Bank to abandon its project.

Second, that the circulation, among the masses of the people, of coin which would (by Sir Thomas Gresham's law) be displaced by small notes, constitutes the best possible reserve for the banks issuing notes. In his work published in 1826, Mr. Tooke quotes Mr. Baring's evidence before the Committee of 1819 as showing, by the example of the Bank of France in 1817 and 1818, "the comparative facility with which the coffers of a bank which has suffered too great a reduction of its reserves by imprudent issues of paper, may be replenished out of a circulation consisting in great proportion of coin, notwithstanding a coincident demand for large payments abroad."[1]

"Their bullion," said Mr. Baring, "was reduced by imprudent issues from 117,000,000 francs to 34,000,000 francs, and has returned, by more prudent and cautious measures, to 100,000,000 francs. It must, however, be always recollected that this operation took place in a country every part of the circulation of which is saturated with specie."

And it is at this point that a fair criticism of Prof. Price's position respecting small notes suggests itself. On the assumption that bank-notes are convertible, that able writer throws not a little ridicule upon the small-note-prohibition. If convertible £5 and £10 notes are good, why not convertible £1 and £2 notes? But the specie circulation which the £1 and £2 notes would replace is one of the prime means relied upon by many economists of Prof. Price's own school, for making the higher notes convertible. If a paper money is convertible, it is, as Prof. Price admits, not because it is called so, but because it is made so and kept so.

The third argument of those who advocate small-note-prohibition is that, while the small notes are imperfectly convertible, being liable to be put out and kept out in excess in ordinary times, owing to the want of information on the part of holders, or their inability to present the notes for redemption promptly and in the right place, the very ignorance of the masses may at times render this the most dangerous element of the money of a country, since the uneducated are the first

[1] State of the Currency, p. 111.

subjects of panic, and, after tolerating bad money for a long period, are apt, on the occurrence of any alarm, to rush to the opposite extreme and give way to unreasoning apprehensions, besieging the doors of the bank, beyond all control or influence by argument or persuasion, and bringing down mischief upon themselves and the community. The issue of small notes, said Mr. Horsley Palmer, "renders the bank liable to a very great sudden demand. . . . The holders of small notes are the lower orders of the people, whose fears are more extensively acted upon in times of distrust." It was the testimony of the officers of the Bank of England that this portion of the issues was the main source of danger in 1825.

The argument, in this connection, from the higher claim which the poorer classes, by reason of their helplessness, have upon the consideration of government, is mainly a political argument and we need not entertain it here.

The argument from the greater facility of counterfeiting[1] in the case of small notes, is at least worth noticing. The Act for authorizing the Bank of England to stop payment, in 1797, was followed, as a matter of necessity, by an Act enabling the Bank to issue notes under £5. The result was a monstrous increase of forgery. In the twenty-one years preceding 1797 there had been but five or six executions for this crime. In the twenty-one years between 1797 and 1818, 313 persons suffered death for counterfeiting bank-notes.

---

[1] "Doubtless, too, they can be more easily forged; and this is a practical reason of great weight. Still it is not a reason derived from any principle of currency; it is a reason of mechanics, of manufacturing, on which a political economist need not dwell, when expounding the principles of currency."—[Price, Principles of Currency p. 155.]

## CHAPTER XX.

### CONVERTIBLE PAPER MONEY IN ENGLAND.

SUCH, with the incidents described, being the issue between the two schools of English economists, advocating, severally, what are known as the Currency Principle and the Banking Principle, let us trace the progress of the doctrines of the former school up to their embodiment in the Bank Act of 1844.

In 1819, says Lord Overstone, "terminates the Dark Age of Currency." Up to this date the directors of the Bank had stood on the Banking Principle, maintaining that good banking was all that was necessary to give the country good money; and in the very year named the Bank sent to a Parliamentary Committee a resolution [March 25] in the following words:

"That this Court cannot refrain from adverting to an opinion strongly insisted on by some, that the Bank has only to reduce its issues to obtain a favorable turn in the exchanges, and a consequent influx of the precious metals; the Court conceives it to be its duty to declare that it is unable to discover any solid foundation for such a sentiment."

But the views of the directors did not prevail. "The reports of the select committees of both Houses of Parliament upon the expediency of resuming cash payments, in 1819, were founded upon the adoption of the doctrine of the Bullionists, and from that time it may be said that the principles of currency, as expounded by them, have supplanted the so-called practical views[1] which had previously prevailed, and have been recognized by the public sentiment, as the code of laws by which the monetary system of the country ought to be governed."—[Lord Overstone, Tracts, p. 53.]

"The next well-defined step," continues Lord Overstone, "in the progress of public intelligence upon the subject of currency was at the period of the appointment of the Parliamentary Committee, preparatory to the renewal of the bank charter, in 1832.[2] The evidence given by the most intelligent of the Bank directors on that occasion contrasts in the most extraordinary manner with the evidence given, under similar circumstances, only thirteen years before."—[*Ibid.*, p. 58.]

Yet, notwithstanding this movement of public sentiment and of Bank opinion on the subject, the position of the Bank relative to the money-supply of the kingdom was still, in the opinion of the Currency School, exceedingly unsatisfactory. "The banking reserve was a vague and undefined quantity. It was the power of issuing any amount of notes, until the gold was finally

[1] Lord Overstone [Tracts, pp. 45, 52, 53], though himself a banker, expresses great contempt for the uninstructed "practical views" of the Bank and the City. Prof. Price, who holds widely different opinions, concurs heartily in this sentiment—see his "Principles of Currency," pp. 1–6.

[2] "Many matters of moment date from that inquiry; such as the publication of the accounts of the Bank, the publication of the amount of bullion held by the Bank, and the partial adoption of the principle of currency by which the Bank of England, as well as the country banks' circulation, should be regulated by the state of foreign exchanges."—[Levi, Hist. Br. Com., p. 204.]

exhausted;" while "a reduction of deposits was deemed a sufficient set-off against a reduced amount of bullion."—[*Ibid.*, p. 328.]

The root of the evil, in this writer's view, lay in the union, in the same institution, of the two functions of a bank of issue and of a bank of deposit and discount.

As to the absence of any necessary relation between banking and paper money, there is substantial unanimity among economists.

"This accidental, or rather non-essential, connection of notes with banking," says Prof. Price, "is alas! the parent of interminable confusion. It is the plague spot of all currency; the foreign and insoluble ingredient, which will neither itself crystallize, nor suffer the other elements to crystallize."—[Principles of Currency, p. 104.]

In the same view, Mr. Norman: "No correct notions can ever be formed upon the subject of currency, unless the business of issue be clearly separated in the reader's mind from the other transactions which form the real and legitimate employment of the banker."

"Issuing," says Mr. Nicholson, "is creating money; banking is managing money after it has been issued."—[Sc. of Exchanges, p. 46.]

But no writer has so fully developed the theme that there is no necessary connection between banking and paper money as Lord Overstone:

"A bank of issue is intrusted with the creation of the circulating medium, a bank of deposit and discount is concerned only with the use, distribution or application of that circulating medium. The sole duty of the former is to take efficient means for issuing its paper money upon good security, and regulating the amount of it by one fixed rule. The principal object and business of the latter is to obtain the command of as large a proportion as possible of the existing circulating medium, and to distribute it in such a manner as shall combine security for repayment with the highest rate of profit."—[Tracts, p. 31.] "The principles upon which these two branches of business ought to be conducted are perfectly distinct and never can be reduced to one and the same rule."—[*Ibid.*, p. 63, cf. pp. 30, 115, 139, 142, 181, 219.]

While, however, economists are substantially agreed as to the absence of any necessary connection between banking and paper money, Mr. Tooke and the advocates of the Banking Principle do not admit that the union of the two functions in the same institution is in any way objectionable. On the contrary, it may not only be more economical; it may better serve the wants of the community, each function being more fully performed by reason of the other being carried on under the same management.

The advocates of the Currency Principle, on the other hand, hold the union of the two functions to be productive of evil. The banker inevitably sympathizes with expansive speculations; therefore he should not issue currency.[1] The union of the two functions, of circulation and of deposits, is bound to cause confusion, both in reasoning and in action.

The separation of the banking and the issue departments of the Bank of England was, therefore, the first object of the economists of the Overstone school, as rendering possible a regulation of the Bank issues ac-

---

[1] Lord Overstone, Tracts, cf. pp. 32, 39, 63, 115, 143, 177, 249–50

cording to their principles. "A repeal of the Union," Lord Overstone wrote in 1840, "is essential to good government in monetary affairs." . . . "The common crown may still rest upon the brow of the sovereign of Threadneedle Street, and she may be permitted to wield one sceptre of authority over her separated departments. But she must consent to hold a Committee of Treasury in the Bullion Office, as well as in the Discount Parlor, and must govern them through the instrumentality of a distinct system of laws, appropriate to each and in harmony with their respective purposes. The interest and well-being of the one must no longer be interfered with or endangered by influences or affections connected with the other."—[Tracts, p. 145.]

That repeal was effected by the Act of 1844,[1] and the two departments of the Bank of England are now as distinct as the customs and internal revenue bureaus of our own government. By that Act the Bank is allowed to issue £14,000,000 of notes upon its securities. It is, moreover, provided that, on provincial banks ceasing to issue notes, the Bank may be empowered, by Order in Council, to issue upon securities two-thirds of the notes which such banks had been authorized to put forth. Under this condition,[2] the secured issue has risen to £15,000,000. But for every other note which the Bank may put into circulation, an equal amount of coin or

[1] Supplemented by the Act of 1845. I shall, however, speak of the whole body of this legislation as the Act of 1844.

[2] Mr. Maclaren states that the application on the part of the Bank of England, to issue notes in lieu of those no longer issued by the country banks, did not originate with the Bank directors, but was made by them at the instance of the government.—[History of the Currency, p. 282.]

bullion must be paid in. Nor is it for the directors to say whether more notes shall thus issue or not. The Bank is bound by law to buy bullion from whomsoever offers it, at £3 17*s.* 9*d.* per oz.

It is in view of this entire exemption of the issue department from the will of the directors, that Prof. Price speaks of the Bank as "The Automaton."—[Principles of Currency, pp. 138, 144.] "It is not," he says, "a department of the Bank in any sense. It is a self-acting institution of the State, working on the Bank's premises, and directed by rules laid down by the State, and absolutely beyond the control of the Bank directors."

In the language of Mr. Neaves, former Governor: "The issue department is out of our hands altogether. We are mere trustees under the act of Parliament to see that these securities are placed there and kept up to that amount, and in no case can any creditor of the Bank touch that which is reserved for a note-holder."

In the provisions regulating the note-issues which have been recited we have the second grand feature of the Act of 1844, viz., the establishment of the paper circulation upon a basis which, in the view of the Overstone school of economists, secures the exact conformity of its movements, in rise and in fall, to those of metallic money. The amount of secured circulation being fixed at an amount (£15,000,000) below that to which it is reasonably to be supposed the metallic circulation of the country could, in any event, be reduced, the fabric above that is built up wholly out of specie.[1] Not a £5

[1] All notes over the secured circulation, are "only so many certificates of the deposit of a corresponding amount of bullion."—[Nicholson, Science of Exchanges, p. 44.]

The bank is permitted to hold one-fourth its specie reserves in

note can be issued from the Bank of England unless the corresponding quantity of bullion has been deposited. Not a £5 note can disappear, except by accidental loss, unless a corresponding quantity of bullion has been taken away in exchange for it.

In Lord Overstone's phrase, the principle of the Act is: the amount of securities invariable; the fluctuations in notes to correspond to fluctuations in the specie on deposit.[1] This, in his opinion, constituted "free banking" in the best sense.

"If they [the people] bring in gold, they increase the circulation; if they take out gold, they diminish it. In this respect they are perfectly free agents: neither law nor authority interferes with them; and thus the regulation of the amount of the currency is strictly in the hands of the public."—[Tracts, p. 320.]

Thus we see that the greatest bank in the world is not, as a bank, an issuer of notes, a manufacturer of paper money. Nor are the joint-stock banks of London, with their enormous deposits and discounts, dependent in the smallest degree for their power or their profits on note circulation. No London bank can issue notes, nor can any bank which has been chartered since May 6, 1844, while the issues of the English banks then existing are limited to their ordinary outstanding circu-

---

silver, but is not obliged to buy silver as it is obliged to buy gold. Accordingly, the Bank in the crisis of 1847 refused to buy silver or make advances upon it. Lord Overstone justifies this action: "In a country where the standard is gold, silver is a commodity, and must be treated as any other commodity. It is not expedient that the Bank should be compelled to make advances on commodities."—[Tracts, p. 299.]

[1] Tracts, pp. 6–7 27, 60, 77–8.

lation before that date. The Irish and Scotch banks,[1] however, can issue bank-notes above the amount of their circulation in 1844, provided that for every note so issued they possess a corresponding amount of coin.

Here we have the third great feature of the Act of 1844, viz., the restriction, so far as was deemed consistent with vested interests, of the country bank circulation. It was in this part of the paper money of the kingdom, prior to 1844, that the advocates of the Currency Principle found the main source of the evil of excessive inflation or contraction.

"We impose upon the Bank of England," wrote Lord Overstone in 1837, "the duty of regulating the value of the currency and providing for the payment of the whole of it in specie, without giving to that body the exclusive power of issuing the paper money, or investing it with any direct control over the conduct of rival issuers."[2]

"This is the vital objection to our country issues," he wrote in 1840, "that they expand and contract with prices, contrary to what ought to be the result upon sound principles, and would be the result with a metallic circulation." Col. Torrens had said: "When the Bank of England decrees contraction, the country banks of issue, instead of resisting, obey and suffer." "It would," rejoined Lord Overstone, "have been more consonant, as we conceive, to the real course of events, had he said the country banks of issue first resist, then suffer, and in the end submit."[3]

---

[1] In Ireland and Scotland bank-notes are not a legal tender. In England Bank of England notes are a legal tender everywhere except at the Bank or its branches.

[2] Tracts, p. 12, cf. pp. 14–5, 91–6, 179, 221, 256, 350–1.

[3] *Ibid.*, p. 101.

"It is of the nature of the circulation of the country banks," wrote Mr. Tooke in 1826, "to be extended under circumstances favorable to speculation, upon the prospect of an advance of prices, or upon the opening of new fields of enterprise, and to be diminished under the opposite circumstances."

"In periods of excess," wrote Sir James Graham at the same time, "the issues of the country bankers have greatly exceeded the rate of increase by the Bank of England; and in periods of contraction the diminution has been more violent and unlimited."

Within the limits imposed upon the issues of the English country banks and the Irish and Scotch banks, the secured circulation, exclusive of that of the Bank of England, authorized by the acts of 1844 and 1845, was as follows:

| | |
|---|---|
| England and Wales, - - - - | £8,689,937 |
| Scotland, - - - - - - | 3,063,000 |
| Ireland, - - - - - - | 6,354,494 |
| Total, - - - - - | £18,107,431 |

The amount of bank-notes so authorized at the date, June 30, 1866, was £16,360,140. The amount actually issued was £14,687,546.[1]

[1] Hankey on Banking, p. 12. The return of the circulation on October 27, 1875, shows that the English banks, which cannot in any case exceed their fixed issues (as previous to 1844), were below that amount £1,365,910. The Irish and Scotch banks, which can exceed their issues of 1844 so far as they hold specie for all additional notes, had taken advantage of that provision, the Irish to the extent of £1,884,369, the Scotch, £3,489,146. The gold and silver held by the Irish banks at this date was £3,393,001; that by the Scotch, £4,401,849.

## THE OPERATION OF THE ACT OF 1844.

The Act of 1844 has been the subject of passionate controversy. Mr. Bagehot makes the animosity which subsists on this subject the excuse for omitting all discussion of it in his interesting work, "Lombard Street.'

"If you say anything about the Act of 1844, it is little matter what else you say, for few will attend to it. Most critics will seize on the passage as to the Act, either to attack it or defend it, as if it were the main point. There has been so much fierce controversy as to this Act of Parliament, and there is still so much animosity, that a single sentence respecting it is far more interesting to very many than a whole book on any other part of the subject. Two hosts of eager disputants on this subject ask of every new writer the one question, are you with us, or against us? and they care for little else."[1]

Prof. Price asserts that the Act of 1844 did not make the Bank of England note any safer. This may be conceded by the advocates of the Act, for it is of the essence of the Currency Principle that something more than good banking is needed to give the people good money; that issues may take place under perfectly sound banking which will involve production and trade in great perturbations, and even bring them down in disaster and ruin, while yet the individual note-holder has no reason to doubt the ultimate solvency, or even the immediate solvency, of the bank, which reaps a profit from its inflated issues in the period of prosperity, and in time of stringency and pressure may, by the exercise of firmness and good judgment, secure exceptionally high rates of interest without danger.

---

[1] Lombard Street, p. 2.

In other words, the Currency Principle assumes that the interests of the general community, and of the commercial and manufacturing classes in particular, are not necessarily identical at all times with the interests of the banks, in such a sense that the observance by the latter of their own interests in the issue of paper, will subserve the interests of the former, without restriction or regulation devised for the public good.

But while Prof. Price asserts that the Act of 1844 has added nothing to the safety of the Bank of England note, he freely concedes the merit of that Act in the regulation of the country circulation.

"The matter," he says, "is quite otherwise with the notes of country banks throughout England. These banks had failed by hundreds. They were bad bankers and often lost their means; and then those who held their notes were involved in ruinous losses. . . . Bankers who conducted their business ill were manifestly unfit persons to be intrusted with the function of supplying public money. They were bad makers, bad manufacturers, unfit to be trusted with the work; as bad as a mint whose sovereigns could never be relied upon for quality. The remedy came in the Act of 1844, and whatever may be said of the Act then passed, it is certain that, so long as it remains in force, the special disasters of 1825 can never recur."[1]

Here comes out strongly the antagonism of the Banking to the Currency Principle. The country issues were formerly mischievous, because issued by "bad makers, bad manufacturers." The rules of good banking were not observed. The currency manufactured was not, in fact, convertible. This admission saves the

---

[1] Principles of Currency, pp. 136–7.

principle that good banking will give good money, and that, if notes are truly convertible, they cannot be maintained, or even issued, in excess.

On the other hand, the authors and advocates of the Act of 1844 have felt bound to prove that the operation of the Act, aside from its effects on the country circulation, has been beneficial to the production and trade of England; and this is not only in the very nature of the case a hard thing to do, but there are some very ugly facts in the way.

These facts are, first, that the fluctuations in the rate of discount are much more frequent in England since than before the Act of 1844, and are more frequent in London since that Act than in other monetary centres of Europe;[1] secondly, that the operation of the Act has been thrice suspended by the intervention of government, as a necessity of the financial situation.

Let us take these objections in inverse order. The fact of the necessity of the occasional suspension of the Act, the writers of the Currency school refuse to accept as affording any disparagement of its usefulness; and they certainly have a controversial advantage in that they can show that this opinion is not an afterthought; but that the question of the possible suspension of the Act was entertained before its passage, and incidentally to the discussion of its principles. Thus, Lord Over-

[1] Mr. Robert Baxter adduces the following facts: For the first eleven years of the operation of the Act the changes of the rate of interest were 28; in the second series of eleven years, 106. The average amount of change in the rate for the first period was under 1 per cent.; the average of the second period over 3 per cent. While in the twenty-two years between 1844 and 1866 there were 134 changes in the rate of interest at the Bank of England, there were only 52 at the Bank of France.—[The Panic of 1866, pp. 12–5.]

stone, in 1840, drew up and printed his "Thoughts on the Separation of the Departments of the Bank of England," which was reprinted during the pendency of Sir Robert Peel's bill in 1844. In this pamphlet he dealt with the question, whether a drain might not, in exceptional circumstances, be carried so far as to render the maintenance of a fixed rule mischievous and even highly dangerous to the community, reaching this conclusion: "If the danger is deemed to be of such a nature as to require an efficient provision against it, this is to be found, not in a general abandonment of the attempt to place the management of the circulation under some fixed principle, but in that power, which all governments must necessarily possess, of exercising special interference in cases of unforeseen emergency and great state necessity."—[Tracts, p. 282; cf. pp. 301–2.] Having thus admitted the possible occasion for a suspension of the Act prior to its passage, the advocates of the Currency Principle can argue, without any discomfiture in the result, that the three suspensions of 1847, 1857, and 1866 were only the proper administrative relaxations of a rule of conduct which they declare to be, in general, sound and beneficial.

What is meant by a suspension of the Act of 1844? It is popularly supposed in this country to imply the suspension of specie payments; and it is not unusual to meet with statements to the effect that the Bank of England has failed three times since 1844. The suspension of the Act of 1844 does not touch the obligation of the Bank to pay bullion for its notes on demand. This it has never failed to do since the resumption in 1821. It is not from any stress upon the issue department, but from the exigencies of the banking department, that the necessity for government interference has in every case arisen.

The suspension of the Act of 1844 amounts simply to this: whereas the law says that the Bank shall issue notes above £15,000,000 only upon the actual deposit of corresponding quantities of bullion, the government has in the three specific instances referred to authorized the management to act, temporarily, without reference to this restriction, though still subject to full responsibility for the redemption of notes in specie on demand Out of the three instances the Bank has actually taken advantage of the permission afforded but once, viz., in 1857, and then only to the extent of £800,000.

To the charge that fluctuations in the rate of discount have become more frequent in England since 1844 than they were before, and are more frequent now in London than in other monetary centres, the advocates of the Act of 1844 reply that the increase since 1844 is due to the growing extent and complexity of commercial relations and the greater facility of communication; while the fact that London suffers more frequent changes than any other monetary centre is due to the high and responsible position which she occupies in international transactions, the effects of all disturbances being felt there as they are felt nowhere else, the disadvantage arising herefrom constituting the necessary price of the great advantage which London enjoys as, in the language of Burke, "the Exchange of the World."

We have now reached the point where we may inquire rather more precisely than we have yet been able to do into the *rationale* of the scheme for governing the monetary circulation of England. Prior to 1819 the Bank directors professed[1] to be governed, not by the

---

[1] See Bagehot Lombard Street pp. 175–6.

state of the exchanges or by the price of gold, but by the demand for discount, having reference to the amount already advanced to the individual, to the solidity of the paper, and to the appearance of its being wanted for strictly commercial purposes. These were good and sufficient banking rules. We have already seen that the Court, in 1819, passed a resolution declaring that they saw no grounds for the sentiment that the Bank had only to reduce its issues to obtain a favorable turn in the exchanges and a consequent influx of the precious metals; and that the Act of that year was passed in opposition to the views of the Bank. By 1827, however, the directors had been so far moved from their position as to rescind the resolution of 1819. In 1832 occurred the Recharter, when the Bank directors showed a still further change of views on the subject of the regulation of issues; and from that time to 1844 the following was the accepted principle of management: The issues were to be regulated in amount with constant reference to the state of the foreign exchanges; and the increase or diminution of gold in the hands of the Bank was to be taken as the only certain and safe test of the favorable or unfavorable state of the exchanges. Consequently the amount of paper issues was to be made to vary with direct reference to fluctuations in the amount of bullion in the Bank. This having been from 1832 the theory of the management of the circulation, the Act of 1844 was regarded by the Overstone economists as enabling and requiring the theory to be simply and surely realized in practice.

## FOREIGN EXCHANGES.[1]

"The phrase 'Foreign Exchanges,'" says Mr. Göschen, "is in itself vague and ambiguous, being more frequently used to express the rates at which the exchanges in question are effected than the exchanges themselves—the prices rather than the transactions. That which forms the subject of exchange is a debt owing by a foreigner and payable in his own country, which is transferred by the creditor or claimant, for a certain sum of money, to a third person, who desires to receive money in that country, probably in order to assign it over to a fourth person in the same place, to whom he in his turn may be indebted."—[Pp. 1–2.]

The dry goods importers of New York, let us suppose, sell to Chicago in a given time English goods to the value of $5,000,000. The grain exporters of New York send abroad $5,000,000 worth of grain received from Chicago. Shall the New York grain exporters send $5,000,000 to Chicago, and the dry goods dealers of Chicago send $5,000,000—perhaps the same notes in unbroken packages—to New York? Clearly this would involve waste and unnecessary risk. Instead of this, the dry goods dealers of Chicago, having sold their stock into the country at a profit, pay upon the order of the New York importers of dry goods $5,000,000 to the grain shippers of Chicago, who, out of this sum, pay the

[1] Four excellent works on this subject are available: Göschen's "Theory of the Foreign Exchanges"; Nicholson's "Science of Exchanges"; Tate's "Cambist, or Manual of Exchanges"; Seyd's "Bullion and Foreign Exchanges." Wm. Blake's work, "Observations on Exchange," published early in the century was the best work on the subject in its day, but all it contains will be found in later publications.

grain growers and realize their own profit. The New York grain exporters, selling the grain in London at a profit, pay, on the order of their Chicago creditors, $5,-000,000 to the New York importers of dry goods. But since these latter have to pay the West of England manufacturers, not in New York but in London, they arrange with the grain exporters not to bring home the proceeds of their sales in Mark Lane, but to transfer to them the right to draw for the amount upon the purchasers. This is done, and the New York dry goods importers, now become the creditors of the English grain importers, direct these by letter to pay the claims of the English manufacturers of kerseys and broadcloths. Here we have a simple case of direct exchange, domestic and foreign. It is seen that no money passes between Chicago and New York, or between New York and London.

As an illustration of indirect foreign exchange, we might take the relations of England, China, and the United States.

The United States sell little to China and buy much from her, and are therefore debtors largely to the Chinese; England buys largely from China, also, but sells to her even more largely, and is therefore the creditor of the Chinese. China, through the operations of exchange, says to the United States: Pay to England, upon this my warrant, what you owe to me. It is done, and the actual transfer of money, first from New York to Canton, thence to be shipped to Liverpool, is avoided.

"This circuitous method," says Mr. McLeod, "is called the Arbitration of Exchange. . . . When only three places are used in the operation it is called simple arbitration; when more than three are employed it is called compound arbitration."

It thus appears that what is termed Exchange is merely the familiar principle of the cancellation of mutual indebtedness, applied to trading communities and nations. As, however, it ordinarily involves the calculation of indebtedness in foreign moneys, the technical term, exchange, is retained, even when no actual changing of domestic for foreign coins is required, and, indeed, where the whole transaction is performed without any transfer of money.

I said "without any transfer of money." This may be done when the indebtedness between one country and another, or between one country and all others (when the arbitration of exchange is resorted to), is equal in amount and coincident in time. But it will easily appear that the chances are very small, under modern commercial relations, that such an equivalence of debts should occur. While many elements[1] have to be taken into account in ascertaining the balance of international indebtedness arising from all the transactions of a year, it is clear that the failure of coincidence in the matur-

---

[1] The cause commonly looked to, to explain a divergence between the amounts of debts owing by a country and the amounts falling due to that country, is the excess of imports over exports, or *vice versa*, as shown by the customs returns of trade. But this mode of ascertaining the balances of international obligations is insufficient. The other elements indicated by Mr. Göschen are (1) Freight and Insurance, since the goods may be carried both ways, and both voyages insured by the shippers and insurers of one country. It is in this way the balance of payments is made so often to turn in favor of England. (2) Interest on bonds held abroad, and commissions and profits earned by resident foreigners to be remitted abroad, also sums earned in wages to be sent back to relations. By all these ways American indebtedness is largely increased. (3) The expenses of foreign travel. (4) The disbursements of fleets on foreign stations and armies in foreign countries.

ing of obligations may introduce further divergence as to the amounts owing and falling due at any given date within the year. Two nations might conceivably come under equal obligations to each other during the course of the year, and yet one have a great balance of payments to make in the spring, and the other in the autumn.

When the payments between any two places or countries, at a given time, exactly balance each other, exchange will be at par. In the instances given above, London owing New York as much as New York owes London, every New York merchant will be able to purchase a debt owing in London at its face-value, and *vice versa*. Exchange between two places is at par when, by paying gold in one place, you may have an equal quantity of fine gold paid to your agent, or on your order, in the other place; or by paying silver[1] in the one place, you may have the command of an equal amount of fine silver in the other.

On the other hand, if, at a given date, there is a larger sum to be paid in the United States by English merchants than in England by American merchants, every American merchant who has the right to receive money from England can sell his right to some English merchant who is bound to pay money in the United States for more than the face-value of his claim, because there will not be enough of English claims on America to satisfy all American claims on England.

---

[1] There can be no true par of exchange between countries having a different metal as the legal standard, only "a usual rate."—[McLeod, Econ. Phil., ii, 290.]

"Gold," says Mr. Göschen, "is simply merchandise in such countries as have a silver currency, and silver is merchandise in such countries as have a gold standard; and according to the price of the merchandise at a given moment, so will the exchange fluctuate."

On the other hand, every English merchant who has the right to receive money from the United States will sell his right for less than its face-value.

To what extent will the premium on "bills" rise? To that only which will induce an export of bullion. When, in the instance given, those American merchants who hold claims upon England demand more than the cost of purchasing gold in England, shipping to the United States, insuring it on the voyage and paying certain incidental charges, English merchants having to pay debts in the United States will send bullion.[1]

It has been said that exchange between two places is at par when a man in one place by paying in gold can have an equal amount of fine gold paid to his agent or order in the other place. It will be observed that exchanges are effected with reference to the fine gold contents of the coins of the several countries.[2] If, therefore, the coinage of any country be debased, the effect on the exchanges will be immediately felt. It was in the sense of this evil that the first banks of Northern Europe had their origin.[3]

---

[1] "When the French exchange is at 25 francs 10 centimes to the pound sterling, it pays to send gold from England to France. When the exchange is 25:35, it pays to send gold from France to England. The mint par being taken at 25:22½, we have, thus, a margin of 12½ centimes, or ½ per cent. either way, and 25 centimes or 1 per cent. between the two extreme points."—[Seyd, Bullion and Foreign Exchanges, p. 394.]

[2] "When British goods, sold abroad, are paid for in money, it is not the denomination of the foreign coin which the merchant regards; it is the quantity of gold and silver it contains."—[James Mill, Commerce Defended.]

[3] "Chose singulière! L'établissement destiné à consolider la rigoreuse précision de la monnaie métallique, a servi de point de départ à l'invention qui la menace!"—[M. Wolowski, Journal des Économistes, Oct., 1868.]

"Before 1609," says Adam Smith, "the great quantity of clipped and worn foreign coin, which the extensive trade of Amsterdam brought from all parts of Europe, reduced the value of its currency about nine per cent. below that of good money fresh from the mint. Such money no sooner appeared than it was melted down, or carried away, as it always is in such circumstances. The merchants, with plenty of currency, could not always find a sufficient quantity of good money to pay their bills of exchange; and the value of those bills, in spite of several regulations which were made to prevent it, became in a great measure uncertain.

"In order to remedy these inconveniences, a bank was established in 1609 under the guarantee of the city. This bank received both foreign coin and the light and worn coin of the country at its real intrinsic value in the good standard money of the country, deducting only so much as was necessary for defraying the expense of coinage and the other necessary expense of management. For the value which remained after this small deduction was made, it gave a credit in its books. This credit was called bank-money, which, as it represented money exactly according to the standard of the mint, was always of the same real value and intrinsically worth more than current money. It was at the same time enacted that all bills drawn upon or negotiated at Amsterdam of the value of six hundred guilders and upwards should be paid in bank-money, which at once took away all uncertainty in the value of those bills."

Where the money of a country consists mainly of debased coin, we have seen that the effect on the exchange is unfavorable to trade. Much more injurious is paper money which is not convertible upon demand into coin. We have already cited Mr. Bagehot's remark that "any depreciation, however small, even the liability to depreciation without its reality, is enough to disorder exchange transactions;" and we saw that to this cause Mr. Bagehot attributes the fact that Paris has, since 1871, ceased to be one of the two exchange centres of the world, and that practically the whole of this great agency, with its important franchises so directly affecting the control of commerce, has come into the hands of London bankers. If this be true of a paper money slightly depreciated, the effects of greatly inflated and rapidly fluctuating paper must be mischievous in the highest degree. No advantage that could be alleged in favor of Inconvertible Paper Money, even allowing for the saving of the entire first cost of the circulating medium, would compensate any progressive country for the disturbance of commercial relations and the uncertainty introduced into all international monetary transactions by this cause.

With this brief glance at the general theory of the subject, we are prepared to take up again the English scheme of regulating the bank issues with reference to the exchanges.

### NOTE-ISSUES AND THE EXCHANGES.

"When the exchanges are in an unfavorable state," said Lord Overstone, "I apprehend that is evidence that the relation of the money of the country to the commodities of the country is such that it is more profitable to export money than to export commodities; and the action on the part of the managers of the circulation ought to be directed to restoring such a relative state between money and commodities as shall render it the interest of the community at large to export such a quantity of commodities as shall prevent a further export of money."—[Evidence on Banks of Issue, 1840.]

This doctrine, it will be seen, is based directly on Ricardo's position that a country will not export bullion instead of goods unless there is an inflated circulation.

Again Lord Overstone says: "The only safe course is to consider a continuous drain of gold from the Bank as conclusive evidence . . . of the necessity of effecting[1] a corresponding reduction of circulation."

But if the policy of regulating the note-issue by the state of the exchanges was the avowed policy of the Bank in 1832, wherein lay the importance of the Act of 1844? It was that, until the function of deposit and discount was separated from that of issue, each was certain to be "endangered by influences or affections connected with the other."—[*Ibid.*, p. 145.] The banker inevitably sympathizes with expansive speculations; therefore he should not issue currency. The managers of the Bank, in its compound character, were certain, not more in their published accounts than in their reasonings and calculations, to "blend together deposits and circulation on the one side; gold and securities on the other" [p. 33], and thus deceive themselves and impose upon the public with an appearance of

---

[1] AT ONCE: cf. pp. 23, 75, 242, 247, 253, 265. "A system of early, steady and continuous contraction, in the place of that which has been late in its commencement, sudden and violent in its operation, and irregularly carried out."—[P. 243.]

"Thus, probably, calm, deliberate and judicious preparation from 1833 to 1836, whilst the bullion decreased from £11,000,000 to £6,000,000, would have obviated the confusion and despair which ensued in 1837, when the alarm occasioned by a very low state of the bullion acted abruptly upon an unprepared community."—[P. 260.]

strength which the circulation proper did not possess; while the banking reserve would remain "a vague and undefined quantity, the power of issuing any amount of notes until the gold was exhausted" [p. 328], a reduction of deposits being deemed a sufficient set-off against a reduced amount of bullion [p. 34]. The separation of the departments made it impossible for the Bank managers to mislead the public or misunderstand their own situation. Moreover, it substituted for a policy of the directors a rule of law, which could only be changed by the act of a responsible government.

How far has the Act of 1844 accomplished its avowed object of regulating the note-issues with reference to the exchange?

"It was expressly declared," says Mr. McLeod, "that it was the purpose of the Act to cause a withdrawal of bank-notes from circulation, *i. e., from the public,* exactly equal in quantity to the gold withdrawn from the Bank, in strict accordance with the 'Currency Principle,' and it was supposed that, if the directors neglected this duty, the 'mechanical' action of the Act would compel them to fulfill it.

"No occasion arose for testing the powers of the Act till April, 1847. The well-known disasters of 1846 caused a steady drain of bullion from the Bank to commence in September. But the Bank made no alteration in its rate of discount till January, 1847, when the bullion was below £14,000,000, when it raised it to $3\frac{1}{2}$. Having lost another million in a fortnight, it raised discount to 4 per cent. But it made no alteration till it had lost £3,000,000 more, and then it raised discount to 5 per cent.

BANK-NOTES.

| | Held by Public. | Held in Reserve by the Bank. | Total Amounts of Bullion. |
|---|---|---|---|
| Aug. 29, 1846, | £20,426,000 | £9,450,000 | £16,366,000 |
| Nov. 7, | 20,971,000 | 7,265,000 | 14,760,000 |
| Jan. 9, 1847, | 20,837,000 | 6,715,000 | 14,308,000 |
| Jan. 30, | 20,469,000 | 5,704,000 | 12,902,000 |
| March 6, | 19,279,000 | 5,715,000 | 11,596,000 |
| April 3, | 19,855,000 | 3,700,000 | 10,246,000 |
| April 10, | 20,243,000 | 2,558,000 | 9,867,000 |

"These figures show the utter futility of the idea that as the bullion diminishes the Act could compel a reduction of notes in the hands of the public, for the notes in circulation were within an insignificant trifle as large in amount when the bullion was only £9,867,000, as when it was £16,366,000. . . . Whence did this failure arise? From this very simple circumstance. The framers of the Act supposed that there is only one way of extracting gold from the Bank, namely, by means of its notes, and that, if people want gold, they must bring in notes, and consequently as the gold comes out, notes must go in. But as a matter of simple banking business, there are two methods of extracting gold from the bank—namely, by notes and checks. Those persons who have credit in its books may go and present checks, and thus draw out every ounce of gold from the banking department, without a single bank-note being withdrawn from the public.

"In fact, instead of withdrawing the notes from the public, as was intended by the Act, the directors threw the whole effect of the drain of gold on their own reserves, and that happened in this way: The public has two methods of drawing gold from the banking department, namely, by notes and checks; but the banking department has only one method of drawing gold from the issue department, namely, its notes in reserve. And when the Bank felt a drain on its banking department[1] for gold, it had to replenish it by giving up an exactly equal amount of notes, and thus the whole drain fell on its own reserves."

But can we conclude with Mr. McLeod that the Bank Act is a failure because it does not secure the reduction of the amount of notes in circulation, correspondently with a reduction of the bullion in bank, during a foreign drain? Doubtless the authors of the Act expected this, and in so far the Act may be said to have failed. Mr. Ricardo and, following him, Lord Overstone and Mr. Norman, had regarded the bullion in the country as practically all money in circulation, affecting prices. If, then, bullion was imported,[2] it resulted that prices

[1] "The remedy for this state of things, which involves such serious disturbances from foreign demands for gold and from recurring panics, is to disconnect altogether the issue department of the State from the banking operations of the Bank of England, so that the State shall issue and find gold to redeem the paper as asked for, and that the Bank may, like every other bank in the kingdom, confine its responsibility to the receiving and returning its customers' capital, without concerning itself with the currency at all."—[Robert Baxter, Statistical Journal, June, 1876.]

"To say that the amount of notes should only be equal to what a metallic currency would have been, is a very intelligible proposition; and, as we have observed, several banks have been constructed on that principle. But no bank constructed on this principle ever did, or by any possibility could, do a banking business for profit. These banks were pure banks of deposit; they did no discount business whatever."—[McLeod, Econ. Phil., ii, 474.]

[2] "There can be no great addition to the bullion of a country, the currency of which is of its standard value, without causing an increase in the quantity of money."—[Ricardo, Reply to Bosanquet.]

were raised and the importation of goods was in that degree encouraged. If bullion was exported, prices fell, and the exportation of goods was in that degree encouraged.

The position of the opponents of the Act of 1844 was that bullion might come into the country in large amount without entering into the circulation[1] as money, and hence affecting prices; while, in another situation, when there should be a drain caused (as they assert, in opposition to Mr. Ricardo and Lord Overstone, a drain might be caused) by a great demand for foreign expenditure on the part of the government, or by a large exportation of capital for investment, or by a failure of crops in the countries from which the raw materials of manufacture are imported, or by the loss of domestic

---

[1] "Only that portion of coin, or money, which is at any time in the hands of the public employed in performing the exchange of commodities, is entitled to be deemed *circulation.*"—[Wilson, Capital, Currency and Banking, p. 17.] Again, the internal circulation may diminish coincidently with a large import of bullion, under certain circumstances.—[P. 21.] "This is in direct opposition to the principle of Sir Robert Peel's Bank Measure, and of the doctrine of currency so ably advocated by Mr. Loyd [Lord Overstone], Mr. Norman and Col. Torrens, who, in common with Sir Robert Peel, place implicit confidence in the effect of an import of bullion to increase the circulation, to raise prices, to encourage imports and to correct the exchanges."—[P. 22.]

"It may not be deemed an extravagant supposition," says Mr. Tooke, "that there might occasionally be, under a perfectly metallic circulation, fluctuations, within moderately short periods, to the extent of at least 5 or 6 millions sterling, in the import and export of bullion, perfectly extrinsic of the amount or value of the coin circulating as money in the hands of the public, and perfectly without influence on the general prices of commodities, as equally without general prices having been a cause of such fluctuations."—[Hist. of Prices, 1839–47, p. 225.]

harvests, the bullion or coin for export will be taken out of the reserves of bankers and out of hoards,[1] and not from the coin actually circulating. Thus Mr. Wilson, in 1847, claimed that no drain in England had ever gone so far as to touch the money in the hands of the people.[2] It is manifest that economical opinion has turned strongly towards the belief that bullion, often and to a considerable extent, leaves a country or returns to it without reference to the state of the currency[3] and without affecting prices.

It appears to me that the merit of the Bank Act of 1844 is in its influence upon the circulation, not in crises, but in times of prosperity, when the seeds of evil

---

[1] Mr. Fullarton, in his "Regulation of Currencies," assumes the existence of extensive hoards of metallic money out of which, under the metallic system, drains are met. This is probably true to a considerable extent of France.

[2] "When a drain sets in, which merely means, when it becomes profitable to export the commodity, gold, such demand will act on the stocks of bullion, and on the coin in the reserves of bankers, but not directly on the coin constituting the actual circulation, at least until all those reserves were actually exhausted, and then a struggle would commence between those who required coin for circulation and those who required it for export. To this point a drain never yet has proceeded with a convertible currency, nor can we conceive any circumstances under which it is likely to do so."—[Capital, Currency and Banking, p. 65.]

"Au moyen de ces réserves [de caisse], des payements très-considérables peuvent s'effectuer de peuple à peuple, sans que la circulation, ni, par conséquent, le prix de l'argent, en soient de part ni d'autre le moins du monde affectés."—[Roscher, Wolowski's Transl., §125.]

[3] "It is a fact now beginning to be recognized, that the passage of the precious metals from country to country is determined much more than was formerly supposed by the state of the loan market in different countries, and much less by the state of prices."—[J. S. Mill, Pol. Econ., III, viii, 4.]

are being sown in a soil apt to receive and ferment them.

"Fluctuations to a greater or less extent," wrote Mr. Tooke in 1826, "are inseparable from the course of commercial affairs. The business of production or supply proceeds wholly upon anticipation; it is dependent on the seasons and on an endless variety of casualties; while consumption or demand may be influenced by changes of habit, fashion, legislative enactments, and by political events. The contingencies which may excite a spirit of speculation and enterprise on the one hand, and disappoint expectation and defeat calculation on the other, are therefore innumerable."—[State of the Currency, p. 65.]

The advocates of the Currency Principle, who maintain that there is a liability to excessive issues of paper; that, when speculation is once on foot, the public will receive and retain a larger amount of bank-notes, which will enter into the circulation, raise prices, and thus still further stimulate the speculative impulse, leading to overtrading and distorted production, may still fairly assert for the Act of 1844 an important and salutary influence.

It would be quite enough to justify the Bank Act if it could be established that its "mechanical" action is to put commercial crises further apart, and to diminish their intensity when, in spite of its conservative action, they occur. No power inheres in any monetary system to prevent excessive speculation with its evil results on production and trade. Money is, at the most, but a tool of commerce. We have seen abundant illustrations of its power to work mischief when perverted from its right uses, but the office of a true money is simple and its influence limited. It does a great work in saving labor in the exchanges of commodities, and in measuring and registering the mutual obligations of the parties to contracts; but this is all its legitimate service. Having almost unlimited power to curse, its beneficence is bounded by its normal function, as it has been described.

Granting the possibility of issuing and maintaining bank-notes in excess, it appears to me that a salutary effect, in restraining issues during the times when speculation is insidiously preparing future convulsions of trade and productive industry, may justly be ascribed to the Act of 1844. Its failure by purely mechanical action, irrespective of the discretion of the directors, to reduce the note-issues correspondently with a loss of bullion on the occasion of a drain, only illustrates the proposition of Mr. Bagehot,[1] that the problem of managing a panic is primarily a mercantile one.

## THE TREATMENT OF PANICS AND CRISES.

When panics and crises occur, as they will under any monetary system, though not with the same frequency and severity under all, they are to be dealt with, not by the heroic method of contraction, but on the principle of re-inforcing the parts first and especially assaulted with the most liberal support from the whole industrial and commercial body. Whether paper money occasioned the mischief or not, the mischief has already been done when the panic begins. Curative and sanative measures are not necessarily in the line of preventive measures. It was superstition which in the Middle Ages gave to the weapon which had made the wound a peculiar efficacy in performing the cure.

---

[1] Lombard Street, p. 52.

A panic implies, sometimes, previous overtrading and the distortion of productive industry; sometimes, the unduly rapid conversion of circulating into fixed capital[1] of limited uses, or, not infrequently, of no use at all.[2] Paper money may or may not, in the given instance, have contributed to this result; but, however it came about, when the panic is once upon the country there is only one thing which can be done, and that is to spread the strain as widely as possible. This is to be done by borrowing. Even if the paper money did the mischief, it is, in the presence of a panic, of no more consequence than the knife which gave the wound from which the patient lies bleeding. The knife may be of great interest to the coroner; it is worth nothing for the purposes of the physician.

Panic indicates, we repeat, either[3] that the proportion

---

[1] See Mr. Wilson's account of this process in England during the railway mania which preceded the catastrophe of 1846–7.—[Capital, Currency and Banking.]

[2] In his evidence before the Committee on Banking and Currency, at Washington, 1874, Mr. Forbes remarked concerning the New York Banks in 1873: "Their capital needed for legitimate purposes was practically lent out on certain iron rails, railroad ties, bridges and rolling stock, *called* railroads, many of them laid down in places where these materials were practically useless."

Mr. Condy Raguet remarks respecting the early "internal improvements" of Pennsylvania: "The process which has in reality taken place has been the mere transmutation of stone and lime, wood and iron, from a form in which they possessed a value, into one in which they possess no value; and the conversion of a large quantity of bread and meat, whisky and rum, butter and milk, sugar and coffee, coats and jackets, coal and wood, hay and oats, into roads and canals, without the possibility of a reconversion to those original elements." —[Currency and Banking, p. 63.]

[3] I am supposing that the solvency of the bank-note is not in question among the mass of holders, in such a way as to cause a run

existing between fixed and circulating capital has been profoundly disturbed by speculative investments, or that the relations between the different classes of commodities which make up the circulating capital of the country have been distorted and perverted by speculative overtrading, and consequent overproduction in certain lines.

At once to re-inforce the parts which have been weakened by such disturbance of relations between fixed and circulating capital, or between the different classes of circulating capital, and in time to distribute the strain as far as may be over the entire system: this is the problem in a panic. This is to be done, as was said, by borrowing, generally through the banking agency. Of course, what is thus borrowed must ultimately be repaid. No expedient can restore the wealth which has been squandered in the extravagant living which a period of overtrading inevitably induces, or replace the capital which has been, to all present, practical purposes, lost by being directed prematurely and excessively into speculative enterprises. Nothing but industry and frugality will suffice to repair the waste of energy and resources of which a panic, such as occurred in England in 1866 and in the United States in 1873, is the certain retribution; but the very salvation of the existing machinery of production and trade may depend on the ability to distribute the strain over a larger surface than that which is first attacked, and to give time for the forces of repair and restoration to operate. This is done by

upon the bank for redemption. This sort of panic is now not known in England. We have seen that Prof. Price, who severely criticises the Act of 1844 in many respects, concedes that it has placed the country circulation above the discredit which attached to it in 1825.

RAISING THE RATE OF INTEREST.

"When the exchanges," says Mr. Göschen, "are manifestly against any country, and it is perceived that a balance of indebtedness is the cause, the equilibrium can be restored only in two ways; the one being the increase of exports and diminution of imports, the other an advance in the rate of interest.

"When the payments for imports continue for any length of time in excess of the receipts from exports, the redress of the balance can only take place by ceasing to incur liabilities, that is to say, by a change in the course of trade. . . . But what we are at present most concerned to examine is the operation of a high rate of interest in those more usual cases where we have to deal with temporary fluctuations and sudden emergencies, such as may be caused by the loss of a harvest, or by a period of general national extravagance, ending in a critical inflation of prices, or by excessive warlike expenditure.

"In such times, when the resources of a country are crippled for the moment and its debts increased, it is most desirable, and indeed absolutely indispensable, that not only bankers and merchants, but also the public at large, should clearly understand how quick and effectual a relief may be afforded by a high rate of interest, which is, indeed, the natural result of such a state of things. Those who imagine that what is called an oppressive rate of interest adds to the losses and difficulties against which the community have at such periods to contend, seem very much in error. . . . The efficacy of that corrective of so-called unfavorable exchanges, on which we have been dilating, has been most thoroughly tested since the Bank of England has adopted the system of varying its minimum rate of discount more rapidly and more extensively than was its practice in former years. The fact has been that almost every advance in the bank rate of discount is followed by a turn of the exchanges in favor of England; and, *vice versa*, as soon as the rate of interest is lowered, the exchanges become less favorable. . . . Foreign creditors give their English debtors a respite, and prefer to wait longer for remittances, gaining interest meanwhile at the profitable English rate." Mr. Göschen concludes: "It is clear that there is no corrective of a drain of gold and all its attendant consequences more powerful and effectual than a rapid advance in the rates of discount. It is the only mode by which that which is on the point of being lost may be retained, or that which is actually gone may be replaced; and its natural effect is, not to produce a scarcity of money,[1] . . . but to remedy and correct this scarcity by offering a premium to the rest of the world to send their capital or money to the dearest market."—[Foreign Exchanges, pp. 128–48.]

Such is the theory of regulating the exchanges which is at present generally accepted in England, and which has, since the panic of 1847, governed the action of the Bank in periods of drain. It will be seen that it differs widely from the scheme of correcting the exchanges which was maintained by Mr. Ricardo, Mr. Norman, and Lord Overstone. Not that the two schemes are necessarily antagonistic in practice; but setting out with different explanations of the cause of the drain, they proceed to treat the evil with different remedies.

---

[1] Mr. Göschen doubtless means a scarcity of "moneyed capital."

But it may be asked, is not the existing rate of interest the necessary outcome of the existing supply of, and the existing demand for, capital? If so, how can the Bank of England, or any other fiscal agent, control that rate? It must be confessed that English writers are much inclined to speak after this fashion. Even Mr. Göschen gives way to the tendency so far as to make admissions, which, if confirmed, would take from his philosophy of drains and the exchanges all value as a guide in practical conduct.

Thus he writes: "It may be said that an advance in the rate of interest has been spoken of as if money could artificially be made dear. But the fact is, as has already been pointed out, that, when a considerable efflux of specie is taking place, the rate of interest will rise in the natural course of things. The abstraction caused by the bullion shipments will of itself tend to raise that rate; and banking establishments will, in their own interest (which will be identical with that of the public), accelerate this result as far as lies in their power."—[P. 132.] So again: "Not that it is to be supposed that the Bank of England itself can make money dear or cheap;" and again: "The real importance of a variation in the minimum rate of the Bank does not consist in the power exercised over, but in the indications afforded by, the money market."—[*Ibid.*, p. 133.]

In contrast with such weak admissions by Mr. Göschen, which are really destructive of his own theory of the exchanges and of foreign drains, it will be instructive to read these sagacious words from that sagacious economist, Charles Babbage. "The principle that price at any moment is dependent on the relation of the supply to the demand, is true to the full extent only when the whole supply is in the hands of a very large number of small holders, and the demand is caused by the wants of another set of persons, each of whom requires only a very small quantity."—[Economy of Manufactures, p. 141.]

Mr. Bagehot presents the matter thus: "A very considerable holder of an article may for a time vitally affect its value if he lay down the minimum price which he will take and obstinately adhere to it. This is the way in which the value of money in Lombard Street is settled. The Bank of England used to be a predominant, and is still a most important,[1] dealer in money. It lays down the least price at which alone it will dispose of its stock, and this for the most part enables other dealers to obtain that price or something near it."—[Lombard Street, p. 114.]

This is a just view of the relations of the Bank of England to the rate of discount, and it gives significance and practical importance to Mr. Göschen's theory of the regulation of the exchanges.

---

[1] "At Dutch auctions an upset or maximum price used to be fixed by the seller, and he came down in his bidding till he found a buyer. The value of money is fixed in Lombard Street in much the same way, only that the upset price is not that of all sellers, but that of one very important seller, *some part of whose supply is essential.*"—[Lombard Street, p. 115.]

## CHAPTER XXI.

### CONVERTIBLE PAPER MONEY IN THE UNITED STATES.

In turning to the United States we are required at once to deal with a question which has been intimated at several points in preceding chapters, but which I have thought it best not to move until now. We have marked the antagonism of the two schools of English economists, professing severally the Currency Principle and the Banking Principle, upon the question whether Convertible Paper Money can be issued in excess.

But what is Convertible Paper Money? Just how much is implied in convertibility?[1] We cannot proceed far in our discussion of American paper money unless we reach a precise understanding on this point, for it is to be noted that some of the strongest advocates of the Banking Principle in England charge that the paper money of the United States has, to a very great extent, not been convertible in any true sense; and hence they give warning that their conclusions relative to the impossibility of excessive issues and permanent depreciation do not apply to our case.

Since our English cousins are inclined to deny the convertibility, in their sense of that term, of our paper

[1] "Convertibility in the Currency is like conscientiousness in a man; it has many grades."—[Sumner, Hist. Am. Currency, p. 116.]

money, let us ask what were the peculiarities of our American system, say between the resumption of specie payments after the war of 1812–5 and the outbreak of the civil war in 1861, which tended to defeat the full convertibility of our bank issues; the convertibility, that is, not in the legal, but in the economical, sense.

In the first place we had the fact of competing issues. This was the consideration most strongly insisted upon by Mr. Webster and the advocates of the Second Bank of the United States. In quoting Mr. Webster's speech on the Bank Lord Overstone said:

"The very existence of specie payments in this country at the present moment is attributable to the influence of one predominant issuer, charged with the responsibility of maintaining the convertibility of its notes. Without the Bank of England to warn by its example and to control by its power, the paper issues would have been regulated in no degree by the state of the exchanges, but solely in accordance with the apparent wants of commerce and the demands of the trading world. Increasing issues would have accompanied decreasing bullion, until even the appearance of a mutual connection would no longer be presented."[1]

In the second place we had the fact of the want of any traditional habit, maintained by the force of a strong public sentiment throughout the banking community, for the due exchange of bank-notes among the banks themselves.[2] This is the point Mr. Wilson especially insists upon.

"By an agreement between the different banks, they

---

[1] Remarks on the Management of the Circulation, 1840.

[2] It is from the want of a system of mutual exchange of notes that, in American Banking statistics, the column, "Notes of other banks," assumes so much importance.

never called upon each other to pay their notes in specie; and thus each bank always held large quantities of the notes of other banks for which they did not demand payment; and such was the political prejudice against the payment of specie, that any private individual who demanded the payment of specie to any large amount was marked as a common victim by the banks." --[Capital, Currency and Banking, p. 268.]

There was no time when this statement of Mr. Wilson would have applied without qualification to banks in all sections of the United States; yet it holds true in a high degree of the banks of the country as a whole during a considerable portion of our financial history. The earliest and most important effort to secure a prompt and regular redemption of notes was through the so-called "Suffolk Bank system" of Massachusetts, afterwards extended throughout New England, by which all the country banks were brought, by threats of outlawry against their circulation, to keep a deposit in the Suffolk Bank ample to redeem their notes on presentation. The effect of this system, which became the great distinguishing fact of the New England paper money, was to give the bank-notes of that section a wide acceptance all over the Union.

The third feature of the paper money system of the United States which militated against convertibility was the issue of small notes.[1] This affects convertibil-

---

[1] "Small notes," said Mr. Webster in his speech on the Bank, in 1832, "have expelled dollars and half-dollars from circulation in all the States in which such notes are issued. On the other hand, dollars and half-dollars abound in those States which have adopted a wiser and safer policy. Virginia, Pennsylvania, Maryland, Louisiana, and some other States, I think seven in all, do not allow their banks to issue notes under $5." A sketch of the history of small-note issues is given by Mr. Raguet, [Currency and Banking, pp. 137–40.]

ity in two ways: first, the notes pass chiefly in the hands of those persons who are least of all likely to present them for redemption, except under the influence of panic. Second, they expel the specie which should "saturate the circulation"[1] and afford a supply, in case of need, to the reserves of the banks. In England notes are not allowed under £5 ($25). In Scotland the "small-note system" prevails, but there no notes are issued under £1; while in the United States notes of $1 and $2 have at all times formed an important element of the issues, and in many sections notes for fractions of a dollar have been issued, driving even the smallest pieces of silver out of circulation.

A fourth fact in the paper-money system of the United States during the period of which we speak, was a public sentiment always unfavorable, and at times actively hostile, to the presentation of notes for redemption.

The natural pressure of trade upon the dealer, or the laborer, to receive bank-notes without scrutiny of their character, is at the best so strong as somewhat to impair convertibility, even where no artificial obstacle is interposed.

"The taking of them in payment," says Prof. Price, "is not so purely a voluntary act as the taking of a check. There is a kind of semi-compulsion pressing on the man to whom they are offered. The tradesman who rejected them would run the risk of losing his customer, who might be tempted into the rival shop where no objection would be made to his money; offense might be given to the numerous friends and customers of the bank throughout the town. No doubt there is always

---

[1] See p. 441.

the remedy of demanding gold for them; but the habit of the world is against that process."—[Principles of Currency, p. 133.]

"Everybody knows," says Mr. McCulloch, "that, whatever notes may be in law, they are in most parts of the country practically and in fact legal tender.[1] The bulk of the people are without power to refuse them. The currency of many extensive districts consists in great part of country notes, and such small farmers or tradesmen as should decline taking them would be exposed to the greatest inconveniences."—[Commercial Dictionary.]

But there was more than the unavoidable pressure of trade to compel the citizen of the United States to take bank-notes without scrutiny, and to allow him in turn to pass them off in exchange without presenting them at the bank for redemption.

"The habit of calling for specie," says Prof. Sumner, "had never been formed, and it was sternly discountenanced by public opinion."[2]—[History of American Currency, p. 157.]

---

[1] "It was the catastrophe of the year 1814," says Mr. Gallatin, "which first disclosed, not only the insecurity of the American banking system as then existing, but also that when a paper currency, driving away and superseding the use of gold and silver, has insinuated itself through every channel of circulation and become the only medium of exchange, every individual finds himself in fact compelled to receive such currency, even when depreciated more than twenty per cent, *in the same manner as if it had been a legal tender.*" —[Considerations, etc., p. 6.]

[2] Of the power of public opinion in such a matter the people of the United States have recently had a striking illustration in the practical exclusion of greenbacks, during and since the war, from ordinary circulation on the Pacific Coast. Though legal tender, no man dared to offer United States paper money for a debt contracted

We have noted certain characteristics of American paper money prior to the forced circulation given to United States treasury-notes in 1862, which distinguish it in a marked degree from that of England during the same period, and especially from the later form of English paper money as organized under the Bank Act of 1844. The features noted were all such as to impair more or less seriously the convertibility of the bank-note, and thus, even in the view of the advocates of the Banking Principle, to take away the security which they think they find for the conformity of paper to metallic money; while in the view of those who hold the Currency Principle, the features of the American system, as noted, must have aggravated in a high degree that tendency to excessive issues, and hence to depreciation, which, as they assert, inheres in all paper money not based, as was the paper money of Hamburg and Amsterdam, through many generations, cent. per cent., on the precious metals; but which evils may be brought within narrow limits in a system like that of England, where the circulation is controlled by one dominant institution; where banking traditions enforce the frequent interchange and mutual redemption of paper; where issues are restricted to notes of the higher denominations and the circulation is thus surcharged with specie in the hands of the people and of the small dealers; and, lastly, where both law and public sentiment make it the unchallenged right of every holder to demand specie[1] at

---

in United States gold money; and all the large commercial transactions of that section went on upon a gold basis, under the sufficient protection of a consolidated public sentiment, which did not lose its power over the debtor even in face of a premium of 150 per cent.

[1] "Convertibility is not enough, if it is only nominal, and if no one tests its reality because public opinion frowns on such an act, or bank displeasure follows it."—[Sumner, Hist. Am. Currency, p. 186.]

his own pleasure, and the obligation of every bank at all times to pay specie, without condition, without demur, and without retaliation.

The writers of the earlier period of our history who were most conspicuous in their opposition to issues of paper not severely restricted and regulated to prevent excess were Messrs. Wm. M. Gouge, and Condy Raguet, both of Philadelphia, and Prof. Tucker, of Virginia.

The near contemplation of the evils of excessive issues and oft-recurring bank suspensions made the first mentioned of these writers somewhat less discriminating than was just in his strictures upon banks and the issue of paper money, and while his "History of Paper Money and Banking in the United States" forms a valuable portion of our economical literature, its generalizations, and at times its specific statements, require qualification. Mr. Raguet's work is founded upon the doctrines of the English Banking School, as to the impossibility of issuing and maintaining an excess of convertible paper; but the author clearly apprehended the fact that the American bank issues did not meet the requirements of convertibility[1] in the economical, if they did in the legal, sense.

---

[1] "In the management of the numerous banks of the United States an inexcusable ignorance of first principles has been repeatedly manifested, and hence we have seen repeated expansions and contractions of a highly prejudicial nature. . . . The ignorance of some, the speculative avarice of others, and the desire common to all to amass large profits, are constantly operating to effect an expansion of the currency *to the utmost limits of tension.*"—[Currency and Banking, p. 106–7.]

Prof. Tucker, also, found that the American system of paper issues suffered from the lack of genuine convertibility; and that, in consequence, the circulation was now inflated and now deficient, with very mischievous effects upon trade and production.[1]

In a later period of our history Prof. Amasa Walker has upheld the views of the English Currency School, maintaining not merely that the American system lacked the requisite of convertibility; but that paper money issued in excess of the specie held for its redemption, under whatever system of management, tends inevitably to fluctuate otherwise than metallic money. In his pamphlet on "Money," published after the panic of 1857, and in his treatise, "The Science of Wealth,"[2] published after the Civil War, Prof. Walker maintained this proposition with an earnestness and force which have had a great effect in checking the assent which Mr. Tooke's defection from the Currency Principle had done much to secure to the doctrine of the English Banking School, that paper money redeemable in specie on demand cannot be got out, or kept out, in excess of the volume of metallic money, which under the same circumstances would have been in circulation.

---

[1] "Whatever may be the mischiefs of overtrading and a gambling, speculating spirit in the community, and they are for the time very great, banks must be considered responsible for a large portion of it. . . . The banks, by affording aliment to this spirit, give it a force and vigor of mischief it could not otherwise attain."—[Money and Banks, p. 188.]

[2] "Nous ne saurions taire l'expression d'une admiration sincère pour cet ouvrage capital: *Science of Wealth*, ouvrage digne d'etre mis au premier rang de ceux dont l'étude de l'économie politique peut le mieux s'enorgueillir."—[M. Wolowski, Journal des Économistes, October, 1868.]

The following is Prof. Walker's statement of the vital principle of a Convertible Paper Money, or, as he terms it, a Mixed[1] Currency:

"IT IS NOT GOVERNED BY THE LAWS OF VALUE.

"The great principle of value is: demand creates supply; supply satisfies demand.

"A mixed currency is not regulated in this way. In so far as it has not value, it is not controlled by the laws of value. It is put out by bank managers at their pleasure and for their profit. It is not produced by labor. This last fact removes the gravitation which alone can secure a currency. It makes it a thing to be blown about by every breeze, carried up or carried down with the currents or whirled around in the eddies of trade. It should be stable, and not sport for the winds. There should be a reason for the putting out or taking in of every dollar of money; and that reason should be found in the laws of value.

"Now, these laws control the expansion or contraction of money, or a value currency. If it is increased, as it may be in the natural course of commercial transactions, it is because actual money has been brought into the country by the balance of trade; but a mixed currency is increased by the voluntary and interested action of bank managers, without regard to the laws of value, and without the addition of a dollar to the real money or wealth of the country. The increase of money [metallic] by importation takes place in obedience to causes that are gradual and appreciable; and any

---

[1] Compounded of value and credit, in uncertain proportions. The same term was frequently employed by Mr. Norman, in England.

one who watches the course of commerce can anticipate its arrival. If it comes in excess from any unusual source, it easily and naturally passes off to other countries till the balance is restored. . . .

"We have found that the quantity of a mixed currency is not governed by the laws of value. On the contrary, we find laws positively mischievous substituted for the wholesome operation of supply and demand.

"First, of expansion. The more there is issued of a mixed currency, the more will be wanted. The supply does not satisfy the demand, it further excites it. Like an unnatural stimulus taken into the human system, it creates an increasing desire for more. There are two reasons for this: one, that, as the currency is expanded, prices are raised correspondingly, and more currency is demanded to effect the same exchanges; the other, that the speculation inevitably following the rise of prices leads to an enormous extension and repetition of indebtedness, which requires for its discharge a greatly increased amount of the circulating medium. . . . All this is quickened and helped by the fact that the manufacturers of the currency are ready and eager to crowd upon the public all it will take.[1]

---

[1] That bank managers make distinct efforts to enlarge their circulation is notorious. Chalmers, in his "Estimates," says: "The country bankers tried various projects to force a greater number of their notes into circulation than the business of the nation demanded." Macpherson, in his "History of Commerce," in speaking of the country banks, says: "Whose eagerness to push their notes into circulation had laid the foundation of their own misfortune." Mr. Wakefield, in his evidence before the Agricultural Committee of the House of Commons, in 1821, says: "Up to the year 1813, there were banks in almost all parts of England forcing their paper into circulation at an enormous expense to themselves, and in most instances it had been done to their own ruin. There were bankers who gave com-

"Secondly, of contraction. We have seen the forces that raise the currency higher and higher. . . . The cause which limits the expansion and finally produces contraction, is the liability of the notes to be presented for payment in money.

"The occasion for this cause to operate may be almost anything—a political convulsion, an adverse balance of trade, a failure of some large trading or banking company, or an unaccountable mood of the popular mind. We will take that which is most common and sensible—an adverse balance of trade. If it be large, the demand for specie which it occasions will create a pro found sensation among the banks. With actual money there is under these circumstances no reason for excitement or alarm; ten millions of dollars of the currency will discharge that amount of debt abroad, and the currency at home is reduced but so much.

"A mixed currency has in itself no power whatever to satisfy a foreign creditor. If ten million dollars are to be paid abroad, it must be taken from the specie of

---

missions, and they sent persons to the markets to take up notes of other bankers." Even the Bank of England, Mr. Tooke says, adopted in 1823 "new modes of accommodation to individuals in order to induce them to borrow at 4 per cent."—[State of the Currency, p. 73.] The forms which these efforts have taken in the United States have at times been almost ludicrous. Enterprising banks have sent agents hundreds of miles to exchange their notes at hotels, stores, railway offices, etc., for those of other banks. Mr. Raguet refers to the practice of loaning notes, with the express understanding that the borrower was not to put them into circulation within a certain distance of the place of issue. "Some new writer upon the wealth of nations," said Mr. Charles Francis Adams in 1837, "might make an edifying chapter by explaining in more detail all the tricks that have been resorted to for the purpose of puffing up the circulation."—[Reflections on the Currency, p. 16.]

the banks, the basis of the currency is so much diminished, and the circulation must be curtailed accordingly; that is, notes must be brought in and not put out again till the basis is restored. If the proportion of specie, as is the case on an average in this country, is only as one to five of notes, then the export of ten million dollars must cause a contraction to the extent of fifty million dollars at home. The removal of so much currency causes stringency, and stringency causes suspicion. Vague apprehensions abound; everybody becomes prudent, many are scared. Here is another reason for contraction. With a value currency, the fact that it was especially wanted would be a reason why it should stay. Not so with credit money; it won't bear to be looked in the face.[1] . . .

"It should be borne in mind that these contractions and expansions are not imaginary, not possible only, not merely occasional, nor at all local; but they occur frequently and everywhere within the field of such a currency.

"But, it may be asked, are there not natural tides in business, irrespective of a mixed currency? Certainly; but they are never aggravated or intensified until they end in panic or ruin. They are calculable and healthful. They are tests of business character. They may go to the extent of exposing the emptiness of bad concerns, but never destroy those that are good. When they occur, money will be wanted to pay debts; but, when one debt is paid, there is just as much money as before with which to pay others. The pressure does

---

[1] "Dans un sauve-qui-peut, tout système fondé sur le crédit doit s'écrouler, car le sauve-qui-peut est le négation même du credit."—[Chevalier, La Monnaie, p. 67.]

not annihilate any part of the currency. The party who receives a payment does not put the money away in vaults, not to appear again till the crisis is past. The means of payment can be reduced only by the amount actually sent out of the country. Gold and silver are as little injured by panic as by fire."—[Science of Wealth, pp. 155–60.]

We have seen what was the character of the money of the American colonial period: at first, cattle, corn, wampum, and bullets, slowly superseding a barter trade; then, small supplies of silver and copper, brought in from the West Indies and from Europe, constantly complained of as inadequate; then, bills of credit, an inconvertible paper money, beginning with the Massachusetts issues of 1690, extending in 1709 to the other New England colonies, and to New York and New Jersey, and soon overspreading the whole settled country from New Hampshire to Georgia. This money more or less fully maintained itself, in spite of the inhibitions of the royal governors, the Crown, and Parliament, until the outbreak of the Revolution caused the issue, in overwhelming amount, of the soon depreciated and discredited "Continental Currency."

In 1790 there were three banks in the United States: the Bank of North America,[1] in Philadelphia, the Bank of New York, in the city of that name, and the Bank of Massachusetts, "established in the Town of Boston" [A. Hamilton, Report on the Bank]. In 1791 was chartered the First Bank of the United States, with a capital

[1] This had been Robert Morris's bank during the last years of the Revolution. It had gone under a Pennsylvania Charter, and is still doing business under the National Banking Act.

of $10,000,000, having power to issue notes payable on demand in specie. It is significant of the administration of public affairs in this country at that period that, though the act chartering the Bank provided that a report of its condition should be laid before the Secretary of the Treasury whenever required, "but not oftener than once a week," the records of the Treasury Department do not show that any formal reports were ever rendered during the twenty years of its existence; and the only balanced statements to be found showing the state of the Bank are two contained in letters of Secretary Gallatin, March 2, 1809, and January 24, 1811.[1]

On the refusal of Congress to recharter the Bank[2] in 1811, large numbers of State banks sprang into existence, almost all of the usual American joint-stock type, on the principle of limited liability.[3] The outbreak of war in 1812 caused the failure of nearly all of these, outside New England which still maintained specie payments, drawing silver in large amounts from the States in suspension. The funds of the United States, which had been deposited in the insolvent banks, were in great measure lost.[4]

The check of redemption, even to the very limited ex-

---

[1] Report of the Comptroller of the Currency, 1876, pp. 8–9.

[2] "It is our deliberate opinion that the suspension [of 1814] might have been prevented at the time when it took place, had the former Bank of the United States been still in existence."—[Gallatin, Considerations, etc.]

[3] "The banks in America are under limited responsibility, while in this country, with the exception of the Bank of England, the Bank of Ireland, and one or two of the chartered banks in Scotland, the issuing bankers are liable to the whole extent of their property."—[Tooke, Hist. of Prices, 1839–47, p. 257.]

[4] Nearly $9,000,000 of Treasury funds were, in 1814, in suspended banks.

tent in which it had existed, being withdrawn by the suspension, the banks continued to pour out their notes until the issues, which stood in 1811 at $28,000,000, reached, according to Secretary Crawford, $62,000,000 to $70,000,000 in 1813, and $99,000,000 to $110,000,000 in 1815. The vague form of these statements is significant, not only of the absence of all regulation of issues, but even of public intelligence respecting the facts of issue. The action of the banks in a state of suspension, under the wretched system of easily condoning bankruptcy which has done so much to pervert the trade and production of the United States, to lower the national standard of morality, and even to infect our politics with dishonesty, is thus described by Mr. Raguet:

"Banks, when they default in their payments, not only never ask the indulgence of their creditors for any specified extension of time, but they do not even think themselves under obligations to pay interest to their creditors for the funds they forcibly detain from them; *nay, they very frequently, in the midst of their insolvency, declare dividends* of the very profits which actually belong to their creditors, who, and not the stockholders, are entitled to interest for their withholden funds. Excepting where legislative enactments have forbidden dividends under a suspension of payments, instances are extremely rare wherein a sense of justice on the part of the directors of banks has led them to refrain from such manifest injustice, and the consequence has been that *a direct inducement is thereby created for taking no steps towards a resumption of payment.*"[1]—[Currency and Banking, p. 158.]

---

[1] A few States sought to remedy this evil by a heavy fine on banks remaining in suspension. Thus, the discount in Boston on New

Of course, in a country where such things could be done, much more in a country where such things were done frequently and without rebuke, it was rank nonsense to talk of convertibility.[1] In 1814 Mr. Dallas, Secretary of the Treasury, wrote:

"The multiplication of State banks in the several States has so increased the quantity of paper currency that it would be difficult to calculate its amount, and still more difficult to ascertain its value. . . . There exists at this time no adequate circulating medium common to the citizens of the United States." The depreciation of the bank paper at the close of the war reached in some instances twenty or twenty-five per cent. Throughout 1816 the banks continued to issue largely their discredited notes, while floods of unchartered paper were poured out, in notes of all denominations from six cents upwards.

The war with Great Britain had given rise to the treasury-note system, which was extensively resorted

---

England bank-notes having gone up in 1809 to 10, 30, and in some cases 50 per cent., the legislature of Massachusetts passed an Act in January, 1810, affixing a penalty of 2 per cent. per month, payable by the bank to the bill-holder, for refusal or failure to redeem notes on presentation.

[1] "By convertibility of the paper, according to the ordinary signification of the term when applied to bank-notes in this country, is meant that the holder of a promissory note, payable on demand, may require payment in coin of a certain weight and fineness, *and in the event of refusal or demur, such payment is enforced by law against the issuer to the utmost extent of his property. The issuer, whether a private or joint-stock banker, is considered to have failed; the circulation of his notes is at an end, and he is subject to the process usual in cases of insolvency; while anything like fraud on the part of the banker is visited with severe penalties.*"—[Tooke, History of Prices, 1839-47, p. 251.]

to[1] and contributed to the general excess of the circulating medium. Of this measure Mr. Calhoun was always a strenuous advocate.[2] This measure the banks, naturally enough, opposed. The treasury-notes were not of forced circulation; they failed to be paid at maturity; and general distrust and commercial distress ensued.

The evils of the financial situation led to the establishment, in 1816, of the Second Bank of the United States, with a capital of $35,000,000, notes not to be issued below $5. The regulation of the circulation was looked for from this powerful fiscal agent. But the country was already on the verge of a crisis. The State banks began to fail in 1818, and a second general suspension occurred in 1819, extending through the two years following. The paper money afloat at once ran down, as estimated by Secretary Crawford, from $99–110,000,000 in 1815, to $45–53,000,000 in 1819. The Bank of the United States sustained heavy losses, and its financial condition was only re-established by an importation of $7,000,000 in specie, at the expense of half a million. Still another shock was experienced in 1825, but this manifestly had not originated in the United States, having been communicated from England, where the suffering was far more severe. In the United States

[1] And, again, 1837–1843, so that between 1812 and 1843 the treasury-note issues aggregated $84,611,828.—[N. Y. Banker's Magazine, July, 1861.]

[2] "It is like an individual using his notes of hand, having a short date to run, to meet his engagements. The return of these would soon embarrass him; to avoid which, to enable him to plunge more deeply in debt, the resort, on the part of the thoughtless, is usually to a mortgage. Such, I apprehend, is the case in the present instance; for what is a permanent loan but a mortgage upon the wealth and industry of the country?"—[Speech in opposing the Loan Bill of 1841.]

the crisis was not particularly a bank crisis. Most of the banks that suspended proved to have failed utterly. Again, in 1828 and 1829, considerable pressure was experienced by the money market, as the consequence of extensive overtrading in 1827.

The office which had been expected of the Bank of the United States was performed only in part. How far the management was at fault for the degree of failure which occurred it is not our part to inquire.[1] Practical inconvertibility characterized the issues of the joint-stock banks of the United States down to 1834. Looseness of management, the want of legal regulation, the absence of any authoritative and effective business traditions and maxims, with, in not a few cases, purposed swindling of the most outrageous character,[2] committed always with entire impunity, make the early history of paper-money banking in the United States exceedingly discreditable.[3] The popular term, "Wildcat Banking,"

---

[1] President Van Buren, in his message of 1839, arraigns the Bank as follows: "At every period of banking excess it took the lead. In 1817 and 1818; in 1823, in 1831, and in 1834, its vast expansions, followed by distressing contractions, led to those of the State institutions. It swelled and maddened the tides of the banking system, but seldom allayed or safely directed them."

[2] Prof. Sumner gives the following brief but eloquent account of the Farmers' Exchange Bank of Gloucester: "Its capital was $1,-000,000. Only $19,141.86 were ever paid in, and of this the directors withdrew what they paid in, leaving $3,081.11. One Dexter bought out eleven of the directors for $1,300 each, paid out of the bank's funds. He borrowed of the bank $760,265. When it failed it had $86.46 in specie; bills unknown; the Committee estimated them at $580,000."—[Hist. Am. Currency, p. 62.] See also Mr. Raguet's account of the Newbern and Cape Fear banks of North Carolina [Currency and Banking, p. 118].

[3] "La triste histoire des banques des États Unis n'est que trop connue: elle a été si féconde en désastres que des hommes consid-

not inaptly describes much, the greater part, indeed, of the operations of American banking of a period reaching even down to 1837. The worst faults of our national genius here made their worst manifestations. Those who should only know the people of the United States through the banking of that age might well have the most contemptuous idea of them.

The vices of character which permitted the discreditable operations which have been known as banking in pretty much every part of the country, by turns, and in some from first to last, may be indicated as follows:

1. The national haste to be rich. Americans are not avaricious. No people expend what they acquire more liberally, whether for personal gratification or in public benefactions. But if an American is going to be rich any time, he wants to be rich right off. He is impatient of everything which does not yield immediate results. There is, however, no work in which the present has to be more distinctly subordinated to the future than banking; none in which habit on the part of the public, and reputation on the part of those who solicit patronage, have so much to do as in deposit banking. The reputation of the banker, the habit of deposit among the community, can only be slowly built up.

---

érables, des financiers de premier ordre, Gallatin, par exemple, en étaient venus, en dernier lieu, à se demander si les dangers qu'entraîne le billet de banque, ne devait pas faire renoncer à l'emploi de cet instrument de la circulation."—[Wolowski, La Question des Banques, p. 381.]

"The farmers of Illinois, Michigan and Wisconsin, would rather encounter war, pestilence, or famine than the old style of unsecured or imperfectly secured bank-notes, by which they were robbed at frequent intervals during the twenty-five years preceding the war.' —[Horace White, International Review, Nov., 1877.]

2. The national arrogance, combined with the ignorance of finance which characterizes both our statesmen and our men of business, creating a contempt for the wisdom of the ages and the experience of other peoples in all that relates to industry and trade.

3. The rapidity of the national growth, which would have outstripped the natural development of any banking system, however well and fairly founded. The same cause has compelled us to put up with rude and clumsy contrivances, or mere make-shifts, in many departments of activity besides banking.

4. A false view of money which regards coin as the proper subject of governmental regulation, but considers the manufacture of paper money, which will drive coin out of circulation and take its place, as a branch of ordinary business with which the state has no right to interfere.[1]

So completely without regulation, or even inspection, was the so-called Convertible Paper Money of the United

---

[1] "If," said Mr. Hamilton, in his Report on the Bank, "the paper of a bank is to be permitted to insinuate itself into all the revenues and receipts of a country; if it is even to be tolerated as the substitute for gold and silver in all the transactions of business, it becomes, in either view, a national concern of the first magnitude."

"Is it not," asked Mr. Ricardo, "inconsistent that government should use its power to protect the community from *the loss of one shilling in a guinea;* but does not interfere to protect them from *the loss of the whole twenty shillings in a one-pound note?*"—[Proposals for a Secure and Economical Currency.]

Per contra, M. Courcelle-Seneuil, who favors the American system, says, in his "Opérations de Banque": "Les droits régaliens . . . n'ont rien de commun avec les émissions de billets payables à vue et au porteur."—[P. 352.]

States in this period, that it is scarcely possible to recover any of the facts of banking capital, circulation, deposits, or specie reserve. Hardly a statistical fragment survives as an indication to the student of money. It is impossiblê to tell accurately what was the total circulation of the country at any time. There is only too much reason to suppose that the officers of many banks did not themselves know the liabilities of the institutions whose affairs they were conducting. I have alluded to the astonishing fact that but two returns of the First Bank of the United States are in existence or are known ever to have been rendered. One of these was manifestly trumped up[1] after the date.

When such a state of things could exist in regard to the national bank of the United States, intended as a

[1] This is easily seen by comparing the "round numbers" of the one with the exact figures of the other.

| RESOURCES. | January, 1809. | January, 1811. |
|---|---|---|
| Loans and discounts, | $15,000,000 | $14,578,294 |
| U. S. 6 per cent. stock, | 2,230,000 | 2,750,000 |
| Other U. S. indebtedness, | —— | 57,046 |
| Due from other banks, | 800,000 | 894,145 |
| Real Estate, | 480,000 | 500,653 |
| Notes of other banks on hand, | —— | 393,341 |
| Specie, | 5,000,000 | 5,009,567 |
| | $23,510,000 | $24,183,046 |
| LIABILITIES. | | |
| Capital stock, | $10,000,000 | $10,000,000 |
| Undivided surplus, | 510,000 | 509,678 |
| Circulating notes outstanding, | 4,500,000 | 5,037,125 |
| Individual deposits, | 8,500,000 | 5,900,423 |
| U. S. deposits, | —— | 1,929,999 |
| Due to other banks, | —— | 634,348 |
| Unpaid drafts outstanding, | —— | 171,473 |
| | $23,510,000 | $24,183,046 |

regulator of the general circulation, and subject to immediate supervision by the Treasury Department, it is matter of small wonder that the numerous small and scattered State banks furnish no data for the student of money. Notes issued under such a system, or lack of system, were, in every economical sense, inconvertible The pretense of conversion[1] could only be maintained under a general consent not to apply the test of redemption; a consent enforced upon recusants by a stringent public opinion, and, in border communities, there is reason to believe, by a sharp compulsion.

The state of things described in the foregoing pages almost justifies the severe language of Mr. McCulloch:

"Had a committee of clever men been selected to devise means by which the public might be tempted to engage in all manner of absurd projects, and be most easily duped and swindled, we do not know that they could have hit upon anything half so likely to effect their object as the existing American banking system. It has no one redeeming quality about it, but is, from beginning to end, a compound of quackery and imposture." —[Commercial Dictionary.]

"No person," says Mr. Fullarton, in his "Regulation of Currencies," "who has given any attention to the evidence respecting the state of the American paper circulation, will venture to affirm that, even previous to the universal and spontaneous suspension of cash payments in May, 1837, that circulation was really and practically convertible."

Of the war made by President Jackson on the Bank of the United States, of the criminations and recrimina-

---

[1] Mr. Crawford, Secretary of the Treasury, in his report of 1820, speaks of States "where the convertibility is not even ostensible."

tions of that scurrilous period, of the merits or demerits of the Bank management, our present purpose does not require us to speak. The Bank was killed, whether by the stroke of justice or the hand of the assassin. The removal of the United States deposits, by the will of the President, and the selection of State institutions as depositories of the public funds, incited the formation of many new banks and a rapid increase of issues. It is about this time that we begin to have reliable statistics of the paper money of the United States. The aggregated circulation of the banks, exclusive of that of the Bank of the United States, had been estimated at $61,000,000 in 1830. By 1834 it had risen to nearly $95,000,000, while it was further increased to $149,000,000 between that date and 1837. As the result of the panic of the latter year, the circulation fell off to $116,000,000. The year following it rose to $135,000,000, only to fall to $107,000,000, as the result of the crash of 1839, sinking to $84,000,000 in 1841, and to $58,500,000 in 1843.

The panic of 1837, the second and heavier shock of 1839,[1] and the long and dreary prostration of industry lasting until 1843, were the result of speculative overtrading, mainly after 1833, leading to a general distortion of productive industry, and to speculative investments, especially in western lands and mines, in railroads and canals, in corner lots and river fronts, which, even had they been intelligently made, would have far

[1] "The New England and New York banks held out bravely, but, taking the country over, this was the real collapse of the banking system which had been growing up. Three hundred and forty-three out of eight hundred and fifty banks closed entirely, and sixty-two partially."—[Sumner, Hist. Am. Currency, p. 151.]

outrun the possible growth of the country, locking up in unremunerative enterprises the capital needed to conduct the manufactures and trade of the nation. Language could not well exaggerate the extent to which this misapplication of capital and this distortion of production had been carried. The whole head was sick and the whole heart faint. Few things remained sound, and these were not unsuspected. Even the ordinary commercial machinery of the country was carried away in the crash which followed. The train was wrecked upon the track, and it took years to clear away the debris and get the ordinary agencies of trade, viz., exchanges, commercial correspondence, business good-will, and in some cases even the facilities of transportation, again in working order.

That the evils of the period 1834 to 1843 were in great measure due to vices of paper-money banking is not to be questioned. The opening of the "great West" would doubtless have led to much wild adventure, industrially and commercially; and it is of the American genius to take large risks boldly. But the facility of issue, without the reality or scarcely the pretense of redemption, made the banks, even those which had been reasonably well founded, reckless as to the nature of the enterprises which they assisted; while the money thus put into circulation, without "reflux," enhanced prices and still further stimulated both speculative investments and speculative trading.[1] When the audacity of the better

[1] Prof. Sumner expresses the opinion that between 1833 and 1837 "the bank expansion only kept pace with the speculative expansion and rise of prices, and that the issues, although opposed to all sound rules of banking, and sure in the end to prostrate bankers and dealers together, were not made faster than they were called for."—[Hist. Am. Currency, p. 157.] Doubtless they were not. The ques-

institutions failed, hundreds of "wildcat" or "'coon-box" banks, without capital, without a constituency, with no past and no future, whose managers risked nothing and had nothing, came forward with offers of notes to speculators who planned to build cities in the wilderness, or contractors who wished to construct roads and bridges without materials, tools, or means of paying wages. Again, as in early New England,[1] a bank meant a batch of paper money.

The severe experiences of this period led in some States[2] to legislation designed to place the issue of bank-notes on a sounder basis. New York led off with an enactment, afterwards widely imitated in other States, which secured to its paper money, though still convertible only in a very limited sense, far more stability than it had before possessed.

New York had already been the scene of an effort to secure the liabilities of banks. Under Gov. Van Buren an Act was passed, in 1829, establishing the so-called "Safety Fund System," under which forty banks were organized. A common fund was to be created by contribution, annually, of one-half per cent. of the capital of each bank, until three per cent. of such capital should have been paid in. This fund was to be made applicable to the payment of the circulation and other indebt-

tion is, whether these issues increased the aggregate circulation above the amount of metallic money which would have come into the country and stayed in, had the paper not been issued. If so, while the bank expansion kept behind the speculative expansion, it allowed the speculative expansion not only to precede but to proceed. In the language of Tooke, it did not kindle the conflagration, but it fed the flames.

[1] See p. 317.

[2] Massachusetts had, in 1829, passed a general banking law which limited the circulating notes to 25 per cent. in excess of the paid-up capital.

edness of any individual bank contributing which should become insolvent. In 1841–2, eleven of these banks failed, their aggregate liabilities far exceeding the total Safety Fund. An extraordinary levy had therefore to be made, the amount required being advanced by the State out of the proceeds of a special loan. After 1842 the Safety Fund was made applicable only to the payment of circulating notes.

In 1838 the Free Banking System of New York was established, under which the circulating notes were to be secured by a deposit of United States or New York stocks, or bonds and mortgages on improved and productive real estate. In 1840 a law was passed requiring each bank to redeem its notes at an agency of the bank in New York City, Albany, or Troy. Two of the strongest banks in New York City about this time inaugurated a plan of redemption similar to that of the "Suffolk Bank System" in New England. These provisions did not, however, prove sufficient to secure even the ultimate, much less the immediate, convertibility of the paper issues. Previous to 1843 not less than twenty-nine banks organized under this system had failed, their aggregate circulation being about $1,250,000, while the securities held for redemption brought less than half that sum. Subsequent acts of the legislature increased the proportion of securities to notes issued.

This is the scheme of *Secured Circulation*, known as the New York system, which, as stated, has been widely imitated in the legislation of other States, and on which, to a considerable extent, the present National Bank law of the United States was framed.

The plan of basing a circulation upon securities[1] is

---

[1] "Monnayer la rente est tout aussi périlleux que de monnayer la terre."—[Wolowski, La Question des Banques, p. 397.]

not economically approved. It does not give convertibility, in the sense of preventing excessive issues, even in the view of the advocates of the Banking Principle It does not even secure the perfect acceptability of the notes as a medium of exchange, since the receiver desires to be assured that they will, at any moment, be worth what he takes them for, whereas the New York system, at the best, only gives him a pledge that, at a future date, when the bank shall be wound up and the securities disposed of, he will receive that which he may need for this day's subsistence of his family, or to meet the present pressing wants of his business.

Indeed, it is to be noted that the New York system, even as amended by the subsequent legislation referred to, did not profess to secure precise convertibility.

"*Redemption* in the New York law," says the Comptroller of the Currency, in his report of 1873, "*meant discount.* It was to be a redemption in specie, and it was founded upon the avowed principle that specie was worth more, and was more desirable to hold, than the circulating notes authorized."

But, while the New York system can not be accepted as based on sound principles of money, or even of banking policy, it proved, at the time, so great a check upon the wild and reckless paper-money banking that had prevailed almost universally throughout the country, and it had so clear an effect in educating the public mind to more correct views of the banking function and of the responsibilities attaching to note-issues that it should be spoken of with respect by the historian of American money.

Even more important was the system of mutual redemption, first instituted in New England by the voluntary action of the Boston banks, and by the New York law of 1840 made compulsory upon the banks of that great commercial State.

"The rates of discount in the New York market," says the Comptroller of the Currency in the report just quoted, "upon the bank-notes issued and in general circulation varied from $\frac{1}{8}$ of 1 per cent. to $1\frac{1}{2}$ per cent., while many bank-notes that had a local circulation were quoted at from 5 to 10 per cent. discount. *The notes of the New York and New England banks,*[1] *only, circulated throughout the whole Union, like the National Bank currency of to-day.*'

The painful experience of 1837–43, and the discussions regarding money and banking which that experience called out; the reduction in the average term of commercial credit;[2] the growth of a public sentiment to criticise and condemn excesses in paper-money issues, and the formulation of maxims and precepts more or less fully recognized by bank managers as binding upon them; the dying out of the rage for Western speculation, and the general conviction, inspired by the sufferings of the preceding period, that wealth is to be produced, not

[1] The 5th Annual Report (1858) of the Board of Managers for the Suppression of Counterfeiting brings out the fact that the devices of New England banks were especially affected by the counterfeiting fraternity, on account of the freedom with which the notes of that section passed everywhere without particular scrutiny.

[2] "Long credit is not one of the least of the bad effects of paper money. . . . Long credit, thus obtained, does in turn forward a bad currency. . . . Insensibility of discredit does naturally follow long credit."—[Tract, The Currencies of the British Plantations in America.] It would be difficult to put more moral and economical philosophy into three sentences.

discovered; and, lastly, the legislation which has been described, though far from fulfilling the requirements of either good banking or good money: all these causes combined to place the trade and industry of the United States on a sounder basis between 1844 and 1860. Yet the paper money still tended to excess on the occurrence of every speculative impulse. Rising prices inevitably distorted production, creating an excess of those commodities which first felt the force of the upward movement, and, in the end, disturbing the foreign exchanges of the country. Excess was surely followed by deficiency, expansion by contraction, as the downfall of promising schemes created suspicion and alarm, or as the outward drain of specie brought upon the banks the necessity of reducing their liabilities to meet impending danger. By such oscillations trade was made highly speculative, often to the verge of gambling; the terms of contracts were altered, to the loss now of one party and now of another; false impulse and false direction were frequently given to labor and capital, entailing great waste of productive energy. Believing, as I do with M. Wolowski, that, of all human agencies, money is that one which costs least for the work it performs, I cannot doubt that the United States by the use of such a vicious medium of exchange lost every few years, through misdirection of effort, waste in expenditure, and impairment of industrial force, enough to have provided a metallic money of full value, adequate to all the demands of their domestic trade.

As an incident of the Civil War, a system of national banks was created, and the notes of the State banks were taxed out of circulation. As the new banks came into existence when the country was in a state of suspension, and their notes have in the fourteen years intervening been redeemable, in fact, only in the legal-tender bills, an account of them does not belong to the department of Convertible Paper Money. In the fact of a uniform law for all the issuing banks of the United States is found for the first time in our history the possibility of regulating the paper money circulation of the country, should specie payments be restored according to the pledge of the government. It is not, however, to be expected that a people so impatient of slow gains, so deeply penetrated, moreover, with the belief that in the domain of wealth something can be made out of nothing, and much easily out of little, will bring themselves to submit to the restraints of law and tradition which in England, France, Germany and Sweden reduce the evils of paper issues to a minimum.

In the present mixed condition of the money of the United States,[1] there are seven distinct species in circulation, or known to the law.

1. Gold coins, legal tender to any extent; but, in fact, at present used (except per force of special contract) for but two purposes: in payment of customs duties, and of interest on the public debt.

2. Silver and nickel coins, a token or subsidiary money; legal tender only in limited amounts.

3. Legal-tender notes issued by the National Treasury, known popularly as Greenbacks, limited in amount by law.

4. The small residue of paper "fractional currency," which has not been superseded by the new debased silver coinage.

---

[1] See article, "Our National Currency," by Prof. Amasa Walker, in the "International Review," March, 1874.

5. National bank-notes, issued by 2089 banks,[1] under a degree of regulation by government; redeemable in lawful money of the United States; secured by deposit of United States stocks.

6. Coin-bank notes. By the Act of Congress of July 12, 1870, the Comptroller of the Currency was authorized to issue to "any national banking association depositing the bonds of the government bearing interest payable in gold, circulating notes of different denominations of not less than five dollars, to an amount not exceeding eighty per cent. of the par value of the bonds deposited; which notes shall bear upon their face the promise to pay them in the gold coin of the United States." By the official report of 1876 there were nine of these banks, all in California, with an aggregate capital of $4,450,000 and a circulation of $2,090,500.

7. Gold notes, in denominations of twenty dollars and upwards, furnished by the government to all who deposit coin for that purpose with the Treasurer of the United States. These notes, like the former paper money of Genoa, Hamburg and Amsterdam, are simply receipts for gold. They form the ideal circulating medium, a money combining the convenience of paper with the security and stability of coin.

### OTHER EXAMPLES.

The country which, next to England, makes the greatest figure in discussions of paper-money banking, is

---

[1] Report of 1876.

| | |
|---|---|
| Capital, | $499,802,232 |
| Surplus, | 132,202,282 |
| Undivided profits, | 46,445,216 |
| Loans and Discounts | $927,574,979 |
| Circulation, | 292,166,039 |

Scotland. The remarkable success of the Scottish banks[1] and the high degree of convertibility maintained by their paper, has afforded the advocates of unrestricted issues their favorite illustration. And to those who hold that paper-money banking inevitably leads to bankruptcy, as has so often been the case in England and the United States, the example of Scotland is a sufficient answer. But we have seen that, conceding the solvency of the banks, conceding them to "good makers, good manufacturers"[2] (Price), and to be able abundantly to protect their own interests and to secure their note-holders, the question remains whether there is not the liability to an excessive issue of notes under speculative impulses in the commercial or industrial body, giving fuller scope and freer play to such impulses than they could obtain through the use of metallic money, and thus leading to overtrading and the consequent distortion of productive industry, or to extravagant investments and the consequent depletion of the circulating capital available to conduct the current business of the community.

---

[1] Mr. McCulloch remarks: "The destruction of country banks in England has upon three different occasions, in 1792, in 1814, 1815 and 1816, and in 1825 and 1826, produced an extent of bankruptcy and misery that has never perhaps been equaled, except by the breaking up of the Mississippi scheme in France. In 1826 forty-three commissions of bankruptcy were issued against country bankers, and from 1809 to 1830 no less than three hundred and eleven. *During the whole of this period not a single Scotch bank gave way.*"

[2] "The difference between the two results in no way proceeded from any variation in the systems of currency adopted in the two countries. The method of issuing notes and providing for their convertibility was identical in both. The failure in the one case and the success in the other were exclusively events of banking, in no degree events of currency. . . . The Scotch issuers of notes were good bankers and kept their money; the English were bad bankers and lost it."—[Principles of Currency, p. 128.]

Upon this point the success of Scotch banking proves nothing either way. Were we discussing the principles of banking,[1] no country could afford more instruction. In the discussion of the principles of money it has only a secondary importance. Prior to the Act of 1844 Lord Overstone was able to assert that "all the evils to which a trading community is exposed: fluctuations of prices, recurrence of commercial pressure, stagnation of markets, losses by insolvency, occur with as much frequency and intensity under the Scotch System of Currency, as under that which exists in England."[2]

To the paper money of France,[3] however, even this

---

[1] An account of Scotch banking is given by Mr. Inglis Palgrave, in his "Notes on Banking," pp. 10–26; cf. Gilbart on "Banking," 311, 319, 424–5; Tooke, "History of Prices," iii, 205, 263; Nicholson, "Science of Exchanges," 45–9; Wilson, "Capital, Currency and Banking," 2, 3, 97–8, 102, 234. Two facts are of especial importance in explanation of Scotch banking successes. The first is that all land is registered (as is not the case in England), enabling the public easily to ascertain the amount of real property possessed by the partners of the bank who, except only in the case of the Bank of Scotland and the two chartered banks, are bound jointly and severally; and, on the other hand, enabling the bank management to ascertain the amount of real property owned by persons applying for loans. The second consideration is the fewness of the Scotch banks and their great individual strength. In 1873 there were but eleven banks, with eight hundred and one branches. By the evidence before the Committee of 1841 it appeared that one bank in Scotland had 20,000 depositors. Perhaps quite as important to be remembered in this connection as either of the above considerations, is the shrewd Scottish sense and the strong Scottish will.

[2] Tracts, etc., p. 114, cf. pp. 111, 274.

[3] The Bank of France was established in 1800. Previously to 1848 the Bank had sustained competition in issues from joint-stock banks in the large cities; but in that year, these became, by force of law, branches of the Bank of France. Thus the Revolution brought about

redoubtable champion of restricted issues is compelled to concede a quality as stable as belongs to metallic money. "Probably," he wrote in 1840, "the circulation of that country undergoes no fluctuations but such as would occur with a circulation exclusively metallic."[1] We have seen with what caution and firmness the Bank has on two occasions maintained the currency of its notes, even in a state of suspension. Mr. Seyd makes the statement, as quoted by Mr. Nicholson, that on a mass of commercial paper held by the Bank of France between Aug. 13, 1870, and July 6, 1872, amounting to 868,000,000 francs, there had been a loss of but one-third per cent. Financial abilities such as are indicated by a result like this, and a circulation "saturated with specie,"[2] have combined to secure the close approach, if not the exact conformity, of the paper money to the movements of coin and bullion under the operation of supply and demand, in spite of the fact, which according to the views of the Currency School would seem to render such an achievement impracticable, that the Bank considers good mercantile bills a sufficient basis for the issue of notes.

Mr. Bagehot, in his work, "Lombard Street," calls our attention to the fact that, while the law contemplates a branch of the Bank of France in each

---

the centralization of the banking system in France, as the Civil War did in the United States. M. Courcelle-Seneuil says: "La banque de France n'est pas un établissement commercial seulement; c'est aussi, et avait tout, un instrument politique, une banque d'État."—[Op. de Banque, p. 212.]

[1] *Ibid.*, p. 206.

[2] Down to 1848 the Bank of France issued no notes of less than 500 francs ($100). In that year issues of 200 and 100 franc notes were authorized.

department, branches in fact exist in only sixty out of eighty-six departments, so slowly does the banking system make its way in that country. This is the more noticeable because in the French colonies banks of issue have acquired no small importance, prosperous institutions existing in Martinique, Guadaloupe Reunion, Guiana, and Senegal, while within two or three years a bank of issue has been created at Noumea in New Caledonia.

We have said that the issue of convertible notes was first undertaken in Sweden, nearly forty years before the Bank of England was established. Mr. Palgrave, in his interesting "Notes on Banking," seems disposed to place Swedish paper money first in point of merit as well as of time.[1] By the Act of 1874 the power of paying bank-notes with other paper was taken away. Even the notes of the Bank of Sweden do not satisfy the demand for redemption. Notes when presented at the head office of an issuing bank must be paid unconditionally with the lawful gold coin of the realm.

Sound banking principles have long been traditional in Holland, and the Bank of the Netherlands maintains a reputation hardly second to any. Its management is notable for the large specie reserves, which are said to be greater proportionately than those of any other bank in Europe.

---

[1] "If we except Italy, where for two or three years past the system of monthly bank statements has been carried out, there is not in Europe any country whose bank statistics are more carefully compiled, or more general, than Sweden."—[N. Y. Banker's Magazine February, 1877.] The excellence of the Italian accounts is due to the eminent abilities of Prof. Louis Bodio, the chief of the Central Statistical Bureau of the kingdom, whose contributions to economical and political science have been many and great.

Prior to the unification of Germany nearly every State possessed a system of paper-money banks, all of one general type, though with varying provisions for the security of the shareholder, the depositor, and the note-holder. Thus, while in Bavaria a specie reserve of only one-fourth the circulation was required, in Leipsic the reserve was two-thirds. The more usual proportion of specie required by law, or established by banking tradition, was one-third. Of all the German banks the Royal Bank of Prussia, with its numerous branches in the commercial cities of the kingdom, was the most important. Both the proper operations of banking and the issue of notes for circulation were habitually conducted by the banks of Germany with great care and good judgment. Since the French war a new bank law has been promulgated. The most important feature is the creation of a Central Bank of Issue for the empire.

Of the scheme of the new bank, the "Economist" remarks: "It looks as if its framers had consulted the books of all the principal schools of banking and currency, had seen what they recommended to make banking safe, and had taken something from each." The principle of limiting the "uncovered circulation," borrowed from the English Bank Act of 1844, appears in the Bank Act of Germany, the Bank being authorized to issue only 250,000,000 marks[1] beyond the coin held for redemption; but this check upon issues is greatly impaired by a provision that issues above the maximum may be made by the Management under the penalty of a tax of five per cent. on all such excess.[2] The principle of the separa-

[1] The other banks, thirty-two in number, coming under the New Banking Law, are allowed an uncovered circulation of 135,000,000 marks.

[2] Of the liberty of increasing the issues under a tax of 5 per cent., an arrangement which Prof. Jevons terms the "Elastic Limit Sys-

tion of the departments of banking and issue, which, we have seen, was held to be of vital importance in the English Act, is not adopted in the German law. Upon this failure to take the one principle of the English Act with the other, the "Economist" comments: "First, there are no special securities and bullion set apart on which the notes are issued. There is no ground for saying that the convertibility of the note is in any special way maintained; the note-holder and the depositor are on a par. Secondly, what strikes even deeper at the principle of the Act of 1844 according to its original idea, a decrease in the amount of coin and bullion, is not necessarily followed by a decrease in the note circulation. The first principle of the Peelite legislation, that a combined currency of the precious metals and notes should fluctuate as if it had been exclusively metallic, is not complied with."

The new Imperial Bank is to be in the highest sense a government institution. The shareholders neither reign nor govern; they have neither the form nor the essence of power. Respecting this great fiscal and political agent, the article we have already quoted, from the pen of one of the first of recent authorities on banking, the late Mr. Bagehot, makes the following suggestive remarks: "In any other country such a bank would be the most dangerous of all institutions. The government would be a bad banker, and would be a worse

---

tem" of circulation, that author says: "This provision is designed to avoid the suspension of the law during times of crisis, and it is quite possible that we might with advantage introduce a similar modification into our own currency law. But the fine, or tax, upon the excessive issue ought surely to be much more than 5 per cent., and in this country should not be less than 10 per cent."—[Money and the Mechanism of Exchange, p. 319.]

government because it was a banker; it would waste the money of its subjects, and waste it in ways which injured them. And how such an engine may be worked in Germany during a time of civil trouble no one can foresee; but at present we believe it will work very well." After referring to the highly successful management of the Bank of Prussia, which is absorbed into the new Bank, Mr. Bagehot continues: "We believe that the new Bank will carry on its business in the same cautious way, because its managers will be much the same men and guided by the same motives. The Bank will be safe—not because its constitution has resemblances to that prescribed to the Bank of England by the Act of 1844, for those resemblances are unreal; nor because it contains a theoretical provision for the benefit of note-holders, for that provision could not be worked for their benefit and might hamper the Bank; nor because its business is cramped by stiff and foolish rules.[1] It will be safe, if it is safe, because it is, in the last resort, ruled by a most cautious and able administration, which will heed everything, which will waste and venture nothing, and which, above all things, will keep an immense sum of actual cash in store,[2] in readiness for, and as a security against, trouble. And this is a most characteristic example of many cases in which, under a most pedantic exterior, the German mind conceals a most simple, rude and tremendous essence."

---

[1] Such as requiring three signatures to all bills discounted, etc.

[2] The Bank of Prussia, at the last return quoted by this writer held 72 per cent. in specie upon all its deposits and circulation.

## CHAPTER XXII.

### THE THEORY OF CONVERTIBLE PAPER MONEY, CONCLUDED.

The account given in the preceding chapter will perhaps allow us with advantage to recur for a moment to the theory of Convertible Paper Money as presented in Chapter XIX.

The question of supreme importance in this branch of our subject respects the Reflux. Is the check on overissue sufficient, under good legal regulation and with good banking administration, to keep such a money strictly within the bounds of metallic money?

We saw in the United States a paper money, nominally convertible, at times seemingly in great excess, and again brought by a rapid contraction under the influence of panic to a point which we must believe to have been below the amount of specie which would have circulated had it not been replaced by cheaper money. Yet, notwithstanding the apparent excess of paper in the periods of relative inflation, we do not find that a premium on gold habitually existed, or was recognized in the quotations of the market. In small amounts, for exceptional purposes, gold could almost always be had for notes at par.

Now if these two facts did really co-exist as appeared, the doctrine of Lord Overstone and Mr. Norman found here a practical illustration. The whole mass of the money of the country, specie and paper together, was depreciated.

How could this be? Why did not gold, if it was depreciated in comparison with the mass of commodities, go abroad where it had a greater purchasing power? This is the question with which the advocates of the Banking Principle assume to close the discussion.

An answer covering a part of the ground of the objection has already been offered. If, as the accounts given by Prof. Cairnes and others of the movement of the gold supplies make it appear, gold may from its own excess reach a local value distinctly below that which it has elsewhere, and may maintain this value through considerable intervals, it certainly may be true that gold, reaching a lower local value through excess of paper, may remain under depreciation for a period sufficient to allow no slight effects to be wrought on industry and trade through the enhancement of prices operating, as every such cause does, very irregularly upon the mass of commodities in the market and upon the wages of different kinds of labor, and also through the incentive given to speculative investments depleting the capital requisite for current production in favor of a thousand wanton schemes for great and sudden gain.[1]

---

[1] Mr. Charles Francis Adams, in 1837, expressed the opinion "that there may be a particular stage of currency not narrowly observed as yet, when, the paper having increased very rapidly, and the gold and silver not having yet taken its direction into the foreign trade, such an unusual quantity of the circulating medium may exist for a time as to force up the price of commodities and thus communicate a prodigious impulse to the speculating enterprise of a community." —[Reflections upon the present state of the Currency in the United States.]

But another economical cause remains to be adduced, which will account for the protraction of this lower local value of gold (as part of a monetary circulation) through periods long enough to allow the most serious mischief to be wrought.

We have quoted from Mr. Tooke's pamphlet of 1826 the following sentence: "It not unfrequently requires an interval of some length before *the commodities which are interchangeable with other countries* are affected by an excess in circulation in such a degree as to produce the effect of increased export." Let us dwell on the words which have been emphasized.

All the commodities produced in a country are not equally and indifferently the subjects of foreign trade. Every country pays for its imports with certain commodities in preference to others. Of two articles that may be exported, a reduction of price in one will often quicken the export far more than a proportional reduction in the other; while as between two articles, one of which is habitually exported and the other not, a slight reduction in the former case may prove sufficient to cause a vast increase of shipment, while a large reduction in the latter case may not start the movement of a pound, a bushel, or a yard. "Currents of trade," said Locke, "like those of waters, make themselves channels out of which they are as hard to be diverted as rivers that have worn themselves deep within their banks." Only a great flood suffices to produce an overflow.

Now, nature had clearly pointed out what should be the chief exports of the United States, in the period to which we refer, that is, in what class of commodities, predominantly and by preference, we should pay for the goods we purchased, or discharge the debts we had contracted. These were the products of the field, the farm, and the forest, in respect to which the United States enjoy advantages nowhere equaled. The cost of production of these articles was so low, owing to the extraordinary natural endowments of the country, that the American agriculturist, after paying the cost of transportation to European markets, could bring home as the proceeds of his sales what enabled him to live with a degree of comfort and enjoyment known to the manual labor class of no other people in the world. A vast volume of such products have flowed from the United States, year by year, through the whole history of their foreign trade. These were the natural, one might say the necessary, exports of the country.

From this condition of our agriculture it resulted that corn and cotton, provisions, lumber and naval stores, continually tended to become the cheapest commodities which we had to export. Gold might through excess of paper issues become cheaper here than abroad; but the products enumerated were cheaper still. Gold, of course, would go abroad under no other motive than the desire to make purchases or pay debts, but for these purposes other commodities were in a higher degree available.

The effect of the employment of such money upon the interests of the agricultural class may be indicated as follows: The price brought by that portion of the crop which was exported was, of course, the price at which the whole crop was sold. But in carrying on their production and in their domestic consumption, the agricultural class found themselves compelled to purchase the products of other occupations and trades which produced goods which were to be consumed wholly within the country, and produced them, moreover, under protection from foreign competition, either through a high cost of transportation, as in the case of bulky articles, or through heavy imposts laid for revenue or with the avowed purpose of excluding the foreign article In the case of such products there was clearly nothing but domestic competition to keep down prices; and the money of the country having been, as we have assumed, depreciated from excess, the prices of these products would stand at a higher level, relatively to cost of production, than the prices of the products first enumerated. If the situation has been correctly given, there has been throughout our history a tendency to deplete the agricultural classes and all engaged in producing exportable articles, for the benefit of the classes which were engaged in producing articles to be consumed at home under conventional or natural protection; and the prime agent in this operation has been our bank paper money.

Such was the theory of the case advanced by Prof. Amasa Walker, and it seems to me to account for the existence of the depreciation which he alleges occurred at intervals in the money of the country, while yet no premium on gold appeared. What, but for the condition of things recited, would have been the premium on gold, was levied as a tax on the agricultural interest. Their products were made cheaper than gold or silver, and thus became the preferred exports of the country, while other trades and occupations sold their goods within the country at prices which were advanced by the excess and consequent depreciation of the local money.

### DOES IT "PAY"?

Rejecting the plea that elasticity is a desirable element in money, we have seen that two advantages are claimed for convertible paper: one, its higher convenience in use, owing to the great weight of the masses of metallic money, even of gold, required in the larger transactions of commerce, which, were the metal to be actually employed, would cause difficulty in transporting, handling, and counting money, besides inviting by so open a display of treasure to crimes of violence; the second advantage claimed for such money being its comparative cheapness, a portion only of the gold or silver which would form the metallic money of a country being retained as the basis of paper issues.

The first of these advantages would clearly appertain equally to a paper money like that of Hamburg and Amsterdam in former times, like the rouble notes once issued by the Commercial Bank of St. Petersburg,[1] and like the present coin-certificates of the United States Treasury. The only advantage remaining, then, for a paper money issued in excess of coin and bullion held for redemption, over a paper money based on the full amount of specie which it promises to pay, is its comparative cheapness.

Is such a money really cheap? Does it "pay" to substitute credit for value in the circulation?

I shall not undertake to argue that a money of bank paper only nominally convertible, like that of the United States before the Civil War, issued upon a minimum of specie even after the bitter experiences of 1837 and the reformatory legislation which followed, is not cheap. I apprehend that there are few thoughtful and intelligent Americans who will not accede to this statement of Prof. Perry: "There can be no hesitation in affirming

[1] In 1840 the bank had outstanding notes based, cent. per cent., on reserves of coin and bullion, to an amount not less than 114 million roubles or about $95,000,000 of our money.

that the expense of maintaining a gold and silver money for all the wants of the whole country might have been met, many times over, from the losses resulting from this bank paper system."—[Pol. Econ., p. 306.]

If, as may fairly be affirmed, the utmost amount of metallic money which would have circulated in the United States between 1816 and 1860 would not have reached ten per cent. of the aggregate annual income of the country, a single commercial disaster checking production to the extent of one-third only, through a period of four months, would involve a loss equal to the cost, out and out, once for all, of a metallic money sufficient for all the wants of the country. How often have the mills and furnaces and factories of the United States been on three-quarters, two-thirds, one-half time, and that, not through months, but through years! Bad money has not done all the mischief, but it has done enough completely to justify Prof. Perry's assertion.

But turning from the United States, where value and credit were so compounded in the circulation that the mixture became, like Lady Smart's ale, "strong of the water," only, let us ask whether there is true economy in the substitution of credit for value in the money of a country where sound banking principles are observed, where the banks frequently exchange their paper and ample reserves are maintained to secure the redemption of notes on demand by a public which is not intimidated by mob-violence, by public sentiment, or by bank persecution.

M. Wolowski estimates[1] the saving by the use of

---

[1] La Question des Banques, p. 155. Mr. Hankey computes the gain by the issue of bank-notes by the Bank of England to be: To the Government, £200,000 nearly; to the Bank, somewhat less than £100,000.—[On Banking, pp. 4, 9.]

credit as an element of money in Great Britain and Ireland at $\frac{1}{320}$ of the capital, and $\frac{1}{1000}$ of the revenue of the United Kingdom. If, however, purely banking principles were to prevail as to the volume of reserves,[1] with the issue of £1 and £2 notes as recommended by Mr. Wilson and Prof. Price, the saving could undoubtedly be made twice or three times as great, without involving any sensible increase of risk to the noteholders of the kingdom. Would this be true economy? Of course, if the reader is prepared to accept the proposition of the economists of the Banking School, so ably maintained by Messrs. Tooke and Wilson, that Convertible Paper Money cannot appreciably vary from the course of a metallic money of full value, he must regard such a saving in its first cost as an object of great importance, which it would be inexcusable to neglect. If money is merely a tool of trade, it should be made no more expensive than is required for its highest efficiency. On the assumptions of the Banking School, a paper money secured by a reserve of coin and bullion to the full value of the circulation would be as wasteful as ivory-handled forks in a hay field, or nickel-plated spades in a railway cut.

But if, on the other hand, there is reason to believe that a paper issued above the amount of specie held for redemption, however carefully managed, tends to excess in greater or less degree, we must, I think, conclude that there is no true economy in effecting such a saving in the first-cost of the circulating medium. No money

---

[1] Prof. Price mourns over the large reserves of the Bank of England under the Act of 1844. He holds the circulation to be "needlessly and excessively, and therefore wastefully, secured."—Principles of Currency, p. 143, cf. pp. 190, 193, 201.]

is cheap which does not perfectly answer its purpose,[1] for money, as M. Wolowski has said, is of all societary institutions that which accomplishes its work at the least relative expense.[2]

Perhaps the best illustration we could offer on this point is one taken from the foundation of a large building, say a cotton factory. The builder opens the ground and digs till he gets below the reach of frost, perhaps till he comes to solid rock. He puts in stone and mason-work at the cost of thousands of dollars, which will form no occupied part of the structure, will furnish no room for spindles or for storage. The system of paper-money banking in the United States attempted the same kind of economy as if the builder of the cotton factory should lay its foundations so grudgingly that it would from time to time settle downwards, causing wide seams to appear in the upper stories, exciting alarm in the minds of employer and workmen, involving costly outlays for shoring up walls, bracing floors and putting in new partial foundations at great disadvantage, with the result, at the best, of a weak, shaky structure, liable at any time, and certain at some time, to come down in ruins.

---

[1] "To dispense with barns would be a greater annual saving than that which arises from the substitution of a paper to a metallic currency. Some favorable seasons occur when the farmer might thresh his wheat on a temporary floor exposed to the weather, and dispense with a barn. Yet, in our climate, every prudent farmer prefers security to a precarious advantage, and would consider it a most wretched economy not to incur the expense necessary for that object. Similar is the economy of that expensive instrument, the precious metals, if the substituted paper currency is insecure."—[Gallatin, Considerations, etc., p. 20.]

[2] "Aucune invention humaine n'est plus utile que la monnaie; aucune institution sociale n'impose moins de dépense."—[Journal des Economistes, October, 1868.]

Such folly as this the writers whose views we are considering would denounce as earnestly as the most strenuous Bullionist. But they still insist that the foundation may be reduced greatly in its extent and in the quality of the material used, not only without bringing the factory down in a heap, but without showing a crack from cellar to garret. All this might be while yet with such a foundation the factory would shake under the tread of a thousand feet and the pulsations of its powerful engines sufficiently to cause a great loss of power, great waste of stock, and to interfere largely with the uniformity of the product, on which depends much of its commercial value.

So is it, I am disposed to believe, with credit introduced into the money of a country. It may cause no catastrophe, may threaten no disaster, while yet it may jar the whole structure of industry and trade, and cause the machinery of production and exchange to operate with less of precision and force than would otherwise be the case.

The great fact of modern industry, under the wide diversification of production, the localization of trades and the minute subdivision of labor, is waste of industrial power through the tendency to a divergence of demand and supply, leading now to an overproduction which is never fully utilized; now to a cessation of industry which is carried by the timidity of merchants, manufacturers, and bankers far beyond what is necessary to equalize production and clear the market. Oscillations in demand and supply are indeed inevitable in the nature of things; but our modern system, by which two or three towns make half the goods of a certain sort which the whole world consumes, extends these oscillations into wide-reaching fluctuations, which in the aggregate largely reduce production from its economical maximum, and render the employment of labor irregular and precarious. This tendency must, as it appears to me, be in a greater or less degree, but always with unfortunate results, aggravated by the issue of paper money not based, cent. per cent., on the money of international commerce.

But it is difficult for one to contemplate such stores of gold and silver as would be required for the basis of a paper circulation into which no proportion of credit should enter, without feeling that here is waste. Prof. Price looks down into the cellars of the Bank of England, where lie £20,000,000 of gold, and exclaims: "A spot more identical with the deep Australian mine cannot well be imagined."[1] Identical! No two places on earth have so little in common, and the difference between them is all the more striking because of the presence of the same metal in both. In the Australian mine the gold has no value: it will not answer one human use; it is not available to purchase a single commodity or pay the smallest debt. In the vault of the Bank of England the gold has an immediate value; it embodies a vast amount of labor expended in raising it from the mine, in reducing it to a state of commercial purity and in bringing it half around the world; it will command in exchange the most precious products of English labor; it is ready to be shipped east or west, north or south, to purchase the teas of China, the grain of America, the furs of Siberia, or the spices of the Indian Ocean.

But, says the same writer, in speaking of the withdrawal of gold from the Bank, "it is the idle, the unused,

---

[1] Principles of Currency, p. 193: "Transferred from a mine to a cellar."—[P. 201.] Prof. Price frequently brings up the same image.

the temporarily-annihilated resources, slumbering in the cellar, which are lessened."—[P. 219.] Is the gold in the vault idle, unused, temporarily annihilated? Is the bridge which bears up the train of freight or passengers less busy than the snorting, puffing engine which draws the cars? Are blocks of stone unused when laid deep under ground in the foundation of a building which serves the purposes of industry, of art, or of government? Surely there is lack of scientific imagination in that view of the gold in the vaults of the Bank which regards it as idle and unused, when its true and faithful symbols are running their busy course above ground and outside the walls, effecting the daily exchanges of thirty millions of people!

# INDEX.